Zen

AND THE ART OF

Fatherhood

Zen
AND THE ART OF
Fatherhood
LESSONS FROM A
MASTER DAD

Steven Lewis

A DUTTON BOOK

DUTTON
Published by the Penguin Group
Penguin Books USA Inc., 375 Hudson Street, New York, New York 10014, U.S.A.
Penguin Books Ltd, 27 Wrights Lane, London W8 5TZ, England
Penguin Books Australia Ltd, Ringwood, Victoria, Australia
Penguin Books Canada Ltd, 10 Alcorn Avenue, Toronto, Ontario, Canada M4V 3B2
Penguin Books (N.Z.) Ltd, 182–190 Wairau Road, Auckland 10, New Zealand

Penguin Books Ltd, Registered Offices:
Harmondsworth, Middlesex, England

First published by Dutton, an imprint of Dutton Signet, a division of Penguin Books USA Inc.
Distributed in Canada by McClelland & Stewart Inc.

First Printing, June, 1996
10 9 8 7 6 5 4 3 2 1

Illustrations by Harry Trumbore

"Moon Birth" originally appeared in the *Poughkeepsie Journal*. "Nothing Is to Blame" originally
appeared in *Exits off a Tollroad*, Pentagram, 1974. "Have a Cigar!" originally appeared in *L.A.
Parent*. "Circumcisio" originally appeared in *Seattle's Child*. "Bayou Grace" originally appeared
in *Parents Magazine*. "The Zen of Diaper Dunking" and "The Rules of the Road" originally
appeared in the *Huguenot Herald*. "Who Wears the Belt in Your Family?" "Seven Facts for
Father's Day," and "Zen and the Teenage Girl" originally appeared in *Dutchess Magazine*.
"Where's Papa?" originally appeared in *New York Newsday*. "Outside the Garden" originally
appeared in *The Reporter*. "The Zen of Getting Clean in Rural Connecticut" originally appeared
in the *New York Daily News*. "A Father's Numerology" originally appeared in *Wisconsin*.
"Biting Off the Matter with a Smile" originally appeared in *Commonweal*. "When Bad Things
Happen to Innocent Children" originally appeared in *Parenting Magazine*. "Looking Out for
Number One, Two, Three . . ." originally appeared in the *New York Times Magazine*.

LIBRARY OF CONGRESS CATALOGING-IN-PUBLICATION DATA

Lewis, Steven M.
    Zen and the art of fatherhood : lessons from a master dad / Steven Lewis.
        p.   cm.
    ISBN 0-525-94147-9
    1. Fathers—United States—Anecdotes.   2. Fatherhood—Religious aspects—Zen Buddhism.
I. Title
HQ756.L493   1996
306.874'2—dc20
                                                                            96-3783
                                                                            CIP

Printed in the United States of America
Set in Simoncini Garamond
Designed by Leonard Telesca

This book is printed on acid-free paper.

CONTENTS

FOREWORD

Fathering is a dreamy road trip full of contradiction and paradox, meandering summer lanes behind the leather-wrapped wheel of a green Alfa Romeo that become—in a wet sneeze—windy mountain passes slick with ice as you steer a beige Astrovan full of screaming kids. Every time you think that you know where you are, you're not there anymore.

For me, becoming a father—and being a daddy—has sometimes felt like getting lost in Queens. You know you're in New York City, but frankly it doesn't look like it's supposed to look—and at least half the people on the street don't speak the same language or dialect as you—and admitting that you're disoriented to the scowling presence on your right is more than your pride can bear—and, anyway, you're not really lost, you simply need to find a familiar landmark. So you just keep driving. As Tobias Wolff's clueless stepfather says in *This Boy's Life*, "I know a thing or two about a thing or two. . . ."

A thing or two.

As such, fatherhood to me is the perfect oxymoron, pure contradiction. *Zen.* And like Zen, there's no adequate way to describe it. Alan Watts says, "Zen Buddhism is a way and a view of life which does not belong to any of the formal categories of modern Western thought. It is not religion or philosophy; it is not psychology or a type of science. . . ." Neither is the art of fathering.

I am a man who, through something akin to serendipity, has found himself at the wheel of the family Vanagon sputtering across some vast unknown highway where it seems I am doomed to seek what I never shall find; where ambition and purpose is exposed daily as vanity and vexation; but where dark purposelessness is revealed to me through my restless family as crystalline joy.

Over the past twenty-six years, as family matters have grown exponentially more complicated and busier with the birth of each of our seven children, my inner life has paradoxically become simpler and quieter. Is that Zen? I don't know. In 1977 when my third daughter was born and the children suddenly outnumbered my wife and me by a ratio of two to one, I awoke to the knowledge that, despite any illusions to the contrary, we were no longer in control of the family. That's when all my notions about what it means to be a father dropped like a toy boat over a raging waterfall—leaving me sharing a crowded inner tube floating down a slow-moving creek with an extraordinary feeling of freedom. And it was then that I began to grasp the elusive notion, as expressed by Alan Watts, that the "perfection of Zen—or *fatherhood*—is to be perfectly and simply human." Nothing more. And as Hermann Hesse wrote in *Siddhartha*, "everything is necessary." Everything.

I'm sometimes told that as a father of seven I appear to have the wisdom of the ages. To my kids, however, I am as big a fool as I am a wise man. And to my inner self (and often to my wife Patti), I am a pure fool foolishly tripping over myself trying to play the role of the wise man.

Yet in the end—as in the end of another day in which I ponder the imponderables of a life with seven children—I feel like I
really do have some enlightened experience to share with other
fathers who find themselves as lost in this whole inscrutable
process as I am.

1

Before Father Time

MY FATHER, MYSELF

How I learned the value of presence from a father who was rarely around

No snowflake falls in an inappropriate place.
—ZEN SAYING

My father was not what you might call a New Age nineties dad. When I rewind the boyhood tape, the only moving image I can conjure up is the distinctly 1950s look and smell of my businessman father going to work each morning: the row of brown and gray suits in the closet, the white starched collar, the smell of Aqua Velva, the dark tie pulled off a crowded rack, the big Windsor knot, the heavy herringbone overcoat, the line of hats on the top shelf in the hall closet. And then the door closing. After a long day in which my young life went through more changes than a chameleon—and still stayed the same—the rough scrape of his face when he came in from the cold late each night lingered for hours.

He was a dad. A man. He worked. He worked in New York City from early morning to midevening six days a week. And when he came home, he ate dinner alone and then sat down in the den in front of the black-and-white Sylvania television and did paperwork. Sundays he tended to the lawn or fixed the radiators or regrouted the tiles in the bathroom—and then did more paperwork. The closest we came to doing "stuff" together was when he'd call me all the way into the house from a tight stickball or football game on the street to run down to the basement and get him a wrench or a hammer.

That was it.

Or at least pretty much what I recall about me and my dad when I was growing up in suburban Roslyn Heights, New York. Except that he used to hold my hand while we drove silently in the car.

Not that I expected anything else. He was just like my uncles (Mac, Murray, and Herman), who were scattered around Long Island. And he was no different from Mr. Jayson down on Westwood Circle or Mr. Weil and Mr. Diamond across Candy Lane (yes, Candy Lane), good men who never once strolled into the games that boys play to learn how to be men. They were men. They worked all the time.

The men in my neighborhood didn't go on fishing trips with their sons. They didn't play punchball in their shirtsleeves out on the quiet streets. They didn't lie out on the grass on buggy summer nights, fireflies lighting up the air, watching for meteors and talking earnestly about the possibility of life on other planets. They didn't sit on the edges of our beds on cold winter nights reading chapters of *The Call of the Wild* or *The Hardy Boys*. They didn't go to our Little League games. And years later, long after the first solitary shave and the last innocent kiss, they didn't take us out to the local tavern for a coming-of-age drink and some gravelly man talk about girls and women and children and work. They worked.

And somewhere along the unbroken line—after I left for college in Wisconsin and realized that the textures of life differed according to geography and circumstance—I felt the reconstructed loneliness of a lost boyhood without a fabled Norman Rockwell dad. I promised myself that when I married and had kids I wouldn't allow my days and nights to be consumed in work—no matter what the cost. I would not get trapped in Kenneth Patchen's "murder into pennies round" of daily existence. I'd be free, I'd be around, a kiss on the top of their heads, a hand on their shoulders, an encouraging slap on the butt. I'd go to Little League games, I'd take them to concerts, I'd play ball, I'd go fishing, I'd lean back in bed and read a chapter to them each night, I'd laugh with them until my sides ached: I'd be a pal for my children.

And then I got married and had kids and more kids (and even more kids), and I changed diapers and danced with toddlers on my feet and played ball and went fishing and agonized with them through recitals and blowout soccer games and laughed until my sides ached, and even sat around scraping out the insides of Oreos and ruminating about life and love. But along the way I also discovered that I'd never be their pal.

I learned that unsettling truth as my oldest son, Cael, and Randy McCrory made a secret clubhouse in the barn (and didn't invite me in); as my oldest daughter Nancy and her friend Eva whispered and giggled behind closed doors from night till morning (and didn't let me in on the joke); as Addie fell head over heels in love with another *man* (Tony Ciliberto) in seventh grade; as one by one (by one) my children grew up and found their own pals beyond the solid walls of this house with whom they rightly shared their suddenly private lives.

And through their silence I found out that being a pal isn't the essence—or the alpha and the omega—of fatherhood. Friendship is nice, like icing or gravy, but it's not *it*. *It*, it turns out, is mostly about going to work and coming home each night. It's about being around. Like a dad. Like my dad.

Somewhere along the meandering parental way I understood that what my children want most from me—aside from money and rides and carte blanche to do anything they want—is to be there as they walk through the kitchen door panting and sweaty and hungry for dinner, or when they call home for a ride late Friday night, or as a cushion to lean into on the couch while the

TV does its mindless work. Or, like my father, to reach over out of nowhere and hold their hand in the car when there is nothing in the world to say to each other.

More than forty years later I can still feel his big rough hand holding my small smooth paw as we drove silently in the Chevy station wagon. The truth is that I had nothing to say to him. And, as far as I can figure, he had nothing to say to me. I don't think we knew each other very well when I was a kid. He just held my hand. He treasured me. He let me know that no snowflake falls in an inappropriate place, that I was his.

My father, who it seems was never there, taught me the Zen value of presence: how to not be there and be there at the same time.

SOMETHING IN THE
WAY SHE MOVES

Stumbling into love

Wind moving through grass so that grass quivers. This moves me with an emotion that I don't even understand.
—KATHERINE MANSFIELD

Patti's a patrician, a blue blood, raised in the Garden District of New Orleans, groomed at Miss Edith Akins Little School and later refined at the Louise S. McGhee School on Prytannia Street. She actually understands noblesse oblige.

I'm a New York Jew, spawned out of the generational pickle juice of Brooklyn and raised in a suburban development of quarter-acre ranches bulldozed out of a Long Island potato field. I went to public school in a cranky yellow bus, scratched my way through Wheatley High in an ugly succession of mohair sweaters, and learned about obligations by way of the adolescent charms of a girl named Judy Goldstein.

Patricia Charlee Henderson and I met purely by accident in September 1964 as newly arrived freshmen at the University of Wisconsin. I thought she was beautiful: gorgeous face, long brown hair, the sway of her back that left me with a permanent yearning in the hollow of my throat. I have no idea what she thought about me, but it wasn't until more than three years later—a long uninteresting story—that we had our first date: December 10, 1967.

I know the exact date because I had two tickets to see the great Otis Redding. That night Mr. Redding's plane crashed into the frozen waters of Lake Mendota. Certainly an inauspicious beginning to the relationship, but we nevertheless were married the following August.

Twenty-six years later I still don't understand. We have none of the ordinary things in common. Nothing. Sports, plays, music . . . nothing. (I later found out that she didn't even like Otis Redding.) I speak only for myself then when I say I am drawn to her daily in vast unspeakable ways, a vague sense of biological inevitability when we pass in separate cars. Or later when I inhale her scent. Her breath in my ear.

I like her. I like who she is. We somehow share the same vision of life. Beyond that it's pure mystery.

If you'd have asked me to describe my ideal partner twenty-six years ago, it could have been almost anyone but Patti Henderson. ("Beautiful but not my style.") Yet since the moment I first haltingly placed my lips on hers, she was the one with whom I always had to be. No one else. No one else. I can't repeat that too many times.

I have tried in vain to explain to my friends and even some nosy strangers about the desire and the ambivalence at the root of a relationship that not only permanently connected us but inspired us enough to bring seven children into this world. As Stella says to Blanche in *A Streetcar Named Desire*, "There are things that happen between a man and a woman in the dark. . . ."

Things.

And, mostly, things in the dark, though I don't only mean things sexual. There's much more than that. Much more. Although it's hard to be more specific. Patti and I are together all this time *and* have seven kids because of who we are and who we are to each other. As far as I can see there is no more acceptable explanation for our choices than there is about why some people like their oysters from the Chesapeake and others from the Rockies.

And to give this fishy stew a really bizarre flavor, let me add this: while Patti always wanted a large family—it was from the earliest awareness of her sense of connection to the earth—I know myself well enough to realize that had I married someone else, I probably wouldn't have had so many children. It's even possible that I would actually have married someone who didn't want kids and would be now writing a reflection on our matched pair of Harley Sportsters.

But of course I didn't.

Cael was born while we were still undergraduates in Madison. Two years after Nancy graced our lives in Milwaukee, we had Addie in upstate New York. Then Clover. Then Danny. Then Bay. Six years ago Elizabeth Bayou-Grace completed the set. (I think.) Every day I wake up amazed at it all.

It looks like it should make sense.

But after all these years, I still don't get it.

FAMOUS ZEN LAST WORDS I

"I will not marry until I'm at least thirty-five."

Words, as is well known, are great foes of reality.
—JOSEPH CONRAD

It is early November 1967. My college roommate and I are sitting in Ella's Delicatessen on State Street in Madison, Wisconsin. I can't remember now whether it is very early morning or very late evening—probably both—but it's cold and dark outside and I'm on my fifth or sixth cup of java, running at the mouth and soberly contemplating the meaning of life as only fourth-year sophomores can do without feeling completely ashamed of themselves.

I am twenty, in unrequited lust with a provocatively strange and morose brunette named Jodi who has just given me the heave-ho for not being quite strange or morose enough. To complete the picture, I am bent over in my finest sensitive poet's pose, sucking on a Lucky Strike between gulps of coffee and liberally quoting from Hermann Hesse's hippie classic *Siddhartha*, a book I carried in my hip pocket like a flask from 1965 to 1968.

There may have been no more earnest person in Ella's at that moment. There may also have been no less earnest person in

Ella's at all. If I remember correctly, the late sixties turned unc-
tuousness into a public art form.

Anyway, we were slurping up the coffee and blowing out the
smoke and no doubt talking about the cruel and meaningless
cycle of life, the vainglorious, futile despair of bourgeois American materialism, and, of course, freedom—our three favorite subjects—when my roommate asked what I thought of marriage.

Which is when I uttered my undeniable vow, spoken with all
the conviction of an antiwar placard: "Marriage is a middle-class
trap. I guarantee you that I won't get married until I'm at least
thirty-five."

I said that without even a facial tic, without a moment's reflection that it might not be true. I was that sure. After all, I was
twenty, my tuition and rent were paid by my utterly confused
mother and father who lived a thousand miles away, and I was
as free as a cold Wisconsin breeze across the vast prairie—and
determined to stay that way until I was too old to make it matter
anymore. Which was thirty-five.

Until that fateful point, freedom was the only state of existence worth pursuing. My first obligation was to live. Really live.
Be alive. Be on the road. Be me.

It was commonly assumed back then that life was, for all in-
tents and purposes, over on your thirtieth birthday. You sold
out or were sold out. Either way, you were no longer trustworthy.
And by thirty-five you were so far gone—so unfree, so uncool—
that it didn't matter anymore whether you got married or not.
I'd seen countless others trade in their black T-shirts and black
Levi's and engineer boots for white V-necked undershirts and
Hush Puppies and Sansabelt slacks. I'd watched as the hippest
of the hip, the most angst-ridden of a generation of sufferers,
climbed that fateful hill and walked down the other side in poly-
ester suits with plastic smiles on their close-shaved faces, striding
hopefully toward nine-to-five corporate jobs, wives in curlers,
2.3 children, Chevy wagons, Levitt houses, riding mowers, golf
in jackass pants, and, all in all, the paunchy side of life.

At thirty-five, I would stop smoking. I would stop drinking. I would go to sleep after the eleven o'clock news. I would settle down, marry, and die.

My roommate nodded forlornly.

And, as long as I was on a roll, I took a long drag on the Lucky, rolled the smoke up through my nostrils, and blew it out through my dark bearded lips in a thin blue line, muttering like one of Hemingway's Lost Generation heroes, "And I will never have kids. Never." Affecting the high moral tone, which may have been the most useful thing I learned as an undergraduate, I said, "It would be a terrible thing, the cruelest of jokes, to bring an innocent baby into such a painful existence. A world fraught with war, disease, phoniness. Ultimate meaninglessness. [Yes, I believe I used the word *fraught*.] Never."

He understood totally. Of course. He was as miserable as I was. And that was that. I pushed the burning butt into the over-flowing tin ashtray and dropped a few crumpled dollars on the table, and we walked back through the silent streets to our apartment and slept till noon.

Three weeks later I tripped and fell hopelessly in love with my roommate's ex-girlfriend, the girl he never wanted to see again. Patti. The attraction was as transforming as it was unintended, but that was the end of our deep understanding—and the end of our friendship. Freedom be damned. I was in love! And nine months later I found myself standing in a living room in New Orleans with a haircut, a trimmed beard, a white linen suit, watching the most beautiful girl I had ever seen in my life walking my way in a white wedding gown.

And ten months after that, July 17, 1969, three days before a man walked on the moon, Cael Devin Lewis was born at St. Mary's Hospital in Madison, thus proving that words are indeed great foes of reality. And thus the quasi-Zen koan: Never say never without saying never.

I've told that story to all my children and to countless thousands of students over the years. All in the name of teaching them the truth. They actually think it's funny or cute or whatever—or they pretend it's funny or cute—and then toss the intended aphorism into the garbage with An apple a day . . . and A stitch in time . . . and the rest of the bourgeois nonsense adults heave their way. They'll learn.

MMM, HE SMELLS GOOD, THIS ONE

The earthy wisdom of southern grandmothers and the power of good gumbo

> *Everything in the universe is connected, everything is osmosis.*
>
> —TAISEN DESHIMARU

I knew immediately upon stepping out of the plane into the thick hot air that I was a fish out of water—or, more appropriately, since fish could probably live in the humid atmosphere of the delta, I was simply out of my element, a wooly panting mutt whose paws get stuck in the swampy muck every time he tries to take a step.

I was dizzy. I was sweaty. I was close to an out-of-body experience.

I was in Louisiana to meet Patti's mother and father—and grandmothers and aunts and uncles and cousins and friends and ex-boyfriends—a daunting task for an aggressively shy beatnik poet whose social graces might best be called stunted.

And soon enough I was failing miserably at the task of winning over my new family. Though Patti's mother, Nancy, loved me immediately for reasons that remain way beyond my comprehension, my tongue grew swollen when I tried to talk with Cousin Bobby or Uncle Bruce and his wife, Red. My ears filled with swamp water when I tried to understand the lilting voices of Patti's friends Clydia, Kingsley, and Amalie. I squirmed and sweated like a malaria patient while we had afternoon tea in her wealthy grandmother's parlor. My long hair frizzed into an Afro of continental proportions. And the hot shrimp creole her mother prepared felt like burning tar in my tender meat-and-potatoes mouth.

The final blow came when I met her father a few days later. An inveterate angler who to this day manages to fish (ocean, stream, pond, or rain puddle) 365 days a year, he had been down on the gulf when I had arrived, so Nancy had arranged an extended family picnic at Lake Pontchartrain where he would meet us on his way back to New Orleans.

Charles Crawford Henderson arrived in a grayish Chevy wagon and strode right across the grass right in my direction, arms swinging, face lined and burned, a vision of southern manhood, right hand extended. Although I managed the manly grasp, I also noticed my hand looked like a dead whitefish in his reddish brown mitt.

And his very first words to me were, "So, do you fish?"

If it was possible to grow paler than I already was, I'm certain I blanched. "Well, yes, no, I mean I've been fishing, but I'm not really . . ."

He looked angry. "Well, do you hunt?"

"Ummm, no . . ."

Now he looked confused. My throat was clogged, my mind a swamp. Finally I uttered the only thing that made it through the tangles: "Patti and I rode horses over at Audubon Park today."

"Oh." He lit up. "You ride horses?"

"No, not really." I sank in the muck. "It was my first time."

He shook his head and looked haplessly over at Uncle Bruce. "Well, you don't fish, you don't hunt, you don't ride horses— what do you do?"

While looking for a tree to back up against in case I fainted or got attacked, I scurried around behind my glazing eyes desperately searching for some manly conversation to please the old man. A fourth-year college sophomore didn't seem quite impressive enough. A former high school athlete who hadn't run across a highway in at least three years didn't seem to be the key. A bourbon drinker might have been a possibility, but it was too risky.

My mouth opened but nothing came out. The family was leaning in my direction, waiting. Patti's father had his hands on his hips, waiting. I was drowning.

Then from behind, right over my left shoulder like a fairy godmother, came Patti's mother's soft southern voice: "Why, he's a poet, Charles."

His eyes rolled back into his head, and the groan he suppressed might have created a tidal wave on the lake. I don't remember anything after that.

Alone in the guest room bed several hours later, I made plans to pack it all in and race back to New Yawk as fast as I could, my tail between my legs. I lay there muttering to myself in cinematic New Yorkese: *I'm outahere . . . I'm outahere . . . I shoulda just stayed in my own backyard with my own kind . . . I coulda been a contenda. . . .*

But the next morning I was awakened early, had a cup of muddy French Market coffee poured down my throat, and was shuttled into the backseat of the family car before I was lucid enough to tell everyone I was going home. We were already across the Mississippi line when I realized we were headed to Biloxi to meet Patti's grandmother, Eleanor Magruder Sharp. Patti called her Damma.

Damma lived in a little brown bungalow on Lee Street, about a block and a half off the old two-lane U.S. 90 and the Gulf of Mexico. As we pulled into the narrow sandy driveway, Damma was outside with a nearly blind old man named Sam who was supposed to be trimming her rather anorexic-looking hedge. A short grandmotherly woman with a massive tilting pile of white hair on the top of her head and an enormous bosom, she walked right up and grabbed me by the forearm, yanked me down, and gave me a wet kiss.

While she still had me bent over, she turned to Patti and said, "Mmmm, he smells good, this one. I'd keep 'im." Then she added with a wink, "I didn't like the last one. And the old one—what's his name?—was a good boy, but I like this one better. He smells good."

And that was that. She let go and I stood up, a member of the family. Nothing else seemed to matter.

We went inside and she served us her gumbo out of an overflowing soup tureen, a dark pond filling my blue-and-white bowl, fish and oysters and shrimp and okra and whatever else she could find to chop and slice and dump into the witch's brew that transformed me with the first spoonful.

I had never tasted anything so dark and spicy and suggestive of the sensuous bottom of the sea. I understood more with every spoonful what Patti had been talking about all the months I really knew her. I tasted what she tasted. I learned the language. I ate well. I smelled good. I loved her more than ever. Everything was suddenly connected.

And the next day when we drove over to Pascagoula to meet Uncle Jimmy and Aunt Jane (and Covington, Brucie, and Lucie), I even rectified my image a bit with Charles. Weary of pleasant conversation and looking for any excuse to escape the scrutiny of the adults, I offered to shoot hoops with Covington. That's when my future father-in-law found out that I had played on my high school basketball team and decided I wasn't quite as completely worthless as he had assumed.

I had become a *contenda*.

THE WEDDING OF
NORTH AND SOUTH

New York Jews in dark suits, girdles, and frizzy blue hair mingling with New Orleans Episcopalians in white linen suits and breezy countenances and red noses

The first sensation that staggers August visitors arriving in New Orleans is the intense, dizzying humidity. Stumbling down the ramps off air-conditioned Delta jets or Greyhound buses, they look like they're going to faint.

The second thing that happens is that their carefully coiffed hairdos blow up like bags of burned microwave popcorn before they even make it out of the airport or bus station.

And so it was for the Levy-Lewis hordes crossing the Mason-Dixon line like Hannibal crossing the Alps to see Sammy's boy Stevie—yes, at twenty-two they still called me Stevie—get married to the—shhhh . . . shiksa—from down south.

New Orleans (pronounced New Orlyuns with the accent on the Or not the Lyuns or Leans) isn't like Florida, where everybody is really from New York. It also isn't some backwater Georgia speed trap off U.S. 95 where so many snowbirds from New York spend a few expensive hours en route to Florida. It isn't like anywhere else in the world. Entering New Orleans is like entering some foreign protectorate.

At the wedding, held in Patti's house in the Garden District, there was no confusion about who belonged to whom. If we had had a theme like some contemporary weddings seem to do, we could have called it Cognitive Dissonance. The natives were breezily dressed in their white linen suits and dresses. They mingled together in bemused, understated casualness, sweating drinks in napkined hands, watching in controlled horror as the invaders schmoozed and schpritzed through the beautiful (*be-yew-tee-ful*, as Aunt Betty used to say) but un-air-conditioned home.

And my people were indeed schmoozing and schpritzing, wrapped in the dark suits and heavy sequined dresses of the neo-traditional bar mitzvah or wedding or twenty-fifth-anniversary affair held at Leonard's on Northern Boulevard. The women's blue hair frizzed into big pelican nests; the men mopped their considerable brows.

There was Uncle Max—the man who defined the plaid-on-plaid-with-argyle-kneesocks look at summer barbecues—with his massive cigar talking at commodities trader Sam Livaday with those broken capillaries highlighting his pale cheekbones and nose. It was clear to anyone walking by that they didn't speak the same language—Max talking like rapid gunfire out of the side of his mouth ("Yaddayaddayaddayaddayadda . . ."); Sam nodding in polite confusion and then slurring out a rather slow but measured generic response designed to fit any social repartee.

And there was Aunt Betty, trapped in her girdle like the rest of my aunts, pinching the cheeks of sophisticated adults who had not had their cheeks pinched since they were knee high to a grasshopper. That warm round face, that wonderfully massive Victorian shelf of a bosom, those unbelievable salamis swinging from her upper arms.

Then there was Patti's great-uncle Charlie, the one who lived alone in his mansion on First Street, drool on his bright yellow tie, wandering around with a confused countenance, no doubt wondering if this was just a Jewish costume rehearsal for Comus; her uncle Bruce drawlin' on about fishin' and shrimpin' and huntin' and crabbin' and, of course, crab bawls and pee-can pies to my best man and official nonoutdoorsman, Richard Gaynor, "one toke over the line, sweet Jesus."

My favorite moment, though, was Uncle Murray handing out his business cards—MURRAY A. LEVY, FIRE ADJUSTER—to all the profoundly bewildered Garden District gentry ("Hey, ya never know . . .") who thought they'd had one bourbon too many and walked into that recurring dream of currency.

And then, of course, there was Patti and me, the living embodiment of love's oxymoronic nature, the yin and yang of earthly constitutions, the Zen paradigm of opposites being twins, stuck on the receiving line for hours on end getting drunker and drunker with each gracious handshake and polite well-wishing— Patti swilling and spilling champagne down the front of her wedding dress, catching the flowers on fire as she lit a cigarette—the two of us leaving the reception for the rest of our lives long before the party was over.

We spent the night in the elegant Royal Orleans Hotel down in the French Quarter, ordered room service fit for the adolescents we were, and watched Hubert Humphrey take the Democratic nomination for president in Chicago.

Everything was perfect—perfectly bizarre—exactly as it should have been. Nothing fit, not even the white linen suit Patti's mother bought for me after seeing the wool suit I'd brought to get married in. Like a deformed man, I pondered grace.

I still do.

FAMOUS ZEN
LAST WORDS II

"Let's wait to have a baby until we graduate."

Do I contradict myself?
Very well then I contradict myself.
—WALT WHITMAN

In late September 1968, three or four weeks after returning from our three-dollars-a-day honeymoon in Wales, London, and Paris, Patti and I threw off the wrinkled sheets of connubial bliss and had our very first serious talk about the future. I mean The Future, as in what we were gonna do when we grew up and got real jobs and car loans and a mortgage and had, like wow, a family.

Far out.

It was a pretty bold concept for two young hippies who had difficulty seeing around the corner of the next weekend. We were then fourth-year sophomores on the unofficial six- or seven-year plan at the University of Wisconsin (enroll a semester, drop a course or two, drop out altogether, re-enroll). Patti was a psychology major with absolutely no interest in becoming a mental health counselor of any kind. I was an English major who thought it would be nice to make a living as a poet. Meanwhile, I was washing dishes at Mama Brava's.

You might easily surmise that we were ill-advised to get married—or even be enrolled in college. At the time, I think everyone we knew, except perhaps a close college friend majoring in psilocybin, was surmising the same thing. But, of course, we were in love, profoundly deaf to the whispered warnings of others, and blinded by desire to any danger signs they planted in the road ahead of us. We went right ahead over the cliff.

So, there we were in Middletown, living in a rental cottage the size of the small room in which I am now writing, arriving late to evening classes, discussing as earnestly as we knew how the one topic we were least knowledgeable in: mature married life.

The career angle was simply too abstract, so we just left that behind with a sort of dumb blind faith (a shrug and a smirk) that things would work out in the end. As Confucius wrote, "It does not matter how slowly you go so long as you do not stop."

Then there was the baby question. On the surface, that was even easier to figure out. It has long been common wisdom that having a baby before you are stable emotionally and economically is a blueprint for marital distress and failure. Both desperately trying to be mature, she nodded and I nodded.

We agreed that we would just wait until we were ready. (I'm pretty sure that meant waiting till both had graduated and I was making big money as a poet.) The mere thought of being a father at my tender age was still a bit bizarre for me—how could *I* be a father when I was still battling my own? That was the mature, reasoned side of the discussion that evening.

However, there was also a palpable sadness that passed between us at that very reasonable moment. During our brief but wonderfully romantic long-distance courtship (for most of those nine months, I was in Cambridge, Massachusetts, and Patti was in Madison), we had fantasized again and again, as young lovers do, about our future home together: a big white wooden house with wallpapered rooms and porches and porch swings all around set at the edge of a stream in the middle of a lush green meadow, the heartwarming, soulful sounds of twelve kids laughing and playing in the flowered yard. Yes, twelve kids.

Having both come from small families, the dozen children vision was nothing less than complete and utter fantasy. And actually the fantasy was mostly Patti's, a deeply ingrained sense of destiny that she had had since she was a little girl. I, who had once dreamed of becoming a hermit in Nova Scotia, basically traveled along with her fantasy and eventually even adopted it as my own, no doubt because I loved her more than I had ever loved anyone or anything in the universe—and the vision made her happy. And if she was happy, I was happy. Simple as that.

And it was simply sad to have to acknowledge that we'd have to put off our vision of paradise, at least for a few years.

Which was when Patti looked at me, head tilted and eyes twinkling, and shrugged and smiled and held out that elegant hand for me. I reached over and touched her skin and suddenly loved her in a whole new way. It was like a dream of opening a door you've never seen before and, upon opening it, discovering a wonderful summer porch off your bedroom where you feel more at home than you've ever felt in your life.

And in that moment, holding each other's hand like two children at the brink of the wilderness, we silently agreed that while our life together was already full of questions and contradictions and questionable motives and unbelievably poor decisions, there was no time like the present to be pregnant and have a baby. We felt as large as the universe. We contained multitudes.

2

Zen Pregnancy, Zen Birth

MOON BIRTH

Cael is born; a man walks on the moon

> *Nothing is born, nothing is destroyed. Away with your*
> *dualism, your likes and dislikes. When you have per-*
> *ceived this, you will have mounted the Chariot of the*
> *Buddhas.*
>
> —HUANG PO

Much to my youthful surprise, the earth-shattering news on July 17, 1969, was not my son's birth.

In the delivery room at St. Mary's Hospital in Madison, Wisconsin, the nurses smiled behind their green masks and the fatherly obstetrician patted Patti on the knee and then shook my shaking hand. But that was it.

There were no heartfelt embraces. No tears. No champagne. This was a birth like any other birth in the obstetrical ward at St. Mary's—and judging by the way everyone scooted out of the delivery room, there was bigger news going on outside.

Out in the corridors it was as still as outer space. I'm not sure what I expected when I puffed up my boyish chest and pushed my way out of the swinging doors, but there were certainly no bands. No fireworks. No reporters from the *Capital Times*.

As I walked down the hall that afternoon peeking into opened rooms I saw what the quiet was all about: patients and staff were all pugged into the airborne Zeniths, and from there into the cosmos, where Neil Armstrong was less than seventy-two hours away from walking on the moon.

Frankly, I have never been much excited by rockets and space travel. The appeal of Superman, Captain Video, and later, Captain Kirk had passed me by like a far-off meteor whizzing above my head as I was looking down at my feet. I always saw life in more earthy—or earthly—terms: the Brooklyn Dodgers, Camp Deerwood, the bounce of a leather basketball, my pal Richard. Later it was Muddy Waters, a green Morgan 4/4, William Carlos Williams, a pitcher of beer, the Vietnam War, Patti. Patti. Patti.

And then there was Cael, purple-faced and mush-headed wailing like a police siren after a grueling twelve-hour labor and delivery. He was a beauty.

After phoning my mother, who did surprise me by crying, I called everyone else I ever knew in my entire life all over the country, but most of them were not home. Then I raced over to the Rathskellar in the Student Union and found a halo-haired boy named Art Ohlman and a few of his friends sitting around a metal table on the shoreline terrace at Lake Mendota. I told them of the miracle of Cael's birth. Art smiled broadly and said his best "Far out!" and gave me a big bear hug, but then there was nothing more to say. He was as far from the experience of young fatherhood as I was from walking on the moon.

And several hours later, Madison growing dark and crickety and the moon beaming through the hospital window, Patti, Cael, and I sat alone in a semiprivate room with the powerful and terrifying knowledge that we had created life—and that life was suddenly here, not coming in nine months or next week or, as it sometimes seemed, eventually coming like some kind of messiah.

He was here, he had a name, crying and suckling on her breast, and in the space of one yowling moment the enormous unencompassable universe was transformed into something as small as the hospital bed where the three of us were huddled together in fearful awe of what Patti had just done.

The next morning before going to the hospital, I stopped at

Rennebohm's Drug Store on State Street for a cup of coffee. On the stool next to mine was a copy of the *Wisconsin State Journal*. The front page was all Apollo 11, as were pages two and three—even the Vietnam War was buried on page four—but I sat there and flipped the noisy sheets until I got way back to the birth announcements, my finger moving down the small print, desperately seeking our names.

Of course, the words and the names weren't there. As I know now, birth announcements are listed a week or weeks after the fact. Still, I was stunned that there was not even a mention of my wife's Artemisian effort to bring new life into the universe or Cael's courageous presence among the newly born. I had witnessed the miracle of the ages right in town, and it seemed nearly as miraculous that the local paper was so focused on a few astronauts soaring off to a dead moon 238,000 miles away from the hospital that they didn't notice the real news.

Two days later, though, on July 20, 1969, Patti and I watched wide-eyed from her hospital room as Neil Armstrong stepped off the landing module and spoke his immediately immortal lines. Everyone cheered in the corridors. Patti cheered. Cael yowled. Even I felt stirred inside by the magnitude of the event, but I was eternally annoyed that the fireworks and bands and corks popping all over the country were for the crew of Apollo 11, not for Patti and Cael.

That evening I sat alone on the rickety pier of our cottage on Lake Kegonsa, sunnies flipping out of the water, and looked up at the moon and understood, perhaps for the first time, just how absurd and wonderful human beings can be.

I dipped my bare feet in the cool water, the moon rippling out beneath the pier, and cheered for all of us: the fireworks and America and Neil Armstrong, but mostly for Cael and Patti, who had given up all dualism and mounted the chariot of the Buddhas.

NO SEX, NO LIES,
NO VIDEOTAPE
Zen facts of pregnant life for fathers

> *Certainly nothing is unnatural that is not physically impossible.*
> —RICHARD BRINSLEY SHERIDAN

I know that I should be a little more high-minded about these things, but as everyone knows, early on in most relationships it's all about the body. The flesh. Rubbing up against each other in the dark. The ooooooh. And the aaaaaaaaaaah. The extraordinary capacity for pleasure one experiences through the shared communion of physical love.

And that's the way it should be. It is, so it should be. Just as Siddhartha couldn't escape the world by joining a group of ascetics who lived in the forest and preached the denial of the self—he had to learn the ways of the body to find his way to the soul—I believe that sex is one path, among many others, that enables us to achieve true spiritual or transcendent union with another human being. Carnal knowledge is, after all, knowledge.

So I knew Patti and Patti knew me—just as it is written in the Bible. And knowing each other in that way was a lot of fun. Actually, a whole lot of fun. And educational, too. Although we were good friends long before we were lovers, I don't think we knew each other very well in our souls.

Frankly, I don't think that makes us any different than most newlyweds or newly somethings. Young couples have sex anywhere, anytime, in any position, and any number of times during any given day. And so it was with us.

Until Cael was conceived. Then the X-rated video of connubial bliss turned to an R (morning sickness, fatigue, language), which was still very nice, but, you know, not quite the spontaneous anywhere, anytime, any which way it had been. And, yes, it all came as a bit of a shock for me; it was difficult to imagine or admit, but her mind was sometimes other places than in bed with me.

I'd say sex maintained an R rating for much of the first trimester, but, unbeknownst to me, there were still deeper and more profound changes awaiting us in the second three months of that pregnancy. Along with some back pain, hormone changes, and a growing connection to and obsession with the tiny life growing in her young body, Patti turned down the heat and led us right (or left) into the realm of PG-13 for the next three months—i.e., a lot more talk than action.

Then, in late April or early May, just as she was making the transition from waltzing sensuously and proudly across campus with her round belly pushed out in front of her to complaining about feeling like a guernsey and waddling (right hand in the small of her back, left hand wiping the sweat from her brow, eyes looking everywhere for a place to sit), our sex life achieved as close to a PG rating as one can get and still be termed marital relations—mostly hand-holding, shoulder rubs, and dreamy internal monologues of how it used to be.

And then, of course, there were the totally celibate G-rated six weeks before and after the birth itself. No more needs to be said about that period.

Considering the most recent findings that young men think of sex every fifteen seconds, over the course of the pregnancy I increasingly had a lot of time to ponder (and grow morose about) Patti's lack of interest in me. And she had an equal amount of time to ponder the pimply adolescent scowl on my face.

Thus, over the surprisingly hilly course of those forty increasingly celibate weeks—and refined over twenty-seven years of marriage and seven full-term pregnancies—I learned nine important Zen facts of pregnant life for husbands:

1. Nine months may be an eternity but it is not a very long time.
2. Extraordinary sex may be sexless.
3. All men are not nearly as irresistible or understanding or sensitive or unique as we think we are—in or out of bed.
4. Absurd as it may sound, a man is not his penis.
5. A man does not die from sexual frustration.
6. A man does not die from leaving his boyhood sexual illusions behind.
7. Pouting is not only unmanly, it gets you nowhere, especially with sex.
8. A man's lust is not self-limiting. Nothing is unnatural that is not physically impossible.
9. Sex, like good wine and deep love, gets better with age.

SEASONS OF BLOOD

Affirmations of life and love after two miscarriages

The world is impermanent. One should constantly re-member death.

—SRI RAMAKRISHNA

Our second-floor apartment on North Newhall Street in Mil-waukee was yowling with life: three dogs, two cats, and little mop-headed Cael, fifteen months old and gearing up his consid-erable lungs for the ascent into the terrible twos. Life, it may be said, was full of life. And so was Patti: pregnant, a blossoming flower for all to see.

Although her mother's untimely death (just a month before Cael was born) had been a wrenching reminder for all of us about the terrible and awesome and paradoxical cycle of exis-tence, in that early fall of 1970, while Lake Michigan was grow-ing colder by the day, preparing to transform black water into white ice, the east side of this overgrown factory town was so full of blue sky and warm color that you could easily fool your-self into believing that winter would never come.

In the small and worn backyards fronting the alleys, onion grass still sprouted like hairs on a balding man's head. Even along the tired and bereft brick foundation walls of the two-family house where we lived, throngs of chrysanthemums warmed the cold earth. And although the Brewers had recently thrown the sheets over the box seats at County Stadium, the windowless door at Tony's Bar was still held open with a cinder block on sunny afternoons.

Life was good. Damn good. Despite all the calendar-driven evidence to the contrary, everything was ascending, blooming, sparkling, vibrant. That fall I was teaching at a group home for delinquent teenage girls and doing graduate work at the University of Wisconsin-Milwaukee. And with our two-bedroom flat growing smaller by the day, Patti and I started dreaming of buying one of the small charming older homes in the neighborhood. To quote an absolutely awful song from that era, "Everything is beautiful in its own way." And I truly believed it. Everything I saw walking back from the college each day reminded me of the living, breathing embodiment of the eternal, immortal nature of life. (Did I mention that I was an ascending youthful poet?)

So when Patti walked out of the bathroom one evening with worry scribbled across her lovely face, I figured she was concerned about matters more mundane than life and death. Even when she said a few moments later that she was spotting, I remained undaunted; I put my arm around her shoulders and whispered in my most manly warble that everything would be okay. And, of course, I meant it. I felt as invincible as the spring that seemed to be able to leapfrog over the winter that supposedly lay out ahead of us. I *knew* in my heart that everything would be fine. How could it not? When you're young and in love, pregnancy is nothing less than a certain sign that everything is right in the world. We were in tune with nature and nature was about the consummate power of life. We were indomitable.

But nature, we were to discover once again, is not just about life and regeneration, it is also about the inexorable rhythms of existence, including degeneration and death. It is about dark spots on white toilet tissue turning bright red; it is about silent rides up to Whitefish Bay to find that white-coated doctors are as powerless and ignorant as the flannel-shirted crowd in dealing with the inscrutable logic of nature; it is about blood dripping down the inside of alabaster thighs; it is about the lonely wailing after the profoundly quiet passing, walking aimlessly through the incontrovertible streets day after grieving day.

A miscarriage is about one of you mourning a dream and the other grieving what was once real and suddenly is not; it is about turning on a light in our separate corridors of grief and finding that at the end we are all together in our aloneness.

And, some months later, in due time—in due time—it is about healing and falling in love again and getting on with the unfettered hopefulness of life (though with slightly less exuberance this time). It is about planting the seed and making the phone calls and planning the nursery and making yourself believe again in the indomitable power of life. . . .

And then watching hopelessly, hopelessly, angrily, as the dark stains reappear and then turn bright red and begin to flow like a river across a crumbling dam of our most youthful life-affirming assumptions. The very ones you thought you'd left behind the first time around.

The very same ones you've come to rediscover—as if for the first time—when she miraculously grows pregnant again, her eyes bluer than blue, her belly round as fruit. Then you know that it is in the nature of nature to let us know that we are as immortal as we are mere mortals. We die and we do not die.

And so it is also about how fragile we are, and strong; how, as Nietzsche suggested, life will break you, but if it doesn't kill you, it will make you stronger in the places where you've been broken; it is about how we come through tragedy to know in our hearts that we need each other over and over again to withstand the vagaries of this life; it is about how love is the one and only redemptive force.

It is, finally, about how damn good it was to hear fat little Nancy yowling the third time around. It is about how every time I see her, I am reminded of our impermanence on this earth and how I see so suddenly the eternal loving space she occupies in my life. And it is then that I feel most alive.

NOTHING IS TO BLAME

Waxing unpoetic

> *A poem should not mean but be.*
> —ARCHIBALD MacLEISH

With each child's birth I wrote a poem. To be kind to myself, which every Zen father should be, I wrote each of the poems out of the gush of loving feeling that accompanied the startling vision of my eternal other releasing a child that I helped create from her extraordinary body into the thin air of this existence.

To be unkind to myself, which every Zen father should also be, I wrote the poems, I've come to see, as a way of stealing a little of the spotlight away from Patti (Hey, look at me!), whose act of creation was so much more profound and magical than anything—anything—I could make or do.

In either case—or, more to the point, in both cases—in reading back through the seven pieces, the poems tell more about my development as a father than they do about birth or anything else, for that matter. I still feel the first (for Cael) as deeply as I do the last (for Elizabeth), though the language of each makes them almost unrecognizable as expressions emerging from the same person.

In the poem for Addie you can see my awakening to the utterly plain, ordinary, earthy nature of the most sublime moment in the universe.

When she was conceived we were living in upstate New York, in a two-hundred-year-old brick home just a mile or so from the craggy base of the Shawangunk Mountains. Just as the rest of the sixties counterculture had gone "back to the land," so had we.

On the property were a barn, a rickety carriage house, a tumbledown chicken coop, and a fenced-in pasture that, at first, felt as big as the Ponderosa back forty. (Later on it miraculously shrunk to a single acre.) In addition to the dogs and cats, we added rabbits and goats and, for good measure, allowed a neighbor's horse to live in the field.

I was writing the great American novel and feeling prematurely wizened by the horrors of Vietnam, the revelations of Watergate, and the act of homesteading (more symbolic than actual) in a place where we didn't know a soul. As naive and idealized as my vision of life still might have been at the time, I was first seeing daily existence in all its raw beauty. With Cael in public school, Nancy in diapers, and dirt under my fingernails, there were no more romantic illusions of how the world should be. No more smoke-filled dreams of utopian existence. No more Age of Aquarius.

As Aaron Neville implored each of us who would listen to him, I wanted nothing more than to "tell it like it is." I felt strong and full of the joy and pain of life I had just seen Patti deliver into the world. The title of the following poem comes from "Why I Laugh When Kai Cries" by Gary Snyder.

Nothing's to blame . . .

Ah Addie,

You made it so quick and sloppy,
your first breath, a squeal, a squeal
between your Mama's thighs, your body
still unborn inside
came gushing out, dripping
with all the mess we have
tucked under skin, hidden
behind closed eyes, wiped
away with fluffy towels. And how funny
you looked, scrawny legs folded up
like a curl to your fat belly
and then stretched
upside down
by your ankles
to drain the muck
from your lungs, the pink
insides of your mouth. What
an unaffectionate word *suction* is,
but how lovely to watch the suctioning,
clearing the canals for the air
that minutes before smelled so antiseptic
and then and now smelling clearly
of you and your Mama clearing the air, ah
Addie, I would have licked you clean. You
wailing your song over shiny gums, tongue
wagging inside, trembling
with the fury of a whole world, 7 pounds
10 ounces of clenched and raging anger
that twice before shook my bones,
shook them like an angry father
full of fright and apologies, which left me

laughing deep in the belly,
deep belly laughing for you, Addie
because it is true, nothing is to blame, after all
the fancy words, it is simply this:
one whole person
turning, squirming, pushing and
sliding naked into this life.
No more. No less. All of a sudden.

Just like that.

isn't like anywhere else in the world. Entering New Orleans is like entering some foreign protectorate.

At the wedding, held in Patti's house in the Garden District, there was no confusion about who belonged to whom. If we had had a theme like some contemporary weddings seem to do, we could have called it Cognitive Dissonance. The natives were breezily dressed in their white linen suits and dresses. They mingled together in bemused, understated casualness, sweating drinks in napkined hands, watching in controlled horror as the invaders schmoozed and schpritzed through the beautiful (be-yew-tee-ful, as Aunt Betty used to say) but un-air-conditioned home.

And my people were indeed schmoozing and schpritzing, wrapped in the dark suits and heavy sequined dresses of the neo-traditional bar mitzvah or wedding or twenty-fifth-anniversary affair held at Leonard's on Northern Boulevard. The women's blue hair frizzed into big pelican nests; the men mopped their considerable brows.

There was Uncle Max—the man who defined the plaid-on-plaid-with-argyle-kneesocks look at summer barbecues—with his massive cigar talking at commodities trader Sam Livaday with those broken capillaries highlighting his pale cheekbones and nose. It was clear to anyone walking by that they didn't speak the same language—Max talking like rapid gunfire out of the side of his mouth ("Yaddayaddayaddayaddayadda . . ."); Sam nodding in polite confusion and then slurring out a rather slow but measured generic response designed to fit any social repartee.

And there was Aunt Betty, trapped in her girdle like the rest of my aunts, pinching the cheeks of sophisticated adults who had not had their cheeks pinched since they were knee high to a grasshopper. That warm round face, that wonderfully massive Victorian shelf of a bosom, those unbelievable salamis swinging from her upper arms.

Then there was Patti's great-uncle Charlie, the one who lived alone in his mansion on First Street, drool on his bright yellow tie, wandering around with a confused countenance, no doubt wondering if this was just a Jewish costume rehearsal for Co-mus; her uncle Bruce drawlin' on about fishin' and shrimpin' and huntin' and crabbin' and, of course, crab bawls and pee-can pies to my best man and official nonoutdoorsman, Richard Gaynor, "one toke over the line, sweet Jesus."

My favorite moment, though, was Uncle Murray handing out his business cards—MURRAY A. LEVY, FIRE ADJUSTER—to all the profoundly bewildered Garden District gentry ("Hey, ya never know . . .") who thought they'd had one bourbon too many and walked into that recurring dream of currency.

And then, of course, there was Patti and me, the living embod-iment of love's oxymoronic nature, the yin and yang of earthly constitutions, the Zen paradigm of opposites being twins, stuck on the receiving line for hours on end getting drunker and drunker with each gracious handshake and polite well-wishing—Patti swilling and spilling champagne down the front of her wed-ding dress, catching the flowers on fire as she lit a cigarette—the two of us leaving the reception for the rest of our lives long before the party was over.

We spent the night in the elegant Royal Orleans Hotel down in the French Quarter, ordered room service fit for the adoles-cents we were, and watched Hubert Humphrey take the Demo-cratic nomination for president in Chicago.

Everything was perfect—perfectly bizarre—exactly as it should have been. Nothing fit, not even the white linen suit Patti's mother bought for me after seeing the wool suit I'd brought to get married in. Like a deformed man, I pondered grace.

I still do.

BRINGIN' IT ALL BACK HOME

Home-birthing Clover

*Observe things as they are and don't pay attention to
other people.*

—HUANG PO

Giving birth in the late sixties to early seventies wasn't quite the
lighthearted experience that Mrs. Brady or Mrs. Nelson or Mrs.
Reed led us all to believe it should be. Accompanying the accounts
of the joyful births of Cael, Nancy, and Addie, it should also be
said that Patti was angry (overwhelmed, uncomfortable, frustrated,
humiliated) about the uncompromising, patronizing institution-
alism she found in every admissions office and nurses' station and
doctored phrase in three different hospitals in two states.

She not only deeply resented having to go from the warmth
and comfort of our home and drive to a cold institution while
she was in labor, she loathed leaving one baby behind with a
baby-sitter while she went away for days to birth another. She
hated the senseless and inhumane shave and enema that was at
that time standard procedure. She was irate at the internals performed in the middle of contractions. She despised the fact that
she had to be rolled on a narrow stretcher from a labor room
down the hall to a stark white delivery room while she was in

transition. She abhorred the medieval delivery table and those awful stirrups. And she was aghast at the cavalier attitude of the obstetricians who showed up just in time to do an episiotomy, catch the baby, and take credit for all the work.

Of course, it should also be said that beyond all that was deplorable about hospitals, she was thrilled beyond description about birthing her babies.

By 1977, however, she was thirty years old, the mother of three, and felt strong enough and had read enough and knew enough about pregnancy and birth and the arrogant nature of too many obstetricians to make the audacious promise to herself that the next baby would be born at home. And it was audacious; very few women outside of communes in northern California and The Farm in Tennessee were doing home births.

Practically everyone from worried sisters to angry obstetricians to acquaintances who knew us only as Cael's parents said it was the wrong thing to do. Practically everyone said we weren't considering the consequences. Practically everyone said we were being selfish. Practically everyone told us that hospitals had changed and that birthing rooms were every bit like bedrooms, just safer.

Well, she observed things as they were and didn't listen to anyone else. And practically everyone was wrong.

Clover, who was conceived in front of the living room fireplace, was born in our upstairs bedroom on Coffey Lane, with the bumpy plaster walls covered in flowered yellow wallpaper and sunlight pouring in through old poured glass windows.

The day was beautiful, sunny, and warm. In the early stages of labor Patti walked around the property and picked wildflowers for the room, capturing the swooning scent from the big lilac at the corner of the barn. And when her labor grew more intense, we called Patti's friend Cathy Fosnot, who would be her birth attendant, and Herb Weinman, the family GP who, against his own "better judgment," had agreed to monitor the birth. Herb brought his wife, Arlene, along as an assistant; she had never before witnessed a birth, not even her own children's.

It was truly Patti's day. From letting each of us know precisely what she needed—and when—to figuring out the most comfortable position to birth the baby, she was in total charge. We cooked them dinner while Patti labored upstairs; Cathy bathed the kids while I took care of the animals; and later I put the kids to bed with the promise that by the time they woke, they would have a little sister or brother.

I won't go into more pastoral descriptions of the day or the radiance of Patti's presence (she was radiant) or even the unforgettable sensation of catching Clover in my own hands as she emerged into our world (after Herb exchanged places with me soon after she had crowned). Suffice it to say, I still get chills recalling the yellow bedroom and the moment of life and the extraordinary power of the woman who pushed that life into the world.

But what I remember as much as anything else about that day and night was the next morning when Cael, Nancy, and Addie shuffled shyly into the bedroom to see their mother and their new baby sister.

They climbed onto the bed and snuggled in. Patti held each of them—and they held their tiny little sister. And everybody cooed and laughed and made horrible faces when Clover scrunched up her tiny mug and filled up her diaper.

What was so heartwarming for me and Patti was that they clearly didn't feel abandoned and confused, as Nancy and Cael had felt after the earlier births. There was no anger, no manic behavior or saccharine sweetness. They actually seemed to like baby Clover.

And then, because they were little kids and had no more than a five-minute span of concentration—and maybe they got bored and hungry because the baby just lay there like a lump—and also because they knew Patti and the little wrinkly thing weren't going anywhere—I took them downstairs to the kitchen for breakfast. Just like any ordinary morning.

Cael went to school and told everybody that he had a new

sister—and that she was born at home. And when he jumped off the school bus that afternoon, he raced upstairs and discovered that his mother and his baby sister were actually still there, and unleashed a smile that could have melted the polar caps. He went up to see them, funfered around a bit, and then raced down the steps to eat some cookies and go out to play. Just like any other day. As Mike Myers would say as Linda Richman, "No big woop."

And, such as it was, it was the biggest woop of all.

HAVE A CIGAR!

An apology for the rhetoric of modern birthing fathers

If it were possible to talk to the unborn, one could never explain to them how it feels to be alive, for life is washed in the speechless real.

—JACQUES BARZUN

When Cael was born I was just about as full of myself as my young wife had been full of baby. I was the first father allowed into the delivery room at St. Mary's Hospital and was justifiably proud of myself for coaching Patti through twelve grueling hours of labor.

However, I am thankful that I wasn't listening to me when I recounted the joys of that first birth as if I were the one in labor. Shameless is the only word that comes to mind. In fact, with the first five kids, born between 1969 and 1979, I sprinted out of the various birthing rooms, purposely without a stash of cigars, but with an enormous and unabashed arsenal of sensitive phrases, quietly, insistently announcing the wonder and beauty of "our" births.

With each, adopting a voice I still do not recognize, I emotionally described how we struggled through the early stages of labor, how we barely survived transition and then pushed the baby out in what was certainly the most "beautiful moment of my life." I'm sure that I always added, "It was a miracle."

It would have to have been a miracle.

Of course, I was not sitting on an inner tube while I spoke, nor had I felt nauseated during the first ninety days of our pregnancy, slept on my back for six months, felt like a guernsey during the last few weeks, had a ten-hour muscle spasm in my belly, endured the dry heaves in transition, or had anyone surgically slice my perineum. Also—as long as I'm telling—I had no real plans of getting up for many of the two, four, six, eight (ad nauseam) feedings because *we* nursed our children.

Frankly, I'm not sure how Patti stood by and maintained a smile as I told practically the whole world how I had done her job. One woman I know has suggested that as men are unaccustomed to finding themselves in supporting roles, the shared birth rhetoric may realistically be considered a veiled attempt to steal the show. I can't disagree.

In my heart, I always knew that there was something wrong with all that talk of sharing—even as I was doing it and incidentally getting complimented for my sensitivity—but it was not until Patti became pregnant with Bay (number six), that I began to feel seriously out of place mentioning our cracked nipples. I was climbing over the rhetorical hill. Or perhaps I was already over the hill at thirty-nine and, like many men my age, just beginning to truly discover my own place in the world. In either case, it was an entirely new experience for one who should have been an old hand at such things.

Over those nine months I grew to understand that I had been neglecting what was truly mine as a father and a man. By denying my rightful place at my wife's side, not in the stirrups, I was cheating myself out of an experience that connected me not only to my own father but ultimately to men of all ages.

I slowly became more aware of my distinctive place in the whole generational process, more painfully aware than ever before of the fragile life growing within my wife's uterus and of my immeasurable responsibility to the woman and child I had touched in my own indelible way.

And I respected that pain as the source of my strength, strutting down Main Street upstate in New Paltz just as my father must have done on 172nd Street in Queens during the early spring of 1946, passing out cigars and blowing smoke. And that was almost like being born. Or being a father for the first time.

3

Zen and the Mindless Little Person in Your Bed

THOSE DREAMS OF FALLING

*When three in a bed is not
a ménage à trois*

Reality is where we are from moment to moment.
—ROBERT LINSSEN

Picture this: You've just spent the last hour and a quarter (not that you're counting) pacing back and forth across the living room doing the daddy jiggle, a hip-dislocating reverberating great ape walk that men magically acquire with the birth of their first babies: back and forth, back and forth, back and forth, large paw of a hand on that tiny delicate head, milky drool soaking your shirt while you hum an indecipherable version of Bob Marley's *Redemption Song* over and over until the screaming collicky infant is first calmed and then finally falls asleep long enough for you to lift the little doll hand to see if it drops in total dreamy unconsciousness. Finally. Finally.

And then, of course, you had to keep the bump 'n' jiggle going down the hall and into the dark nursery, the air scented with baby oil and a reminiscent dash of ammonia, humming and jiggling all the way to the crib, where you gently pried the little monkey from your shoulder and lowered him what seemed to be three or four or five feet down to the bunny and kitty mattress, careful not to jangle the damn airplane mobile, humming, jiggling, patting, patting, patting more and more softly until you're just patting air and tiptoeing backward like some doofy cartoon character out the door, which you leave open a crack so you can check his breathing every twenty-five minutes later on.

And then you're finally in your own bed, nothing between you and the beautiful naked woman who stole your heart a long time ago, the one who can still scratch your itch and who, by the way, you have not been with (in the biblical sense) for more than two months (not that you're counting the four weeks before the birth when she let you know in no uncertain terms that coitus was no longer in her dictionary and the six weeks afterward when words like episiotomy scars, hemorrhoids, and sore nipples replaced the extraordinary "Mmmmmm" in that same dictionary).

Tonight, however, she has let you know in broadly suggestive terms that the book has been reopened, and the pages are fluttering in the wind from her breathy lips, and you are every bit as excited and lusty and nervous (yes, nervous) as you were when you were fifteen and you were in a constant state of excited, nervous lustiness. And no doubt it's that excitement, coupled with an hour and a quarter of jiggling, that has made it absolutely necessary to run to the bathroom before . . . well, just before, you know . . . but, hey, the baby is finally asleep and the night is still night and there's music in the air. . . .

Unfortunately, in the short time that it took you to stumble to the bathroom, do your business (being careful not to flush and wake the little bugger in the next room), and then do the naked racewalk back to the silky comforts of the marriage bed, the song has miraculously changed from Dylan's *Lay Lady Lay* to Simon and Garfunkel's ode to romantic futility and humiliation, *Cecilia*: When you come back to bed, someone's taken your place. La la la la la.

In fact, he's not only taken your place, he's pressed up against her luscious naked body! And he's sucking on her magnificent breast! And worse still, she looks perfectly content, not strung tight like the shrieky violin that has recently taken up residence in your head and makes your hair stand straight up with each draw of the bow.

She smiles at you and blows you a kiss as if to say "This will only be five minutes, don't lose the mood darling. . . ." So you slide under the covers and lie down on your official six-centimeter slice of the marital bed and wait the five, ten, fifteen, twenty minutes (not that you're counting) in near frenzied expectation when you suddenly realize that the slurpy sounds of nursing have long since stopped and have been replaced by a lilting duet of rhythmic breaths—and then you look over in complete despair and see that little Oedipus and his mother are fast asleep.

And in that instant all those visions of bacchanalian lovemaking that have sustained and kept you edgy lo these many weeks fall into the trash heap of another cold, lonely night full of dreams of falling. Falling out of windows. Falling off cliffs. Falling from the back of speeding trains.

Only this night the dream is not really a dream at all. You have fallen—out of bed. In the final act of domination, Little Big Oed, who is fully sated with breast nectar, has scooted around sideways on the mattress, pressed his stubby but steel-like toes into your ribs, and pushed you out onto the floor.

I almost wish there were something to say that would enable new fathers to avoid the inevitable frustration and humiliation that surely awaits them, but as the man says, "Reality is where we are from moment to moment." And the reality is that life is never the same after a baby alters the symmetry of love.

Accept it and move on to the next reality. Sex returns—in many ways more deeply satisfying than it was before—but you'll never again be totally alone in bed with your one and only—even if the door's locked and the children are asleep (or grown and out of the house).

WHEN "IT" FINALLY OCCURRED TO ME

The "withness" of the first night home

We have no right to assume that any physical laws exist, or if they existed up to now, that they will continue to exist in a similar manner in the future.

—MAX PLANCK

My guess is that Patti grew up gradually over the nine months she was pregnant with Cael. The profound changes to a woman's psyche that must by nature go along with a life stirring within her body must also bring with them an extraordinary sense of the "withness of the body," to quote Alfred North Whitehead, and a deep enduring awareness of one's connection to the ebb and flow of the universe.

Frankly, I didn't know much about "withness" or connection or even that deplorable word *maturity*, primarily because as a male I spent those same nine months in the same boyish hormone-driven heroic ("Bottom of the ninth, bases loaded, Lewis comes to bat . . .") fog that I'd spent the previous twenty-two years. I was still a kid. I was not only witless, I was withless.

So while Patti was gearing herself up mentally, spiritually, and physically for the impending, if idealized, visions of birth and life with an infant, I don't think I was working on any vision at all. I think I just assumed that after the baby was born, everything would pretty much return to normal: we'd stay up till the early hours of the morning, sleep till noon, go to afternoon classes, party, work when absolutely necessary, rock 'n' roll. If there were any visions rattling around in my hairball of a head, they might only have been about how cool it was going to be to have a little guy in OshKosh overalls, and a blue Brooklyn Dodgers cap and a pint-size Rawlings glove on his tiny hand.

I do remember noticing small but significant changes early on in the pregnancy (besides the watermelon that was turning her belly button from an innie to an outie), like the strange motherly voice I sometimes heard on the phone—and her newly acquired propensity to be on time to appointments—and, most shocking of all, her sudden need for more than three hours' sleep a night. But I also remember thinking that they were temporary aberrations and would disappear as soon as the nine months were up.

And through the next few months of agonizing crib and layette shopping (and doll-size clothes scattered around the house and doctors' appointments and Lamaze classes and, of course, that enormous protrusion between the two of us as I tried valiantly to carry on a sex life), all of which should have alerted me to the fact that my life was never going to be the same again, I'm pretty sure that I remained clueless.

Withless. Even on that spring morning when we were rushing to get to classes on time and she glanced disparagingly down at our two-seater British racing green P1800 into which she had to drop her not inconsiderable girth—and from which she would later on extract herself.

"What?" I asked.

She glowered at me like I was a dithering child. "We need a new car, Steven . . . one that has a backseat and is more than six inches off the ground."

I looked over at the two-seater, a real honey of a Swedish automobile when Swedish cars were still fun to drive, and wondered if it was financially possible to put the 1800 up on blocks and get an old clunker until she came back to her senses. As I said, clueless.

So, it was a stunning moment for me the night after the morning we brought Cael home from the hospital (in our brand-new used station wagon!). We were sitting on the floor—just the three of us where there had only been two just a few days before—in the bare living room of the cottage on Lake Kegonsa, crickets filling the spaces of the warm night outside, water lapping at the shore, both of just staring at this marvelous wailing producer of poop, when it finally occurred to me that I was his father. His Dad. The Old Man. Daddy. Pops. Moneybags. The Doofus Hiding in the Bathroom. The Ride Home from the Dance. And I would never again be the same innocent and childish and footloose and irresponsible and ignorant hipster that I had always aspired to be.

Which is when I turned to Patti in a mild sweat and said, "Let's run into town and get something to eat." It had been common for us in those days—especially as the pregnancy wore on and Patti grew increasingly ravenous—to leave the lake at all sorts of bizarre hours to search for doughnuts in twenty-four-hour places in Madison.

Patti looked at me like I was crazy. "It's almost midnight and I just got him to sleep. I'm completely exhausted. Let's go to bed."

It was as if the avenging angel had swooped down on Stoughton, Wisconsin, and lifted the gummy veil of childhood from my eyes: out ahead lay diapers, two a.m. feedings, baby-sitters, work, health insurance, nursery school, career, middle-school chorus concerts, college tuition, thinning hair, and a paunch. Tea and cookies at eleven o'clock each night. Sansabelt slacks. A condo in Florida. Eternity.

And no more three a.m. doughnuts.

When Patti and Cael fell asleep in our bed soon thereafter, I walked barefoot to the lake and sat down at the edge of the rickety dock, feet dangling in the dark water. I felt old, more deeply tired than I'd known possible at the early hour of one a.m., heavier in spirit than ever before in my young life. I used to think I could walk on water. On that night, a few days after men had walked on the moon, I realized that if I eased myself off the dock, I would slip into the black lake and sink like a stone all the way down to the muck at the bottom.

And that night the water felt cool on my hot skin, my toes pushing off from the muck and my body rising to the moonlit surface and floating off into an extraordinary new life.

CIRCUMCISIO

Some thoughts on circumcision

Do not seek to follow in the footsteps of the men of old;
seek what they sought.

—MATSUO BASHŌ

In 1979 when Danny was born and routinely circumcised by the doctor, Patti took one look at the painful lesion on his tiny penis and swore tearfully that if we *ever* had another boy she would never again allow such a cruel and barbaric mutilation of one of her babies. There was no medical reason for it.

Although reluctant to agree, for reasons still not perfectly clear to me, I nodded sympathetically—and looked away. In truth, I believed it was a nonissue. Danny was our fifth child—and supposed to be our last.

Despite the screaming, the red raw tip of his penis, and a worrisome infection that followed, the fat baby boy eventually healed, and the painful experience was replaced by the joys and anxieties of watching a young child grow. And by 1984 when he entered kindergarten, circumcision was as far from our thoughts as the idea of having a sixth child.

Which is all we were thinking about after watching Danny take that giant step up to the school bus—and we walked back into an empty house. So, in February of 1985 when Patti was six weeks pregnant, the issue instantly became relevant again.

Patti was quick to recall the painful memories of Danny's first few days of life. And I agreed right away that we should talk it over. Sometime. What can you say about something that feels so wrong and so right at the same time?

I tried almost nightly to express my confusion, but every time I opened my mouth, the voices of some angry old men took up residency in my vocal cords and shouted me down. Then one evening I closed my eyes to all the shouting, hoping to visualize a transcendent solution—or something—and when I opened them again Clover was standing in front of me. The resolution.

At that hopeful moment I convinced myself that we were going to have a girl, and as winter turned grudgingly into spring and spring hesitantly into summer I parlayed that resolution into nearly six months of silence on the subject.

In early September, however, when the midwife of our "refresher" Lamaze group wrote CIRCUMCISION on the board, I knew that the comfortingly discomforting silence had come to an end. And after she finished a rather compelling argument against what she called a "cosmetic procedure with significant medical risks associated with it," Patti turned my way as if to say "Well?"

On the ride home there was nothing but silence as I drove down the dark country roads trying to find my voice amid all the shouting going on in my brain. When I was finally able to utter some sounds, I hesitantly told her that it troubled me deeply that the baby—if it was a boy and I was sure it wasn't—would look different from me, his two older brothers, and the vast majority of boys at school. I admitted that even though I had not attended services since I was thirteen, I still felt that it would be a betrayal to go against what has been done to Jewish baby boys for thousands of years. I was concerned that my parents would not understand. As time went on and the gas gauge neared empty, I even admitted, somewhat sheepishly, that I preferred the way circumcised penises look. However, none of those reasons felt exactly right.

Later that evening, disrupting an awkward silence that had lasted for hours, I told Patti the other truth: that despite my obvious wish to avoid the subject altogether, as the father, the burden of the decision should be more mine than hers. It would be me with whom he would have to contend to establish his own identity as a man.

I expected a serious rebuttal—Patti is a strong, self-willed person—but after some private thought of her own she reluctantly agreed, reminding me again of the screams and the raw lesion and the dangerous infection. I nodded.

Had I been totally honest that evening, however, I would have admitted that I knew that the right thing to do was to leave the foreskin intact but that the right thing for me was to have him circumcised. But I could not utter the words. All I could do was hope we would have a girl.

On October 6, Bay Steven was born. It was a wonderful birth; his three sisters, one brother, an aunt, his godmother, and I were all in the birthing room as he emerged into our world. My joy was as pure as I had ever experienced at any birth.

I waited, of course, until the last possible moment to admit to myself and to Patti that I had (long, long ago) decided to follow the old men. On the evening of the second day of his life, I chose circumcision for my infant son.

By the time I arrived at the hospital the next morning, it had already been done. Patti was teary and angry. Bay was crying. When I lifted the small gauze, his tiny penis was red and painfully raw. And for what? The old men who tell that circumcision is a sign of initiation into the community?

There was nothing to do but hold my baby, to accept his pain as my own and welcome him into the confusing community of men, boys all of us, following our fathers' giant footprints in the sand. That night, as I rocked him back and forth, I thought ahead to his days in the tangled woods with his best pals . . . to his afternoons in damp locker rooms with friends and enemies . . . to the hazy light of hanging out on street corners with the guys . . . to the quiet darkness of sitting in a rocker with his own son. That night I understood that the old men were not wrong, but they were not right. Initiation happens every day of a boy's life when we seek what they sought.

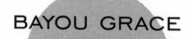

BAYOU GRACE

*Enduring the biggest fright
in a parent's life*

Zen is simply a voice crying "Wake up! Wake up!"
—Maha Sthavira Sangharakshita

On top of Patti's cluttered dresser is the swirling ultrasound Polaroid taken at the amniocentesis. I don't remember the details of that day, only the sense of well-being I felt driving away from the clinic in New Haven. Of course I had doubts about being a father for the seventh time, but as I had always harbored a feeling in the depths of my soul that we were somehow watched over, I felt in my bones that my family would *always* be protected from anything too painful to endure.

A few weeks later, a genetic counselor called to say the baby was fine. "Perfect," I said to Patti, despite the fact that this was already not a perfect pregnancy. At nearly forty-two, Patti was tired and nauseous much of the time, not quite as resilient as she had been at twenty-two with Cael or at thirty-two with Danny. And to my surprise, the older kids were not exactly thrilled with the idea of another sibling squeezing into our crowded den. At two, Bay was ignorantly blissful, but Danny and Clover, then eight and ten, were concerned about new room arrangements;

Addie, twelve, felt displaced—again; Nancy, fourteen and long past thinking her parents had any self-control, shrugged; and Cael, eighteen, was simply embarrassed. "Oh no!" he blurted out when I called him at college.

Nothing could rock my confidence, though. After six kids nothing could surprise us. Toxemia, labor, hospital birth, home birth, circumcision, colic, sleepless nights, croup, sibling rivalry, and more—we'd been through it all.

So when Elizabeth Bayou-Grace arrived on a warm May day, I imagined her born into a state of grace, cradled by the rippling waters of a bayou in my wife's native Louisiana. She was a gorgeous baby. In fact, everything seemed so right with the world that when the pediatrician detected a condition called congenital hip dysplasia—dislocated hips—I was rather cavalier about it, even as I watched her fitted into a harness that held her knees up to her belly like a frog. I was thankful it was not worse, my optimism rising with the temperature through the summer visits to a specialist at the Hospital for Joint Diseases in New York City.

The fall was a rainy one, however, and the simple joint problem seemed quickly to skid out of our shaky control. First the news that the harness didn't work—both hips were still out of joint—then the frustrating cancellation of several diagnostic tests because of a suspicious low-grade infection. And then, so suddenly it seemed, the soft measured voice of a pediatrician saying to my unbelieving soul that the blood tests indicated a problem totally unrelated to the hip disease: perhaps acute lymphocytic leukemia. He could not confirm it, though.

Through two decades of dark nights in emergency rooms, holding desperately feverish or injured children in my arms, I had never known the helplessness or terror—or betrayal—I felt when I heard those words. I began to wonder how I ever could have seen the world with such certainty.

As the rain turned to snow and ice outside, it was recommended that we move along on the joint problems again and keep a close watch on her blood levels. Elizabeth was placed in traction and was to stay that way for two weeks. Patti warned me on the phone about what to expect when I arrived at the hospital, but how do you prepare yourself to see a beautiful and innocent five-month-old baby flat on her back with her little legs separated and strapped to a pulley-and-weight apparatus attached to the top of a metal crib? I had to step out in the hall to catch my teary breath when my heroic wife climbed up into the crib and leaned bare-breasted over Elizabeth so the wailing baby could nurse.

This was definitely not the way it was supposed to be. During the next two weeks, Patti spent twenty-four hours a day in a cramped hospital room entertaining our frustrated baby and I put nearly three thousand grueling miles on the car commuting between our upstate home, work, and the hospital.

Along the way my older children kept me from skidding off into despair; Nancy, Addie, Clover, and Danny provided mothering and fathering for Bay (and each other) during the many hours I was away; Cael called often from college; and we combined weekend trips to the zoo and the Moscow Circus with visits to the hospital armed with balloons, stuffed animals, and drawings the kids made. Soon the sterile hospital room began to take on some of the warm semblance of home. And Elizabeth's smiling good nature through her ordeal made us all feel as if things were going our way again.

They were not. The traction failed to keep her hips in place, and she was sent directly from X ray to surgery. Hours and hours later when our little baby returned dazed and hurting from recovery, the needle marks, bruises, and horrid incisions we saw provided final proof to me that the protection I had once imagined had never existed at all.

On the way home from the hospital that night, I pulled off the road, laid my forehead on the wheel, and wept as I had not wept since I was Danny's age. I had always thought my most important job as a father was to protect my family from harm, but sitting alone in that cold car, I realized how powerless I was to stop her pain or the cancer. I had no claims on special treatment, no matter what I did or who I knew or how loud I raised my voice in protest.

I felt as forlorn as little Bay, who woke each morning with the same question: "Is Mommy home yet?" And the older kids, weary of worrying, eating at neighbors' homes, baby-sitting and begging rides, began to withdraw from the daily soap opera behind their closed bedroom doors. The eagerly awaited Christmas was approaching, but I walked through the big house shivering in cold pockets of silence.

In retrospect, I think Elizabeth and Patti came home just in time to save us all. As much as they yearned to be surrounded again by family, dogs, cats, ducks, and thirty acres of red and gold fallen leaves, we needed a mother and baby to hold us together. Invigorated by their presence, we put our energies into creating accommodations for a baby in a bulky body cast that went from her armpits to her ankles: car beds out of wicker dog beds, car seats created by sawing away the sides of standard restraints, and a high chair cut out of a butcher-block table on wheels. We decorated for her first Christmas.

The girls often took Elizabeth into their rooms as they talked on the phone or did homework. Danny read books to her, and Bay hovered around his baby sister as if she were his best friend. And most amazing was Elizabeth, who woke singing each morning, actually learning to creep and even climb in the heavy cast by using her small hands to grasp the rug or a chair or a leg and hoist herself along.

The baby who was the focus of my most desolate fear made Christmas '88 as clamorous and wonderful as any in memory. We sat her in the butcher-block high chair and she giggled and squealed through the entire high-voltage morning, paper and ribbons flying everywhere, unaware and unconcerned that her ordeal was not over. At all.

From this vantage point seven years later, I know she had much more ahead of her: another hip operation, more excruciating blood tests, the exhilarating news that she did not have leukemia, the icy disappointment of learning that after all she'd been through, only one hip was in place and she would be confined for more than three years to a heavy brace that held her legs wide apart, her feet in a virtual plié. I know now that the joints would never heal perfectly and that physical therapy would become a way of life.

Yet the baby who lit up that cold Christmas in 1988 eventually got up on her haunches and started crawling in '89; and from there climbed up on Bay's scooter and, using her feet like flippers, began dashing recklessly around the house. Scooting, bumping down stairs, hitching rides on sore hips, or directing us with a vocabulary born of necessity, she became a lesson to all about getting around in an unsteady world.

By Christmas 1990, she actually walked in her brace across the festive living room to the cheers and tears of her screaming family. And in January 1992, Elizabeth Bayou-Grace walked into nursery school without a brace. It was not just a great day. It was a miracle, especially to me, who once let ordinary miracles pass me by.

So as Christmas approaches this year, the energy levels wavering near the paternal red line, it's no surprise that at the center of the frenzy of anticipation here is a seven-year-old who still runs rather unsteadily yet provides enough of a surge to light the densely ornamented spruce in the corner. She has indeed become the spirit of Christmas in our home, the baby who leads us to accept our fragile places in this world without assumptions. A healthy reminder to her father, in this snowy, slippery world, to "Wake up! Wake up!"

ZEN IN THE ARTLESSNESS OF GIVING NAMES, PART I

What's in a name? That which we call a rose
By any other name would smell as sweet.
— SHAKESPEARE

On May 14, 1979, while sitting or, more precisely, squatting on my lap at the edge of our four-poster bed, Patti let forth an archetypally mammoth groan and pushed out one fat little baby boy between her spread thighs, squishy and howling and altogether rather cute despite his bald head.

Patti's sister Leigh was there with us. So was her friend Kitty. And so was Dr. Wooten, home birth doc from the famed Woodstock (where in keeping with the Zen-ness of this book the Woodstock festival was not held). The doctor was kneeling on the rug dressed in an orange jumpsuit. He caught the baby in his sure hands just as the little guy felt the first forces of gravity in his young life. It was all pretty extraordinary.

And, yes, pretty ordinary, too. A simple holy moment. As Milwaukee poet James Hazard writes: "It is an ordinary thing to be holy. We do such extraordinary things not to be." And so it was.

Ordinary, that is. Cael, who was ten at the time, was pretty excited the next morning about finally having a brother after all those sisters, but probably no more so than about the fact that it was Saturday and he didn't have school. However, Nancy and Addie, six and four respectively, in their footed pajamas, thought it was absolutely terrific to have a real live doll baby in the house. And Clover, at two, was clueless but quite happy that her mama was there just like she was there every morning of her life. That was it, though. Life went on unimpeded.

The baby who had been inside her mother for so long was now outside. Simple as that. Suddenly—and generally uneventfully—we went from six to seven in the family. The house was as homey and messy as it had always been. Emma the dog rolled over on her back and begged shamelessly for a scratch. The goats needed feeding. The grass needed mowing. Everything was fine and dandy—and ordinary.

Until Nancy and Cael realized that we hadn't named the little orangutan. Then all hell broke loose.

Frankly, I don't know how we made it forty weeks without figuring out an official name for the new baby, but as you might have gathered by now, we're a little laid-back about some things in our family. We did choose several names for both sexes that each of us liked. It just turned out that we never agreed on the precise one.

And then so suddenly he was born. I figured that it might be a neat idea to try out a few names for the first few days and see how they fit—sort of like a thirty-day free home trial. Patti actually liked the idea.

The kids, however, thought we had lost our marbles. On Sunday, the day after the birth, they were horrified at their parents' blatant irresponsibility. They implored us to give "it" a name.

And early Monday morning when the tubby little muffin still didn't have a real name, they were on the verge of reporting us to the authorities for dereliction of parental duty. "He needs a name!" Cael burst out self-righteously over his oatmeal, sounding a lot like my father.

"How could you not name him?" Nancy snarled, dripping cereal and contempt at our immaturity. As the only truly organized person in the family, she's never been able to abide our messes.

"Yeah," added Addie, our little bulldozer who always spoke the truth. "How are they gonna go to school and tell everybody?"

Ah, we realized, that's the essence of the problem. They were far less concerned about the poor nameless baby than about having to show up at school and admit that their parents were classless jerks. And the problem thus unfurled, Cael forged right ahead with my father's patented either/or stance on life. "We can't go to school and tell everybody that our parents didn't get it together to give our new brother a name." He scrunched up his nose and glared at us. "Either he gets a name or we stay home!"

"Yeah," piped in Nancy, who wasn't sure that this was going to work. "A person needs a name!"

"Yeah," said Addie, who wasn't going to school that day anyway.

Patti and I don't normally take well to being extorted by our children—see the chapter on Zen spanking—but in this instance I admit we understood their abject humiliation and shame. Reasonable or not, it would be embarrassing to have to tell everyone that your parents couldn't figure out a name for your new baby brother more than two days after he was born. The jokes would never end.

So, just before Nancy and Cael walked out the kitchen door that morning, the fat little baby boy got called Daniel Clay Lewis. (Just for the record, there is no significance, personal or otherwise, to either name, and furthermore, we had no idea at the time about Daniel Day Lewis.) They all agreed that they liked that, though I'm sure we could have called him Rin Tin Tin and it would have been all right.

But it was even better than that; it was a regular name, not something weird like Cael or Clover or Adelyn. It was Danny, an all-American name that you could bring to school and not have to hear snorts or snickers or howls.

And he smelled very sweet.

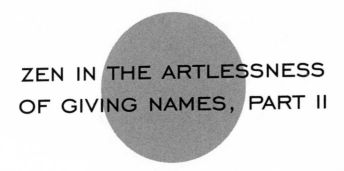

ZEN IN THE ARTLESSNESS OF GIVING NAMES, PART II

Our names are the light that glows on the sea waves at night and then dies without leaving a signature.
—RABINDRANATH TAGORE

Of course, that was not the end of the issue when Danny finally got his name. One thing that you learn early and well in a large family is that nothing is ever simple.

Saddled with a father who for reasons beyond their understanding (and my own) rarely calls his children by the names inked on their birth certificates, they waited expectantly to hear what Danny really would be called.

At the time that Danny was born, for example, I was calling Clover Poochie, which was short for the unwieldy Perchmont Robert Haldanish. Don't ask why. Zen names are beyond understanding. And since that time she's had a wide variety of aliases, from the pithy Flodunkus to the more je-ne-sais-quoi Florky-Dorky (or its derivative Flumkin-Dumkin) to the stately Foofie.

Honestly, I don't know. She responds to any of them, though.

And, of course, Clover is not the only one with unusual tags. Cael is Bubba, but he was Ralph Barco for years. Nancy has evolved to The Turtle from previous incarnations as Puppy Turtle,

Turkey Puddle, The Scooper, and Woopy Woop for a Full Year till She's Full Grown (which I eventually shortened to Wooper). Addie has worn, among several other monikers, Aderlwyn Yacht, Yetso Yurt, YD, The Bulldozer, and most recently Al-Edward, or Edward for short. Danny, who was Graybadge and E-Man (Encyclopedia Man) and Danzek and Dansak and most recently Darzulu or Zule, is now Donald. Yes, Donald.

Things got simplified with the last two. Maybe I'm just getting old, but the names fit so well, I've just never had the need to transform them again. Bay is The Boofer, first, last, and always. He couldn't be anything else. And Elizabeth Bayou-Grace has been simply (and, I believe, rather elegantly) Bishy for all seven years of her life.

It's been with a mixture of horror and an odd sort of endearment that the children abide my quirks. I can tell you, though, that in that big family stock-in-trade of calling children by their sisters' and brothers' names—"Hey, um, Nancy, Addie, Clover, Danny, whatever your name is, please turn off the light."—I never trip over the private names, the ones destined to be recalled in embarrassed whispers when the children are grown with children of their own and reflecting back on their lost youth.

Yes, everything comes and goes, even names, like the light sparkling off the sea waves at night. They grab our attention, they lap at the sides of the hull, but they are not who we are, except to the one who calls us in the dark. Maybe then.

THE ZEN OF
DIAPER DUNKING

*There is a proper way to swish
cloth diapers in a toilet*

The Way is Not a Way.
—GARY SNYDER

I'm no shirker. I changed diapers for more than twenty-one years. Seven kids and a lot of dirty bottoms later, I'm pretty much of an expert in the field. In fact, estimating ten thousand diapers per child from birth to toilet training, Patti and I have probably lifted more bottoms than the entire academy of plastic surgeons.

Back in the old hippie days, when the earth seemed big enough to absorb all the world's garbage without so much as a queasy equator, we used the first varieties of paper diapers. They were pretty primitive by today's standards—rather bulky, they had no elastic and no tabs, didn't absorb well, and didn't hold much in—but they were disposable. And even more important, you didn't have to dip them in the toilet, a truly awful job, certain to cause most grown men great grief. We loved disposables, especially when we were traveling. If they weren't so costly (relative to washing our own cloth diapers at the laundromat) we would have used them all the time.

As the years, family income, and number of children mounted

proportionally, however, we began to use paper diapers exclusively. In the seventies, when "single-use disposables" achieved space-age performance and convenience, we became a major supplier of solid waste to the local landfill. I estimate that twelve years must have passed between the time that I dunked (and dunked and dunked and dunked) my last cloth diaper in a toilet and the day Bay (number six) was born into the world's burgeoning awareness of a garbage crisis.

The facts about the world's solid waste problems—and the single-use diaper's role in filling and contaminating earth and water—are well known by now. I won't drive down that road. My point is that after Patti and I decided to return to cloth diapers as one specific solution to try to keep the world spinning cleanly on its axis, I was suddenly back dipping diapers in the toilet.

And whining in a most unbecoming fashion.

Frankly, I didn't want to be in my sophisticated forties and be seen hunched over the porcelain throne holding the one clean corner of a messy diaper between thumb and forefinger, dunking and swishing (dunking and swishing), wondering how I was going to wring out the excess water when I was finished without getting my hands dirty. I'll admit that on a few occasions I actually dropped the diaper in the toilet and walked out, leaving the awful job to the next unsuspecting person who stumbled into the bathroom to, of all things, go to the bathroom.

I yearned pathetically for the old disposable way of life. Being an English teacher, I might even have moaned something like "Something is rotten in the state of Denmark" when that old familiar odor wafted its way across the room. I pined out loud that life was already messy enough, hoping that someone would come to my rescue and do the dirty deed.

And as the months went on and I continued to try to weasel out of changing Bay's diapers, my wife and kids began to look at me with disdain. Nancy's scowl reminded me of Claudius's words about the melancholy Hamlet of the same rotten Denmark: "T'is unmanly grief."

And so it was. Though the Bard's words reflect much weightier matters than a load in an infant's pants, the meaning is the same for all fathers: whether it's revenge for your father's murder or wiping the schmutz off your baby's bottom or cleaning up the environment, there is a proper way for us to approach the unpleasant realities of fatherhood.

Unfortunately, there is no way to wring out a sopping wet diaper with the tips of two fingers on one hand. I've tried. You have to get your hands dirty. The art of it is, as mothers have always known, that there is no art.

Diaper dunking is done mindlessly. You take a deep breath and plunge right in. Dunk and swish until the diaper has nothing stuck to it and then, without even a second's pause, grab it with both mitts, fold it once, wring the sucker out, and slam-dunk it into the diaper pail. That's it.

And don't forget to wash your hands—and keep your nails short.

The Suchness of Life
with Toddlers

SURVIVING THE TERRIBLE TWOS

A road map for the lost and weary

'Tis as manlike to bear extremities as godlike to forgive.
—JOHN FORD

Included with the basket of diapers and lotions that are sent home with every infant from every maternity ward in the country should be a three-year supply of fortune cookies with two separate messages inside:

> Throw away all those how-to-parent books. Just keep in mind who is the parent and who is the child. Nothing else matters.

> Every two-year-old exists solely to test your sanity. Be as patient as the universe but don't be quite so limitless.

Two-year-olds are really cute. Really cute. Moppy hair and OshKosh overalls and brand-new stubby teeth and short chunky little legs and sweet little raspy voices that call you Daddy.

They're so cute that when they stand in front of you, hands on nonexistent hips, bellowing out an adamant NO!, we actually laugh. They're so cute, in fact, that I think there's a Darwinian survival mechanism involved in their cuteness. Otherwise they'd never survive.

They're cute, but they're bad.

So, there's no irony or transcendent double entendre in the designation terrible twos. Two-year-olds are terrible. You've seen them in the grocery stores, in the malls, in churches and synagogues, in your own living rooms. They touch everything they can reach; they break everything they can touch; and they throw tantrums every single time they can't reach something they want to touch and break.

And they say NO! to everything in the universe.

I'll skip the psychobabble about independence and the inner child and self-esteem and separation anxiety and gender identification. Let's just define the two forms of a tantrum: *home* and *away*, just like in sports.

A *home* tantrum involves lying on the floor and kicking your legs and screaming (often screeching) and sometimes holding your breath until you turn an odd shade of blue or gray, depending on your cultural diversity factor. For most adults it's a no-brainer. Any reasonable parent will simply walk out of the room, thus ending the tantrum. A tantrum, like a tango, takes two people.

Just a side note: if you think that you can outyell or out-tantrum a two-year-old having a tantrum, give it up. You can't. As the saying might go, any self-respecting two-year-old can tantrum any grown man under the table, which is where your wife will find you when she gets home, babbling to yourself like Tony Perkins in *Psycho*.

And here's another one: trying to reason with a toddler having a tantrum is such an absurd concept, it doesn't even warrant further comment.

An *away* or public tantrum is very different. It involves being sprawled on the floor of the supermarket or the mall or a family friend's living room and kicking your legs and screeching and sometimes holding your breath, just like a home tantrum. The difference, of course, is that there are adults besides your parents around to scoff and snicker at the scene.

Most parents are painfully embarrassed at the sight of their kids writhing on the filthy floor, and try to make lame explanations to the other adults gawking on in smug disapproval like "I've never seen her like this" or "He must be coming down with something." Then they try to get their unruly children to stop and behave, either by making unenforceable threats ("The store manager is going to call the police") or talking in that sickly sweet voice that you hear on PBS kids' shows. Either way the parent loses. The kid's got a rapt audience and the harried parent's complete and undivided attention—and the tantrum won't stop until she or he has your power of attorney.

I hate to be so definitive—and so traditional—and so un-Zen—but there are only two possible courses of action to save you from abject humiliation—and along the way maybe even do your kid a favor. The first is to walk away, just like you do at home. (You might say something patently parental like "I don't listen when you act that way" if that makes you feel better. It actually doesn't matter what you say.)

If walking away is not possible—for instance, when your tot is disturbing other people, like in a movie (been there) or a restaurant (seen it) or a friend's living room (done it)—then Plan Two goes into effect. You simply pick 'em up, turn 'em sideways, and hoist 'em onto your better hip (head forward, kicking feet back) and remove 'em from civilized society. A car is a good holding tank. So is a park or a backyard in warm weather. Two-year-olds calm down very quickly when they realize a tantram is not working.

Then they get remorseful—and cute: tear-stained faces, wet matted hair, and grubby little paws up in the air begging a hug. The sight is so cute that you are instantly filled with tenderness, hugging them as if they've been lost for days and just been found. And in that wonderfully warm (and probably wet) moment you wonder how it's possible that you were so furious with them just a few moments ago.

Which is precisely when, of course, the little imp smirks over your shoulder, knowing she has just earned the upper hand for the next tantrum coming down the pike.

WHAT IS THE SOUND OF ONE HAND SPANKING?

Some non-PC thoughts on discipline

A master, Gutei, whenever he was asked the meaning of Zen, lifted his index finger. That was all. Another kicked a ball. Still another slapped the inquirer.
—HUSTON SMITH

When it comes to the more sticky realms of parenting, like whether it's okay to spank the little urchin for crimes against parental humanity, I generally turn to my wife as guide or guru. She knows more than I do.

I know I'm not supposed to say that, but it's true. Given the undeniable fact that mothers and babies share organ systems for forty of the most meaningful weeks in a person's life, it's reasonable to conclude that most mothers know more about children than most fathers, which does not necessarily mean that they make better parents. They just know more intuitively. Patti certainly does—plus she's not really the enigmatic type, which is a great help for me when I find myself in an ethical or moral morass about things like the spanking issue.

Her sphinxlike advice? "Swat 'em when they need it."

She draws most of her good knowledge from observing animals. Animals, she says, don't ponder correct behavior, they live it, drawing on eons of knowledge of survival. In Zen terms they know what is—they have "isness."

In contrast, far too many childcare experts (with M.D.s and Ph.D.s dangling off their names like price tags off sale rack clothing), deal only with what *should* be. Despite those same eons of evidence that human beings are aggressively territorial, they believe we *should* be able to live meat-free as well as aggression-free. Karen Horney, my favorite social theorist, called it "The tyranny of the shoulds" and suggested that the should system is directly responsible for the formation of self-destructive behavior patterns in children and other living things.

Anyway, Patti says it's okay to spank if the situation warrants it and you don't leave any marks. She says "Look at how dogs and cats (and monkeys and lions) handle their babies when they get obnoxious." They growl or snarl first and then out comes the paw and they swat 'em. Not hard enough to hurt, but hard enough to let 'em know they've been scolded. And the pups or kittens pick themselves up and go away—presumably without any psychological scars or damage to their self-esteem.

The central fact of life with toddlers is that it is virtually impossible to communicate via pure language with them. If you think men and women speak different dialects—and it's pretty clear that we do (read Deborah Tannen's *You Just Don't Understand*)—then toddlers and adults speak entirely different languages. So when your kids do something *really* outrageous—like running out on a busy street or yanking on the cord and knocking over the Mr. Coffee or smothering the new baby or punching the mailman in the groin—logic does not work. You can't explain right and wrong to two-year-olds. They just have to know in no uncertain terms that whatever it is, it's not okay.

Of course, yelling (or a good growling) works up to a point, especially if you can work up something really deep and stern. And so does banishment, though all of my grown kids later informed us that being sent to your room with all your toys and books is not really punishing. But nothing is as swift and sure and pointed as an open palm swatting a covered bottom.

The technique itself is very simple: take the toddler's upper arm in your left hand, turn her sideways, and then swat her with your open right palm on her bottom. Never anyplace else, never on bare flesh, and never hard enough to knock her out of your solid but nonsqueezing left-hand grasp. Sometimes it's good to follow it up with a "Don't ever do that again!" but I don't think it really matters. What matters is that they understand.

At some point, generally before kindergarten, spanking bottoms gives way to more reasoned forms of punishment. You can actually talk to them or yell at them and banish them at that point—and it means something. Or other.

Then the only form of corporal punishment allowable after toddlerhood is the *automobile swat*. It is an effective means of discipline when you are alone in the car with one or more screaming ninnies roughhousing in the backseat. I'm sure you've been there—either in the backseat of your own childhood or in the front seat more recently.

The technique again is quite simple. You begin with the peremptory growl or yell, then growl or yell louder, and then just when you think they will drive you out of your mind—and off the road—you put your left hand tightly on the wheel, hoist your right arm up and over the seat back, and while looking straight ahead at the road (very important), start swatting at anything you can hit.

Feel free to swat as hard as you can because the angle makes it almost impossible to have any real force behind it—and besides, after the first or second knee has been slapped, all the kids in the backseat have lifted their legs and are scrunched back toward the seat belts—way out of your reach.

Sometimes children laugh at parents doing the backseat swat because adults look ridiculous twisted around like that and because the slaps are so ineffectual. In those cases you have to do it again as soon as their legs are back down. And that will take care of that.

Finally, don't worry about turning your kids into ax murderers if you occasionally swat their bottoms. It seems to me that ax murderers come from truly abusive homes or homes where plain old everyday aggression is aggressively denied. Unlike many over-educated adults who have lost connection to the "isness" of the universe, children and little animals understand in their bones that aggression is a natural function of life—it cannot be obscured or denied, just appropriately directed. And with that knowledge they learn when aggressiveness is okay and when it is not.

Not a bad lesson for these violent times.

ARE YOU A WIMPY DAD?

Who wears the diapers in the family?

You Know You're a Wimp When . . .

- You have to ask your child's permission to go out Saturday night.

- Every other sentence in your phone conversation is to the little tot standing next to you.

- You're not sure if it's right to punish your child for painting the living room wall because you don't want to stifle his creativity.

- Your grocery cart is full of Twinkies, Cocoa Crispies, Cheese Doodles, Gummy Bears, Mountain Dew, and Hawaiian Punch.

- Your explanation of why it's not okay to hit Daddy is more than five words long. ("Don't ever do that again!")

- You ask your child to set the table and she says, "In a minute," and walks out of the room.

- Being alone with your kids makes you nervous.

- You clean your child's room while she's messing up the play-room, and vice-versa.

- Your child hides under his friend's bed when you arrive to pick him up . . . and the friend's mother is the only one who can get him out.

- Your three-year-old has the baby around the neck in a bear hug and you say, "He just loves her so much."

- You actually believe that the preschool teacher who says your child doesn't cooperate well in class is being insensitive to her needs.

THE ZEN OF TOILET TRAINING

Floating away on a dream

Just as eating against one's will is injurious to health, so studying without a liking for it spoils the memory, and it retains nothing it takes in.
— LEONARDO DA VINCI

The evolution of potty training from child to child in most homes is a lot like the disappearing snapshot phenomenon.

You know how it goes: with the first child every moment of wakeful drooling and angelic sleep is recorded simultaneously by video and still cameras. With number two, however, the video cam is likely no longer functional and the album is predictably less ambitious and lacks the pithy commentary. And with number three (four, five, six . . .) the production of pictures grows proportionally smaller until at some point the album is replaced by a carton full of miscellaneous photographs of several unidentifiable infants, one or two of whom may be your own.

And so it is with potty training. With number one, the preparation begins long before the onset of the "new semester" in the tot's life. Books are read, pediatricians consulted, extensive equipment purchased, and a schedule devised to best meet the needs of parent and child without one impinging on the other's well-defined notions of self-determination and intestinal fortitude.

This is serious business; everyone in the early childhood game agrees that this is a most delicate and important developmental stage in a child's life, and one does not want to scar the little poop production machine forever with an inappropriate or insensitive approach to what is a natural and healthy human biological function.

With number two, however, the high anxiety has been dropped a notch or two. Basically you're too tired from having two kids to use up all that energy being detail oriented. Second round parents still schedule potty sessions, and still read four or five Berenstain Bears books per session, but not with the same enthusiasm and certainly not with the same degree of conviction.

By the advent of number three (and four and beyond), however, the total extent of parental involvement in potty training often consists of tossing a pair of training pants on the unmade bed and saying, "Your diaper days are over, Bucko. Get yourself dressed and ready for breakfast—and don't have any accidents."

And so it was for us (vis-à-vis pictures and toilet training). Cael, Patti, and I spent a month's worth of hours in the bathroom, reading books, sounding bright and cheery and supportive when there was nothing coming out, and cheering with great pride when something did. And, yes, there were several occasions when Cael was so proud of his production that we didn't flush for a long time so that we could all admire his good work. Along the way, we grew quite concerned when Roz and Dennis Read's overachieving son Evan was diaper-free (day and night!) while Cael still considered the world his toilet. But he eventually made it.

With Nancy we still had all the old equipment from Cael (the bathroom potty, the living room potty, the van potty, etc.) and even used it occasionally and cheered when she made it to the bathroom without an "accident," but we had lost our illusions that we were building her self-esteem; we just wanted to get her out of diapers because Addie was already born and filling them with abandon.

As for Addie, I think she pretty much toilet trained herself. I don't remember. Same thing with Clover. Anyway, they both figured it out somehow.

My revelation about the Zen of toilet training came with Danny. He was just past his third birthday and probably 90 percent trained, and whether or not he was psychologically and physiologically ready to gain 100 percent control of his excretory functions, we certainly were.

We were on our way home from Hatteras Island and had stopped for a picnic just before getting on the Chesapeake Bay Bridge Tunnel when little Danny had an accident. While it didn't seem to faze him a bit—he was running around, chasing his sisters and brothers, falling on his butt, and laughing some more—his siblings were totally grossed out.

"Change his diapers!" they yelled. "He stinks, pee-yew!"

"He doesn't wear diapers," I said calmly, as if that had anything to do with the stench that hovered in the humid air around our littlest boy.

"So, change his underpants! Just please clean him up!" Nancy, the neat and tidy daughter, was making gagging sounds, followed by Addie and Clover, who looked like they might puke. Thirteen-year-old Cael couldn't believe that he was stuck in a family like this.

And so I cleaned him up, but not happily. And not without some grave concern for the lateness of his development in this area. Driving over the bridge, I began to wax psychological, wondering if the periodic accidents were a form of passive aggression against his large busy family who didn't pay him enough attention; I worried that we hadn't scheduled enough potty sessions, that we hadn't read to him, that we didn't cheer loudly enough when he succeeded, that we flatly refused to save his gargantuan efforts afterward.

Midway across the twenty-three-mile span I grew panicky that they wouldn't allow him in nursery school in September, that he'd be frightfully humiliated on the playground and, spinning out beyond reason, much later on in high school. I broke out into a cold sweat with miragelike visions of a grown man wearing adult-size Pampers, rubber pants, and extra-large overalls with pockets full of diaper wipes.

I promised myself that I'd make an appointment with the pediatric psychologist as soon as we got home.

But as we approached the second tunnel on the span, the bridge disappearing out ahead and the massive Chesapeake Bay all around, I first panned the rearview mirror at Danny's four older siblings (and the miserable job we had done with their basic training) and then straight ahead at the endless line of cars full of children heading toward Virginia Beach—cars full of smart parents, stupid parents, hip parents, square parents, good parents, bad parents, black parents, yellow parents, white parents—and suddenly understood that probably 99 and 44/100 percent of their children get potty trained. What's the difference between twenty-six months and thirty-two months? Mostly, everyone gets potty trained in this life.

It was a real revelation.

As we drove across Fisherman's Island, I finally understood that Danny would be totally ready when he was totally ready. I caught his eye in the rearview mirror and blew him a kiss. He didn't understand, I'm sure, but he blew me one off his chubby little paws. And that was the last time he had an accident.

A COMMODE IS A COMMODE
IS A COMMODE
A belated apology to Sears

Zen has no secrets other than thinking about birth and death.

—TAKEDA SHINGEN

As I've previously suggested, Patti and I have little to offer new potty trainers except the conviction that whatever well-meaning parents do to help their kids will eventually work. The problem, as the following story shows, is that no one knows precisely when it will work.

In the fall of 1971, shortly after Patti and I became home owners of a fifty-year-old beauty (a white Victorian with green trim on a double city lot on the east side of Milwaukee), we proudly went shopping one afternoon for a toilet seat, towel bar, bath mat, and shower curtain at Sears. Tagging along behind us was our little two-year-old terror, Cael. He was dressed rather nattily in his Wrangler elastic waist jeans, a Brewers T-shirt, a pair of blue-and-red Keds—and underneath it all were brand-new Winnie the Pooh training pants, which seemed to function as a training tool 50 percent of the time and as a sieve the other 50 percent.

So, somewhere between some absurdly intense discussions

over the worthiness of ceramic towel bars as opposed to plastic or metal and an argument over the value of double as opposed to single shower curtains, Cael wandered off and we temporarily lost sight of the little jock.

At first neither of us was terribly concerned when we didn't see him in the immediate vicinity—after all, it was 1971 and it was Milwaukee—but we did want to find him before he broke something or suddenly realized that we were no longer in his sight and began to howl like Elmer Fudd befuddled again by Daffy Duck. I called his name. Patti called his name.

There was no answer.

So while I checked bathwares, Patti roamed through appliances, and when we met up again in hardware and plumbing neither of us had found him. "Where is he?" I demanded, as if it were Patti's responsibility alone to be watching him every second. She had a terrified look that must have mirrored my own.

It was then that we turned and saw the young prince. I can't describe the relief that instantly washed over me, but it was very short-lived. There he was on his throne, only it wasn't quite a throne, it was a floor model of a light blue Kohler toilet. And his Wrangler jeans were no longer stretched tight around his fat belly, they were down around his red-and-blue Keds. And his cute little face was not that alabaster smoothness that we loved to catch in Kodacolor, it was bright red and scrunched up as if he was taking a crap.

And that, we realized a microsecond later, was exactly what he was doing.

Patti and I dropped the shower curtain and towel bars and raced down the aisle in a desperate attempt to try to stop him before anything unseemly occured, but the earthy aroma that greeted us as we approached our smiling urchin signaled our failure.

"Look! Look! Look!" he said hopping down off the throne. "I did it! I did it! I went potty!" I looked down into the shiny waterless bowl. Yes, he had. And with a vengeance, I might add.

Now, there was a real moral dilemma facing us. Our little potty matriculant had finally made it all the way to the bowl on his own after I can't tell you how many near misses. He had climbed to the top. He had grabbed the brass ring.

What were we going to do? Yell at him? Punish him for doing exactly what we'd been begging him to do for months? Besides, how could we ever explain the difference between a real potty and a floor model?

And another thing, what were we going to tell the store manager? What the hell could we tell the store manager?

We looked around. No one was there. We glanced at each other like high school sophomores who had just broken a window at school, silently mimed the universal *eek!* expression, and while Patti pulled up Cael's pants, I put the lid down on the toilet and the three of us racewalked out of the store across the parking lot and into the Dodge van.

It was a terribly immature thing to do, I'll admit. And I've often thought of the dozens of shoppers who imagined they smelled something rancid ... and the hapless customer shopping for a light blue commode who lifted the lid on the floor model ... and the horrified look on the salesman's weary face ... but what else could we have done?

I don't know. I simply do not know. *Mea culpa. Mea culpa. Mea maxima culpa.* In that moment I achieved the heart and soul of a little child. If you could see me now, you'd see my arms open wide, palms up in the universal pose of cluelessness.

ZEN AND THE ART OF GETTING UNSTUCK

Getting a penis unstuck from a zipper

The foolish reject what they see, not what they think; the wise reject what they think, not what they see.

—HUANG PO

Pain is unavoidable in this life.

I'm not sure whether that is a Zen principle or an axiom of life that spans all theologies and cultures, but, as nearly all parents understand, there is no greater pain than the pain of a child. And no more soul-splitting sound than that of a toddler screeching in agony in the next room.

Children, especially small children, find themselves in excruciating pain perhaps twenty or thirty times a day. They stumble into the sides of tables, they stub their little toes, they bite their tongues, they burn their tongues, they cut themselves, they touch hot stoves, they skin their knees, they get splinters, and they get the double whammy of splinters gouged out by their needle-wielding mothers or fathers.

(Actually, I said fathers just to be fair and enlightened, but other than my friend Bruce Schenker I don't know any dads who do the home surgeries, even dad doctors. Perhaps it's because fathers pride themselves on being able to fix things for their families, and a child's pain is generally unfixable until it fixes itself. Perhaps it's got something to do with how women, by way of childbirth, truly understand that pain, like everything else in life, really does pass. Frankly, I don't know the answer. In my New Age Zen, however, not knowing is knowing.)

Anyway, with seven kids, I have been a party to the entire pantheon of minor childhood scrapes and bruises, from bleeding heads to fingers caught in car doors to broken bones and mind-altering concussions. But, trust me, there is no pain, no howling, no sense of fatherly powerlessness like a little guy with his little penis stuck in a zipper—and his mother out for the afternoon. Trust me.

Cael was five—Nancy a tubby ball of oneness—and the three of us were just hanging around the warm house on a cold fall Saturday afternoon while Patti was out for a few hours. I was in that Zen zone of fatherly unconsciousness—playing without playing, hearing without listening, speaking without talking, agreeing to everything without agreeing to anything.

Suddenly there was an otherworldly cry of agony from the other side of the house. I won't recount for you the horrors that I imagined as I raced through the kitchen of our old farmhouse, clomping through the dining room and bursting into the bathroom where the howling was growing in strength and intensity like an air-raid siren.

The look on my little guy's face as he stood paralyzed in front of the toilet was a study in Job-like pain. If it could have been translated, it would have said, "I didn't do anything bad. Why is this horrible thing happening to me?" And the yowling was almost unearthly.

As a member of the local rescue squad, I was somewhat accustomed to *acting* calm in the face of medical emergencies. But seeing my little boy with his little penis stuck in a zipper (a small piece of skin caught between the metal yanker and a tooth) I immediately lost my enlightened detachment: I spun around to yell for Patti (the needle wielder, the walking Heimlich maneuver,

Ms. Calm-in-a-medical-storm), and then spun back in the horrific realization that I was alone in the house—and I alone had to do something to stop the pain. And the yowling.

At first glance I thought that all I needed to do was what I figured Patti would do: simply give a brief but utterly painful yank on the zipper to set him free. And he would be free. But on closer inspection I saw that the piece of skin was caught firmly in the metal teeth. Who knows what would come off if I just yanked? I was not prepared to deal with the possibilities.

I momentarily considered calling the rescue squad, but the idea of the dispatcher's voice crackling on scanners all over town saying "Penis caught in zipper at One Coffey Lane" convinced me that the problem was best solved privately. Meanwhile, Cael was screeching, spinning around and around while I was pacing back and forth in the small bathroom, praying that somehow—miraculously—the penis had unstuck itself.

It hadn't. I picked him up. He screamed. I put him down. He screamed. The only thing I could think of was how the weight of the jeans on his stuck penis only increased the stinging pain. So I reached into the drawer and pulled out a pair of big sewing scissors. Cael took one look at the long shiny blades and the screaming turned to squealing.

He tried to run away, but with a penis stuck in a zipper, well, you know. I started cutting from the cuff of one leg and snipped up to the crotch along the seam of the zipper and through the thick waistband. A few more snips and then down the back side and one leg was removed.

By the time I was finished cutting, Cael was standing there bare bottomed with a three-inch square of jean and zipper hanging off his raw penis.

And he was still screeching.

Now what? I thought of pliers. I thought of Vaseline. I thought of Wesson oil. I meditated on the unique properties of penises the world over. I thought about how penises have lives of their own. I thought of my own penis. I scooped him up and strode over to the bathtub, turned on the cold tap, and waited until there was half a foot of frigid water and laid him down in the cold tub. He squirmed. He yanked on my hair. He pleaded to get out. He yowled as if I were torturing him.

And two seconds later the patch of zipper was floating on the surface of the suddenly still water. And the look on his face was of pure cosmic relief.

The blissful ahhhhhhhhhness of getting unstuck.

UNTANGLING THE KNOTTED STRANDS OF LIFE

The Zen of getting bubble gum out of hair

Action should culminate in wisdom.
—*BHAGAVAD GITA*

Patti was down in Florida visiting her father. There was nothing remarkable about the trip or the fact that I was alone with the brood for several days, but I was admittedly a little concerned about four-year-old Elizabeth. She was still so cosmically attached to Patti that mere separation had the potential to tip the homeostatic balance.

(The previous time Patti went away, Elizabeth's cold escalated into a 104-degree fever and we sat up all night shooting hallucinogenic monsters out of her delirium.)

I was spending a typical spring Saturday going to the dump and taxiing kids all over town, ending up down in Wallkill with Bay and Elizabeth to watch Danny play soccer. And I was prepared, as a father of seven should be prepared, with a blanket, a few well-chosen politically correct toys, some wholesome snacks, ten percent 100-percent-pure fruit juices, sun block, and a trusty bag of candy and gum if things got testy.

I won't go into the particulars of how we got to the candy

and gum stage so early in the second half of the game—any parent can easily conjure up an applicable situation—but we were there nevertheless. Bay, who had grown bored watching packs of twelve-year-old boys fruitlessly chasing a round ball, was playing in a dirt pile with some other dirty kids, and Elizabeth was happily chewing on some (sugar-free) bubble gum at my side. And, as such, I was enjoying my first few unfettered moments of the game, which was suddenly the most interesting and important event in my life.

I actually began to care if *we* won(!), and thus lost conscious awareness of the portable voice machine at my side. She was babbling on as if we were actually having a conversation, and I was nodding and adding an occasional clueless *hmmmmmm*, and the game (and the day) was heating up, and I was growing increasingly annoyed at the crowd of enemy parents nearby who kept cheering every time one of the Wallkill kids made a good play.

So it was a good five minutes before I looked down to see why Elizabeth had suddenly grown quiet. But five minutes was enough for her to have taken the wad of well-chewed pink gum and stretched it in both directions across her face, around and around her neck and up into her hair and down the other side. Up, down, across, and sideways—and then back again. All over her face. In her ear. The skin on her neck wrinkled and pressed together. Her long hair a tangled mass of deranged clumps.

All I could think of in the horror of the moment was Patti stepping off the plane in two days and seeing her baby girl with a crew cut. (I'm not sure if it was my mother or someone else's mother, but I do have a motherly voice hidden deep in the audiotape files of my memory saying, "We're going to have to cut that gum out of your hair!")

However, from years of experience with bubble gum stuck to noses and lips, I did know that if you rubbed the chewed gum on the pieces stuck on the skin, the stuck parts should come off.

So I snatched what was left of the wad out of her mouth and started rubbing her face and neck (and arms and legs). Owing to some principle of anatomy that I don't understand, the gum came easily off her nose and lips and limbs, and easily enough off her red ears, but the neck was a totally different story. The stuck gum just grew dirtier and dirtier as I rubbed and scoured and stretched the tender skin. And when Elizabeth began to whimper and plead for me to stop—and the Wallkill parents glared at me as if I were a child abuser—I turned to her hair, trying in vain to separate the tangled sticky strands until she let out a shriek that sounded like the town fire whistle.

At the end of the game (we lost), I gathered up Bay, who was covered with a sweaty paste of dirt, Danny, who was one massive grass stain after spending the entire game perfecting his slide tackle, and whimpering Elizabeth, and headed silently to the car and home, the bath, and the scissors.

Driving has always been a transcendent experience for me, a chance to zone out and go on automatic pilot while I consider the vagaries of existence. It's a Zen state that many fathers attain, they just don't know it's Zen. And the drive up Route 208 that afternoon was no different. Somewhere between Ireland Corners and Dressel's orchards I recalled someone someplace saying something about peanut butter and gum in hair. I think it was Donna Ciliberto who heard about it from Linda Ackert.

I had nothing to lose. As soon as we got home, I snatched the Skippy out of the pantry, reached three fingers into the wide mouth, and grabbed a fistful of the creamy stuff. Elizabeth looked equally horrified and amused as I spread the gooey stuff on her neck and then all through her hair, massaging it into her scalp as if it were shampoo.

She giggled like we were kids doing something really bad behind Mom's back. And I laughed as I squished my fingers through her hair because she wasn't crying, because it felt like we were doing something bad behind Mom's back, and because the tangles were actually coming unstuck! It was magic!

When Patti came home two days later, Elizabeth and I picked her up at the airport with clean, brushed hair, smirks on our faces, and the knowledge that action does indeed culminate in wisdom. And thus my advice: while I can't in good conscience endorse a specific product relative to the untangling of one's "stuckness," any brand probably works as well as any other, but I'd stay away from chunky or the kinds that mix jelly in the jar.

BUDDHIST (AFTERNOON) DELIGHT

Sex, lies, and Cocoa Crispies

If we achieve satori and the satori shows, like a bit of dogshit stuck on the tip of our nose, that is not so good.
—TAISEN DESHIMARU

Another axiom of parental life: when children get wind of sexual electricity buzzing between Mom and Dad—and it definitely is in the wind—they will do everything in their power to cut the lines and sabotage the glorious event.

It's not that the little imps want to rob parents of whatever small pleasures adults find in life—although I don't really think that parental pleasure is on any healthy child's agenda—but I do believe that all children understand intuitively the perilous ramifications of sex between parents. That's why babies always seem to wake up or toddlers barge into your room just when things are really heating up. They know in their fragile little bones that sex equals baby and baby spells danger, not only for the infant who must protect her or his milk supply but also for older children who comprehend the economics of food and time and the profound impact of one more sister or brother on family dynamics.

So, it's in their best interests to keep you celibate.

But life, of course, has its own devious pleasures. Just about the time that coitus interruptus seems like the only coitus there is in young parents' lives, the joys of "napping" in the afternoons opens up to them like lotus blossoms. And, indeed, there is nothing quite so lovely and spiritually elevating as a Saturday or Sunday "nap," you and your sweetheart alone and unfettered for an hour or more of afternoon delight.

Naps are wonderful oases for young parents because, in general, toddlers not only need and want their daily siestas, they don't resist them with the same steely ferocity as going "nigh-nigh." Even infants know from their limited experience that a nap is only a temporary respite from the joys of driving parents crazy, and that when they wake up there's still a whole day of pooping left to achieve purpose in life.

When Cael was a toddler it was easy to achieve that kind of satori in the afternoon. If the opportunity and desire arose, we would simply slip in the sack as soon as he curled up with his "banky" in the crib. Sometimes we even slept, another kind of satori for the diaper weary.

The problem with achieving afternoon delight comes with the addition of one or more children into the household. Unless they all nap—and nap at the same time—those private little thirst-quenching oases from the rigors of parenting threaten to become little more than memories or mirages or mmmmm-rated fantasies disappearing in thin air.

And that's when you have to be opportunistic, sneaky, dishonest, and utterly libido-driven. Like a teenager. Which is what you are in your heart anyway. Which is when the quest for the next level of satori truly begins.

As men and women all over the planet know from their own devious teenage years, there is nothing steamier, sexier, or quite so frustratingly exciting as making out on the couch after your parents have gone to sleep—or gone out for the evening. But, as we also know, such pleasures involve planning and higher-level consciousness of the metarealities of hidden sexual conduct. Parents must also think ahead.

The technique for achieving Stage Two afternoon satori is not very complex, but does involve strict adherence to four simple rules:

RULE 1 : Be certain that your partner is on the same page of the same Anne Rice book as you are. There is no greater sense of worldly disappointment than setting up a romantic tryst and making a swan dive into the marriage bed only to find that she really does want to take a nap.

RULE 2: No one except the conspirators should ever get wind of your plans. No public displays of affection. All kissing, petting, rubbing against, grabbing, snorting (and all other animal noises) must be held in check. You must be utterly parental in your demeanor. And foreplay must be accomplished in total privacy: in the next room, in the bathroom, behind the kitchen counter, anywhere but in front of your children. Remember, it's in the air. Be careful.

RULE 3: Don't get creative. The tried-and-true nap scam is the only reasonable path to follow. Children will snicker right in your face if you say something like "Mom and I will be doing some important work in the bedroom, so don't disturb us." They don't have a great deal of respect for work, especially since the two of you complain about it in front of them all the time. And they certainly won't allow you to slip away unnoticed for as long as it takes to accomplish your mutual goals. All children have a built-in sonar detector that drives them to seek out and find lost parents every ten to fifteen minutes.

However, kids understand that a sleeping parent is almost always better than an alert one. They want Mom or Dad around in case something bad happens, but they also know that a sleeping parent will never know if they do fun bad things like sneak into the cookies or play in the sink. Plus, they know you'll be up soon, so their own sense of illicitness will give them almost as much pleasure as your own sense of illicitness will give you. It's perfect.

RULE 4: Cocoa Crispies. There's no reasonable excuse for keeping sugary cereals in the house, except for moments like these; and then they become an integral phase of the final plans. Before leaving the room, you snap on your fatherly voice and recite everything that they must not—ever—touch or do, and then say, "I'm going to pour you a cup of Cocoa Crispies in case you get hungry." Of course they take the bribe. That way they not only get rid of you but get paid for it. And it keeps them busy for at least a little while.

And that's it. You disappear behind the locked door and experience the pleasures of the here and now while your children are discovering new and devious ways to entertain themselves.

One last caveat: neither you nor your partner (nor the bed or the floorboards) must make a sound while you're in the throes of impassioned pleasures—and you must not say anything or look too blissful after it's all over. If they even think you're doing something so outlandish under their noses, you'll look like you have dogshit on your noses and you'll never again know the secret pleasures of afternoon satori.

5

Early Satori: The Peaceful Era Before the Teenage Wars

THE ZEN BROWNIE LEADER

How a father leads a troop of little girls into the wilderness when there is no mother in sight

> *Zen teaches nothing; it merely enables us to wake up and become aware. It does not teach, it points.*
> —D. T. SUZUKI

I am one of the few men in North America—perhaps the world—who can recite the Brownie pledge, sing "I've got something in my pocket that belongs across my face . . ." (complete with correct hand movements), order and bestow badges, teach the principles of Juliette Low, as well as choreograph and direct a solemn but Kodak-cute moving up ceremony that includes a scripted and abridged three-minute version of "The Brownie Story." And I know which snacks refresh but do not stain.

Patti became the Brownie leader of Troop 242 in 1979, when Nancy was a first grader. And if I may say so, she was—and remains—the quintessential Brownie leader, as comfortable with papier mâché as tying knots and digging latrines. During those early years I was the dutiful dad and husband, attending all ceremonies with camera in hand, setting up the yard for the campouts, and maintaining consciousness during Nancy's stirring monologues about badge acquisition and campfire safety. But I was not, I admit, a Brownie aficionado. I just went along to get along.

For some reason, though—I can't remember which pregnancy got in the way—she had to step aside for a year and the troop was left leaderless.

So, without much prodding and even less comprehension of the duties that go along with the job, I undertook the hallowed position of leader. Actually, Patti deftly positioned me so that I thought I actually wanted the job: she mentioned offhandedly one day that another local father, Dick Geuss, had been a Brownie leader for several years. Then, several minutes later, she wondered aloud why more men didn't have the "stuff" to lead a troop of first-, second-, and third-grade girls.

My manhood and my fatherhood thus challenged, I immediately enrolled in a Brownie leader workshop with a dozen women of all shapes, sizes, and social fortunes. As I walked into that first meeting, every woman in the room glared at me with a curious mixture of cautious wonder and extreme distrust. Behind the smile and the limp handshake of each mother was the (neon) flashing sign: OH LORD, ANOTHER DICK GEUSS, ONLY THIS ONE HAS LONG HAIR. And behind that: *What the hell is he doing here? My husband wouldn't be caught dead in this place!*

But I persevered the way that men always persevere with women when we're out of our manly element: we act inept. By the second meeting practically every woman in the group was vying for the chance to help me make a "dream catcher." If I didn't win their respect, I did win their approval—and their certification.

From there on, I organized Brownie meetings, I sang the Brownie songs, I pledged the Brownie pledge, I served the Brownie snacks, I did Brownie crafts that I didn't think men were capable of doing, and in the spring I went to a council meeting and announced my intentions to take the girls into the woods to learn to identify animal tracks.

My announcement, which I anticipated would be met with great enthusiasm, was followed by a most uncomfortable silence and a jittery leap to the next item on the agenda. A few days later the processed word came down from "council" that I was *not* allowed to take the girls for a hike without chaperons. A single adult male was not sanctioned to be alone in the woods ("To the woods! No, not the woods.") with innocent little Brownies.

I guess they figured that in the basement of the Reformed Church I would be able to keep my dark side in check, but out in the mountain wilderness of New Paltz I might forget all civilized restraint and . . . what? *(He does have all those kids!)*

Deeply offended—and full of the self-righteousness of false accusation—I prepared to take on the council. I'd write letters. I'd threaten to go to court. I'd go to court. I'd take it all the way to Washington. This was defamation of character, institutional bias, reverse discrimination of the worst sort! And, besides, what the hell was I going to do with the little buggers now that it was warm outside?

Patti, who fully intended to return to scouting the next year—and who understood the parochial machinations of Girl Scout leadership—advised me against making a federal case out of it. "Just do it," she said. "No one up there will ever find out."

(I feel I should mention that she said "Just do it!" a decade and a half before the cynics at Nike made it sound like we were hearing it for the first time.)

And so I did it. We wandered the woods and swamps and saw deer tracks, bunny tracks, raccoon, and maybe (just maybe) bear tracks, and by the end of the day no one could remember or recognize what they saw, except the deer droppings, which looked a lot like bunny pellets. But it was fun (even if I had to carry Olivia Harrison practically the whole way because she didn't want to get mud on her white shoes) and I learned a real lesson about the way children learn. You invite them along into the wilderness and they learn things they never knew before. You just do it. Everyone finds something to take home with them. Even if it's poison ivy.

THE ZEN SOCCER COACH

And the demonic inner child in a lawn chair

You don't need Little League. You don't even need nine kids. Four is plenty—a pitcher, a batter, and a couple of shaggers. You can play ball all day long. My kids used to try to get me out there, but I'd just say 'Go play with your brothers.' If kids want to do something, they'll do it. They don't need adults to do it for them.

—YOGI BERRA

When Cael was old enough to play for the local Little League team, I had to decide between joining the elite coaching ranks of gruff-throated fathers with whistles around their necks or the lawnchair brigade of baby boomer dads. It was a non-choice.

As a former three-sport "star" at Wheatley High (blazing more brightly with each passing year), long-suffering Dodger fan, and perennial boy inhabiting the shell of an aging man's body, I knew all too well about fathers and sons and whose co-gliones are really on the line when a little boy steps up to the plate. (At the time, I was still quite naive and did not know that sports moms also have *cogliones*.)

So I chickened out. I was afraid that I didn't know enough about skills development, game strategy, and fostering the necessary toughness to serve parents whose sons were destined to be the future Pete Roses of the western world. It would be humbling for me—and abject humiliation for Cael—if I stood in front of a pack of bulldog-faced sires and tried to explain my philosophy that sports are supposed to be fun.

However, when Nancy was nine and the newly enlightened coed town soccer league was searching (i.e., begging) for coaches to lead their teams, I strapped on the whistle and the jock strap and headed into the fray. At the time most people didn't know squat about soccer, so I figured the parents wouldn't know if I was doing a good job or not. Besides, as the father of a daughter I'd be cut a lot more slack for my wimpy managerial style.

Actually, the first few weeks of practices as the head of the Blue Raiders were murder. I don't know what happened, but in the time it took for me to receive my whistle and stick it in my mouth, I was transformed from a happy hippie coach *(winning isn't everything)* to the reincarnation of Vince Lombardi *(winning is the only damn thing)*.

I spent hours planning for the ninety-minute practice sessions, devising fun but educational ball handling exercises, interspersing pep talks with skill development modules, interjecting strategy discussions into scrimmages punctuated with well-chosen insights about the meaning of sport and life. I told them that while there was nothing wrong with losing, we really *had* to win.

Honestly, it was awful. I spent most of the practices trying to make them all listen to my pearls of soccerly wisdom—and they wwouldn't listen. I felt like a substitute teacher forcing the kids to do homework after working all day long at school. I was miserable. And the kids, who only wanted to run around and yell and play soccer in the crisp fall air, were miserable.

Then came our first game. Shortly after the opening whistle it became apparent that they didn't remember anything I had told them about positions and passing. They didn't even remember how to do a proper throw-in. And apparently the opposing team didn't remember a thing their coach told them. On the green field were two packs of chimpanzees, distinguishable only by the color of their shirts, chasing a ball that kept skidding away from them. It looked like a lot of fun.

And it might have been fun, except for the parents behind us. Hordes of them in lawn chairs lining the field, cheering one child's domination over another, berating the poor volunteer refs, screaming venomously when a sixty-pounder side-stepped a hundred-pound charging bull, and groaning in undisguised disgust when an easy goal kick was missed or when a child reasonably shied away from a three-mile-high header.

In the second half, an exasperated father stormed over to me and started drawing attack strategies in the dirt with a stick. I thanked him and said I was just happy at this point if they were all going in the right direction. He looked over at another red-faced father and shook his sorry head as if I were not only beneath contempt but beyond any hope for salvation.

At that moment I decided to stop being a coach and allowed the kids the same pleasure of playing soccer I had when I was a kid and there were no adults in sight. And we did okay, winning nearly as many games as we lost, celebrating the end of the season at JD's soft ice-cream stand.

Two years later with Addie's team, I coached less, encouraged more, and gradually learned to enjoy the dance of life from the sidelines. Thanks in no part to my coaching style, we went undefeated. With Clover's team, which might have gone winless except for a couple of really lucky breaks, I began to achieve a state of coachless coaching.

So by the time Danny came along, I would spend one practice session working on various kicks and the rules of the game—and then set them free for the rest of the season. During scrimmages I occasionally mentioned moving the ball in the right direction (a major victory with at least two of the kids), playing your position (as opposed to everyone on both teams swarming around the ball), and the benefits of passing (forget it). We won as many as we lost. Not bad at all.

If the league ever allows me to coach again, I think my managerial strategy will be simply to give the kids a ball and allow them to play soccer. They'll figure it out. I'll sit on the sidelines with a cup of coffee and a newspaper just in case someone gets hurt or needs to go to the bathroom.

And before the first game, I will schedule a mandatory parents' contest where the kids will sit in lawn chairs on the sidelines and yell like obnoxious children when the players fail to charge an opponent or shy away from a tall header or miss an easy kick—or get tired and rest for a minute.

As Yogi says, the kids figure it out by themselves.

JUST SAY YES

When yes is no and no is yes

There is no way you can use the word "reality" without
quotation marks around it.

—JOSEPH CAMPBELL

Nearly ten years ago I was sitting on the back deck, half sleeping, half listening to a group of kids on the swing set. One
yelled, "Let's pretend that yes is no and no is yes!" The rest,
dangling and sliding and spinning wildly, screamed with such
glee at her suggestion that I was struck dumb—i.e., awakened—
by the simple beauty of the vision.

The message was so elegant: yes is no and no is yes. All kids in
all times have done the same thing, turning the world inside out
to see the world as it truly is. Moments later they raced up to the
deck and stood in front of me, smiling, dirty-faced, and panting.

"Hi. Are you all having fun?"

"No." A few giggled.

"Would you like a drink?"

They looked at each other and giggled some more. "No."

"Would you like some cookies?"

"No!" they roared in unison.

"Would you . . . like to wash the dishes?"

"Yes!!"

"Mop the floor?"

"Yes!!!"

One more question about cleaning the toilets and they were rolling on the rug, squealing hysterically.

The encounter soon fizzled, however, because the kids were sophisticated enough to know when to take the cookies and scram. They left and I went back to the window to digest an emerging epiphany about the nature of reality. Indeed, yes is no and no is yes.

But it was not until Elizabeth actually demonstrated the principle many years later that I truly understood its application in real life.

It was probably Patti who discovered the little puddles of water around the algae-encrusted fish tank. In truth, it doesn't matter. After determining that there was no leak from the tank, she wiped up the water, checked the fish in the murky tank, and found one missing. Just one.

She quickly convened a family meeting where we all stood around the bubbling tank like men stand around the open hood of a disabled car trying to bluff their way through a problem they simply do not understand.

The older sleuths (Clover, Danny, Patti, and I) soon pointed our collective fingers directly at Sammy the cat. All the evidence suggested Sammy, a real scoundrel if there ever was one, was the killer. He slunk away as if he still had the taste of tropical fish in his mouth.

Bay, who likes to believe the best of everyone, including cats like Sammy, wondered if the fish could have just jumped out of the tank all by itself. Danny made a face. "If the fish jumped out of the tank, Sherlock, where is it now?"

That's when we first heard Elizabeth's little voice behind us: "The fish is not in my pocketbook."

"What?"

"The fish is *not* in my pocketbook."

Ahhhhhhhh. Patti raced over to the playroom and found Elizabeth's pocketbook and the little fish, which was miraculously still alive, and quickly returned him to his home in the murky depths.

And with heart full of joy I ran to the mirror and read my lips: "No, yes is no. And yes, no is yes."

No? Yes.

THE RULES OF
THE ROAD

*Telling Danny the truth about
the way adults tell the truth*

Do as I say, not as I do.
—EVERY PARENT

Nine-year-old Danny and I were zipping along on the New York State Thruway, radio blaring, not saying a word to each other. Out of nowhere, it seemed, he leaned over and checked the speedometer and then made the simple but pointed observation that everyone was speeding. It was true. I was going my normal "law abiding" sixty-three miles per hour and we were in the slow lane. Practically everyone was passing us.

In the face of the abject truth, it seemed pointless to make up excuses ("They don't really mean fifty-five") or outright lies ("Speedometers are often ten miles per hour incorrect") or, worst of all, offer him the "Do as we say, not as we do" speech. I turned down the radio and flatly agreed that most people don't follow rules exactly as they are laid out. I then tried being a good father and slowed down to fifty-four miles per hour, which felt more like twenty-four, and judging by the swerving cars I saw in my rearview mirror, almost caused several pileups.

When we arrived home, it took an extended visit to my "office" (you know, Dad's office with a sink and toilet and lots of magazines) to figure out what to say or do to explain the adult world's hypocrisies to a savvy nine-year-old—and still have him follow the rules.

As a member of the "Question Authority" generation, I guess I haven't been much of a rule follower myself, although I have made the usual accomodations along the way: I go to work, pay taxes, mow the lawn, honor my marriage, yadda, yadda, yadda. By and large I live between the lines. You know.

On the other hand—and solely for the purpose of making a point here—I'll admit that, among a host of other petty crimes and hypocrisies, I roll through stop signs and toss apple cores out the window into the woods, indiscretions that apparently have not eluded my errant boy.

In fact, being a smart kid, not much of the world's double standards have passed him by. At nine, he had already observed the big belly on the coach; he had complained that some of his teachers didn't do *their* homework; he knew from watching TV about corrupt politicians, child-molesting priests, drug-abusing athletes, depraved movie stars.

As such, I knew how difficult it would be to impress upon a fourth grader the importance of following rules when it is apparent that the rule makers break them as easily as little kids chomp into jawbreakers without a single fracture. I figured the truth was my only out.

So the next day Danny and I returned to the thruway to find out the truth about speeding in America. It was my job to keep the car at a steady sixty miles per hour, and it was Danny's job to count the number of cars that we passed as well as those that passed us.

He began counting as a carload of old ladies from New Jersey streaked by like a pace car leading a culturally diverse parade of two-, four-, and sixteen-wheeled vehicles that left us in the dust. At the Harriman toll plaza, thirty-two miles from our upstate exit, I figured the point was made.

Danny added up the numbers. It was a romp, a KO, a humiliating blow for the forces of law and order: 122 to nothing. Zip. I didn't pass a single vehicle on the entire stretch of highway. I didn't even brake.

We looked at each other and—what else was there to do?—laughed like little kids. And on the way home, each of us lost in the backroads of life's contradictions, Danny observed—all by his nine-year-old self—that most of the cars had not been zooming past us, and none were careening out of control. We figured that most of them were going sixty-five to seventy miles per hour. Then he wondered out loud what would happen if the speed limit was raised to sixty-five and soon thereafter answered his own question: everyone would go seventy-five to eighty.

We agreed that the world is a funny place. It isn't what it's supposed to be, but it actually resembles itself quite a lot. We returned home that day, my arm around his slender shoulders, going a steady fifty-nine, an acceptable compromise for two guys who had learned a lesson in real-world limits.

WHO WEARS THE BELT IN YOUR FAMILY?

Achieving complete misunderstanding with one's child

If the doors of perception were cleansed every thing to man would appear as it is, infinite.

—WILLIAM BLAKE

Sitting cross-legged on the unmade king-size bed, Bay looks much smaller than his five years. He is watching me very intently, round chin resting in the smooth cup of his soft hand. I am putting on my dark pinstriped suit, absorbed in ponderous thought, barely aware of the youthful brown eyes that observe my every move.

This is a significant event for both of us, if only for how seldom it occurs. I rarely—rarely—wear a suit. As a teacher for more than twenty years, I have "passed" with that tweedy patches-on-the-elbows look. As a writer, I have gotten by with considerably less.

In fact, I have only owned one suit since I got married in 1968. Around the house it's jokingly called my wedding and funeral suit. Unfortunately, this morning I am not getting dressed for a wedding. Staring through the oak-framed mirror into my own deep-set eyes, I am searching for a clue to a question that does not form in my mind or lips.

I have been to several funerals lately. I suppose that happens when you reach your midforties. The world seems considerably smaller to me now than it used to when I imagined everything was possible.

As I button the sleeves on my crisp white shirt, I am uncomfortably reminded of the dressing of the corpse in the beginning of the movie *The Big Chill*. A shiver runs like a frightened rabbit across my shoulder blades as I imagine myself a cold and helpless participant in my own final dressing for the world. "Joy to the World" is playing discordantly on the soundtrack.

In the mirror I see Bay tilt his head as I start to hum the tune "Jeremiah was a bullfrog . . ." and for a moment his soft quizzical countenance makes me sadder than I already am. A man's time with his children—his babies—is so short. It's never enough. Even with seven children spanning a whole generation, the years are not long enough, the days racing by like windows in speeding trains, their soft baby faces growing more angular and wary with each passing hour. I was not much more than a boy when Cael was born. I will be sixty when Elizabeth Bayou-Grace graduates from high school.

Stepping into the dark pressed trousers, I promise myself with great solemnity to spend more time with my family while I still have a chance. There is no better proof than this funeral for the father of one of Cael's friends that no one knows when his or her time will come. I make a covenant with my reflection to be fully alive in every passing moment of my days, not buried in my work or drugged by the TV. Life is no joke; not even a second is to be squandered frivolously.

As I pull up the zipper, press the button through the hole, and begin to thread the black belt through the loops, Bay slips off the big bed. By the time I yank the shiny buckle tight against my growling stomach, he is standing right next to me, his little face a few inches below my hip. As I reach for a tie, I see his mouth forming a thought.

"Dad?"

"Yes, Bay?"

"Dad, when I grow up," he says cranking his head to the side, "I want to be just like you."

The tears that wash over my eyes come on so suddenly that I must kneel, reaching for the slight shoulders and little head covered with soft brown hair. I ache to press him so close to me that we will never be apart, but he leans back as if there is still more to say, something that will illuminate the rest of my days: "Yup," nodding just like his older brothers, "when I grow up, Dad, I want to wear a belt every day!"

It was a perfect send-off to a funeral, though I'm not sure how successful I was in swallowing the smirk that kept sneaking through my lips like a cheap one-liner. When I got home and Bay jumped up into my arms, I hugged him for the one I missed earlier and also for the wonderful and terrible good sense that he brings to my life.

Then I threw off the suit and we sat around, wasting time.

IT'S NINE O'CLOCK: DO YOU KNOW WHERE YOUR CHILDREN ARE?

Forgetting Clover at the Vermilyes

When the mind is nowhere it is everywhere. When it occupies one tenth, it is absent in the other nine tenths.
—TAKUAN

Patti met Kitty Vermilye more than twenty years ago when she answered an ad in the local weekly for mothers interested in starting a play group. As Nancy and Lydia played together that first morning, the two mothers found a companionship of spirit that soon evolved to dragging their workaholic husbands to weekend get-togethers that their also socially resistant husbands tried desperately to avoid. And so, just as most married men would never have friends without their companionable wives, Steve and I became lifelong friends despite the fact that we've always been too busy to do anything together, except perhaps eat.

I don't recall exactly when the tradition began, but at some point in the late seventies, the Lewises and the Vermilyes started to eat Sunday dinners with each other, alternating houses by the week. Lopsided as it was (they have only two kids), Sunday evenings with Steve, Kitty, Lydia, and Jamie soon became a valued respite from the traffic of our increasingly busy and complicated lives.

One Sunday evening in 1984, like so many other Sunday evenings after a dinner full of the usual good laughter and spilled drinks and bad jokes, I nudged Patti and reminded her—as I often did in those days—that I had hours of papers to review before going to bed. It was Sunday night, but I was already completely absorbed within the crisscrossing realities of a Monday to be spent teaching at two different schools. We gathered the Lewis herd together, thanked our hosts once again for their graciousness, and piled into the mustard colored Vanagon.

In the time it took to insert *Highway 61 Revisited* into the tape player, my mind was in complete gridlock. I drove the cold van up the dirt road, bumping across the tracks onto Glen Circle, made a left on Forest Glen, another left on Route 208, and was a mile or two past Dressel's orchards when I suddenly experienced an odd sensation of lightness. The van actually felt less stable on the road. The energy felt incomplete. The center of gravity had shifted. Something was missing.

With headlights behind us illuminating the dark shapes in the seats I counted heads: one, two, three, four . . . four . . . four . . . FOUR! I flipped on the overhead lights and saw Cael, Nancy, Addie, and Danny squinting and scowling at the bright ceiling.

"Poochie," I called back over my shoulder, assuming she had fallen asleep. "Poochie? . . . Poochie!"

"Where's Clover?" Patti demanded of the kids, as if they, not us, were responsible for her. Cael, who never quite acknowledged that we had any real children after him, shrugged as if it were an irrelevant question. Nancy, who probably knew where Clover was but enjoyed the parental hysteria, merely looked out the window. And Addie, who was angry at Nancy and didn't hear the question, was still scowling at the light. Just then little Danny spoke up as nonchalantly as if he were talking about the weather, "Oh, she's upstairs playing with Jamie."

I jammed on the brakes, squealed through a jerky U-turn, and roared back up 208, a sickening lump forming in my stomach as we red-lined it back to Bridge Creek Road. Bumping down the dirt lane, Patti and I imagined our delicate little Clover curled up in a corner, crying hysterically, inconsolable, scarred for life, and doomed to an eternity on a psychoanalytic couch—or worse, dribbling and drooling in some asylum run by a man who looked and sounded like Mel Brooks. We skidded to a halt in front of the house and barged en masse through the door like the Six Stooges.

And there was little Clover, standing in the middle of her foster family with a toothless grin and a scowl and an embarrassed fistful of anger that would last for a day or maybe a week. Not a lifetime.

As the person in our family who has always proceeded through life with the fewest claims on the universe, her toothless grin told me a lot that night about the relationship between nowhere and everywhere. She forgave Patti and me our inexcusable lapse of concentration because, even at seven years old, she saw the nine tenths of life that we too often fail to see, and knew that precisely when she was nowhere in our thoughts, she was everywhere. Even before the best-selling book came along, Clover understood the meaning of the "unbearable lightness of being."

6

Nanto (or Hard-to-Penetrate Koan) and Teenage Boys

THE ZEN SEX TALK

The fine line between sex and sport

A young man is so strong, so mad, so certain, and so lost.
He has everything and is able to use nothing.
— THOMAS WOLFE

My own parent-child sex talk in 1959 was brief and to the point: I was sitting on the green Naugahyde couch in the den of the house on Candy Lane (yes again, Candy Lane) and watching the television, when a dark figure passed across the door and an object of awkward dimensions came hurtling through the air and landed to my right. Just as I recognized it as a book, a raspy voice of unearthly quality mumbled, "Read this."

I won't swear to it, but after all these years I think the figure was my mother, and seconds later I heard the same voice trailing off down the hall saying something like, "If you have any questions, just ask. . . ."

I picked up the book, thumbed my way to Chapter One, and closed it as soon as I hit the words *fallopian tubes.* That was it.

Of course, I already knew just about everything there was to know about women and sex from the local brain trust: Marshall Diamond, Steven Weil, and the older wise presence down the street, Bobby Jayson. (This was the same erudite crew that, a few years earlier, had ridiculed and beat up Joe Rappaport for the totally outrageous and revolting claim—during a punchball game—that babies were made by the man putting his penis in the woman's vagina.)

Thus, I swore that when my kids came of age I would have open and honest and unembarrassing discussions with them about the joys and responsibilities of human sexuality.

My first opportunity to step up to bat, so to speak, was just before Cael's thirteenth birthday in July of 1982. My well-orchestrated plan was for us to go out to the woods and pitch a tent and fish and grill raw meat over an open fire and talk like real men. And I'd tell it all flat out. There did not exist a sexual subject I wouldn't cover from A(nuses) to Z(ippers).

We arrived, set up the tent, took a swim, tossed a baseball, did a little fishing, hiked around the pond, made a fire, cooked some dogs ... and all afternoon I kept waiting for the right ("organic") opportunity to introduce the subject. But of course the right opportunity never quite presented itself. Fathers and teenage sons don't normally find themselves talking about sex.

Several times during the day I asked if he had *any* questions "about anything at all," now that we were out in the woods and away from Mom and Nancy and Addie and Clover and Danny. But he had no clue as to what I was talking about. "No," he said, shaking his shaggy head, "I can't think of anything."

I knew in my heart, though, that once we got going on our talk, he'd have a million and one questions for me, and I'd answer every one as openly as I could—and when I couldn't, we'd laugh so hard we'd roll on the ground gasping for breath.

I just needed the right opening.

Hours passed in front of the fire; we talked about everything and nothing—mostly nothing, which is the way boys and their fathers seem to communicate best, faces forward, the road slipping endlessly behind—and still we hadn't touched on the nitty or the gritty.

So, right after some serious words about Thurman Munson's

RBI count, I jammed on the conversational brakes, popped the clutch, and made a hard right down Sex Lane: "Now that you're thirteen, Cael ... you must have some questions...." The groan that escaped his throat went down nine generations.

He locked his eyes over my left shoulder and shook his head. So I began. I skipped the anatomy and physiology lesson, figuring the *Hustler* magazines that I had recently found stashed in the ceiling of the old carriage house had provided enough of the visuals.

Then I talked softly and comfortingly and fatheringly about men and women and lust and respect and masturbation and contraception and, yes, I even threw in a fallopian tube or two, pausing every so often to see if he wanted to "share" something with me or ask a question that would really launch our bonding experience and let him know that sex and sexual thoughts were healthy and wonderful aspects of growing up. Cael sat there, absorbing my every word like a sponge, eyes fixed on some distant object over that same left shoulder.

Forty-seven minutes later I had done the complete Masters and Johnson introductory lecture series, and though it hadn't gone quite as I planned, I felt pretty pleased with myself. I stuffed an Oreo in my smiling mouth, slapped my stomach like George C. Scott in *Dr. Strangelove*, and crooned, "That pretty much covers it, Cael. Any questions now?"

He lurched back from his stupor and glared at me, just like he did when I woke him each morning for school. "Anything?"

"Yeah, Dad"—he looked up and paused—"I have been wonderin' about somethin'...." My heart fluttered. My hands tingled. I was prepared to tell him everything. Everything. He said, "How do you think the Giants are gonna do this year?"

THE ZEN DRIVING SCHOOL
Artless parallel parking

Don't think: Look!
—WITTGENSTEIN

One day you boost them up that first mountainous step onto a yellow school bus to go to kindergarten, and the next day they come home wearing earphones and asking for a ride to the Motor Vehicle office to get a learner's permit.

"You're too young."

"I'm sixteen!"

"No, you're not. You're in third grade. And take those things off. I can't hear you when you're listening to music."

"First of all, (anatomical expletive inaudible), I'm a sophomore in high school, and second, (character expletive inaudible), I'm the one listening to the music, not you, and I can hear you perfectly well . . . although I sometimes wish I couldn't!"

And so it goes. Being the one ahead—as another Zen koan goes—it always seems that you're one or two steps (or grades) behind. But reality is reality, although in this instance reality is nonreality (more on that later), and soon after that stunning bit of psychodrama where you realize that your baby is old enough to drive the family Jeep, you find yourself strapped into the passenger seat making outlandishly paranoid statements like "You must assume that everyone on the road is an idiot or a drunk or a psychotic murderer out to cross the center line and kill you. That's defensive driving."

Every experienced driver knows in his or her mechanical soul that good driving has little to do with proper technique. Technique is mostly learned on that first white-knuckled Saturday that you and your third grader in a sophomore's body drive around the high school parking lot or down the deserted country lane. After that, it's all about attaining a kind of nonthinking communication with the two-thousand-pound metal beast that can hurtle you through space at speeds beyond what the original Maker designed the human body to travel.

Good drivers perform, they don't think. Consider all the times you've zoned out for thirty or forty minutes while driving from one city to the next, absorbed in memory or fantasy or in reconstructing the argument you just lost: you kept the car at a reasonable speed and on the right side of the road, you signaled, you made turns, you braked, and somehow you got where you were going.

Bad drivers think. They drive as if they are perpetually taking their road tests with Big Bertha and her Designed-for-Failure Clipboard. As every experienced driver knows, it is much harder to keep the car within the lines if you're thinking about keeping within the lines than if your mind is a blank.

So learning to drive is not about learning to drive. It is about attaining a state of unconscious oneness with the machine. And so it should be perfect for teenagers, who rarely if ever have a driving thought in their heads.

Yet, put a teenager in the driver's seat, and that is precisely when she or he first experiences focused thought. About the key to ignition. About the cosmic order of transmission. About the mirrors to the immediate past. About backing up to go forward. About obstacles in the road of life. About the way to gain dominion over the tape player and open the window and attain the right elbow angle of calmness and make the sounds in your brain resemble words, all the while trying intently to keep the car in between the lines.

The consequence of all that thinking is situational paralysis. What should be reflexive action in response to the stop sign up ahead is not action but thoughtful indecision, such as when to brake—or not to brake—for the red light, until the Zen teacher has been completely un-Zenned, screaming, arms up across his face, right foot jammed into the pedalless floor, "Not the gas, you fool, the brake! The brake! THE BRAKE!"

The key to getting teenagers to stop thinking while driving is to talk nonstop the entire agonizing driving lesson for no other reason than to get them to listen to you, not to their own inner voices. I also keep the driving lessons short so that their self-contained thoughts don't leach out and confuse me to the point that I lose my edge of pure perceptions and start grabbing for the wheel.

As for parallel parking and other such esoteric skills, the fewer mechanical tips the better. We go through the process several times together and then I tell them everything is done by feel. By visualization. Pull up to the car ahead of the vacant space, line up the steering wheels, and see yourself moving the car back into the space, six inches from the curb. And then do it. Then I get out of the car and leave them to their own process of achieving mindlessness.

Same thing with learning to drive standard transmissions, although I advise doing this after your hot-rodders have already passed the driver's test on an automatic. Show the neophytes what to do, go through the bucking motions a few times, and then have an out-of-car experience. Give them the keys and tell them to find their transcendent spirit. Then stand back and watch as they buck and stall and grind the gears and ride the clutch until they're out of sight.

And when they return later on driving like old pros, yell at them for going too fast.

WHERE'S PAPA?

The importance of being in the picture

Be here now.
—RAM DASS

A hazy one-hundred-degree day. Around four o'clock the small town pool is beginning to fill up with dads. Young dads, old dads, fat dads, black dads, white dads . . . you get the picture. Some are tossing kids in the thick air above the chlorinated blue. Some stand at ease in genital-deep water like sergeants instructing new recruits. Some do laps, seals with goggles and nose plugs. Some never make it to the water; they go right to the frayed beach chair and hide behind the paper.

One thing we have in common is that we all look like dads. You can't buy this fleshy look anywhere. We also sound like dads, barking at kids to settle down, demanding change as we hand out a buck to buy a Bomb Pop, soothing a toddler who has just scraped her knee. There's nothing remarkable here except that there is nothing remarkable here.

New Paltz is a nice place to be a kid—and a dad. The mountains, the college, and a funky main street provide extraordinary playing fields beyond all the green parks and playgrounds. Chil-

dren here are known as much by who they are as by the name
their family has made for itself in local lore.

I tried to imagine on that intensely hot summer day—Bay and
Elizabeth in the shallow section, Clover lounging on a blanket
with friends, Danny tossing a ball with Keith and Jessie—what
would happen if a group of teenagers formed a "whirlpool" here
in New Paltz, as some boys apparently did several years ago in the
Crotona Pool in the South Bronx: locking arms and moving in
circles across the pool, chanting song lyrics, laughing, surrounding a frightened girl, and fondling her.

It didn't take much imagination, though. The lifeguards
would be blowing whistles like crazy and jerking their college-
educated thumbs to order the out-of-control mob out of the
pool. Six foot six head lifeguard Dave O'Neill would scream
bloody murder and throw the group out of the park—maybe
for a week, probably for the entire summer. He'd threaten to
call the police. And, frankly, that would be the easiest part of
the ordeal for most of the errant boys.

Before they made it safely away from Dave—and Bonnie and
Rich and Mike and all the other outraged big brothers and sisters
who sling whistles like guns at Moriello Pool—the whirlpool gang
would have to answer to the fuming dads storming their way, ven-
omous men with bulging veins in their necks who would appear
two earth-shattering steps away from an angry coronary.

I could see dads grown suddenly enormous with massive
hands on love-handled hips glaring down into the terrified eyes of
their suddenly skinny boys; dads with their thick fingers clasped
around the back of boys' chicken necks, pushing them behind the
bath house; dads—red dads, yellow dads, white dads, black dads
(you get the picture)—index fingers jabbing bony chests.

I could feel the boys' silky backs rubbed up against rough
cinder block walls. I could hear the boys crying. I shuddered at
the sight of those wrathful fathers, mouths open like dark caul-
drons of fire, bellowing the way that dads have bellowed at their
bad boys throughout the ages.

And then I looked around at all the dads planted around our local pool and wondered where the fathers of the whirlpooling boys had been that summer. And if they could not be there, what about the uncles and the big brothers? Why wasn't someone right there to calm the roiling waters and save those boys from themselves?

When I closed my eyes, though, all I could see was a circle of panoramic photographs, crowded pools across the country swirling with thousands of perilous eddies, abandoned boys linking hands with each other and singing away their confusion, anger, and pain. And at the center of each of those whirlpools was a terrified little girl—some father's daughter—whose dad had forsaken her to a world where boys never learn to grow up to be men.

As Ram Dass says, Be here now! Now! Presence is all.

SEEKING IDENTITY

*What makes Danny run . . .
and get busted*

> *Trying to define yourself is like trying to bite your own teeth.*
>
> —ALAN WATTS

Whatever psychological issues the fifth (or sixth or seventh) child in a big family may face, there is one distinct advantage for kids on the lower end of the pecking order: from the very beginnings of consciousness, they've seen enough real life to harbor no illusions about domestic bliss. They've had front-row booster seats for some historic family battles and by puberty should know how to navigate the treacherous waters between parents and teenagers.

Take Danny, our current misunderstood sixteen-year-old. He's had a lifetime to observe the assembled crimes and punishments of his older siblings. He's seen Cael busted for partying while the parents are away; he's peeked at Nancy being collared for arriving long past curfew—and he knows all about the midnight call from the local police. No doubt he's contemplated how Addie deftly and sometimes defiantly eluded punishment for crimes worthy of long-term incarceration. And he's been mindfully attentive as Clover learned the value of going about her misdeeds in a quiet and uncontentious manner—and, in doing so, got away with practically everything.

So, life for Danny should be a teenage cakewalk. With all that knowledge and experience laid out behind him, Danny's existence should be grounded in groundlessness. Yet . . .

Beginning with the secret stash of two warm beers and a couple of stale Marlboros we found in the storage shed of the cottage in Hatteras when he was thirteen, and moving on through what has seemed like a monthly smorgasbord of petty family misdemeanors, Dan the Man has probably spent more weekend nights incarcerated at home than any of his brothers and sisters—and perhaps all of them combined.

Danny's life could be read as a minor tragedy, not only because he seems to get caught all the time, but because I know that he's probably done less "bad" stuff than his supposedly innocent sisters. (I'm still finding out about the indiscretions they committed while living under our "jurisdiction.")

There are two nontranscendent reasons why Danny has gotten busted more often than his siblings. One is that although I enjoy teenagers immensely—I love the way they knock over the furniture of our lives as they move toward adulthood; I love their often unlovable music, their unwearable clothes, their unintelligible language, their utterly selfish selflessness—I have no illusions about their innocence.

Nor does Patti. As his four siblings preceded Danny through the gates of pubescent angst, Patti and I were not hiding under the quilts with our hands over our ears. We've seen it all, or at least most of it.

But, we can't take all the credit for Danny's well-grounded life. The second reason for the oxymoronic nature of Danny's predicament has been his search for identity in this big conglomerate of a family. As Alan Watts understood so well, trying to define yourself is both the simplest and most impossible of undertakings; and, if I may add something to the Zen master's observation, trying to define yourself in the context of a big family makes the whole process even simpler and more inaccessible.

Cael was the Cassanova of the family, Nancy the mathematical Einstein, Addie the clone of her mom, and Clover a graceful equestrienne. Danny, too, sought not only an identity from the outside world but a special recognition among his siblings. As such, Danny inadvertently became the James Dean Rebel Without Much Cause in our brood, the one with a good heart who always gets himself into trouble. Consequently, he has always dropped bread crumbs along his felonious path. And while his older siblings might laugh at his ongoing troubles, with each new indictment they've also nodded their heads and said to themselves, "Hey, the little twerp has some backbone. He's all right, after all."

And he is.

A KEG OF BEER, LOAFING ON THE COUCH, AND THE LIVING ROOM RUG OUT ON THE LAWN

Axiom: When parents are gone,
teenagers will party

I'm seventeen: I'm supposed to lie to you!
—C. LEWIS

No sense being coy about it, there is an axiom of family life with teenagers that must be understood by all parents in order for them to attain the next level of spiritual development (i.e., freedom without fear):

When Parents Are Gone, Teenagers Will Party.

This requires no psychological analysis, no social commentary, no spiritual homilies, just a simple story.

When Patti and I told the kids over dinner that we were all going to the beach at Montauk for the long Columbus Day weekend, everyone was instantly excited. Everyone, that is, except Cael. He fell into a grumbling despair, barely finishing his meal with that look of utter disgust that only a teenager can affect.

Actually, I understood his predicament. Like any seventeen-year-old, he was as horrified at the prospect of spending two nights in a couple of mildewy hotel rooms with his five brothers and sisters (Elizabeth was not yet born) as he was humiliated at the vision of walking around in public with giggly girls, a doofy boy, a smelly baby, and two parents who could embarrass a rock.

I actually don't remember whether we took pity on him and decided he was old enough to stay by himself, or if he moaned so insistently about the boredom that awaited him that he wore us down and we relented against our better judgment. It doesn't really matter.

After I extracted several solemn promises from him that there would be no parties ("Dad . . . ," he said, voice dripping with annoyance at my lack of faith), Patti gave him a nonstop lecture on the (two) dos and (sixty-seven) don'ts of staying home alone. Then we gave him a cross-indexed three-page list of emergency numbers; stocked the refrigerator as if we were going away for two months; and Nancy, Addie, Clover, Danny, Bay, Patti, and I left for two and a half beach-filled days at the charmingly downscale Eastdeck Motel in Montauk.

"I know he's having a party," Patti said as we walked the beach on Saturday.

I assured her he wasn't. "He told me he wouldn't. Cael does a lot of things but he doesn't lie."

And so I instantly achieved the Zen state of pure cognitive dissonance when we drove up the long driveway two days later and saw the living room oriental rug spread out on the front lawn. I knew but I didn't know.

Cael met us with as goofy a grin as you'd ever want to see and, after all the yelling and screaming died down, admitted that he'd had a *few* friends over and that the bubble of beer that they had somehow gotten had accidentally fallen off the table and soaked the rug.

Two hours later Patti spoke to Alice Tenuto (our closest neighbor through the woods—about a quarter of a mile away) who said she *heard* the party going all night *and* later found out that practically the entire senior class was there.

Cael was grounded for the rest of his life, and Patti and I

agreed that we would never again leave a teenager home alone for more than a couple of hours.

Except, six months later, which was several months after he had been "paroled" for something akin to good behavior, Patti and I again made plans for another family weekend trip. And of course Cael didn't want to join us, which prompted an emergency meeting at the highest levels of family governance to review public policy. Patti was skeptical, but I argued that since he was properly chastened and punished by the rug-in-the-yard fiasco, it would be a real statement of faith in his character if we trusted him enough to let him stay home.

That evening Cael and I sat down and had a father-son man-to-man heart-to-heart mano-a-mano talk about trust and maturity and the meaning of family. (I don't know what the last had to do with the first two, but I toss it out periodically if I don't know what else to say.)

And Cael nodded soberly and sincerely as if he agreed with every word I had spoken. At the end I said, "Look me in the eye and promise that you're not going to have a party, Cael. That's all I need." I didn't even drop my voice the fatherly three octaves. We were pals now, men of the world.

He looked me right in the eye and said, "I'm not going to have a party, Dad." And we hugged, men of the world together.

Of course you know where this is going. And of course he had a party. And although they didn't soak the living room rug, the big jerk used no-wax floor polish to clean up the pine wood floors, thus creating a dull, thick, hazy finish all over the house. There were spaghetti strands stuck on the kitchen wall, wrinkled sheets on every bed in the house, the heavy clink of beer bottles in the trash.

So, there I was right in his downturned face, veins bursting in my neck as I rose to the essence of my paternal rage: "Worst of all, Cael, worst of all, is the fact that you lied to me! You looked me in the eye and promised you would not have a party."

And he looked me in the eye and said without a hint of deception, "I'm seventeen, Dad: I'm supposed to lie to you!"

Ah, truth.

So Cael was grounded once again for the rest of his life, and Patti and I swore we'd never again leave a teenager home alone overnight. And we pretty much kept our word until Nancy and Addie ("The girls would never lie to us like that!") had an extravaganza several years later that apparently rivaled a Grateful Dead concert—and, as a nice little touch, tripped and poked a hole in the wall with the vacuum cleaner while cleaning up.

THE EMPTY NEST

*What happens when they leave for college
(and can't come home on weekends)*

*When you do something, you should burn yourself com-
pletely, like a good bonfire, leaving no trace of yourself.*
—SHUNRYU SUZUKI

Many parents we know want their children to choose colleges near home. Not so with us. At the risk of sounding a little cold-hearted, we encourage our kids to go at least a state or two away; far enough so that they can't come home on a whim every Friday afternoon.

When I'm taking the high road on these matters I say that in order to find themselves, kids need to leave what is safe and comfortable and predictable. As Chogyam Trungpa says in *Shambhala: The Sacred Path of the Warrior*, "This is your world! You can't not look. . . . Open your eyes. Don't blink, and look, look—look further." Beyond state lines.

On the low road you might hear me say, "Your salad days are over, kid. We love you dearly, kid, but eighteen years of laundry, dirty plates, strange friends, and outstretched palms is enough. It's time to hit the road."

So Cael went all the way down to Tallahassee, Florida, and Nancy flew off to Chapel Hill, North Carolina, and Addie zoomed away to State College, Pennsylvania, and Clover joined Nancy in Chapel Hill. Nobody's closer than four and a half hours by train, plane, or automobile.

In our family there's a two-step process by which one prepares to leave home. Step one occurs years before freshman orientation and involves moving your teenage self and everything you own (and have been able to steal from your brothers and sisters) up to the attic, where there are two bedrooms and a space that might be loosely termed a den with a TV, VCR, and a remarkably uncomfortable dusty couch.

There is no bathroom up there, and it's a three-story walk-up, and it's frigidly cold in winter and suffocatingly hot in summer, and the rooms are more cell-like than roomy, and the rain on the roof sounds like pebbles dropped from the heavens, but the attic is the closest thing to heaven that a teenager can imagine without paying rent. Close the door from the second-floor hall and you're safe from meddling parents and annoying little kids and the embarrassing inanities of family life.

As the oldest in the family, Cael and Nancy staked their claims to the "loft" when we built the house years ago. There was no protest from the other kids; as in most families, there are rights and privileges that go along with age. (Danny was reminded of the hierarchical nature of family life when we were all together last summer on Hatteras. Everyone piled into the Jeep and Danny was "ordered" by the older crew into the "way back" with Bay and Elizabeth. He was nothing short of incredulous: "I'm sixteen! I don't sit with the little kids!" Cael's reply was brief: "As long as we're around, you're number five. Now get in the back." Then he turned to Addie with a sneer and said, "He'll probably be sitting in the way back when he's thirty-six and married with kids.")

So, at the very moment that Cael was closing the lid on the last suitcase to bring to college, Addie was down on the second floor plotting her territorial grab. And as the last of his bags were dragged down two flights and out to the car, the implements of takeover were being stealthily transported up to the attic.

Before he was even out of the house, his bed was dismantled and dragged out of the room.

Addie did make the trek downstairs to give him a kiss and a hug good-bye, and she did stand and wave from the front porch as he left. But then she raced—two steps at a time—to the hot attic paradise that by rights was already hers. And with his body scent still lingering in the air, she painted him out of existence. In pink.

Two hours later, any reminder or reminiscent sense of his time and presence in the room was completely gone. In a form of familial alchemy, it had been transformed completely into Addie's room. (And Addie's room on the second floor was taken over by Danny, who bolted from the room he shared with Bay as if his life depended on it.)

When Cael came home from college that first Thanksgiving and found no traces of his former self up on the third floor—and saw Addie standing symbolically in the doorway with an imaginary Winchester cradled in her arms—he got the picture and took up temporary residence in the tiny sewing room on the second floor. And, as if that wasn't humbling enough, two years later he was relegated to sharing the bunk bed with Danny or any available couch after Nancy left for UNC and Clover immediately planted her flag and her army of ten thousand stuffed animals in the attic room next to Addie.

Nancy, who had observed Addie's expression of manifest destiny, quickly claimed rights to the sewing room before Cael got home for Christmas vacation.

And so it goes. Just as in life, when you go, you hardly leave a trace behind. Everything keeps moving. Everything is in flux. Aside from the photographs all over the walls of this big home—and the memories of the children who grew up here—all of which suggests an immutable sense of place, there are no monuments here, no childhood sanctums, no historic designations.

And, paraphrasing Walter Cronkite, because it is always that way, that is the way it is.

7

Nanto (or Hard-to-Penetrate Koan) and Teenage Girls

ZEN DAD, UN-ZEN BOYFRIENDS

The pimply faced boys who show up at your door

The quieter you become the more you can hear.
—RAM DASS

He shuffles his feet, glances up at the ceiling, coughs, jams his hands in his pockets. Snatches a peek at me out of the corner of his eye. A halting minute later he's trying man-talk with me—cars, boxing, fishing, money, his plans after high school or college.

But I keep my distance. I don't talk much. As he and my daughter finally leave, I offer a low-key "Have a good time." He knows what I mean, though. He knows I'll be staring out the window, watching how he drives away.

I can hear him say to her later, his voice soft at the edges, "Your father doesn't like me."

And I imagine her telling him, "Don't be ridiculous. Of course he does. He likes all my friends."

But she's wrong this time. The barest truth is that I don't like the boy, even though there's a very good chance I liked him last month—that is, the day before he started dating my daughter. In fact, odds are good that I treated him just like I do any of the boys who come around to visit. I welcome them in. I offer them sodas. I laugh at their jokes. I put a hand on their shoulder as a coach or a friendly uncle might do.

Not this one, though. In the timespan of a quick kiss on the lips, he's suddenly found himself, in effect, in a back room sitting on a hard wooden chair with a light over his head. He's suddenly got something to prove to me that has nothing to do with a charming grin or a firm handshake or an intelligent remark or a game-winning goal. I'm not impressed with flowers or jewelry or poetry.

Everybody knows why he wants me to like him: he's attracted to my daughter, and one way or another, I'm an important man in her life. He wants me to like him *only* because he wants her to like him so much that she'll give her heart to him. He wants her to love him.

And while love may indeed be the essence of life—the alpha and the omega—it's also true that nothing in this life can do more damage to a person than lost or abusive love. Everybody also knows that. So any boy who comes to take her heart is going to be seen by me at first as an intruder, a threat, a dangerous snake the moment he first slips through the door.

Frankly, it doesn't much matter to me if his hair goes down to his butt or is clipped marine-close to the scalp. It also doesn't really matter if he's got a nose ring or a class ring, a BMW or a bicycle, a leather jacket or a tweed sport coat. He's come to steal her heart. So he's dangerous.

Love and affection and companionship and sex are all a part of life, so I won't—and can't—protect her from any of it. Any of it. I haven't been and won't ever be a warden to any of my children, but I am going to watch him as insistently as a circling hawk.

And the one thing I'm going to watch most carefully is the way that he treats her when he thinks I'm not watching. The biggest mistake any boy can make—and it's the very one too many of them believe is their right—is to try to be her protector. It's simply not his job; it's mine, and it's the very one that I have been working to walk away from since she was small enough to be cradled in one arm.

I've held her for hours while she burned up with fever; I've rushed her to emergency rooms with broken bones; I've confronted teachers who have hurt her with their words; I've tried to put my arm around her quivering shoulders when some boy broke up with her. I've grounded her when she's done wrong; I've said no a million times. Always to protect her. That's been my job.

Ironically, these Prince Valiants are always fawning at first. Overly attentive and overwhelmingly considerate, they start off treating their girlfriends like princesses who must be shaded from the harsh light of daily life. Some even lack the perspective to keep quiet about how well they'll take care of them.

As soon as I hear the conspiratorially macho "I'll have her in by . . . ," I know there's going to be trouble. And it will be in the form of a jealous boy slowly growing more moody, manipulative, and demanding, eventually becoming a ridiculously macho caricature of his own misguided notions of maleness. At some point his desperation might even become a dangerous weapon.

So I keep my distance. I watch very carefully. I listen.

And not until the moment I see that he *truly* cares for her do I begin to stop watching. When I see a smile of real happiness on my daughter's face when he shows up at the door—not the relief that comes of desperation or fear—I invite him in. When I can hear the joyous sound of them talking, playing, arguing, and laughing as equals, I put my hand on his shoulder.

When he wants to be her friend, not mine, then we'll be friends. Then I'll talk.

POCKETFUL OF GIRL STUFF

The mysterious disappearance of the old man's clothes

The Buddha taught that all things, including his castle, are essentially impermanent and as soon as man tries to possess them they slip away.

—ALAN WATTS

At first, most fathers think it's cute: you pick up your thirteen-year-old daughter at the Middle School dance and find her wearing your favorite blue button-down oxford shirt, sleeves rolled heavily just below the elbow, tails at her knobby knees, a grown-up smirk on her beautiful baby face.

"Nice shirt," you say slyly, walking to the parking lot.

She giggles. "Daaa-deeee . . . you weren't home when I was getting ready—and it looked great on me—and I didn't think you'd mind—and I didn't get any stains on it. . . ."

You don't say much because there's nothing to say and you'd be a fool to try to get a word in edgewise anyway. You just smile like the fool she's playing you for. Then she plants the seed of future incursions into your closet and drawers that will eventually leave you naked and bereft: "You're not mad, are you, Daddy?"

Of course you're not mad. You're actually flattered for reasons beyond your understanding—and, really, she looks so cute.

You laugh and take her delicate little hand in yours and, in effect, give her the keys to the wardrobe. "Not at all, baby girl. Not at all."

In fact, this is bliss: your little girl in your big manly shirt and you acting like the most understanding, hippest dad in town. For a moment you sense some inarticulated danger and revert to the authoritarian "Just let me know when you're borrowing a shirt or something, so I won't think it's lost." Whatever that means. And with that, you think that's the end of it.

It's not.

The next thing I knew, Nancy was fifteen, a little too womanly to be cute anymore, and on her back was a shirt that I vaguely remembered owning but hadn't seen in months. "Is that mine?" I asked like the doddering fool she knew I was capable of being.

"No," she said with unsettling conviction for a girl who was lying through her teeth, "but I think Addie's wearing your sweatshirt." And I turned around to discover that Addie was indeed thirteen and looking as cute as a button (whatever *that* means) in my extra-large Florida State sweatshirt, cuffs down over her fingers, stretched out waistband below her knees. And I was ineffably flattered—and sidetracked—once again, just as I would be enchanted two years later by the sight of Clover dressed up in my Paul Simon *Still Crazy After All These Years* concert T-shirt.

At that point I began to think that perhaps I was crazy because it seemed that I was seeing my clothes—or clothes that I thought I might have once owned—on teenage girls all around this town.

One night I swore I saw Addie's friend Anita in what might have been my North Carolina sweatshirt; and the next week I'm sure I spotted Jessica, Clover's best friend, in a flannel shirt that I hadn't worn in at least two years. Then there was the girl whose name I did not know strolling down Main Street in my Rodanthe Surfshop hat.

But nothing prepared me for the singular experience of arriving at the Listorts' house one night to find Nancy's friend Cynthia wearing my plaid boxers!

I was speechless. What could I say? *What are you doing in my shorts?* I don't think Cynthia had a clue that they were mine. The way these things go, she might not have even known that she got them through Nancy—or Addie. It's quite possible that Anita was wearing my underwear and she lent it to Kristen or Tiffany and one of them lent the shorts to Cynthia.

At that singular moment, my drawers full but completely devoid of me, it seemed to me that I achieved a Zen state of true emptiness.

But I was wrong. My moment of immortality came soon after discovering a favorite jacket (which I forgot I owned) under a six-foot pile of towels on the floor of Clover's room. I was so happy to find it that I didn't yell at her for stealing my clothes again—or for the pile of twenty-three (yes, twenty-three) towels that left the rest of the family drying off with washcloths.

And the next morning I drove off in my newly rediscovered favorite hipster-poet jacket to teach my advanced placement English classes over in the quaint village of Millbrook. When I arrived at the 140-year-old Thorne Building, the old heating system had not quite brought the classrooms up to sixty degrees, so I kept my jacket on while teaching the class.

Midway through the lesson, as I paced back and forth in front of the room, I reached into the pocket and felt something unusual. Something cylindrical. It was hard but covered with paper. I had no idea what it could be.

So, in between some well-chosen insights into the extreme narcissism of Othello and the nature of jealousy, I pulled the alien object out of the depths of the pocket and . . . the room erupted in soul-shaking laughter as I stood there with a slender Tampax in my hand.

In that epiphanic moment I saw everything—the past, the present, the future—and knew in my soul that there was no possible explanation that would do justice to the curious vision of a forty-something teacher standing before a group of high school seniors with a feminine hygiene product in his outstretched hand.

My red-faced silence was an acknowledgment that all things are essentially impermanent, clothing as well as embarrassment.

ARE YOU SAYING I'M FAT?

Teenage girls and their unholy relationship with food

It is an ordinary thing to be holy. We do such extra-ordinary things not to be.

—JAMES HAZARD

Clover looks in a trifold mirror at the department store and frowns. Then she turns around and cranes her head over her neck like a gazelle, gets up on her toes, and mutters, "My butt's too big for this dress."

I'm looking in the same mirror—at the very same moment—and I don't see a big butt. In fact, I don't see a big anything. Mostly, I see this gorgeous, slim-hipped, electric eighteen-year-old girl, a vision of budding womanhood—the girl voted "Best Physique" by the PC-conscious 1995 senior class at New Paltz High School. Not "Biggest Butt."

I asked myself a question to which I already knew the answer: "How could two relatively reasonable people be looking at the same reflected vision and see two distinct and contradictory realities?"

And the answer was at once far too serious and far too ridiculous to answer adequately.

Suffice it to say that because teenage girls are, by cosmic design, narcissists who see the world solely in terms of themselves, they find themselves at the merciless hands of anyone and everyone (boys, men, teen magazines, advertisers) who have a personal stake in making them feel too big. Boys, who are also narcissists, have the exact opposite problem; they see themselves as smaller than they really are and consequently must go around proving how big they are.

I knew the answer, not because I have a great insight into the cosmos of teenage perception but because Nancy and Addie preceded Clover through the valley of the shadow of psychic fat—and, a long ways back, I remember my high school girlfriend Judy at Jones Beach covering her lower half with a towel because her rather compelling thighs were "too fat." (One doesn't easily forget cognitive dissonance like that.)

Nancy, like Clover, was your run-of-the-mill teenage narcissist who saw rolls of blubber in the most unlikely places. She also opened my eyes to another paradox of parenting: a clueless father takes his daughter to lunch, spends hundreds of dollars on clothing she doesn't even need, and somehow, it turns out to be a miserable and demoralizing experience.

Addie, however, brought body misperception to the level of an art form during her teenage years. I don't want to make light of a very serious problem in our society that has led to untold numbers of young women starving and purging themselves to death, but at the less self-destructive levels, there is a Zen resonance in the way teenage girls perceive their weight in the world.

At sixteen Addie not only knew that mirrors lie, she knew how to look through them to see the real truth about her supposedly flabby body. Watching a girl with no body fat do stomach crunches and other painful forms of penance in front of the TV to ward off cellulite and flab made me realize how serious her quest for a perfectly thin body had become. (For the uninformed, stomach crunches are agonizing exercises designed for narcissists of both sexes who want to achieve what is commonly known as a six-pack: a hard and taut belly, which, when flexed, produces a six-ripple effect from the rib cage down to the Calvin Klein waistband.)

However, the awareness of this perfect absurdity came later on. I was innocently walking down the stairs one afternoon and saw Addie sitting against the wall, her feet up on the banister, talking on the phone with her friend Jana.

I suppose I assumed naively that she would just swivel around and let me pass. She didn't. It's possible that she hadn't noticed me towering above her on the narrow step, though it was difficult to imagine that a conversation with Jana could be that riveting. So, all I said was, "Excuse me."

Moving nothing but her eyeballs, she glared at me as if I had just said the most insulting thing a man ever said to a woman. "What?"

"I said, 'Excuse me.' "

"Are you saying I'm fat?" she scowled, not missing a beat.

Stuck on the steps, I stuttered in disbelief, "There's not an ounce of fat on your body, Adelyn, and, besides, what has that got to do with my trying to come down the stairs?"

She swiveled around, stood up, and muttered, "Like you don't know. . . ." Then she pressed her body flat against the wall, leaving a space wide enough for a Mack truck to drive through.

From that point on I understood that it's virtually impossible to argue with teenage misperception. You just give in and wait it out.

That is why, years later on the shopping trip with Clover, I was able to view her megabottom from a more cosmic perspective.

I simply agreed with her, and we went to another store in the mall where they stock dresses that hide one's big butt.

ZEN AND THE
TEENAGE GIRL

How to say one thing and mean something totally different

> *In every truth the opposite is equally true.*
> —HERMANN HESSE

Addie tilts her head. A smirk sneaks across her lips. "You know, I just realized that I can do whatever I want. You don't really have control over me anymore."

She is eighteen, nearing the end of her senior year in high school. She's full of herself: smart, charming, athletic, pretty. In her purse are the keys to a beat-up old Plymouth. On her arm, a boyfriend who makes her parents uneasy. In her folder, an acceptance letter from Penn State. Everything is perfect.

I smile, a standard parental stall, but I know that what she says is true. After children reach a certain age, parents exert only the most superficial control over their destinies. We may continue to inform or lecture them about acceptable behavior, and insist that certain rules be maintained in the home, but when they walk out the door each morning, they make their own choices. They lead their own lives.

Of course I wish it were different; it's a perilous world out there, and part of me would like to be Addie's Schwarzeneggersize Jiminy Cricket, poised over her shoulder in the same watch-ful way that I was when she was four and learning to ride her two-wheeler. But the simple truth is I cannot watch over my beautiful daughter every moment of the day, just as I could not watch Cael and Nancy when they were seniors, just as I will not be able to watch over Clover, Danny, Bay, and Elizabeth Bayou-Grace when it's their time of ascendancy.

I tell Addie all that in a soft, fatherly voice, admittedly feeling more than a little smug that I have come up with a response that is steeped in ageless parental wisdom.

She's not satisfied, though. There is more to this challenge than simply her freedom, and I simply don't get it. "I meant that even if you ground me, I don't really have to listen to you any-more." There is a wrinkle of nervousness around the smirk. I see my bold little toddler sixteen years earlier with that same expression.

"Yes, but . . . there are limits. . . ." I'm not sure what I mean by that, but limits seems a good concept at the moment.

"I mean, truthfully, Dad, what are you going to do if I don't accept the grounding, throw me out of the house? You'd never throw me out of the house, would you?" She glances sideways for the answer.

While scurrying around behind my glassy eyes, searching for some safe wall against which to back up, I see finally that she's not talking about rules at all but rather something like "This is all moving too quickly. I'm supposed to leave everything behind in just a few months. So, I just want to know whether it's possi-ble that I can stay home and behave like an impudent child and still be treated like an adult?"

Conventional Western wisdom (and some subterranean mem-ories of my father speaking to me on the same subject) tell me to say, "No, you can't have your cake and eat it, too." You're either on or off the bus. A boss or an employee. A child or an adult. Set limits. Be consistent. Right is right.

Yet, accompanying my children on their journey through the

dark acned tunnel of adolescence, I have acquired a kind of night vision that allows me to see that nothing is exactly as it seems. Indeed, the parental highway for me has been rather foggy and paradoxical: wrong is sometimes right and right is often wrong. And at the heart of all those contradictions is the most unsettling one of all: that while my children belong to me, they are not mine exclusively.

I don't ever want Addie to think that she is not welcome in my home, yet I don't want her to think that I will allow her to take my home away from me.

So when she asks if I'd ever throw her out of the house, I stutter out a windy yes and then follow with a grunting no and then a quavering yes and no. Finally, in an unintentional paradigm of my own ignorant wisdom: "I don't know what I'd do, Adelyn."

She frowns, disappointed that I haven't concocted a concrete, documentable answer of the on-or-off-the-bus variety. She wants to know whether it's Tough Love Dad or Saint Steven the Martyr. She wants a statement of fact, a simple list of rights and wrongs, the kind that is retrieved from someone's kindergarten teacher or from a wise Jewish grandmother or from some postdoctoral fellow at Harvard interviewed on *Donahue*: good, sane, logical advice on how to be perfectly happy and perfectly protected from the vagaries of an imperfect world.

Stranded in the swirling darkness of this cosmically indefinable problem, all that comes to mind is an aphorism spoken by a man who is neither a Zen master nor a parent: "Love your children most when they least deserve it." Jerry Sherman, a wonderful earth science teacher at Millbrook High School, offered that simple truth nearly ten years ago at a graduation ceremony I attended. And I knew instantly it was the smartest thing I had ever heard. Love is simply not something to be earned or bartered.

So I don't answer Addie's question, saying only that I love her with all my heart, that I will always be her father, in life and in death, reaching across to hold her close, to breathe in that ex-

traordinary essence, just as I did when she was a terrible two
and as easy to embrace as a summer morning.

When we part, she presses her lips together and turns toward
the safety of her cluttered bedroom, a room Danny will claim as
his the day she moves out. Before the door closes, though, she
turns with a sad smile and says, "I wasn't asking if you loved
me. . . ."

I nod, but it's not to her, it's to Jerry Sherman, who knows
the beautiful answer to the question nobody asks.

OUTSIDE THE GARDEN

One night before Nancy graduated from high school . . .

We have it completely backwards: instead of being very strict with little children and gradually opening the gates of freedom as they grow older, we give little children far too much freedom and then try desperately to rein them in when they get older and wilder.

—PATRICIA HENDERSON LEWIS

Nancy was born on my twenty-seventh birthday. I'm not sure if that explains why my memories sometimes seem to get spliced with hers, but her senior year in high school turned on reels of remembrances that had been lost for decades.

In my home movie of the fifties and sixties, Roslyn Heights, New York, was a place of paramount comfort and security. I awoke each morning to two parents, glass bottles of milk outside the front door, a Buick Roadmaster in the garage, and, of course, a perfect little lawn bounded by two other perfect little lawns that encapsulated two other two-parent families who drove big American cars and drank milk every day.

I stumbled happily enough from the I. U. Willets Road Elementary School all the way through Wheatley High without a thought to the good or evil in the world. My innocence was somehow preserved by an insulating layer of Sunday morning bagels, stuffed cabbage, cheek-pinching aunts, a pretty girlfriend, membership in the elite Varsity Club, and an Earl

Sheib–green '56 Ford. All was well with my Donna Reed world.

So it was like the film snapped near the end of my senior year at Wheatley when a classmate, Alan Ibanez, wrote in my best friend's yearbook: "To Richard, one of the good Jews . . . ," the celluloid suddenly flapping, flapping, flapping, flapping, flapping . . . and the inside of my head instantly going blank.

And in the darkness of my shaken soul, I immediately realized three things that I had never before considered:

1. That other people saw me as a Jew first and then as a person.
2. That it was generally considered a bad thing to be a Jew.
3. That it might be a dangerous world out there for Jews.

By the time the lights went back on, I had already left my safe, green, weed-free suburban childhood behind. I walked across the stage, accepted my diploma, and sat back down amid the congratulations of friends and oppressors, right and left. Two months later I left for college with my eyes permanently opened.

So I thought about Alan Ibanez again a few days before Nancy would graduate from high school and it was her turn to enter the "real world." Though she was far more sophisticated than I was at eighteen, I suspected that she was just as naive as to the vicissitudes of life on this planet.

Nancy grew up in a big farmhouse in the middle of the woods with six brothers and sisters—and dogs and cats and ducks and bunnies and goats—and two parents. She spent warm summer days lying in the hammock; she wandered the cool, rocky stream near the house; she kissed her boyfriend Michael on the porch swing. She probably knew more about the profound and passionate drama of life than I did at her age, but I don't think she saw her role in the midst of it all.

The night before her graduation I lay in bed listening to the owls and peepers and the low murmur of voices out in the vine-covered gazebo. Nancy and her friends were hanging out, making the night—that is, their childhoods—last a few minutes longer, their laughter as easy as water gurgling over smooth rocks in the stream. In a breath they would all be off to college, and in the space of another breath the film about small-town life would snap for each of them. And in that darkness each would reckon with unknown oppressors, right and left.

So I wept for my baby girl. I am her father, her protector, yet I knew I could not protect her from what was to come her way. I turned on the projector of memory and recalled the feel of the fat baby in my young arms eighteen years before, the heat of her tiny breaths on my chest, the tiny fingers clinging to my shoulder. I played back the awful ache of leaving her crying at nursery school. I closed my eyes and met again Nate and Craig and Travis and Michael as they came calling at the front door to take her heart away.

I remembered it all, good and bad, real and mythologized, but I could not see where she would go when her Alan Ibanez character would appear and the film would snap and the screen would go blank.

That night I realized that Nancy (and Addie and Clover and Elizabeth after her) would have a double burden after leaving the nest: half Jew, not only would she be counted as a Jew before a person but she would be seen first and foremost in terms of her sex and her sexuality and the ways that she might serve the various self-serving needs of men. For a father, that is an undeniable—and unnerving—truth of life outside the Garden.

I was not so afraid that she would be overtaken by any one oppressor, for I knew she had the strength of her mother, but I was made fearful that evening of the awesome weight on her spirit when she finally would see that oppression is all around, right and left, above and below, ahead and behind. I grew afraid that she might someday sit down just when it is time to stand up and walk out; afraid that she would, in desperation, play a role in someone else's movie of her life.

I lay there wondering if I had done enough to point out to her what she must endure, if I had kept from her too many of the bitter truths one inevitably learns in life.

Yet when the low murmur of voices outside my window disappeared in the roar of a car engine and I heard the front door open and click shut, steps creaking as she tiptoed fearlessly up to her third-floor sanctuary without a care in the world, I gained a glimpse of what my protected childhood had done for me.

The insulated, green, predictable, bourgeois, schmaltzy Super-8 version of life that was Roslyn Heights, allowed me, if arguably little else, the certainty that it was good and proper to be who I am. If I was any less sure of myself and my rightful place on this earth—if I was the least bit scared or ashamed as too many oppressed people are in this world—I might have spent days (or years or even a lifetime) raging against a fool, trying desperately to set the world right again. And Alan Ibanez would still be my oppressor.

So that night, rather than fear that Nancy had not seen enough of the harsh world that surely awaited her, I prayed that the garden we had created would protect her well. I prayed that we had given her the same certainty in herself that I had discovered in myself as a young and innocent boy in Roslyn Heights. I prayed for her good passage.

SHE'S LEAVING HOME, BYE-BYE, PART I

Senioritis

Every parting gives a foretaste of death; every coming together again a foretaste of the resurrection.
—SCHOPENHAUER

Senior year in high school has but one transcendent purpose for young women: to provide ample time for them to grow so irritable and weary and contemptuous of everything associated with home that by spring everyone in the family is awaiting their departure with relief and gratitude.

The process is always the same: the girls spend all junior year looking forward to their time of ascendancy, and by the following summer anticipation has reached such a fever pitch that they are incapable of talking to each other without squealing.

That's as high as it gets, though. By her first day of the last year of school Nancy had already acquired the symptomatic sneer of early senioritis; by Thanksgiving she had "had it" with school and a couple of her old friends; after Christmas she gave up on homework and all household chores; and in February, afflicted with a chronic form of the malaise, she felt so claustrophobic that being in a room with the "fam" for more than fifteen minutes was sixteen minutes too many.

And thus the phrase "I gotta get outahere!" was born—and repeated so often that it became a mantra that carried us through spring, graduation, and early summer, following us like an angel of ironic mercy all the way down to Hatteras for our August vacation.

Nancy's day of deliverance from "the old life" was scheduled for August 14. Hugs and kisses and tears behind us, she and I waved good-bye to the smiling family up on the deck and drove five hours to the university in Chapel Hill. It was, as you might imagine, a bittersweet drive for me. I unloaded the one-ton trunk, four oversize suitcases, and sixteen assorted boxes; got her set up in her dorm; ran errands at the local mall while she attended orientation; had a tender, unsettling last meal at a place called Spanky's on Franklin Street, and headed back to the beach.

The tropical storm Bob I was hearing about on the radio aptly reflected the storm in my heart.

By the time I drove onto the island, Bob was upgraded to a Class 1 hurricane. The following night it was a Class 2. And by the next morning it had made a left sweep, picked up enough steam to be called a Class 3, and was headed toward Hatteras. Two days later we were evacuated.

We didn't want to go home, and motels were booked up a hundred miles in all directions, so we drove to Chapel Hill, rented some hotel rooms, and showed up at Nancy's door at Granville Towers.

Shock, dismay, confusion, nausea, and murderous rage each registered its own particular tic on her pretty face as she stood, speechless, in the doorway.

It was her worst nightmare swirling down the dark tunnel of adolescence. The whole family was following her to college. She would never get away from us, nine of us crowded into a cramped dormitory room barely able to accommodate two.

But like all nightmares, this one came to an end. We stayed a "mere" three days until the evacuation order was rescinded and finally left her alone to live her own life. And she learned her first important college lesson: Thomas Wolfe was wrong—it's not that you can't go home again, you don't ever really leave home at all.

SHE'S LEAVING HOME, BYE-BYE, PART II

Déjà vu

> *We die, and we do not die.*
> —SHUNRYU SUZUKI

Clover got it exactly right in her "Senior Will" in the yearbook: "To my older siblings—thanks for molding me so well. To the young ones—I hope I have done the same for you." The universe is indeed a circle.

From their aggressive style of soccer to their politic manner as the presidents of SADD (Students Against Drunk Driving) to the rivalrous ways they preened for the junior prom, Nancy and Addie preceded and informed Clover about practically everything she would ever experience in high school.

And, like Nancy and Addie when they were seniors, Clover suddenly couldn't stand being around her home and family.

We were sitting at the dinner table and Danny said something pretty innocuous about a teacher at school and she glared at him and snapped, "That's not true." Then Patti said something like, "Stacey said that Kitty told her that Dave broke up with Carrie. . . ."

Fork in midair, sweet, lovable, centered, Zen-like Clover

sneered at her mother like someone from the cast of *90210*: the unbelieving opened mouth, the shake of the head, and then the voice oozing with contempt, "Don't you have a life?"

So when Bay had the audacity to ask her to pass the margarine and when Elizabeth spilled water in her lap, Clover had had enough. She leaped up and scowled, "I can't wait to get out of here!"

We were stunned. Venom like that we could associate with the older crew. Perhaps. But not our sweet little Poochie, who up until that menacing moment had seemed to stroll through life with an aura of quiet at her core.

"Well, before you leave town and change your name," I said, "it's your turn to do the dishes." I thought I was being funny— and it was her turn to do the dishes—but she failed to see the humor in it. She walked out muttering things I'm sure I didn't want to hear. And those of us left behind were once again made to feel like we were residents of a leper colony.

So, there was some cosmic familial justice served up when it came time to grant Clover her wish and take her to college. Ironically, she was following in Nancy's footsteps by going to school in Chapel Hill, and we were again down in Hatteras on vacation, the usual mishmash of kids, dog, parents, boyfriends, girlfriends, coming and going out of the small beach cottage rocking in the wind. And, as it had been laid out four years before, the plan was for me to take Clover over to Chapel Hill midway through the vacation.

It was a beautiful hot day when we first heard about Hurricane Felix being tracked way out in the Atlantic. Clover gasped at the news, but I assured her that lightning doesn't strike the same spot twice.

However, as we tracked the course of the storm from our vulnerable perch on the barrier island, Clover looked on in agitated horror at the unthinkable that seemed to be occurring right before her misting eyes. As if directed by a fate that humbles us all, the hurricane was indeed looping around Bermuda and slowly, surely, almost mindfully, heading for landfall on the Outer Banks.

To Clover's unbelieving dismay, we were evacuated the day before she and I planned to leave.

Poor girl. We packed up the cottage, taped the windows, cleared the decks, and the entire family and the dog drove through wind and rain and flooded roads to take poor old Clover to college. As we trailed her into her dorm room, she looked like she was going to die.

But she didn't.

And along the stormy highway I think Clover learned just what Nancy had learned four years before: you die and you don't die. But you never escape your family.

8

Zen Family Rituals

SEVEN FACTS FOR FATHER'S DAY

Understanding who Father's Day is really for

More wisdom is latent in things-as-they-are than in all the words men use.

—ANTOINE DE SAINT-EXUPÉRY

Into the stupor of half sleep enter footsteps. A covered cough. Something rattling. A whispered *"Hush!"* But the eyelids are heavy. Too heavy. It's Sunday. On Sundays I get to sleep late.

Seconds—or hours—later, with breath sounds close enough to raise the hairs on my neck, I emerge into a dark and dreamy awareness that I am surrounded. Like the child who resides permanently in my soul, I clamp shut my eyes, pretending unconsciousness, hoping the noises and heavy breathing are not from some wild-eyed intruders but from a dream of my own Steven Spielbergian making.

When a sniffling snort pierces the cool morning air, though, one that I instantly recognize as a noise I've heard many times before, and another breathy "Hush!" shakes me to the bone, the synapses click in and I understand in a flash of fear that there are no drug-crazed, knife-wielding criminals in my bedroom. There are no extraterrestrials here. This isn't even a hallu-

cination. Or a nightmare. No, it's something far more frighten-
ing . . . it's . . . it's . . .

FATHER'S DAY!!!!!

A silent scream sends me spinning down a circular shaft that
I have known only in dreams, but in the moments before I hit
bottom (my eyes still closed), I see as clearly as I have ever seen
before in my life. Seven facts of life emerge like answers floating
to the surface on an old eight ball:

FACT I : Unless I throw back the quilt and run wailing
from the room, I am about to be trapped in an early morning
celebration that could rob me of whatever sense of dignity and
youth I think I have left. Depending on who's mad at me, who's
away at college, and who's still sleeping (when I'm not), from
five to seven kids will be grinning as I lift one quivering eyelid to
confirm my suspicions. Behind them will stand my oddly smirk-
ing wife, Patti, who recently had her own "day," holding a tray
of colorfully healthful food I would never consider consuming
on an empty stomach.

FACT 2: I can run but I can't hide. They would wake the
dog and send her out to track me down. They would demand
their due. After all, it's my day and I owe them the once-a-year
pleasure of my extreme paternal gratitude and pride.

FACT 3: I will eat ("Mmmmmmmmm") while Elizabeth and
Bay mouth along with my every bite; Addie, Nancy, and Cael
will twitch impatiently at the edge of the mattress while eyeing
the flashing dots on the clock; and Danny and Clover will con-
spire soundlessly to see who will be the first to jerk my cramped
leg, spilling the juice and then the hot coffee in my lap.

FACT 4: Unless I then trade my role as grateful and benev-
olent papa for the tyrant they always knew I could be, the fruit
of my loins will then turn on their heels as if they had actually
done their duty and disappear before my rudely awakened eyes.
And I'll be left alone to go to the dump, mow the lawn, do some
carpooling, and barbecue up a big family dinner that is every-

one's vision of a Father's Day repast—except mine. Then I'll open the boxes containing shirts, Day-Glo boxers, and various cassettes and CDs that will be swiped, each by its own giver, by night's end.

FACT 5: (My eyes are still closed.) What I think I'd like is very simple: I'd like to sleep until I can no longer stand to stay in bed. I'd like to take a shower until the hot water starts to run out. I'd like to step into the kitchen to the rousing cheers and tears of a grateful family who would prepare—and leave me alone to eat—some grossly cholesterolic slop. I'd like to read the entire Sunday paper out on the front porch, a cup of chicory coffee at my side and a convenience-store pan of gooey sticky buns right next to it, listening to the dulcet tones of birds, frogs, crickets, and lawn mowers. Next I'd like to get a quilt and lie down on the newly mowed grass so that each of the kids could do twenty minutes massaging my back. Then shoot some hoops. Then a nap. Then a beer, two Nathan's hot dogs with mustard and kraut, followed by some baseball on the tube. Then the big kids would take care of the little kids so Patti and I could escape for a romantic evening at a quaint country inn where we would rediscover what it was that made us want to bring all those children into this world, thus making this day a real celebration.

FACT 6: It (Fact 5) ain't gonna happen. It wouldn't feel like Father's Day to anyone except me, and I might not recognize it at all. (My eyes are *still* closed.) Besides, I came to understand nearly twenty-seven years ago that gratitude is an adult invention. It's not going to happen because my kids take me and their mother and this life for granted.

FACT 7: Kids *should* take their parents for granted. I have never been able to abide trying to make children feel grateful for their very existence. It is I who am grateful every single day for my children, not the other way around.

Children are already painfully aware of their extreme vulnerability in this vast, often cold and perilous world. They need to feel safe, not grateful. It's a parent's job to protect them and build them up, not foster their dependence and fearfulness. As I found out from too many of my teachers back in the fifties and sixties, that fear does not breed gratitude, only contempt. And in answer to those who worry that children who don't learn gratitude at an early age will become self-absorbed adults, I have come to trust that the harsher inevitabilities of life itself will eventually provide enough opportunity for them to learn to be grateful for whatever tasty morsels of goodness come their way. Life happens to all of us.

So I figure that there is no better way to show my gratitude than by allowing my children the pleasure of thinking they are pleasing me on my big day while actually satisfying themselves. As Charles Dickens's forgotten father probably muttered aloud in accepting the toy guillotine young Chucky made him for his birthday, "It is a far, far better thing I do, than I have ever done. . . ."

So I open my eyes, force a goofy smile, and await my fate.

HALF JEW, HALF CHRISTIAN, ALL ZEN

Christmas and Chanukah under one roof

Zen is a way of liberation.
—ALAN WATTS

I look at my kids—half Jew, half Christian, part believers, part cynics, blue-eyed, brown-eyed, true mongrels in the organized religion sense of the word—and, finally, believe in God. As any father would, I feel my kids are miracles. Each one a blessing.

So I often wonder with profound dismay how any person or any religious group could actually be arrogant enough to believe that one way—their way—is the only pathway to God. All others be damned. How unenlightened.

Frankly, I prefer Gary Snyder's more Zen-like notion that "the way is not a way." That is, there are untold numbers of paths toward the life of pure spirit that awaits each of us. I take comfort in Rabbi Kushner's belief that God grants life but does not inflict injury. God comforts those afflicted with sorrow. And we take care of the rest.

Patti, as true a believer as one may find in an atheist, believes wholeheartedly in the spirit of nature—and celebrates it through the rituals of family dinners, birthdays, and holidays. And although she does a truly admirable job with celebrations like birthdays and Easter and Halloween, December is when she does her finest work. She choreographs, produces, and directs one of the great quasi-religious events in the hemisphere.

Organizationally speaking, Christmas officially begins in our family sometime in July or August when she sees her first "Elizabeth will love this!" doll or some surf shop sweatshirt that she'll buy in sixes for me and all the big kids. By September, with the Christmas club account beginning to flex its muscles, she is already on the lookout for stocking stuffers. And long before the annual New Paltz Halloween Parade, the suddenly closed-to-the-family sewing room will be smothered in boxes, wrapping paper, bows, and presents of every shape, size, weight—and cost.

By the second week in December every surface in the house is decorated. The banister is trimmed with ribbons of pine, the nine stockings hang from the mantel, and the fat tree cut from Van Alst's farm is completely obscured amid the lights, bubblers, and ornaments hauled down in six cartons from the attic.

From there, it's a slippery snowy slope toward the twenty-fifth: baking Christmas cookies, wrapping mountains of presents, singing discordant, repetitive rounds of "The Twelve Days . . ." in the car. College kids (some ours, some not) arrive in the darkest night to change the chemistry of the house.

Then, as if by surprise, it's suddenly Christmas Eve and we're caroling off-key with the Vermilyes at the Coffeys', wrapping more presents, reading "The Night Before Christmas" and St. Luke to everyone in the family, hauling piles of wrapped presents down to the sparkling living room, and then assembling unassembleable toys until two in the morning.

For a Jewish boy it's an annual revelation of joy to watch the seven of them tumble into our bedroom much too early the next morning, each one five years old again and dragging in the loot from an overstuffed stocking, waiting for the word on high that it's time to go downstairs.

*   *   *

In contrast, Chanukah is slightly more low-key.

I prepare for Chanukah by suddenly realizing that the holiday is upon us and I haven't done anything to prepare for it. I scour the cupboards for the menorah and what's left of the candles from previous years, then go to a place like Mr. Jim's Deep Discount and buy odd and sometimes wonderful and always cheap presents for the eight days of the celebration of the miracle of the lights.

Depending on night classes or high school basketball games or Elizabeth's physical therapy or a gazillion other things that get in the way of orderly family life, Chanukah may or may not get going on that first sundown. No big woop.

And given the varying numbers of people who must take part in the ceremonies, and Chanukah's proximity to Christmas, and Addie's birthday (on December 21), and my cosmically disorganized nature, and whether or not I have enough presents if there's an extra boyfriend or two at dinner, the eight-day celebration is often condensed into six or seven or, as happened in 1988, five days covering nearly two and a half weeks. Whatever. It always gets done, and the kids always end up with eight rather odd presents, ranging from temporary tattoos to Rasta necklaces to cassettes and CDs.

The ceremony itself takes less than five minutes. From oldest to youngest, everyone in the family gets a chance to light the candles and say the prayer in Hebrew. Of course, no one knows what it means, but they all like saying the incantation (which they have committed to transliterated near memory) and lighting the candles. Then they all close their eyes and hold out their open palms to receive their earthly goods while I shuffle through the bags of stuff I bought and place one item in each palm. Then I tell them to open their eyes.

And each night they're surprised and a little bit thrilled to get the nonsense I bestow upon them, although more often than not it's left in the dining room, never to be seen again (unless it's still in the package and then I give it to them again the following year).

Although purists would gag at the conceptual Chanukah ceremony that I conduct on (or around) Chanukah each year and others might scorn the lack of subtlety in the Christmas goddess's
annual extravaganza, both events have become an enduring part
of the way our family lives. In some ways it is an emblem for who
we are: Christians, Jews, children liberated from the ridiculous
dogma that the unforgiving ascribe to God.

THE LAST ANNUAL NEW
YEAR'S EVE PARTY

The times they are a'changin'

> *Don't just do something, sit there.*
> —ANONYMOUS

I can't recall precisely which year it began, the annual New Year's Eve Party for the Homebound and Uninvited, but it was originally devised to save Patti and me and other parents of young children from complete despair on this night of revelry. A noble cause.

New Year's Eve, perhaps the most revered and reviled celebration around North America, is about nothing if not the great second chance. A new beginning. Turning over a new leaf. Redemption. Forgiveness. Pick your banality. Because it has no obvious religious connections, there are no sense of atonement, no apologies, no judgment, no fear; there is only the great relief that one year has passed and a brand-spanking-new one is about to flip up like numbers on digital clocks.

The problem for parents of young children who desperately want to toss away the diaper bag and celebrate a new beginning of civility for just one night is finding a baby-sitter. The entire list of potential sitters scribbled on crumpled sheets of lined paper in the messy kitchen drawer is worthless; they've all got plans.

So, two or three kids into the tribe we call our family, Patti and I were looking ahead to another thrilling New Year's Eve alone with the kids pretending we were having a great time: "It's so much better than all that noise and expense of going out—and for what? It's really about nothing. This is much better." Yeah, right.

That's when some friends, who were as forlorn and homebound as we were, suggested that we cohost a party with them and invite everyone we knew and tell them to bring chips and dips and drinks and, of course, their kids if they didn't have sitters. Unfortunately, the friends were then living in trailers and tiny apartments and couldn't possibly host a party, so we opened our doors.

The house was packed. We ate, we drank, we sang, we danced with babies in our arms, we played puzzles with three-year-olds, we changed diapers, we cleared the linoleum floor and had a dance contest in the kitchen, we crowded into the living room and watched the ball drop in Times Square, we kissed our spouses and kids and other people's spouses and kids, grateful to be out and alive, certain the next year would be easier if not better than the one we'd just survived. At the end of the night the diaper pail was as full as the garbage can.

From there the tradition took on a life of its own. Everyone simply assumed that the Lewises would have the New Year's Eve party. If you didn't have any other place to go—and didn't mind sharing your good time with hippie children who had been taught to be seen and heard—you could always find a party and a dance contest on Coffey Lane. And you could bring your forlorn friends or relatives. Everyone was welcome.

Several years later when Patti and I decided that we definitely didn't want—couldn't afford—definitely would not have—a party, we soon found that the event was totally out of our control. People who we hardly knew would come up to us anytime after Thanksgiving and say, "We'll see you New Year's Eve!"

Anyway, it didn't work. Everyone said New Year's Eve was awful without everyone getting together (at our house), and we should never let it happen again.

And so the party went on like that for years. Then, suddenly(?), the original group of kids grew up and went to their own parties, and their parents, who didn't keep having babies like some people I know, discovered adult, sophisticated New Year's Eves and promptly forgot how much fun we all used to have. And as organically as the party began, it ceased to exist.

The relief was enormous enough to offset any nostalgic notions I might have harbored. The relief was also rather short-lived. Cael, Nancy, and Addie also remembered the wonderful New Year's Eve parties we used to have when they were young and wanted to know what had happened to them. I shrugged, full of hope that their memories were as short as their attention spans.

Yet, as I didn't want them driving on New Year's Eve, I suggested that they invite a few friends over for a "get-together." I didn't want to call it a party, but since we had to chaperon, we invited a few friends over who didn't want to do the typical restaurant–party hopping scene. And the party got a second wind and took on its own momentum.

And sort of left us behind. The first year or two, it seemed to be our affair, with various small pockets of kids sorted by age throughout the house. But then Cael and Nancy were both in college—and Addie and her friends might as well have been— and they were all in the living room, stereo blasting as our rapidly aging friends hid in small pockets in the dining room and kitchen, wishing for earmuffs and waiting uncomfortably until the ball would drop so they could fake some yawns and get the hell out of there.

The passing of one more year brought with it the coup de grâce for the annual fete: hordes of fifteen-year-olds in the basement; throngs of seventeen-year-olds in the attic; twenty-somethings swarming all over the first floor and porches; two nine-year-olds and a six-year-old feigning sleep on the second floor; Hootie and the Blowfish blowing out the woofers on the CD player; televisions flickering all over the house.

And where were Patti and I? Alone, pressed into the far corner of the living room, deserted by the few friends who had come and left before midnight, drinks in hand, speaking fearfully about the cleanup that awaited us and wondering if any of the hordes were going to leave before the bowl games were over the next day.

That was when we decided the tradition was over. *Fini.* As Lou Reed so delicately put it, "Stick a fork in its ass and turn it over, it's done." (However, if our resolve isn't quite what I think it is, and you don't have a sitter, just drop on by. I'm sure we'll be there.)

HERE ONE SECOND, GONE THE NEXT

The importance of family dinners

> *The ritualistic style of conducting one's everyday activities*
> *is therefore a celebration of the fact that the ordinary man*
> *is a Buddha.*
>
> —ALAN WATTS

Back when Clover was seven or eight, she had a most intriguing quality of falling off her chair at dinnertime. One second she'd be right there alongside six or more other bobbing heads, moving mouths, arms and hands spearing broccoli stalks and shoveling mashed potatoes, and the next second there would be a large gap, like a missing tooth, between Nancy and Danny.

Sometimes you could see it happening in slo-mo: Clover slipping ever so gradually down in her chair until her little chin was just at table level and then—*whoosh!*—she'd disappear as if she'd gone down a flume. Or she'd be listing like the Leaning Tower of Pisa—or a ship about to capsize—and then suddenly roll over and sink in the Bermuda Triangle between the wooden chairs.

However, most of the time our little Clover disappeared from dinner without a conscious notice from anyone, just a sixth sense afterward that something was missing, one of us looking around quizzically and wondering, "Hey, where's Poochie?"

And then Poochie would emerge like a Loch Ness cartoon figure from underneath the table with a goofy embarrassed grin squiggled across her beautiful face. No doubt she had hoped to return to her seat as quietly as she had left it to avoid the shaking heads and the delicious jiggling that comes with swallowing laughter, bursting eyeballs, food running out of Addie's nose.

And thus she came to be called Clummo by her remarkably sensitive brothers and sisters.

But that isn't what this anecdote is really about. Nor is it about the way that Patti and I totally missed another child's medical condition (à la finding out that Danny was practically blind when he went for his kindergarten screening—we thought he fell a lot because he was clumsy). Clover did not fall out of chairs because of some neurological impairment or some middle ear problem that disrupted her balance.

She fell because, as one of the quieter members of the household, she would sometimes zone out on all the bantering and conversation flying around her, facts and falsehoods and accusations crisscrossing the table like the illustrations of airline routes across the country. Stand outside of it for a while, and it's enough to make you dizzy.

I bring it up now because it was Poochie falling out of her chair who came to mind as a metaphor while I was driving away from State College, Pennsylvania, tears slipping from my cheeks every few seconds after dropping off Addie for her freshman year at Penn State.

I simply could not believe that my "pal" had been born and had raced through her childhood before I had time to catch my breath. She was there one day, a twelve-year-old with a ponytail and a turned up nose, and then she was suddenly all grown up and hugging me good-bye. Just like that. Here one second and gone the next.

Just the way Clover used to fall out of her chair at dinnertime.

And driving down Route 322 I laughed—and I cried—and I

remembered a thousand and one other wonderfully insignificant meals along the parental roadway that I may or may not have eaten alongside my children—and, honestly, may not have really ever occurred as I remember them. But by the time I was nearing Harrisburg, I could taste the eternally sweet longing and the unquenchably bitter remorse that every father knows in his soul; and it was on that ride back to Patti and the kids still at home that I came to know the utter importance of sitting down to eat as a family.

In contrast to whatever some history professor was predictably going to say to Addie about great events that shape our lives—or the individuals who shape great events—I'm certain that it is only the insignificant, ordinary, seemingly forgettable moments that really count in our lives, and few count as resonantly as the ones at meals.

It is there, around the dinner table, that the daily drama gets its dialogue. It is there where we rub shoulders, tell jokes, make gossip, fight, and sometimes even tell of our days; it is there where we brag about our triumphs, where the emptiness of failure or unrequited love finds a loving, if temporary, nourishment that takes you into and through the next day.

In fact, it is right there, between the bread and the butter, where all the great events in life occur; where we make stupid faces at each other and change the course of history; where we catch the sparkling eye of someone who loves us not for what we do or even who we are, but only because we're there, like we're there every day, because we belong there and nowhere else. As Raymond Chandler wrote about breaking bread, it is "a small, good thing." What else is there?

You almost never hear anyone at death's gate regretting that he or she didn't make more money or work longer hours or kill more enemies or write more books or sleep with more people. None of those things really matter. We regret only the life we didn't lead, the insignificant moments lost in chasing after an immortality that was always ours anyway.

At a time when it seems that fewer and fewer families are not only staying together but eating together, the world grows colder and more lonely with each passing meal. Each of us could do much worse than to sit down and eat with the whole family tonight. (If it hurts too much, take a Rolaids.)

DE FACTO ZEN
PARTY FAVORS

Celebrating the eternal inner child

> *How old would you be if you didn't know how old you was?*
>
> —SATCHELL PAIGE

Ten sets of Little Mermaid paper plates and cups are placed around the big pine table. Behind each plate is a formless collection of Starbursts, M&Ms, blowpops, skinny balloons, blow-up gunk, and a party favor chosen specifically for each of the ten party goers. On the bay window is an impressive stack of presents wrapped in Tweety and Sylvester paper, large rectangular clothing boxes and maybe some books and what might be cassettes and perhaps some toys that are packaged in irregularly shaped wrappings.

On the butcher-block kitchen counter is a lopsided, almost beautiful, homemade chocolate sheet cake decorated with blue and pink flowers and squiggles and thin yellow candles. And on the sideboard is the automatic camera loaded with thirty-six-exposure color print film.

Everything is perfect. Picture perfect.

No doubt you're thinking it's Elizabeth's seventh birthday party. It's not. It's Addie's. She's twenty.

Everyone gets the same family party in our house: theme plates, lots of candy, party favors, a homemade cake, and too many presents. Cael's twenty-sixth birthday this summer was, at least before the presents were unwrapped, no different than Bay's ninth or Danny's sixteenth. And they're all caught on film.

As the dad, I am the official photographer for family events. (That's why you rarely see me in family photographs.) I look through the viewfinder, scope out the heartwarming vision, press the button and the light flashes, the camera motor buzzes. Bay, Danny, Addie, and Addie's boyfriend, Nate, are captured forever in their birthday smiles.

Thirty-five pictures left.

Next is the other side of the table: Clover's boyfriend, Jeffrey, Clover, Nancy, Patti, Elizabeth Bayou-Grace. Flash-buzz. Nancy's boyfriend, Michael, walks smilingly into the kitchen, late from work. He's got a present in his hand. Flash-buzz.

There's one of Nate blowing up the gunk. Another of Addie scowling at Jeffrey. Danny bored. Elizabeth giggling. Nancy and Mike kissing. Flash-buzz. The phone rings. It's Cael calling from North Carolina to speak to the birthday girl. Flash-buzz.

The cake. Flash-buzz.

The birthday girl's mother. Flash-buzz.

The birthday girl's mother lighting the candles, walking through the dim room toward the table, placing the shimmering cake in front of the birthday girl. Flash-buzz. She's making a wish, blowing out the candles, cutting the cake, flash-buzz. She's twenty, but behind the sophisticated, faux-embarrassed veneer, there's a six-year-old filled with joy that everybody's there and looking at her and, best of all, bearing gifts. Flash-buzz. Flash-buzz. Flash-buzz.

Patti, the architect of these juvenile celebrations, says everyone's a little kid on their birthdays. Every single one of us not only deserves a *real* party—not some low-key, boring, adult affair at the local chichi restaurant—but in our heart of hearts we all want one with candy and presents and a gooey cake and, of course, party favors. It's virtually impossible to argue with her de facto logic. Just look at the pictures.

Three days later I'll pick up the photos, look at them with a dopey smile before I even leave the camera shop, wondering as I always wonder why I am not in the stack, and look at them again in the car, and look at them again over Patti's shoulder when I get home, providing annoying color commentary all along the way, picture after picture.

Six months later, however, I won't be able to tell you with absolute assurance which number birthday they reflect. All birthdays tend to look alike in four-by-six color, though despite the smug little five-year-old smile on Addie's face when she opened the gold earrings *(Real jew-ler-ee!)*, you can easily identify her as somewhere in college—or, as most people might think, too old to be eating off of Tweety and Sylvester plates and playing with smelly Tubes of Balloons.

Patti would say they don't understand the boundaries of reality.

A ZEN BIRTHDAY

The nonbirthday birthday

> *Sacred cows make great hamburgers.*
> —ROBERT REISNER

Nancy's old friend and classmate, Whitney, who later became Addie's "squeeze" in high school, a most compelling man-boy who spent an inordinate amount of time in my house playing in the basement with Danny and Bay while he was supposed to be visiting my daughter, taught me about the nonbirthday birthday, or more appropriately, the Zen koan that a truly enlightened individual may indeed have his cake and eat it, too.

I was commandeering a vanload of high school kids to Charlottesville to tour the University of Virginia. I loved—and continue to love—those college trips; out on the open road, tapes blasting, living in motels, walking around all those beautiful campuses, and hanging around with sly, funny, quirky seventeen-year-olds who enable you to remember firsthand how ridiculous adult notions appear to adolescents.

We sat in the rotunda, did the formal tour around Mr. Jefferson's Academical Village, rubbed our hands along the serpentine walls, strolled the charming neighborhood, bought the obligatory UVA T-shirts—and ended up in some college eatery, where the waiters and waitresses had a song-and-dance routine for patrons who were celebrating birthdays. We watched, half amused and half appalled, as the waitstaff burst through the swinging doors of the kitchen doing a kind of bunny hop behind the leader holding the birthday cake and singing a Blue Ridge version of the Beatles' "You say it's your birthday."

We watched as they moved closer and closer to the targeted table, put the cake in front of the surprised and embarrassed and sometimes anguished birthday boy or girl, and then led the entire restaurant in a raucous round of "Happy Birthday to You." Very funny. Pretty awful.

Anyway, we ate, laughed at the birthday train, which reappeared three more times, ate some more, talked college admissions, gossiped, goofed on our fellow diners, and generally acted our age—except, of course, me. And that was it.

Just about the time that I started looking for our waiter to ask for the check, though, the conga line burst into the dining room again, holding a cake and singing, "They say it's your birthday. . . ." We groaned; we laughed; we watched as the line snaked its way around the restaurant, wondering who was the next poor soul to be embarrassed. And I slouched back in my chair, just plain annoyed because I wanted to get on the road and I knew we wouldn't get the check until after the ceremony was over.

The singers danced their way between the tables, seeming to stop for a moment only to tease the crowd and bunny hop along once again, heading toward our side of the room.

I glanced over at the tables on either side of us trying to figure out who was "it," and by the time I looked up again it actually seemed as if they were coming right at us like some calypso-driven tornado, surrounding our table and dropping the cake right down in front of me, *me!* Everyone laughing and singing, all those teeth smiling, fingers pointing, and Whitney Smith suddenly leaping up and yelling, "Happy Birthday Dad, you're the greatest!"

Everyone in the restaurant cheered and sang the song and howled as I turned deep crimson and fought the urge to crawl under the table and bite off Whitney's leg at the knee.

Of course, I didn't tell my fellow revelers that my birthday is not October 22nd, it's April 30th; nor that Whitney is not my son but was spending so much time at my house I was thinking of listing him as a dependent; nor even that I respected the transcendent manner in which Whitney had figured out a way to have his cake and eat it, too.

And then have someone else pay for it.

THE ANNUAL EASTER EGG HUNT

Addie's boyfriend, Nate, a dental student, joins the first and third graders for the annual Easter egg hunt in our backyard

> *In zazen, one is one's present self, what one was, and what one will be, all at once.*
>
> —PETER MATTHIESEN

One of the more remarkable clichés that gets coughed up whenever people find out that I have seven kids is "They must keep you young."

I figure that anyone who would say something like that must be temporarily blinded by the concept of having more children than you can count on one hand. I mean, just look at me: the wild gray hair, the manifest destiny bald spot encroaching on my forehead, the lines around my deep-set eyes that suggest one too many nights spent waiting up for teenagers to get home.

Young seems a rather limited view of my present circumstances.

I'm more inclined to see my age in terms of Matthiesen's vision of zazen, all things at once. There are moments in the midst of every day when I feel so worn out by living my life in nine places at one time that I feel older than my octogenarian parents. But a few minutes later I'm two again and I don't wanna share my tools (clothes, car, food, etc., etc., etc.) with anyone. *Anyone!*

Sometimes, when I'm having a tea party with Elizabeth, I have the extraordinary sensation of being six and sixty-six at the same time. Other times, when I'm just hanging out in the kitchen with Danny or Clover and yammerin' about concerts and movies and who's doin' what to whom, I feel eighteen again, ready to party my semiconscious way through weekend nights at Wheatley High. And when I'm having a catch with Bay, I might as well be nine once more, dripping with laughter and mud, imagining myself climbing the center field wall of Ebbets Field like Duke Snider about to rob the Say Hey Kid of another home run.

Last year's Easter egg hunt provided a particularly instructive manifestation of Mathiessen's principle. On Patti's instructions, the little kids were sent to the basement while the older kids and visiting parents, acting as crew members for her annual spectacular, were out in the yard hiding dyed eggs and chocolate kisses and all the other delicious substances banned by the American Dental Association on tree limbs, behind rocks, in the mesh of the hammock—anywhere out of reach of the sniffing nose of the chocoholic dog.

Then Patti called down to the kids, maybe twenty of them, to come up on the back deck and receive their final instructions for Operation Easter: first graders anywhere in the yard; third graders must search beyond the swing set; fifth graders and all others will confine their hunt to the front yard, the stream, and the woods.

Standing behind and above the hordes on the deck was Nate, Addie's boyfriend: twenty-two years old, six feet four inches tall, about to graduate from Cornell University and go off to dental school. At first I thought he was helping Addie organize the little guys, but then I noticed the same gloriously expectant look in his eyes that lit up the faces of six-year-old Zoe and ten-year-old Craig—not to mention the pink and yellow and blue basket he was carrying. And when he yelled out, "Where do the sixteenth graders go?" I knew that he had transcended time and space and entered Mathiessen's realm.

Like a giraffe among dwarf chimpanzees, Nate raced off the

deck with the rest of the kids when Patti gave the signal to go searching for goodies left by the Easter Bunny. Then I noticed tenth grader Danny and twelfth graders Clover and Jeffrey following close behind Nate with baskets in their hands. (Several minutes later Patti caught them exchanging "good" candy they were just finding with "bad" candy they had already found.)

They weren't the only adult-size children, though. I saw Kathleen's grandmother snarf a marshmallow bunny when she thought no one was looking; I saw IBM manager Joe Ferri stuffing his mouth with the sweets he was supposed to be hiding for the children, looking remarkably like his own six-year-old, Dara. I was even nabbed: Elizabeth wanted to know how I got all that chocolate smeared on my face.

She's too young to know that all things happen at once. I told her that her mother kissed me.

9

Zen Vacations on the Road of Life

OUTER BANKS AT NIGHT

What you see is never what you get

If you meet the Buddha on the road, kill him!
—ZEN SAYING

A popular postcard found in many resort areas is all black. Actually, it's glossy black and on the bottom in small white type it reads "Outer Banks (or Big Sur or Cape Cod or . . .) at Night."

Many people who see it for the first time while spinning the postcard rack at the local surf shop smile and pluck it out to show to someone else. Then the two of them laugh a little conspiratorially. It's funny. And stupid.

But it's also kind of wry, a subtle swipe at the amount of time, energy, and money spent on gathering artificial evidence in the form of snapshots of the ahness of travel. And perhaps even more remarkable is the fact that most people get the joke, five-year-olds as well as seventy-five-year-olds. It is a perfect representation of the Zen of family vacations. The beautiful postcard—as the beautiful photograph—is everything travel is and also everything travel is not.

All of us in our hearts understand the patent phoniness of the photographic image. The blue sky is often softer and bluer than

it really was. In the foamy surf you can't see the perilous under-
tow. There's no accounting in the flat image for the heat or the
humidity or the mosquitoes in the air. The smiles on the tanned
faces of the family suggesting pure harmony often cover the
angst of ongoing family skirmishes. And you never hear dad behind the viewfinder, yelling, "Smile, dammit!"

My most successful vacation in terms of Zen photography
came in 1986. The proof comes by way of the fact that I don't
actually have the snapshots in hand. Or in an album. Yet I'm
sure the pictures were perfect. They were perfect because I know
I had what might best be termed a lapse of consciousness and,
in effect, pressed down a little too hard on the shutter and captured the essence of vacations in a single moment.

Several of the kids and I were at Island Convenience, a Texaco station, tackle shop, grocery store, snack shop, and souvenir
stand run by Mac and Marilyn Midgett, and I was suddenly inspired to take the annual "child pumping gas" shot. It was the
last shot on the roll, the camera automatically whirring its way
through the rewind. And then just as suddenly the automatic
shut-off on the gas gun clicked.

I put the camera on the rear bumper of the van, took the
hose from whichever child was with me, and dribbled in a few
more drops of gas, replaced the cap, and walked my barefoot
way into the cool store. While on line I picked up some candy,
made some weather talk with a fisherman, paid the damage,
walked out into the blazing sun, and hoisted myself back into
the driver's seat. I shared whatever candy I didn't hide for myself alone. I turned the ignition. I clutched, jammed the shift into
reverse (a car was in front of me), turned myself all around so I
could be absolutely sure I wouldn't hit anyone or anything, and
backed up maybe a yard or two until I heard a crack and a crunch
and some kind of minor implosion.

I knew immediately what it was. (You don't have to run this
father over with the facts.) And what it was not.

Upon reflection, I'm certain that roll contained more beautiful photographs than I had ever taken before or have taken since. Being lost in the nothingness of the twisted metal and splintered plastic and ripped celluloid under my F75-14 rear tires, they remain a perfect vision of what a beach should forever be: the family vacation at total eclipse.

THE INEFFABILITY OF
FAMILY VACATIONS
The pain of pleasure

*The only Zen you find on the tops of mountains is the Zen
you bring up there.*

—ROBERT PIRSIG

As an unbroken survivor of all-night drives to the Outer Banks
of North Carolina in a VW van with seven kids (a dog, a roof
rack, a turtle top, four bikes, a moped, and enough bungee cords
to do a successful jump off the George Washington Bridge) as well
as camping washouts in Martha's Vineyard, a car fire in Delaware, brake failure in Virginia, botched reservations in Florida,
barfing children in Jersey, three hurricanes on Hatteras, a midnight call from a constable in London, roseola in the Hamptons,
fever hallucinations in Naples, island hopping in Hawaii, missed
planes, lost directions, lost wallets, lost kids, lost patience, lost
nerve, and lost expectations, I am intimately aware of the darker
pitfalls of family vacations.

Yet there is nothing I yearn to do more than hoist my dadself
into the Vanagon and travel off to the next adventure with my
wife and kids.

Viewed from a detached perspective, vacations for fathers
represent Zen in its purest form: the agony of pleasure. Most of

us spend the entire year (minus two days)—no exaggeration—looking forward to lying back and enjoying some pure unfettered time with the family. No work, no boss, no shoes, no underwear, no shaving, just flyin' kites and buildin' sand castles and fishin' with the kids—and at night renewing the steamy love affair with the woman who inspired the desire to fly kites and build sand castles and fish with those kids.

The oddly wonderful thing about *male vacation envy* is that it's built solely on a mushy foundation of the American Family Togetherness Myth and tempered by the cartoonish stresses brought on by TV family life and hardened into plasticene reality by much-smaller-than-life advertisements for "Family Fun Getaways."

From the day after a man returns from vacation and goes back to work (and has miraculously forgotten the undifferentiated anxiety he experienced less than forty-eight hours before) to the morning nearly a year later that he must pack up the car with enough equipment and clothing to outfit a third-world nation, he believes in his heart that he really wants to go on vacation again.

It's quite sublime, the way the grass keeps growing. And the perennial beauty of it is that as the weeks and months pass by, dads are made increasingly happy by increasingly faulty memories of the previous year's litany of disasters. Desiring nothing more than to get away from it all—and seduced by the patently ridiculous notion that a bad day of fishing (surfing, hunting, bird watching, yadda yadda yadda) is better than a good day at work—dads all over must annually relearn the three universal unkind truths of family travel:

1. Daily life goes on. You don't leave it behind. Kids fight with each other, whine, wake up too early or too late, get sick, get bored, get lost, get your goat, and spend all your money.
2. It takes only twenty-seven minutes to spend all the money you made in fifty-four hours the week before you left on vacation.
3. Family restaurants suck.

THE SPIRIT OF A MEXICAN VACATION

The revenge of Montezuma

He who knows does not speak;
He who speaks does not know.
—LAO-TZU

When the advance-grant (for a textbook I was writing) arrived, we should have promptly put the money in the bank, but it was such a nice even figure and I had a February vacation coming up, and the family tour package to Cancún sounded cheaper than staying home, *and* it seemed like a once-in-a-lifetime cultural experience for the kids. Besides, it was minus twenty degrees in New Paltz.

Plans were hastily made, reservations confirmed, and even though I received a speeding ticket en route to Kennedy Airport, everything couldn't have been more perfect. The nine of us (five kids, two parents, two grandparents) arrived in Cancún and were transported to one of the glitzy hotels along the strip. It didn't look much like Mexico—more like a fancy Miami Beach—but the local people looked Mexican and spoke Spanish and, hey, the water was as blue as in the brochures.

The first problem I encountered involved the difficulty in understanding the clerk behind the reservations desk. The second was revealed when I finally understood why he wasn't giving me the keys to our rooms: the hotel was overbooked.

While Patti opened the suitcases, found bathing suits, and undressed and dressed the little kids in the middle of the lobby (while the older kids hid behind the potted palms in mortal embarrassment), I had an all-American tantrum. I yelled, I cursed, I pleaded, I threatened lawsuits, I tried bribery. All to no avail. *No comprendo, Señor.*

I called the inept travel agent back home, who didn't know what he could do for us "all the way down there." I called the tour company, which wouldn't be open until Monday morning at nine o'clock. I even tried phoning the U.S. Consulate, but no one answered.

I also called every hotel on the beach in Cancún, but they were all overbooked. Late that afternoon, tired of my yelling and afraid that we'd never leave the lobby, the hotel management offered to put us up in the center of Cancún for the night. We had no choice. Suffice it to say that because the replacement hotel was right in the middle of a filthy and vermin-infested neighborhood, it also lacked the gorgeous white sand beach. However, we did find some unlabeled pharmaceuticals in the bathroom and a pair of stiff men's underpants underneath the bed. I stayed up all night guarding my family from bad hombres with crisscrossed gun belts and in the morning called every hotel on the Yucatán Peninsula trying to salvage the already decimated vacation.

In retrospect, I guess I should have known that something was wrong when I found the only hotel in the region with vacancies. But a few hours later we were on the exotic isle of Cozumel, and the hotel lobby didn't look so bad at all and the extraordinarily blue Caribbean was even more beautiful than in Cancún, and even if there was a disconcerting smell as we entered the lobby and the rooms were a little mildewy, I just knew it was going to be wonderful. This was the real Mexico, not some Epcot version of foreign lands. Now the kids would really have a cultural experience.

And they certainly did. We snorkeled all afternoon, spoke halting Spanish to the natives, ate a real Mexican dinner (being very careful not to drink the water or eat fresh fruit and vegetables), walked around the beautiful square in San Miguel, and went to sleep full of the spirit of Central America.

Clover, who was in the room with Patti, Danny, and me, was the first to lose that spirit. In the hopes of keeping this on a higher plane, let's just say that she lost her spirit a few steps before reaching the bathroom. And moments later she was overcome with an almost uncontrollable urge to lose the spirit from a different, deeper, and darker, aspect of her being.

Then, as I was helping poor Clover in the bathroom and Patti was tending to the loss of spirit on the rug, Patti up and lost her spirit. A minute later I lost mine. Shortly thereafter, Clover lost hers once more—in the bed this time. Then Patti. Then me.

And just about the time that we thought the great spirit festival was complete, Montezuma began his rumbling deep in the parental maw. First me, then Patti racing to the porcelain altar like a woman who'd seen the Mayan devil.

Meanwhile, five-year-old Danny, who we affectionately called Dirty Dan because of his abhorrence of the tools of normal hygiene, slumbered as calm and unfettered as if he were cradled in the bosom of the gods.

Practically spiritless by then, I garnered enough energy to put on some clothes and go next door to see how Cael, Nancy, and Addie were faring. When I opened the door, Addie looked absolutely fine, but Cael was already light green and moaning on the bed, alternately threatening and begging Nancy to get out of the bathroom where she'd apparently been meditating on her own spirit loss for the last fifteen minutes.

It was only then, I must add, that things really got nasty.

With no notice and no explanation—*No hablo inglés, Señor*— the management suddenly turned off the water in the hotel! Wide-open taps; unflushable toilets; the transmogrifying aroma of earthly spirit permeating the air.

I won't go into detail about how we had run out of towels and were using sheets and yesterday's shirts to clean up after ourselves, but the final transcendent moment came several minutes later when Addie pushed open our door, took one look around at the devastation, mumbled something about "not feeling so good anymore," and unleashed a projectile offering to the gods that landed all over the curtains.

And Danny continued to sleep through it all.

I eventually made it out to a bodega and bought six bottles of the pink stuff, slugged one down like it was a cool Corona, and returned to administer the nectar to my dis-spirited family. And that afternoon, after the water was turned back on and all of us felt barely well enough to sit on the gorgeous white beach, we watched Danny frolic alone in the surf.

It turned out, as you home repair dads may have already surmised, that the hotel had a problem with sewage leaching into the water supply. In the end, it didn't matter that no one in the family drank the water. And no one ate raw fruit or vegetables. No one even slipped and ordered ice for the drinks. But we did brush our teeth.

Everyone got sick. Everyone, that is, except five-year-old Dirty Dan, who in those days would do anything to avoid bathing or even brushing his teeth. He played all afternoon on the coral reef and ate another big dinner that night—and found in Mexico the perfect place to maintain his spirit through cultural enhancement.

BEING THERE—AND NOT BEING THERE

A trip to the Magic Kingdom

When you put Bay to sleep at night, he boards a space vehicle for transport to his home planet.
—RICHARD GAYNOR, ZEN MASTER

As every parent knows, children are transcendent beings. They are not limited by the five senses or conventional notions of what-you-see-is-what-you-get reality. They are larger than life. And much, much smaller.

In fact, they are pure spirit, like angels. They have (so-called) imaginary friends; they talk to trees, animals, inanimate objects; they make observations about the world that are so nonsensical that wizened adults are suddenly able to see life in an entirely new dimension. In short, they have extraordinary powers of imagination and perception that enable them to envision fantastic visions as true reality.

On a family vacation that could be a real problem.

I'm sure you've noticed—or remember the sensation from your own unforgotten childhoods—that no matter where you take children for the first time, no matter how excited they are to be going there, or how many times they have to pee before they get there, or how often you must yell at them to stop jumping up and down and shrieking in delirium in the backseat of the family van as you approach the palace of their dreams, there is always a profound sense of disappointment in their eyes or the lilt of their voices as soon as you finally get there. Wherever. The circus. Hawaii. Yankee Stadium. The New York City Ballet. Walt Disney World. Wherever. As Peggy Lee sang years ago, "Is that all there is?"

It's a terrible—and indeed terrifying—moment of existential awareness for parents. Yet we have so much invested in our children's happiness, and harbor such tender hidden memories of our own similarly profound disappointments as children, that we constantly strive to bring the light of pure joy into our children's eyes.

Why else would anyone take their children to Walt Disney World?

When Patti and I announced at dinner that we were thinking of taking the family to the Magic Kingdom, it was as if a marching band stepped out of the wallpaper and strobe lights appeared on the ceiling and thousands of little children started laughing and applauding us—the most wonderful parents on the face of the earth.

Thus deified, we flew to Tallahassee to visit Cael at college and then motored down to Orlando, the electricity in the backseats making the rental van glow and shimmer as we hovered above I-75 and passed through Kissimmee, where it seems there are more billboards than people.

We parked in the Goofy parking lot, took the Little Train That Could to the monorail that whisked us silently into the dimension of transcendent fun, and then racewalked through the gates of the Magic Kingdom. Wide-eyed and white-knuckled, the children paused briefly to soak in the magic that appeared before their unbelieving eyes.

Which is when I saw the archetypal flash of disappointment skitter across the smooth faces of the older children. If their expressions were translatable, they would probably have read, *This is incredible, but it's just a big, fancy amusement park. It's not beyond my wildest expectations.*

But not Bay. Opaquely self-centered and translucently selfless, he is the one child among our seven who is seemingly the least entangled by damning realities. Exuberance resonates in all that he does. He is a gift from the cosmos to open up the doors of perception.

So while his siblings paused briefly to acclimate themselves to the less-than-magic reality, Bay was running around in circles screaming that he could see Mickey and Donald and Dumbo—and following his spirited lead, everyone released the tenacious grip on their varied disappointments and had a wonderful time, boarding every ride in the park, buying ridiculous souvenirs, and eating enough hot dogs, french fries, fried dough, Cokes, candy, and ice cream to feed any one of the Epcot-centered nations.

When it was finally time to go back to the motel, we had spent all our money, all our energy, all our good sense—and all our collective disappointment.

I was completely and utterly depleted. I followed Patti and the kids onto the Little Train That Could, happy for the good day we'd had, hopeful that I might never have to have another good day like that again. As we drove slowly back through the Goofy parking lot, I closed my eyes and leaned back in the seat thinking of nothing but the bed in the motel room.

That's when Bay yanked on my shirt and said, "So, Daddy, when are we going to Dismey Whirl?"

My mouth dropped open. "What?"

"When are we going to Dismey Whirl?" Several hundreds of dollars, eight stained shirts, and some serious indigestion after a full day at the Magic Kingdom, and Bay wanted to know when we'd be going to *the* Disney World.

The doors of perception opened a little wider for me at that moment. Bay may have only been three years old then, but he knew that the big smelly mouse wasn't Mickey, that the ridiculous felt duck wasn't Donald, and that Space Mountain didn't really take you into space. Of course.

He'd had a great time, but now he wanted to go to the real thing, the *real* Magic Kingdom.

We couldn't fool him. Walt Disney couldn't fool him.

What could I say? I closed my eyes again and told him what parents all over the solar system tell their kids: we'd get there . . . sometime.

THE ROAD OF LIFE

*How a nine-hour Sunday drive turns into
a thirteen-hour marathon tour of pitstops*

*Flow with whatever may happen and let your mind be
free: Stay centered by accepting whatever you are doing.
This is the ultimate.*

—CHUANG-TZU

Paul Ruff, the Mario Andretti of the family station wagon,
makes the 540-mile drive to Hatteras Island from upstate New
York in around nine hours. I marvel at his paternal control, his
capacity to maintain focus in a steel cage full of children, his
ability to hurtle through space at speeds just below radar detection. More than a man's man, he is a father's kind of father.

As I've heard it described, Paul packs the family (four kids, a
friend or two, and his wife, Lynn) into the Chevy wagon, positions himself in the cockpit, locks the doors, turns up the AC,
and leadfoots his way for three hundred miles or so deep into
Delaware, where he stops just long enough for everyone to rush
to the bathrooms, grab a snack, and race back to the car before
the gas nozzle clicks off—and then he locks the doors again and
barrels down through the Delmarva across the Chesapeake Bay
Bridge-Tunnel and along the coast all the way to the Outer
Banks. That's it. Nine hours. Holy. Holy. Holy.

In striking contrast is my thirteen-hour stop-and-start tour of natural and man-made pissoirs along the Atlantic seaboard. So, just about the time that the Ruffs would be pulling in to Rodanthe, the Lewis clownmobile is predictably located somewhere around Onancock on the eastern shore of Virginia, chugging its way into the fourth or fifth Texaco station, Patti and the children racing knock-kneed for the bathrooms while I'm checking the ropes and bungees and duct tape holding everything together.

I'm not sure whether it's a case of genetically small bladders or chronic urinary tract infections or just simple lack of good old Presbyterian self-control—or perhaps an overwhelming desire to purge the body of toxins—but my family has a patent inability to drive more than a hundred and nineteen minutes without wetting their pants. (That is, everyone except Nancy and me, who not only share the same birthday but the same constitution, including a gallon-size bladder.)

The rest of the group obviously got Patti's three-teaspoon-size organ. Addie, for example, can't make the four-hour drive to school at Penn State without at least one yellow-eye stop, and Cael can't do the two hundred miles from Durham to Hatteras along Highway 64 without stumbling out beyond the tree line once or twice. Even the simple ninety-mile trip to New York City from our home in the Shawangunk Mountains is often punctuated by at least one rest stop; and if Bay is along for the ride, we may have to stop twice.

The good thing about Bay is that, like most boys, he'll go anywhere—in the bushes, behind a tree, behind a Pizza Hut, in the dunes, off a porch, anywhere. Just as the Jeff Goldblum character says in The Big Chill, "That's what I love about the outdoors: it's one big toilet." And so it is for Bay.

Patti, the earth mother, is just like Bay, at least in her willingness to do what comes naturally, naturally. She will drop and squat behind any available tree along the side of practically any road that is not in the Bronx or Brooklyn. Unfortunately, the three older girls in the family consider doing their business along the side of any road an abomination. They would rather turn jaundiced, explode, and die than pee in the woods. They absolutely refuse.

So I stop at the first public restroom on the highway. And 119 minutes later I stop at another. And then another. And another.

But unscheduled restroom stops are not the sole reason why the avatar Paul Ruff beats me to Hatteras by four hours. Five, six, even seven stops along the side of the road to pee would add only an hour or so to the trip. But since we have to find a place with a clean toilet, no less, practically every stop also has a retail purchase element to it, which invariably includes a drink. ("I'm dying of thirst, Dad.")

If I balk at buying drinks, everyone, including Patti, looks at me as if they're one step away from calling 911. And, of course, they don't just buy drinks, they get fries and chips and whatever else is *absolutely* necessary. ("After all, Dad, we're stuck in this van for thirteen hours.") And 119 minutes later we'll have to stop again, where they'll want a whole new round of sodas because all the chips they ate in the intervening two hours made them so thirsty that they'd *die* if they didn't get another drink . . . and so it goes.

Years ago I sopped trying to fight biological and psychic reality. If the trip takes us thirteen hours, then so be it. Crank up Bob Marley or Van Morrison or Lou Reed, get into a travelin' groove, and go with the endless flow of karmic traffic. I might never make it to Hatteras in nine hours, but last year, as we rumbled through Temperanceville, Virginia, my mind flowed so freely that I had a vision of the purity of line, the oneness with the machine, the spiritual connection to the road that Paul Ruff achieves every August: one stop for gas on the way to nirvana. Selah! Selah! Selah!

THE ZEN OF GETTING CLEAN IN RURAL CONNECTICUT

Gender discrimination in a campground shower

God is in the details.
—MIES VAN DER ROHE

Even with charmingly primitive signs nailed to trees and stuck in soft grassy shoulders along the chip and oil roads winding around the gracious Connecticut countryside, we had to retrace our steps several times before arriving at the campground. It should have been as simple as sleeping under the stars: Route 202 to Milton Road to Maple Road to Hemlock Hill Road, but as those of us who have grown middle-aged in the shadows of Ram Dass and Ronald Reagan understand, simplicity is never simple.

The ad in *Woodall's* said we'd find "friendly people, a beautiful setting, and well-maintained modern facilities." And down the long dirt road, that is nearly what we found: friendly people in a nice setting, though a tad swampy down near our campsite.

And that would have been that had I not had this odd misunderstanding about the showers. Not that they weren't reasonably modern and pretty well maintained. But after a restless night punctuated by bullfrogs twanging and a tree root that seemed to follow my every diversionary movement, daybreak filtering into the cold dewy tent along with the voice of someone from a neighboring site calling for my daughter Clover, or, as it turned out, calling for a dog with the same name, I would have settled for a trickling hose. All I wanted was water on my head.

Nancy was the first to make the trek to the facilities but returned shortly with the news that the showers cost a quarter for six minutes. No big deal; we scrounged the floor of the VW bus for coins, and as unspoken family tradition dictated, I waited with the baby and the boys (who never even considered showering) until the women got back.

Finally, it was my turn. Soap, towel, toothbrush, change of clothes, and quarter in hand, I strode into the comfortably campy, lightly mildewed men's room like a gunslinger into a bar. There was a man at one of the sinks shaving all around his pencil-thin mustache. With respect for the ancient ritual, I nodded briefly in the mirror and ducked into the shower stall.

Soon naked, except for my quarter, I looked up. I looked down. I turned around. I turned all the way around again but could not find the coin slot anywhere. One more orbit within the tiny stall and I wrapped the towel around my waist and walked out to the sink area, certain the mechanism must be there. It wasn't.

The shaving man watched me in the mirror as I looked around with a scowl on my face, but he did not say a word. Nor did I, stepping back into the stall and scanning the walls, ceiling, and floor one more time for the slot. It was nowhere.

Of course I felt inept for missing something that should have been so obvious, but as I wrapped the towel around me one more time and stepped out to ask the shaver if he knew where the thing might be, it seemed I had little choice.

He shrugged and said, "I went swimming," as if he owed me an explanation.

I returned his shrug and, with nowhere else to go, walked out into the hall. I'm not sure what I expected to find out there other than a washing machine, a dryer, a bulletin board of local attractions, and a mimeographed list of the day's activities. Two women sorting laundry stopped talking, glared at my towel, and turned away.

Frankly, I was lost. I considered walking back to the campsite to ask my wife or one of my daughters where the mechanism was hidden, but as that would predictably be fraught with laughter and derision, I opted to give the shower one more try. The man arched one eyebrow as I appeared in the frame of the door. I shook my head and disappeared again behind the curtain, dropped the towel, and scanned the white stall. In desperation I decided to simply turn the knobs and see what would happen.

What happened was that the water came on. I nearly shrieked in cold panic, but not being alone, I kept it to myself. I did, however, feel as though I owed the shaver an explanation, so I poked my head around the plastic curtain and called out, "It works! It's free! They must just charge the women"—the absurd reality was just then sinking in, like water swirling down the drain.

He was at the door, turning and smiling like Boston Blackie, the arc of the mustache flattening out across a wide gap-toothed leer. "It's about time we got somethin' for free."

Out of pure orneriness, I took a twenty-minute scalding hot shower and left the water running while I toweled off, dressed, and rehearsed my indignation for the manager.

The camp store was empty, though. At first I considered snagging a few Snickers from a ripped display box as payment for the women's showers but instead picked up a local newspaper off the counter while I waited.

On page three there was a headline from a Gannett News Service story on sex discrimination: STUDY: WOMEN MAKING LITTLE PROGRESS ON PAY SCALE. I nodded. We make them pay every step along the way.

10

More Is Less: The Zen of Living Large on a Small Planet

A FATHER'S NUMEROLOGY

Calculating freedom

Freedom's just another word for nothing left to lose.
—KRIS KRISTOFFERSON

In the weeks following Nancy's birth in 1973, I spent many late nights pacing the living room floor with our beautiful, fat, *howling* baby girl in my weary arms. On one of those long and harrowing sojourns nowhere, I found that I could control my frustration and maintain my sanity by calculating the years that it would take until the collicky baby would grow up—and I would be free again.

I figured that when Nancy reached eighteen—and Cael twenty-two—I would be free. Free, that is, to be me. Me, the well-regarded writer and teacher I knew was my destiny. The day Nancy would leave for college to seek her destiny, I'd set sail on my own journey of self-actualization. I would be forty-five, still young enough to take advantage of the freedoms that would be mine simply by relinquishing my role as worrier and protector—and late-night pacer—a role she would no longer want me to serve. Nancy and I would be friends together in the real world of 1991, not Dada changing a messy diaper, or Daddy booting a soccer ball to his daughter, or even Dad pacing the living room at night waiting for the headlights in the driveway. We would be friends, talking politics or literature or whatever over a beer at Tony's Tavern.

That simple arithmetic helped me get through the colic that evening; and from that vantage point I could foresee a full life ahead to take care of my needs again—to go out when I wanted, to go to exotic places, to sleep late, to sleep long, to be me. Fathering two children, like going to college, was something I did en route to something else. My *real* identity was deeper, more complex than that. It just took some calculations.

And eighteen years later, when I woke up the morning after Nancy's first visit home from college, I remembered those simple calculations and understood with a tired yawn just how wrong they had been. What started out as a small hippie family of four, as you know, blossomed into a not-so-small tribe of seven kids who have defined life and freedom for me in ways I never envisioned on that night in 1973.

Yet all these years have shimmered past like a meteor and I still find myself awake in the middle of the night, up with Elizabeth, who has her own bad dreams, or growling at Bay and his friend Luke to "Go to sleep, now!" or listening almost breathlessly until I hear Danny walk through the front door after curfew.

Through my children's enduring presence, I know myself a little better now than I did when I paced the floor with Nancy all those years ago. I see more clearly my destiny today, even as I am drawn ineffably toward the infinite. When people ask what I do, I still sometimes tell them out of habit or convenience—or some vestige of those days on North Newhall Street—that I am a writer and a teacher, wishing, I think, to add some unnecessary weight to my mere presence. But at the core of my pulsing heart I know I am not a writer or a teacher.

I am a father. I have been a father since I was a few steps out of my father's house. I have been a father for longer than it took John Keats to live a whole life and immortalize himself as a writer.

I am a father when I stand in front of a class, when I sit at a computer screen, coach a Little League team, mow a lawn, plunge a toilet, read a poem, sing a song, sit on a beach . . . as I weep even as I laugh at it all. I will probably be lying awake, pacing the floor, arguing paradoxical points of childhood logic long after I am also a grandfather.

I am a father. That is all I am.

FOOD IS LOVE

The cost of feeding the masses

> *One cannot think well, love well, sleep well, if one has not dined well.*
>
> —VIRGINIA WOOLF

One night this past summer, after a particularly hot and grueling fourteen-hour day of work, I stumbled through the kitchen doorway and headed straight for the fruit bowl.

I yearned only to dump my heavy knapsack, cradle a cool round peach in my palm, walk into the living room, fall back onto the couch, and bite into something that would dribble down my chin and reinvigorate my taste buds and wet my dry throat.

But the wooden fruit bowl on the counter was empty, or practically empty, a few straggly grapeless vines, two wrinkled mangy-looking grapes, some peach stems, and a two-week-old black and purple banana.

I looked forlornly over to Patti, and in my most understanding and deviously needling voice said only, "Didn't make it to the fruit market today?"

"I did!" she snapped, as if she'd seen right through my veneer of sensitivity. But it was just futility speaking. "I spent forty-six dollars and that's what's left, except the damn banana, of course. Why don't they ever eat the last banana?"

I pondered the unponderable. "I don't know." Then I remembered the problem at hand. "How did they eat forty-six dollars' worth of fruit in an afternoon?" I asked incredulously, as if I didn't already know. Patti and I find ourselves often playing the role of the Costello straight man to the other's Abbott when it comes to matters of finance. It's simply amazing to consider how much food can be consumed by a family of nine.

In Patti's tight-lipped response to my incredulity lies the reason: "When I came home they were all sitting around the kitchen counter like vultures, complaining that there was no food in the house. They devoured most of the grapes before I even got them in the bowl."

Craig, Bay's BIG friend, was visiting; and Danny and his pal Keith awakened from their Nintendo-induced stupor in the basement when they sniffed fresh food in the air; and Nate, Michael, and Jeffrey (boyfriends) all showed up just before dinner; and Elizabeth did her usual: she takes a bite of some fruit, puts it down, and promptly forgets about it—and then later gets another piece of fruit and takes a bite out of that one and puts it down. That night I found four pieces of rotting fruit all around the house.

I nodded and tried to figure out how long it takes me to make forty-six dollars, but my brain was too fried. I opened the refrigerator and snatched the one remaining Corona from the six-pack I'd bought the night before, grateful that they had at least left me something cold and wet.

Employing pure logic, you'd think that with Cael grown and moved on, leaving us with eight in the house, we'd consume exactly twice as much as the typical family of four.

Wrong. Food has no logic; consumed exponentially as the numbers around the table increase, Patti says that the cooking itself for eight or nine, which should involve no more work or preparation, is easily more than twice as time-consuming and perhaps three times more costly than feeding a family of four. I know, it doesn't compute.

There are two units of cost factors in any family: consumables and wearables. Wearables, which include shoes, clothes, sports equipment, coats, etc., may be stroke-inducingly expensive, but at least you can cut the cost by shopping for sales and handing things down. Bay, who must have forty T-shirts (no exaggeration), probably has only five that have been exclusively his from point of purchase. Elizabeth is wearing dresses today that were bought in 1973 and worn by all three older sisters. Danny—and the big girls—are continual beneficiaries of the weeding of my closet. Even cars get handed down: Patti's maroon Reliant went first to Cael, then to Nancy, next to Addie, and Clover finally drove it into the ground. Nancy's boyfriend Mike towed it away.

Food, however, is obviously unrecyclable. It comes in, it goes out. (And for those with septic systems, consider the wear on my septic field as our toilets get flushed dozens of times in a twenty-four-hour period.)

I'm not complaining, though. It's not only essential to eat well and have a full belly, it's important to have a full cupboard when kids open the door seeking sustenance in one form or another. More important than a new toy or a fancier car or a backyard pool or a trip to Club Med, a stocked refrigerator and cupboard help to make home feel nourishing, a place of respite from the widespread spiritual famine of contemporary life. Home is a sanctuary from the elements; it is where you break bread with those who share your hungry struggle; it is there where you quench your driving thirst and then tell of your day.

In nineties hip-hop psychology, it is generally understood that food is not love. But it is. It is a part of loving your children, feeding them until they are healthy enough and wise enough to learn how to feed themselves. Whatever the cost.

STOPPING BY THE WOODS

The enriching qualities of human frailty and sorrow

> *Therefore, it seems to me that everything that exists is good—death as well as life, sin as well as holiness, wisdom as well as folly.*
>
> —HERMANN HESSE

More than 150 years ago, the literary behemoths Dana, Alcott, Cooper, Poe, Longfellow, and Hawthorne were turning the reading world on its ear with their passionate writings about the human condition. Now they are all but extinct and forgotten. Their books are too slow, too long-winded, too full of pointless description for the contemporary mind.

Here it is almost 2000 A.D. and we do everything on the go and in pairs: eating takeout, driving while yapping on the cellular, laptopping on the train, reading on the toilet, even grabbing a few winks on the plane en route to meetings in cities we've never visited but go to all the time. We don't have time to read Poe's poignant "Tamerlane."

Contemporary life bears an odd resemblance to a day at Walt Disney World, where for the price of admission, you board the college-marriage-career-parenthood-camcorder-restaurant-movie-midlife-crisis ride and get dropped off at Condo-Land where Olive Oyl turns on the VCR and shows you scenes from a life you forgot you had lived. We do aerobics to relaxation tapes, jog to work, race to yoga classes, dash to shrinks, speed through quality sequences with kids and dogs and aging parents, and wake from sleepless nights to labor for bosses who want us to be in three places at one time. It's enough to make our collective heads spin.

Which brings me to Hawthorne's *The Scarlet Letter* and the perennial question from my students spread far too thin for their young years as to why I make them read it: simply stated, it cannot be read on the run or even at a slow trot.

No, one must sit down in order to have any hope of comprehending its multilayered story. It's a ponderous, repetitive, elusive, excruciatingly detailed drama where, I would be remiss not to admit, little happens. Two hundred fifty pages concerning the question of sin and what happens to our frail and sometimes sorrowful lives. It is humbling both for the oblique nature of its message and the inescapable truth of that message. It commands us to a halt.

Five years ago I watched fourteen-year-old Clover as she returned from soccer practice after school. On the way into the house that afternoon, the phone was ringing; she grabbed the receiver from Addie, and after some coded teenage preliminaries while scanning the refrigerator and paging through the catalogs left on the counter, Clover made hasty plans to meet some friends later that evening.

She was already leaping for the stairs when Elizabeth, our two-year-old with leather and metal braces on her tiny legs, let her big sister know she had a different notion. She just sat in the hall in front of Clover and held up her pink arms. And waited.

The message was inescapable. Clover ceased the forward momentum that had carried her almost nonstop from her first step onto a yellow school bus in 1981, the same force that would have propelled her and her contagious zest for life up the stairs and out of Elizabeth's grasp for at least another day.

But she actually stopped.

She picked up her baby sister, brought that wonderfully soft face to her cheek, kissed her, uttered a few silly words, retrieved the doll she wanted, and moments later, put her down. Not much happened, but Clover's life was once again changed forever by a complex little girl who directs the traffic of our speeding lives like a beefy cop.

At two years old, Elizabeth was still six months away from taking her first wobbly step, yet she commanded enormous power by asking or whining or crying or demanding or cajoling or literally shinnying up our legs. And she maintained an undaunted faith that one of us would always stop.

Every time she held up her hands we stopped.

We stopped to hold her. We stopped to change her. We stopped to carry her on our hip while we did a million and one other things that need doing. We stopped to pick her up, to simply touch her miraculously soft skin, to smell her sweet breath, to do what was important, to remember, to maintain our collective sanity.

Carrying a two-year-old with a metal brace on her legs strains your back beyond belief. Short on mobility and long on language development, she repeated herself endlessly. After spending a full day with her, we all discovered that nothing had happened and our brains were minus several million cells. Yet she became the powerful core of our lives.

Elizabeth Bayou-Grace was—and remains—a constant reminder that, despite all the endless scurrying around this globe with visions of our own puffed-up importance, the world does not work the way we expect it to, that there is sometimes unavoidable sorrow in our fragile lives—and that there is always a rare and wonderful kind of joy in acknowledging our helplessness in the face of all that.

That is why I make my students read Hawthorne.

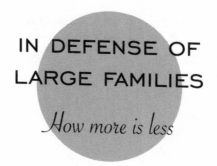

IN DEFENSE OF
LARGE FAMILIES

How more is less

> *All know that the drop merges into the ocean, but few
> know that the ocean merges into the drop.*
>
> —KABĪR

Soon after Clover was born, we began to notice the occasional
raised eyebrow among friends. After all, we had three children
already. Why more?

Danny arrived two years later with the first of the "jokes"
about our sex life. With Bay's birth came the disapproving *tsks*,
which, loosely translated, meant "Get a life." Mostly, I laughed.
One of the great lessons of big family living is to not take things
personally.

However, since Elizabeth graced our lives seven years ago,
the occasional criticisms about "living large" have grown harsher
and less easy to laugh off. The accusing fingers are pointed in
various verbal and nonverbal ways, but they invariably say the
same thing: *By your selfishness you're contributing to the world's
hunger and pain.*

What do you say to that—especially when it's not said?

And so I've occasionally found myself driving aimlessly for
hours around this small college town muttering to myself, an-

swering my accusers, accusing my accusers, trying to find the perfect Rosanne-esque response to the barbs of people from global ecology groups who claim that big families—especially big American families—disproportionately use the world's rapidly diminishing natural resources.

The real problem for me has been that, on the surface, their accusations seem true: the overpopulated earth is growing smaller and more ravaged every day. One look at global population growth rates and it's hard to argue the point. And it is an undeniable fact that Americans simply take more, use more, need more, discard more, pollute more, and ultimately produce more ecological devastation than people anywhere else on earth. It all seems pretty simple.

But it's not. Another singularly important axiom learned from big family life is that nothing is ever simple. This was illustrated to me once again the other day in a seemingly insignificant moment when I saw twenty-year-old Addie scold little Elizabeth for leaving the refrigerator open—just as I or her mother would have done—and then watched as she put her younger sister's hair in braids and the two of them went out to the swings. No big deal, but the world suddenly grew larger. It was an amazing metaphysical event whereby an adolescent was transformed into an adult and, a few moments later, a little child.

And this evening, when I solemnly considered my brood scattered throughout this big house and across this vast country, I understood in that soulful place beyond understanding that there is a dimension of life that exists beyond the realm of numbers, of dollars and cents, of bottom lines and even predictable physical phenomena.

Under our roof there is, in abundance beyond reason, the essence of spirit on this planet. There is the spirit of so-loud-you-can't-think dinners, of tuna casserole realities, of sibling wars fought under tables and behind closed doors, of stealthily borrowed clothes, of never quite getting your fair share, your next turn, your rightful due. And then in the midst of all the furor that drives people and countries to war, there are countless acts of kindness and love that nourish, sustain, redeem, and ultimately expand the universe in which we live.

Going against all laws of physics, my kids, like many other children in solid large families, are simply capable of giving more than they take from the earth. My children understand in their bones what it's like to live under the same roof with many others. They understand better than most adults the economics of sharing. They know from countless meals about not taking more than you can eat. After a lifetime of tagging behind, they know how to follow; and after years of taking little ones by the hand, they know very well how to lead.

Although I can't substantiate it, I am certain that the future scientist—or psychologist or social engineer or basement inventor—who ultimately solves the problem of world overpopulation will come from a big family. (Probably the unbelievably squeezed middle child.) Few others on this planet understand the issues of crowding so intimately and so compassionately.

Only someone who is one of many would know the mystical mathematics involved in proving that more is less is more—that the ocean indeed merges into the drop.

BITING OFF THE MATTER WITH A SMILE

The remains of a Father's Day

Three Silences there are: the first of speech,
The second of desire, the third of thought.
—HENRY WADSWORTH LONGFELLOW

A long time has rattled past since I saw the movie *The Remains of the Day*, but the face of Mr. Stevens, the butler played by Anthony Hopkins, has become one whose shaded eyes and strangled lips I recognize everywhere I go. I have seen him on Metro North trains, in coffee shops, leaning out of car windows. He once served me dinner in a dream.

To stir your memory, the slow-moving, understated film concerns an English butler whose devotion to a life of service keeps him alone, empty, and unfulfilled. He is a man whose dignity in this most undignified age would now be considered less a tragic flaw than an unremarkable character flaw. At the end of his day, all that remains is hollow intention.

It should have been utterly forgettable, yet I cannot escape the remains of that movie.

It was about my father, who devoted the soul of a lifetime to his business. It was about my good friend Steve, a building contractor, who carried on at work through the terrible darkness of his father's death; my nephew Jake in California, who wrote a painful story about a boy's inability to tell a girl he loved her; my closest pal in the world, a photographer who would never ask his famous movie star friend for a lead. It was about my dear sons, who, as they grow older, grow less able to cry out at the awful pain in life. Indeed, they grow less able to double over with laughter at the absurdity of it all.

It was about the silence of men; it was about the way fathers and their sons never really say what they mean.

And so, of course, it was about me, though to look at my raucous, unprivate life with seven children, a sensuous wife, and a healthy disrespect for rules, you'd think that I saw a different film from everyone else. I didn't.

The anecdote I am about to share is as silly and adolescent as it is middle-aged and stodgy, or even elderly and a bit confused. It is embarrassing to tell because it points out how petty I am, how imprisoned I am by my silence.

Some time ago a publisher of some renown bought a weekend place on our rural dead-end road. It was just cause for a lot of local gossip, not only because we suddenly had a celebrity neighbor but because everyone figured that our property values would increase. And I was privately thrilled because I'm a freelance writer. The serendipity of having a famous publisher as a neighbor seemed like suddenly going from fly fishing in a raging creek to dropping a line in a stocked pond.

Logic and reason—and my good wife—urged me to be simply neighborly: walk over there and introduce myself. Once on his doorstep, the fantasy goes, we would find a companionship of spirit. He would be mesmerized by my work and pass it on to his editors with *instructions*. Fame and fortune would be a commission away.

Yet several months passed and I did not walk the half mile to his house through the woods—I did not even know what the guy looked like. Whenever I replayed the neighborly visit scene in my head, it felt fawning. I was certain that he'd think me a phony for being friendly as a means of making a career move. (Of course, I would have been doing just that.) And I hated the thought of my kids seeing me pandering.

So I did nothing. And a few seasons later when I finally met the man by accident—I backed my Jeep (loaded with garbage) into his rental car!—I could not even use the coincidence to my advantage. We laughed about finally meeting "by accident," and he accepted my profuse apologies and we went our separate ways. He didn't say what he did for a living, and neither did I.

In retrospect, I guess it would have been okay to tell him simply that I am a writer, just as I suppose it would have been all right if someone spoke for the butler in the movie and told the maid that he loved her. I suppose. But not really.

After the movie last winter we met some friends at a local café. Each of the women said that they were frustrated and angry with the butler's unwillingness to give in to his emotions, to make that one step, to utter that one sound that would have gotten the Emma Thompson character to complete his life. Finally. But later my friend the building contractor leaned over and said that he wished the film had gone on for hours.

Me, too. A light had been turned on in my own private corridor of silence, and in the shadows I saw the faces of all the men I know. And I wanted to linger there in that quiet hall for a little while longer.

Every day since memory took root—back in the thickening darkness of my own private adolescence—I have had a sense of having to coerce myself through some flimsy curtain that separates me from all that I yearn for: companionship, love, acceptance, approval, joy.

Even now, nearly four decades later, I must urge myself—yes, bully myself on the darker days—through the thin gauzy folds as I come home each night from work to a house and a family I love with all my heart. And I do it. I do it. I do it because I must. I must. But at the risk of seeming overly dramatic (and, of course, a little less a man), it is always done with a sense of peril to my very identity, my sense of duty and dignity, my stubbornly protected privacy.

It is as if in coming home I find myself, like so many other fathers, stepping onto a stage of my fondest dreams, where the lights are suddenly too bright and the floor too slippery and the laughter too loud and the life too livid.

And I do it, although it would feel safer to disappear behind the newspaper. Or hide in the bathroom. Or find some dutied solace in work. The remains of a father's day.

WHEN BAD THINGS HAPPEN
TO INNOCENT CHILDREN
What children really understand

I postpone death by living, by suffering, by error, by risk-ing, by giving, by losing.

—ANAÏS NIN

At dinner some time ago, between forkfuls of pasta, Elizabeth asked me why anyone would blow up a day-care center full of children. She was talking about the infamous Oklahoma City bombing that took place in April 1995.

I was momentarily stunned, scurrying around behind a crooked smile trying to locate some wise and comforting fatherly words to counter the abject evil that had trespassed into her consciousness. Something that would blur the horrifying images of a bleeding child (or an abandoned doll or mangled scooter) that would linger long past the time that the TV screen went blank.

Although it was Oklahoma City that was on her young mind that night, I knew with terrifying clarity the moment I heard her question that there is a new nightmare every day to ponder for seven-year-olds who are full of questions about life—and death. If I could, I would have instantly erased the entire horrific episode from her memory the way you record over an old video,

replacing the Stephen King movie with a cartoon. I'm her father. Her daddy. Her protector. That's my job, beyond all others. If I could I would shield her from all the terrifying images of
contemporary life. I'd toss out the TV, radio, newspapers, magazines. No O. J. Simpson murder trial, no teenage blood on city
streets, no victims of flesh-eating strep virus, no firemen carrying broken babies out of bombed-out buildings.

However, as the shocking scenes on the TV news every night
remind each of us, large and small, there is no escaping the injustices in life, the dark truths that exist just beyond the smiley
faces and rainbows painted on elementary school windows.

And that's what Elizabeth wanted to know: the truth. "Why,
Daddy?"

"I don't know, Elizabeth," I said sadly, taking her hand, the
soft, delicate fingers folded like a rose in my rough palm, hoping
that was enough.

It was not. "But, have the bad men been caught? Can it happen
again?"

I opened my mouth to soothe away her fears with a wishful
lie ("I will never let anything hurt you, baby"). But Patti saved
me from myself, telling her simply, gently, that there are good
and evil people in the world, and adults try very hard to punish
the evil ones and reward those who are good.

I watched Elizabeth's beautiful face closely, afraid that Patti
had told her more than she could handle—or maybe not enough.
But our amazing little girl just nodded and speared some more
pasta. And that was that. She chattered on about Pogs and peewee baseball and her best friend, Kathleen, and along the way
allowed me a glimpse into the simple truth that childhood innocence is, in large part, an adult invention. Of course. Who knows
better than children just how small and powerless one can feel
in this often cold and terrifying world?

When Elizabeth was just an infant she traveled through
Keats's "vale of Soul-making." She knew even then. Now, like
millions of other children, she goes to a school alongside kids

with bald heads from cancer, kids who have been orphaned, kids who are abused. And when she returns each afternoon to her safe and warm home, she finds herself in the middle of the woods with copperheads in the grass, snapping turtles in the ponds, the terrifying screech of natural selection punctuating each and every day. She knows.

After dinner I held my little girl so close I wondered if she could hear the beating of my resilient and frightened heart. And then we went out into the yard for a few moments before dark because I think we both understood how important it is to laugh and play while we can. How terribly important to be part of a loving family that, although they can't protect you from pain, will stay with you until the ache finally goes away.

LOOKING OUT FOR NUMBER ONE, TWO, THREE . . .

Coming home

> *The one is none other than the All, the All none other than the one.*
>
> —SENG TS'AN

A lot of people tilt their heads and ask in that slightly uncomfortable—slightly accusatory—voice, "How can you keep track of so many kids?"

They smile teasingly and want to know if I always remember their names, their birth dates, their favorite foods, their homework assignments. (Yes.) Some wonder with a wry smile if we've ever forgotten one of them à la *Home Alone*. (Well, sometimes.) Others even have the temerity to ask in a whisper if each of our children was planned. (No.)

What they really want to know, however, is whether it's possible to love and care for seven children—or, more to the point, whether there's enough love to go around. *"Doesn't it all get used up by the time you have two or three (or at most four) kids?"* It's not a question, it's a challenge.

I usually smile and make a joke. I tell how I sometimes call one of the kids four or five names before I get to the right one—"Hey, Cael—Nancy—Addie—Clover—what's your name?—

Danny, please pass the bread." Or (for the umpteenth time this year) I recount the night we left Clover at the Vermilyes' house and didn't realize it until I counted heads in the van about five or ten miles down the road. Or the afternoon when Patti forgot that Cael was waiting for a ride at school and she, Clover, and Nancy went to the mall.

That's what most people want to hear. They certainly don't want a lengthy philosophical monologue about the logistics of managing children after they outnumber parents three or more to one. They want affirmation that they did the right thing by stopping at one or two or three.

They also want to confirm their suspicions about large families. As charming as the Waltons might have been—or the Bradfords from *Eight Is Enough*, or the Bradys—everyone knows that things are out of control in big families: we're sex-crazed, we're hiding from life behind our children, we're irresponsible, we're arrogant users of the world's resources, and, finally, the only thing that really matters, we can't possibly provide the love necessary for that many kids.

Yet the truth is that loving your big family is the easy part of having seven kids. In fact, there's nothing even remotely magical or metaphysical about it. It's not like there's a finite amount of parental love doled out to each individual at birth that later gets parceled out among the children—or that you somehow have to create precious love out of base metals so that there's enough to go around. Not at all. You simply love every one of your children with all your heart. That's it. Each one gets the same amount of love: your whole heart. (Which is not to say that you like all of them all the time—or even some of the time—you just love them without question.)

Two years ago Cael came home to the Hudson Valley from North Carolina for a quick visit. The same boy who couldn't wait to escape the pesty little urchins and his oppressive parents in 1987 to go a thousand miles away to college in Florida bought a cheap flight just to come here for a few days—to see eight-year-old Bay's Little League baseball game; to watch six-year-old Elizabeth's tap recital; to "chaperon" Danny's fifteenth birthday party; to pass big brotherly judgment on seventeen-year-old Clover's boyfriend, Jeffrey; to play a round of golf with the old man; to hang out at the local clubs with Nancy and Addie, who had just returned from college; to eat his mother's cooking; to lie back on the couch and watch the Knicks (while Bay and Elizabeth challenged his patience by continually walking in front of the tube).

To be where everyone loves him no matter what.

After the weekend I admit I was beat. As Cael's visit reminded me, with each additional child the house fills up not just by one but exponentially. It seemed that kids were everywhere; on all three floors of this big house—my kids, someone else's kids, kids I didn't even recognize. There were kids on the porches, kids in the refrigerator, kids in the bathrooms, kids on the phone, kids in my wallet, kids in the woods, kids in our bed; teenage boys sneaking a smoke outside the basement door, six-year-old girls leaving the hose running all night, seventeen-year-old girls returning empty juice cartons to the refrigerator, grown boys consuming the air, the couch, the TV, the CD player, the cold beer, even the floor space in the living room.

There was no escaping all of us. Which is just the point here. A big family is profoundly different from a small or even a "regular" family (which we experienced for a brief time between 1969 and 1974). In this house it's never ever about you alone; it's about everyone. Child rearing is not a piece of a grander life scheme; it's not a passage or a phase; it's not even the best part of life. In our time on earth there will be no neat divisions for Patti and me like the infant and toddler years, then the teenage years, then the empty nest years, then the grandparenting years. For us it is everything all at once. There is nothing else out there for us but this big family.

In fact it is so all-consuming—so inescapable—for me that I have come to understand that all my dreams of fame (vast riches, glorious adventure, etc.) are nothing more than fleeting distractions from the daily task of fathering this extraordinary brood. In the diminishing light of my fiftieth year, I see clearly that everything comes and everything goes except this inescapable family.

In an imploding universe where one must increasingly learn to go it alone, where survival depends upon one's ability to look out solely for number one, our children look out for each other. They come home because in a big family someone is always waiting for you.

· A NOTE ON THE TYPE ·

The typeface used in this book is one of many versions of Garamond, a modern homage to—rather than, strictly speaking, a revival
of—the celebrated fonts of Claude Garamond (c.1480–1561), the
first founder to produce type on a large scale. Garamond's type
was inspired by Francesco Griffo's *De Ætna* type (cut in the 1490s
for Venetian printer Aldus Manutius and revived in the 1920s as
Bembo), but its letter forms were cleaner and the fit between
pieces of type improved. It therefore gave text a more harmonious
overall appearance than its predecessors had, becoming the basis
of all romans created on the continent for the next two hundred
years; it was itself still in use through the eighteenth century. Besides the many "Garamonds" in use today, other typefaces derived
from his fonts are Granjon and Sabon (despite their being named
after other printers).

Traumatic Lesions of the Penis

When the penis is exposed, and particularly in the state of erection, it is subject to contusions and open wounds, which are dealt with on general principles and are usually followed by recovery. When the erectile tissue is involved, copious hæmorrhage may ensue even from a small punctured wound. A hæmatoma resulting from a contusion may be slow to disappear.

The penis in the horse may be wounded by the whip. It has been mistaken in the sheath in the scrotal region by the lay castrator for a testicle, and included in the clam, with fatal results from occlusion of the urethra and rupture of the bladder.

The bull may fracture the penis against the ischium of the cow.

In the dog the organ is most frequently injured during coitus by violent separation or by bites from other dogs. Rarely the bone is fractured. As the result of injury, the penis may become more or less distorted and paraphimosis may ensue. The urethra may be concerned in the lesion (see Affections of the Urethra).

TREATMENT varies according to the nature of the lesion, and is on the usual lines for a contusion or open wound. Suturing may be sufficient to arrest slight hæmorrhage, and if an artery is seen bleeding it should be ligatured. The thermo-cautery may be required to arrest hæmorrhage from a deep punctured wound. Erection excites hæmorrhage, and should be avoided by isolating the patient and administering potassium bromide. A suspensory bandage is useful as a support and protection to the organ when it is outside the sheath. Incision of a hæmatoma is contra-indicated here on account of the risk of severe hæmorrhage and the danger of infection in this region. When irreparable injury has been inflicted on the penis its amputation is necessary. Adhesion of the penis to the sheath has been seen as the result of injury and ulceration of the opposing surfaces.

Strangulation of the Penis

Strangulation of the penis arises from the application of a ring or cord round the organ, and is most common in the dog. In the bull the repeated protrusion and withdrawal of the penis may cause the preputial hairs to become twisted round the organ a few inches behind its extremity. When the organ is forcibly protruded the hairs may rupture or become embedded in its surface, acting as a ligature and causing necrosis of the part in front. The gangrenous end of the organ is easily recognised. The urine may escape through several holes in the dead tissue.

TREATMENT.—In all cases remove the cause of the trouble, prescribe antiseptic lotions for the wounded part, and fomentations and gentle massage to diminish the swelling. Cure is the rule when the urethra has not been occluded. When the end of the penis in the bull becomes necrotic the dead portion sloughs off and recovery follows.

Acrobustitis—Balanitis—Balano-Posthitis

Acrobustitis, or inflammation of the prepuce, and balanitis, or inflammation of the surface of the free portion of the penis, may occur independently, but usually they are associated, constituting balano-posthitis. The conditions affect all the domesticated animals, but are most common in the ox, which is predisposed to them by the peculiarities of the sheath. The long, narrow prepuce of the ox, lined by a mucous membrane rich in sebaceous glands, favours inflammation, as does also the fact that the penis is not protruded during urination, thus allowing the urine to come in contact with the preputial lining and smegma to accumulate in the front of the passage. The bull is less liable to these affections than the bullock, owing to the greater calibre of the prepuce and the more frequent protrusion of the penis in the former.

The Horse—ETIOLOGY.—The causes of the trouble in the horse comprise urinating into the sheath, lying in dirty, wet litter, the accumulation of smegma in the sheath, the secretion becoming fœtid and irritant, tumours and swelling of the sheath, and anything which prevents extension of the penis therefrom. In some districts horses suffering from colic or showing difficulty in urination are treated by rubbing the penis with an irritant like pepper, which leads to inflammation, ulceration, and sometimes necrosis of the affected parts. Sometimes a large amount of smegma accumulates around the corona glandis, filling up the urethral sinus and interfering with or preventing urination by pressure on the urethra.

SYMPTOMS.—The inflammatory condition of the sheath is obvious. When the urethra is occluded by smegma in the suburethral sinus, the horse evinces the same symptoms as in a case of urethral calculus. Examination of the sinus reveals the cause of the trouble. The accumulated smegma may be as hard as a stone. Phimosis or paraphimosis may be present.

TREATMENT consists in removing the cause of the condition as far as possible. When it is due to an accumulation of smegma, the horse must be cast, the penis withdrawn from the sheath, and the latter washed with hot water and soap, and then treated with an astringent lotion or an antiseptic emollient powder. When there is ulceration of the affected region, an antiseptic emollient ointment or, better, B.I.P.P. is indicated as a lubricant and protective. When the suburethral sinus is filled with smegma it must be extracted. If the material is in the form of a concretion, it may be necessary to break it with a forceps or dig it out with a stout director. Whenever a horse shows difficulty in urination this sinus should be examined.

The Ox.—In the ox the cause may be some foreign matter gaining entrance to the sheath, such as the head or portion of the stem of grass, or particles of sand ; or an injury, due to direct violence, followed by infection of the injured part ; or a specific infection of the same nature as contagious vaginitis in the cow, and usually contracted during service. The contagion, however, may also be conveyed through the bedding.

Symptoms.—A longish, hot, painful swelling first appears in front of the sheath, and may extend as far as the scrotum. Urination is difficult, and the urine is passed in drops or in a fine stream. The prepuce cannot be drawn back over the penis. Phimosis exists. In the prepuce a grey-black smegma is found, the removal of which gives pain. On rectal examination the bladder may be felt distended and painful on pressure. Colic soon sets in, the patient ceases to feed, and if relief is not promptly afforded will die from rupture of the bladder. Infiltration of the tissues round the prepuce may ensue, and be followed by sloughing of the latter, and perhaps of the penis as well. Recovery may take place even after a portion of the penis has sloughed off.

Treatment.—The first indication is to ensure that there is a sufficient exit for the urine. If the sheath is completely occluded, the bladder must be punctured *per rectum* at once.

The next procedure is to clean out the sheath as follows : Cast the animal and fix it in the left lateral position, with the right hind-limb fixed to the shoulder ; cut the hairs at the entrance to the prepuce, and wash the part with hot water and soap. Smear the index finger with vaseline, pass it into the prepuce, and extract the sebaceous matter collected there, or, if necessary, introduce a blunt curette for the purpose. Irrigate the sheath with warm solution of boric acid or potassium permanganate. Repeat the injections for a few days. In a case of long standing the preputial opening is constricted, and it may be necessary to incise the sheath inferiorly to enable its interior to be cleaned as described.

An alternative procedure in the latter case is to open the sheath at the level of the extremity of the penis, evacuate it of the accumulated material as before, and pass a seton or drainage tube through the anterior portion of the passage. The urine will escape through the two openings while the seton is in position, but when it is removed after a few days the incision will heal.

If the anterior part of the prepuce is permanently occluded, excise a V-shaped piece of the sheath at the level of the point of the penis.

Baldoni advises section of the retractor penis, so that the glans penis will be situated at the level of the entrance to the sheath, and thus avoid urinating into the latter. The operation is performed in the same way as post-scrotal urethrotomy until the penis is exposed, when the retractor is severed behind its insertion into the second curve.

The Pig.—The umbilical pouch in the upper wall of the sheath and close in front of its opening may become distended by its own sebaceous secretion, especially in the castrated animal. The material may become hard, forming preputial calculi.

SYMPTOMS.—Swelling and inflammatory symptoms are observed in the affected region, and local examination reveals the nature of the condition.

TREATMENT consists in cleaning out the sheath in the same way as in other animals.

The Dog.—Acrobustitis in the dog is more of the nature of a catarrh than an inflammation. It is characterised by a greenish, purulent discharge, which moistens and agglutinates the hairs at the preputial opening. The dog frequently licks the part. There may be no evidence of inflammation. It has been erroneously called gonorrhœa, for the urethra is not involved. The catarrhal condition is very common. In well-marked chronic cases the follicles of the mucous membrane become swollen, and the latter undergoes thickening and induration, and may show granular enlargements or vegetations on its surface.

TREATMENT.—Slight cases do not require treatment, but when the discharge is comparatively copious it may be diminished by astringent injections into the sheath such as sulphate or sulphocarbolate of zinc (1 to 2 per cent.), or tannic acid (3 to 5 per cent.), or potassium permanganate, or chinosol (1 in 1,000).

Phimosis

Phimosis, or inability to protrude the penis from the sheath, may be congenital or acquired. The congenital abnormality has been dealt with (p. 748). Phimosis is caused by anything which obstructs or constricts the preputial orifice, such as inflammatory or œdematous swelling, or a neoplasm or cicatricial contraction.

SYMPTOMS.—The symptoms of the cause of the trouble are observed.

TREATMENT consists in dealing with the lesion which has given rise to the condition.

Paraphimosis

Paraphimosis, or inability to withdraw the penis into the sheath after protrusion, occurs occasionally in all animals, but is most common in the dog.

ETIOLOGY comprises inflammatory or œdematous swelling, paralysis, or a new growth affecting the penis. In the dog it may appear after coitus, when it is favoured by the circular erectile swelling round the penis in front of the prepuce. When the organ is being retracted into the sheath some of the preputial hairs may be drawn with it into the preputial opening, forming a wedge between the penis and the sheath,

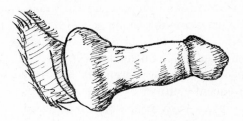

FIG. 312.—PARAPHIMOSIS IN THE DOG.

and tending to prevent complete return of the organ. The swelling which ensues from this constriction aggravates the condition. In the horse a ridge of fibrous tissue may form round the penis as the result of chronic balanitis, and prevent its entrance into the sheath.

TREATMENT.—The obvious treatment is to remove, if possible, the cause of the condition by the adoption of appropriate measures. When it follows coitus in the dog, steps should be taken immediately to return the penis to the sheath as follows : Place the dog in the dorsal position on the table. If the organ is soiled, bathe it with warm water and apply liquid paraffin on its surface as a lubricant. If the preputial hairs are turned in, clip them off. Push the penis backwards with one hand while the other endeavours to draw the sheath forwards over the organ. If the penis is much swollen, use cold or hot applications to reduce its volume. If these measures are insufficient, incise the sheath at its orifice to relieve the stricture and enable the penis to be returned.

48

When due to chronic balanitis in the horse, Vennerholm's operation is indicated (see p. 423).

After service in the bull there has been observed a protrusion of the membrane covering the penis, forming a reddish-brown tumour about the size of a fist in front of the prepuce, with an orifice in its centre through which the urine is passed. The mucous membrane of the sheath at the point of its reflection on the penis does not follow the movement of the organ on its withdrawal after copulation in this case, but becomes detached from it, forming the swelling mentioned. Astringent lotions may be sufficient to reduce the prolapse ; if not, it must be excised after inserting a series of ligatures through the periphery of its base. The writer operated in this way on a yearling Aberdeen-Angus bull in which the tissue removed was found to contain a tuberculous lesion.

Tumours of the Penis and Prepuce

Tumours of the penis and prepuce are fairly common in the horse, mule, ass, and dog, less common in the ox, and very rare in other species. They comprise papillomata, fibromata, sarcomata, melanomata, myxomata, adenomata, carcinomata, and cysts.

The Horse.—Papillomata, fibromata, and carcinomata are the varieties most frequently met with in the horse. Papillomata, warts, or angleberries are particularly common on the sheath. They may be isolated or multiple. They often occur in clusters, and when infiltrated with urine round the preputial orifice give rise to a fœtid odour. Maggots may appear between them in the summer. Fibromata are subcutaneously situated in the form of " apple " or " potato " tumours, which escape when an incision is made over them, or fall out spontaneously in some cases through sloughing of the overlying skin. Carcinoma is usually confined to the penis, forming an angry, fœtid, granular-looking mass round the glans.

TREATMENT.—Complete excision is the only effective remedy. Papillomata may be so numerous and so close together that radical operation would involve the removal of too much skin ; then the operator must be content with excision of them on a level with the latter, and repeat the operation when they recur. Carcinoma or any malignant growth on the penis necessitates amputation of the organ.

The Ox.—Papillomata may form a cluster round the preputial orifice. They may be attached inside and only protrude when the penis is extended ; occasionally the organ itself is involved.

The chief difficulty in removal of growths on the penis is to get the organ exposed for the purpose. It, however, protrudes spontaneously under the influence of epidural anæsthesia (see p. 208). If it cannot be protruded after casting and anæsthetising the beast, it is best to incise the sheath at the level of the tumour, draw the penis partly through the wound with the finger, and then excise the growth. The thermo-cautery may be lightly used to arrest hæmorrhage. When the beast is completely anæsthetised, it is generally fairly easy to protrude the penis from the sheath if spontaneous protrusion does not occur.

The Dog.—Venereal tumours, sometimes called infective sarcomata, are common in the dog, affecting the surface of the penis and more or less of the lining of the sheath. The commonest seat of the growths is the base of the penis and the sheath in this vicinity, but any

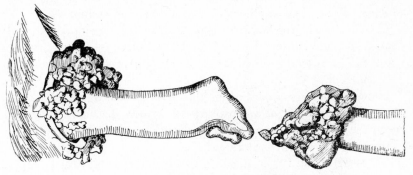

FIGS. 313 AND 314.—VENEREAL TUMOURS OF THE PENIS IN THE DOG.

part of the organ may be affected, and in some instances it is practically covered with them. The disease also affects the vulva and vagina of the female, and is transmitted from one sex to the other by copulation. The condition would appear to be of bacterial origin, but no causal organism has been found in connection with it.

SYMPTOMS.—The first symptom observed, as a rule, is a sanguinolent discharge from the prepuce. When the new growths are well developed, they cause a swelling of the sheath at their level. On exposing the penis, the cauliflower-like enlargements are readily recognised.

TREATMENT consists in complete excision of the tumours. When practicable, it is advisable to suture the membrane over the site of excision. When the tumours are very numerous, successive operations at intervals of a week may be necessary. If there is a suspicion of recurrence in the operation wound, the latter should be cauterised with silver nitrate. It is usually possible to operate even on the base of the penis after protruding it from the sheath, but if necessary the latter may be incised at its depth to facilitate removal of a tumour in that region, the preputial wound being afterwards sutured. Care must be exercised in examining stud animals, lest they be affected with this disease.

Paralysis of the Penis

ETIOLOGY.—Paralysis of the penis may be the result of an injury causing more or less damage to its nerves, or it may be of toxic origin, accompanying some bacterial disease, such as influenza in the horse. The penis in the horse may hang limp as if paralysed when the animal is debilitated from any cause. Numerous cases of this kind were observed in military horses during the First World War as the result of exhaustion. The condition seldom occurs in other animals.

SYMPTOMS.—In the horse the penis hangs inert in front of the hind-limbs. Its skin is generally thrown into transverse folds, and after the organ has been long exposed it may become fissured and ulcerated on its surface.

PROGNOSIS varies according to the cause of the affection. When the result of debility or a constitutional disease, it usually disappears when the patient recovers its normal health. When the nerve supply is permanently cut off the case is hopeless.

TREATMENT consists in prescribing suitable remedies for the cause of the trouble, when it is apparent, and adopting the usual measures for combating paralysis, including massage of the retractor penis between the anus and scrotum, and electrotherapy. When the paralysis appears without obvious cause or is associated with progressive paralysis of the hind-quarters, treatment is of no avail. If the horse is able to work, the penis may be supported and protected by a leather sling or, preferably, it may be amputated. In the case of the stallion, excitement of sexual desire by bringing the horse into the presence of a mare in season may stimulate innervation and favour recovery.

AFFECTIONS OF THE FEMALE ORGANS OF GENERATION

Exploration.—Diagnosis of affections of the genital organs may require careful and methodical exploration. It comprises *inspection* and *palpation*.

Inspection.—To inspect the interior of the vulva and vagina, and the os uteri, insert a vaginal speculum and illuminate the parts by means of an electric torch. Simply everting the lips of the vulva by the hands or fingers will enable a considerable portion of its interior to be viewed.

Palpation may be external or internal. Internal palpation may be vaginal or rectal. It is performed by the hand in the large animals, and by the index finger in the small animals. The patient being suitably controlled and aseptic precautions being taken, the hand or finger, lubricated with vaseline or liquid paraffin, is gently introduced into the vaginal passage.

Rectal examination in the large animal affords valuable information as to the condition of the uterus, ovaries, and Fallopian tubes. In small animals the uterus can be palpated through the abdominal wall by putting the patient on its back and compressing the abdomen with the fingers and thumb between the umbilicus and the pubis. To examine the cervix uteri in the cow, it is drawn backwards outside the vulva by means of a special forceps grasping the lip of the os.

Vaginal Irrigation may be effected by means of a syringe or india-rubber tube and funnel. The solution employed should be made with boiled water and used at the body temperature. Suitable lotions for the purpose are potassium permanganate (1 in 1,000), boric acid (4 in 100), lysol (1 in 100), carbolic acid (1 or 2 in 100), hydrogen peroxide (1 in 4 or 5), perchloride of mercury (1 in 2,000 or 5,000) containing 0·5 per cent. tartaric acid, acriflavine (1 in 1,000), solution of penicillin, etc. Any of these preparations used morning and evening will disinfect the vagina and os uteri when suffering from ordinary infection.

Uterine Irrigation is best performed by means of a rubber tube and funnel, the former being carefully introduced into the uterine cavity. A special bifurcated tube may be used with advantage having an inlet and an outlet portion, so that the fluid escapes from the uterus according as it is introduced instead of accumulating in the organ and requiring to be removed afterwards, as with the ordinary tube. It does not always work satisfactorily. The double-acting pump is also suitable when not worked too forcibly. It can be employed as an injector, and as an aspirator to remove the fluid from the uterus. The solution used should never be allowed to remain in the uterus. If it is not expelled by the expulsive force of the organ, it should be siphoned off or withdrawn with the aspirating syringe.

Toxic irritant preparations should be avoided. The following lotions used at the body temperature are suitable : potassium permanganate (1 in 1,000), biniodide of mercury (1 in 5,000 or 10,000) containing sufficient potassium iodide to ensure its solution, boric acid (3 to 4 in 100), lysol (1 in 100), hydrogen peroxide (diluted with 1 to 4 parts of water), iodine in weak solution (1 in 1,000 or 2,000) or in strong solution (2 or 3 in 1,000), carbolic acid ($\frac{1}{2}$ to 1 in 100). Perchloride of mercury (1 in 5,000) may also be employed, but it is not advisable for cattle, on account of their susceptibility to mercurial poisoning. Iodine solution is the antiseptic agent most in vogue at present for chronic cervicitis and metritis.

When the uterus contains much septic material, it should be first flushed with boiled water or normal saline until the liquid comes out clear ; then one of the agents mentioned can be introduced. Four or five gallons of water may be required to thoroughly wash out the uterus in the mare or cow.

R. H. Smythe (*Vet. Rec.*, July 25th, 1942) draws attention to the facility with which rupture of the bovine uterus can be caused by uterine injections, basing his remarks on experimental injections of methylene blue by means of a Higginson's rubber enema syringe into twelve healthy non-gravid uteri immediately after their removal from the warm carcases. His findings were :

(1) The fluid passing through the rupture does not enter the peritoneal cavity but goes between the double peritoneal folds of the broad ligament.

(2) The minimum amount of fluid to cause rupture was 6 ounces in Guernsey heifers and 10 ounces in young cows which had borne two calves.

(3) The margin of safety would appear to be 3 to 4 ounces in heifers and 6 ounces in multiparous cows.

He concludes that rupture in this way must have occurred in the past not by puncture, but by the force of the fluid. He has observed on several occasions that, using the quantities of liquid usually recommended, pain, straining, loss of appetite, and prolonged cessation of lactation ensued.

AFFECTIONS OF THE VULVA
Contusions

Contusions of the vulva are rare except as the result of injury during parturition. They present the usual features of a contusion, and are dealt with accordingly. A hæmatoma may result similar to that of the vagina.

Open Wounds

Open wounds are usually caused by injuries inflicted during delivery of the fœtus, but occasionally they are caused by external violence. The rig sometimes bites the vulva of the mare.

TREATMENT is on general principles, with the same precautions as for vaginal wounds when following parturition.

Rupture of the Perinæum

Rupture of the upper commissure of the vulva and a varying portion of the perinæum is occasionally caused during parturition, especially in primiparæ. The rupture may be :

1. *Incomplete*, in which the sphincter ani is intact ; or
2. *Complete*, involving the sphincter ani and the ano-rectal mucous membrane, and causing the vaginal and rectal cavities to become confluent, with the result that fæces and urine escape through a common orifice.

In both cases the separation of the lips of the wound and their constant soiling by excrement prevent their union. During progression the entrance of air through the solution of continuity into the vulva or vulvo-rectal cavity causes a noise, and the mare affected with the condition is consequently spoken of in some places as a " fluter." The edges of the wound are often jagged, and after cicatrisation form a fringe inside the vulva. Cicatricial bands may also be formed across the cavity. When the vagina and rectum are in communication, the former will contain fæces and its mucous membrane will be inflamed. The general health of the patient is not affected, but in the case of complete rupture the animal is hardly fit for work. Even when the rupture is incomplete, the " fluting " noise is objectionable and impregnation is likely to be interfered with.

TREATMENT.—Antiseptic lotions are indicated when the case is recent, to prevent septic complications. Immediate suturing of the wound is generally impracticable on account of its very uneven and damaged borders. If attempted, it would be necessary to first excise

the damaged tissues and make the borders even.   When cicatrisation
has already ensued, the following procedure may have the desired
effect in a case not involving the anus or rectum : Separate the mucous
membrane from the underlying tissue for a distance of about $\frac{1}{2}$ inch
from the edge of the rupture and throughout its whole extent. . Bring
the raw surfaces of the skin into apposition, and maintain them there
by Halsted sutures inserted through the base of the flaps.   Unite the
free borders of the latter by ordinary interrupted sutures.   Paint the
lines of sutures with tincture of iodine or collodion, and iodoform or
tinct. benz. co. (Fig. 315).

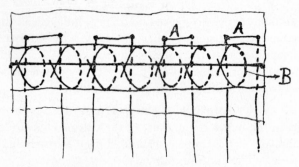

FIG. 315.—PERINEAL SUTURE.
A, Halstead suture through base of skin flap ;   B, interrupted cutaneous suture.

When the recto-vaginal partition has been divided it is more difficult
to obtain healing, but it may be effected by the above method after
first uniting the freshened borders of the divided partition by closely
applied interrupted sutures.

Vulvitis

Vulvitis may be the result of an injury caused by the penis, when the
vulvar orifice is very narrow, or by violence of any kind.   It coexists
with vaginitis, and may be symptomatic of a specific disease such as
horse-pox, dourine, or " foot and mouth disease."

The symptoms are those of inflammation or of the disease from
which it arises and the treatment is carried out accordingly.

AFFECTIONS OF THE VAGINA
Imperforate Hymen—Occlusion of the Vagina

Occasionally in the mare and more frequently in the heifer the
hymen remains imperforate.   It is usually white or roan heifers that
are affected, but the condition is also met with in others.   Occlusion
of the vagina may also ensue from cicatricial adhesion of its opposing

walls, following some inflammatory condition, causing desquamation of its epithelial surface. In either case, the mucous secretion in front of the obstruction accumulates and distends the vaginal cavity.

SYMPTOMS.—Attention is usually first attracted by the animal making violent expulsive efforts. In the case of persistent hymen, this generally occurs at the first œstral period or after being served by the bull for the first time. On rectal examination the fluctuating distension of the vagina is detected, and when the hand is introduced into the latter a partition, varying in thickness in different cases, can be felt traversing the cavity in front of the meatus urinarius, and fluctuation of the retained fluid may be recognised through the membrane. In some instances the hymen bulges outside the lips of the vulva when the patient is recumbent, and then simulates prolapse of the vagina. When the obstruction is due to adhesion between the walls of the vagina, the hand is arrested at this point. Defæcation may be difficult, owing to compression of the rectum, and cause further straining.

TREATMENT consists in giving exit to the retained fluid by incising or excising a portion of the persisting membrane or puncturing the occluded part by a stout, slightly curved trocar and canula about 15 inches long and $\frac{3}{8}$ inch in diameter and flushing out the cavity with an antiseptic solution. It is advisable to fatten the heifer for the butcher at once, as she is not fit for breeding, and, moreover, the condition may recur. The fluid present is generally thick and yellowish, but it may be blackish or reddish, and it is always very fœtid. Its quantity varies ; it may amount to a couple of gallons. Straining continues for some time after the operation, but when the irritation caused thereby passes off it ceases. Vestiges of the hymen in the form of bands stretching across the vagina may persist and interfere with parturition. It is generally sufficient to sever them with the knife or scissors to allow delivery to be effected. The resulting hæmorrhage is insignificant.

Wounds of the Vagina

Wounds of the vagina are most common in the large animals, and are usually produced during parturition by extraction of a fœtus in a malposition or by obstetrical instruments. Occasionally the vagina is ruptured by the penis during service, and several cases have been recorded of sadism in which the passage was more or less severely wounded by the insertion of a stick or some rough instrument, the wounding body in several instances penetrating the peritoneum, bladder, or rectum.

PROGNOSIS.—The possible complications of vaginal wounds comprise :

1. *Hæmorrhage*, which may prove fatal. Post-partum bleeding is usually from the vagina.

2. *Prolapse of the bladder* through a rent in the vaginal floor.

3. *Prolapse of the bowel* through a perforation in the recto-vaginal cul-de-sac.

4. *Abscess formation* in the perivaginal tissues, the abscess bursting, as a rule, into the vagina, or rarely into the abdominal cavity.

5. *Peritonitis*, due to perforation of the peritoneal cavity in the first instance, or to an abscess opening into it, or to extension of vaginal infection, via the uterus and Fallopian tubes.

6. *Occlusion of the vagina* by inflammatory adhesions between its walls.

7. *Recto-vaginal or vesico-vaginal fistula.*

TREATMENT.—Wounds of the vagina which do not perforate the peritoneum are treated by antiseptic irrigations and by the intro-duction into the cavity of antiseptic pessaries. When the peritoneal cavity has been opened these measures cannot be adopted, as the agents employed would gain entrance thereto, and probably give rise to a fatal peritonitis. It is inadvisable to forcibly inject antiseptic solutions into the vagina for the treatment of vaginal wounds following parturition, as the force of the injection might drive septic material into the uterus. Gentle irrigation or swabbing of the affected part should be adopted, followed by the insertion of a pessary.

Recto-vaginal and vesico-vaginal fistulæ are usually the result of dystokia, in which one of the fœtal limbs traverses the vaginal wall. These fistulæ usually persist indefinitely, suturing of the orifice being impracticable except when the fistula is near the vulvar orifice. The author had such a case in a thoroughbred mare after foaling, on which suturing by means of a fully-curved needle was followed by closure of the fistula. It has been suggested to incise the tissues between the anus and the recto-vaginal fistula, and then perform the suturing advised for ruptured perinæum, but the procedure is not to be recom-mended.

Hæmatoma in the Vagina

A hæmatoma is sometimes formed in the connective tissue of the vaginal wall as the result of vascular rupture caused by forcible ex-traction of the fœtus when it is abnormally large or in malposition. When the extravasation is slight the blood is absorbed after a few days but when it is copious the hæmatoma persists and may become infected, terminating in suppuration, gangrene, or general infection. It is the dilated vaginal veins which are ruptured. Isolated cases of the vulvar and vaginal veins being in a varicose condition and bursting spontaneously during pregnancy have been recorded.

TREATMENT.—Cold antiseptic injections are indicated at first, with a view to arresting the hæmorrhage and preventing complications. If, after a couple of weeks, the hæmatoma shows no tendency to become absorbed, it should be incised and evacuated and washed out with an antiseptic lotion. Puncturing the swelling with a trocar and canula is not so satisfactory. Early opening of the hæmatoma, before the bleeding into it had completely ceased, might be followed by profuse and perhaps uncontrollable hæmorrhage.

Hæmorrhage from the Vagina

This usually results from wounds inflicted during parturition, but may be a sequel to the incision of a hæmatoma, as mentioned. It may be arrested by cold or hot douches, or by packing the vagina with sterilised towels, associated with a hypodermic injection of adrenalin or pituitrin.

Vaginitis

The various forms of vaginitis are acute or chronic, simple or specific, and sporadic or contagious. They are also classified, according to the nature of the lesion, as catarrhal, purulent, croupous, phlyctenular, ulcerative, phlegmonous, and follicular. Vaginitis may be primary or secondary to vulvitis or metritis. It may be a symptom of a specific disease, such as horse-pox, glanders, or dourine. In all cases the cause is bacterial.

Simple Vaginitis is commonly the result of injuries received during parturition, but it may also be caused by sadism or the use of irritating vaginal injections.

SYMPTOMS comprise a muco-purulent discharge from the vulva, swelling of its lips, and evidence of pain during micturition and defæcation. On manual examination the vagina is found to be hot, swollen, and painful, and when viewed by the aid of a speculum and torch its mucous surface is seen to be red and perhaps desquamated, or even ulcerated, depending upon the stage of the disease. In the croupous form its lining is covered by a yellowish-grey exudate, associated with necrotic areas and ulcerated spots.

PROGNOSIS.—The inflammation may rapidly undergo resolution, or it may become chronic. Bad cases may be complicated with gangrene which may terminate fatally from toxæmia or septicæmia.

TREATMENT consists in irrigating the vagina with warm, emollient, antiseptic solutions and administering laxative medicine. Any of the agents already mentioned may be employed (see p. 757). Liquid paraffin or linseed tea may be injected into the vagina as emollients. In the croupous form the false membranes must be removed and the affected areas swabbed with a comparatively strong antiseptic agent (hydrogen peroxide, potassium permanganate, etc.). Penicillin is indicated in bad cases, locally and parenterally.

Chronic Vaginitis is only characterised by a continuous or intermittent muco-purulent discharge which adheres to the lower commissure of the vulva. On examination by the aid of the speculum, the mucous membrane is found palish, thickened, and sclerosed, and perhaps ulcerated here and there. In cases following acute forms of the disease, in which there has been loss of substance, there may be stenosis or atresia of the vagina.

TREATMENT.—Astringent and antiseptic injections are indicated, such as sulphate of zinc or alum in 2 to 4 per cent. solution, or iodine (2 or 3 per 1,000), repeated daily until the discharge ceases. If much irritation and straining ensue, they should be discontinued for a while and pessaries used instead.

Contagious Vaginitis may be acute or chronic, and is variously spoken of as infectious vaginitis, exanthematous vaginitis, and granular vaginitis. A similar condition affects the covering of the penis and the lining of the sheath in the male, and the disease is transmitted from one sex to the other by copulation. The disease is dealt with in detail under the heading of " Contagious Diseases " in works on medicine and in those on obstetrics.

Prolapse (Eversion) of the Vagina

There are two forms of prolapse of the vagina, one in which there is merely stretching of the ligaments or tissue binding the vagina to the pelvic walls, and another in which these structures are ruptured. The former usually occurs during pregnancy and the latter during parturition. The condition is met with in all animals, but is most common in the cow and sheep.

ETIOLOGY.—The following are factors in bringing about the prolapse :

1. *Distension of the abdomen* by bulky food or a gravid uterus, or both, causing pressure on the pelvic region and tendency to push the vagina backwards.

2. *Lying in sloping stalls*, which, associated with No. 1, is the usual cause of the trouble in the cow. When the animal is recumbent, the lips of the vulva are everted and the mucous membrane of the vagina is protruded in the form of a pink enlargement of variable size in different cases. At first it only appears during recumbency, disappearing when the animal rises, but eventually it persists, and when it becomes irritated from exposure the patient strains and aggravates the condition.

3. *Expulsive efforts* during a difficult parturition rupturing the attachments between the vagina and the pelvis.

SYMPTOMS.—The prolapse is readily recognised. Occurring during gestation, it usually appears towards the end of the period (seventh or eighth month in the cow) in the form of a reddish tumour between the lips of the vulva, with a depression in its centre corresponding to the lumen of the passage. The mucous membrane is more or less inflamed and secretes a viscid exudate which agglutinates the hairs on the lower commissure of the vulva. The swelling is often soiled by excrement, and may be excoriated from contact with foreign matter. The form appearing during or subsequent to parturition is usually more voluminous and more serious than that accompanying pregnancy. The prolapsed mass may hang down between the thighs, and the opening of the urethra may be seen on its inferior aspect, and its bent position may prevent the escape of urine, distending the bladder and increasing the volume of the prolapse. The part becomes inflamed and painful from injury and exposure, causing the patient to strain incessantly. The os uteri may be visible in the centre of the prolapse. There may be evidence of febrile disturbance. The absence of cotyledons on the surface of the tumour in the ruminant shows that it is not a case of prolapse of the uterus.

PROGNOSIS.—Most cases of prolapse, when attended to early, are treated successfully. The longer the case is in existence, the more difficult it is to deal with. When there has been laceration of the perivaginal tissues and the prolapse is of long standing, new cicatricial tissue will have formed, rendering reduction of the mass difficult or impossible. In rare instances gangrene of the prolapsed part ensues, and sometimes leads to the death of the patient.

TREATMENT consists in cleaning the prolapsed part, returning it to its normal position, and maintaining it there, or if reduction is impossible amputating it. To perform reduction, have the animal with the hind-quarters on a higher level than the fore, push the prolapse gradually forwards, beginning at the part next the vulva, and when it has been returned inside the latter, pass the hand into the vagina and press the fist against the os uteri so as to stretch the vaginal mucous membrane and obliterate its folds, thereby ensuring complete reduction.   A possible accident during the procedure is rupture of the anterior vaginal wall and escape of the bowel, especially in the mare, due to violent straining.   General or epidural anæsthesia is indicated when the expulsive efforts are difficult to overcome.   If the bladder is distended, evacuate it by puncturing or by passing the catheter.   One of the following methods of retention is required to maintain the vagina in position until straining has ceased :

1. *A truss*, by means of which the lips of the vulva are so compressed by a rope that eversion of the vagina is impossible.

2. *Wire sutures* in the form of two stout pieces of copper or galvanised wire, with bayonet points inserted through the lips of the vulva and crossing the passage about 4 inches in from the vulvar orifice, the ends of the wire being then turned with pliers into the shape of rings to keep it in position.   This method answers the purpose well and causes no discomfort to the patient.   Two bicycle spokes with one end sharpened to a point and passed through the vaginal walls and fixed by an ordinary coat button on either end, as used by F. Daly, M.R.C.V.S.(Dublin), suit the purpose admirably.   One piece of galvanised wire passed through the lips of the vulva and having its ends twisted one round the other has been used successfully in the sheep.

3. *Tape sutures* passed deeply through the lips of the vagina, as in No. 2, a simple and effective method.

4. *West's clam*, whose sharp teeth grasp the vulvar walls.   Its application is very painful, and is strongly resented by the patient, but once it is in position it is well borne and proves very effective.   It is made in sizes to suit the cow, sheep, and bitch.

5. *Tying the wool* across the vulvar orifice usually has the desired effect in the sheep.

In all cases care is taken that urination is not interfered with.   The animal should be placed in position with the hind-quarters on a higher level than the fore-quarters, and a sedative draft should be administered to allay straining.

In the bitch, *hysteropexia* may be performed in a case of chronic prolapse of the vagina when other measures have failed.   It consists in performing laparotomy immediately in front of the pubis, drawing the uterus forwards in the abdominal cavity so as to stretch the vagina into its normal position, and then fixing it in this situation by suturing the body of the uterus to the abdominal wall.   The sutures are passed through the serous and muscular coats of the body of the uterus and of the lips of the parietal wound. The latter is closed in the usual way (Fig. 316).

Partial amputation of the prolapsed vagina is indicated in a chronic case which has resisted other methods of treatment and which would not be suitable for hysteropexia. It is effected by applying a ligature round the base of the prolapse, taking care not to include the urethra, and cutting off the portion behind the ligature. The latter may be of silk or india-rubber, the former being more convenient and quite effective. It is generally advisable to ligature the mass in two sections. The operation is most commonly required in the bitch, in which the prolapse usually involves only a portion of the circumference of the passage.

Tumours of the Vulva and Vagina

Tumours affecting the vulva and vagina comprise fibromata, sarcomata, carcinomata, lipomata, adenomata, and cysts. Generally speaking, neoplasms of these passages are rare. Cysts occur in the mare and cow. They may be congenital or the result of a hæmatoma. They vary in volume, are usually pedunculated, and contain a clear or yellowish serous fluid in which some flakes of fibrin may be floating.

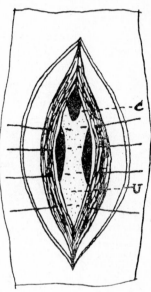

FIG. 316.—HYSTEROPEXIA

U, Body of uterus ;
C, Uterine horn.

The commonest vaginal growths in the bitch are venereal sarcomata of the same nature as described in connection with the prepuce and penis of the dog, and transmissible from one animal to the other by copulation. They cause a sanguinolent discharge from the vulva, and are readily recognised on digital examination covering more or less of the lining of the passage. A vaginal speculum is useful to enable the passage to be inspected to confirm diagnosis by palpation or to show up a suspicious spot that might not thus be detected. Polypoid fibromata are fairly common in the bitch. Carcinoma of the vulva is occasionally met with in the mare and cow, and appears to be more common in ponies than in larger horses. It involves the lips of the vulva and the clitoris. The surface of the tumour is ulcerated and angry, and emits a very offensive odour. Papillomata affect the same region, but do not present the features of the malignant growth. Polypoid cysts or neoplasms may remain undetected until the time of parturition, when straining causes them to appear between the lips of the vulva or protrude behind it.

TREATMENT.—Cysts in the large animals can be removed by the ecraseur when pedunculated. If sessile, they should be largely incised or partially excised, and their interior should then be treated with tincture of iodine, or 5 per cent. carbolic, or 5 to 10 per cent.

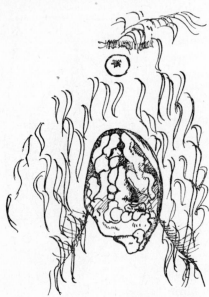

FIG. 317.—POLYPOID TUMOUR IN THE VAGINA OF THE BITCH.

chloride of zinc to destroy the lining of the cyst and promote granulations. Ligation is an alternative method of dealing with polypoid growths, and the most suitable one for the bitch.

Venereal tumours of the bitch require complete excision, adopting the following procedure. Use epidural or nembutal anæsthesia. Evert the lips of the vulva by means of artery forceps and by use of the scissors remove the tumours in the posterior part of the passage. Then grasp the wall of the vagina anteriorly with mouse-teeth artery forceps and evert it so as to bring the tumours there within reach and

remove them in the same way. The curette may also be used to scrape away small granulations. The operation may be supplemented by the application of powdered copper sulphate to the affected parts. It is repeated occasionally as seems necessary. After operation the vagina is irrigated with a suitable antiseptic lotion. The daily injection of liquid paraffin into the passage, as an emollient, is indicated until the wounds are nearly healed. Malignant neoplasms of the vulva and vagina are incurable, but benign growths can be successfully extirpated.

AFFECTIONS OF THE UTERUS

Most of the affections of the uterus are dealt with at length in textbooks on obstetrics, and will consequently be only briefly referred to here.

Atresia or Occlusion of the Os Uteri

This condition may be due to a neoplasm or cicatricial contraction. It renders impregnation difficult or impossible. It is diagnosed on digital examination.

TREATMENT.—When the opening is not completely obliterated, it may be dilated with the fingers or special dilators. The latter are essential for the bovine, in which the walls of the cervix are more rigid than in the mare.

Wounds of the Uterus

Wounds of the uterus may be confined to its mucous membrane or extend more deeply and perforate the abdominal cavity in some cases. It is only during pregnancy, when the uterus is distended and close to the abdominal wall, or at the time of parturition that the organ is liable to injury. The gravid uterus may be ruptured by violent impact of the abdominal wall against a fixed object. Wounds by the feet of the fœtus or by instruments or ropes may be caused during delivery in cases of dystokia. The organ may also be wounded when prolapsed, from a neighbouring animal treading on it, or by bites from dogs or pigs, or it may be ruptured in the act of reducing it.

SYMPTOMS.—Uterine wounds are accompanied by more or less severe hæmorrhage, which may be sufficient to cause death within a short time. When the rupture extends through all the coats of the organ, prolapse of the bowel or omentum may ensue, and death from peritonitis usually follows. Rarely, and most frequently in the bovine, recovery takes place after perforating wounds occurring during parturition. The womb in the bitch is very apt to be ruptured by obstetric forceps if great care is not exercised. When the patient vomits, it is usually a sign that rupture has taken place.

PROGNOSIS.—Death may ensue from hæmorrhage or peritonitis, as indicated. Even superficial wounds at parturition may lead to a fatal metritis. Perforating wounds of the upper wall of the uterus are less serious than those of the floor.

TREATMENT.—In a case of rupture during gestation, all that can be done is to treat for internal hæmorrhage. Non-perforating wounds inflicted at the time of parturition are treated by antiseptic irrigation and antiseptic pessaries. If there is any suspicion that the uterus has been perforated, irrigation should not be adopted for fear of the liquid entering the peritoneal cavity. When the organ is perforated, there is no effective treatment for the condition. The administration of sedative medicine to allay straining may help to bring about spontaneous recovery. When hæmorrhage is profuse, measures to arrest it are indicated.

49

Metrorrhagia

Hæmorrhage from the uterus is usually the result of a wound inflicted during parturition, as mentioned, or it may be a sequel to the tearing away of maternal cotyledons when removing the placenta in the cow.

PROGNOSIS is always grave when the hæmorrhage is profuse, death supervening in the majority of cases. If due to a perforating wound death will ensue from peritonitis.

TREATMENT comprises : (1) Cold douches over the loins ; (2) injections of cold or very hot water into the uterus ; (3) packing the uterus and vagina with sterilised cloths and injecting normal saline subcutaneously or intravenously when the hæmorrhage is very profuse ; (4) the hypodermic injection of ergotin or pituitrin or adrenalin, pituitrin being probably the most effective. The packing material should be removed after twenty-four hours, and the uterus should be subsequently irrigated with a suitable antiseptic solution. Generous diet and the administration of tonics are indicated to recoup the animal's strength.

Metritis

Metritis will be only briefly alluded to as inflammation of the uterus due to the presence in its cavity of pathogenic bacteria, and characterised in the acute form by febrile disturbance, local inflammation, and an offensive muco-purulent discharge from the vagina, and in the chronic form by loss of condition and a constant or intermittent purulent uterine discharge unaccompanied by inflammation.

TREATMENT consists in each case in repeated irrigation by antiseptic solutions, and in the use of antiseptic pessaries, and in administering suitable medicine internally, including penicillin. An autogenous vaccine is indicated in chronic cases. Metro-peritonitis usually proves fatal. The condition is almost invariably a sequel to parturition.

For " Torsion of the Uterus," " Prolapse of the Uterus," and " Retention of the Fœtal Membranes " the reader is referred to standard works on obstetrics.

AFFECTIONS OF THE MAMMARY GLAND

Congenital Abnormalities

Congenital abnormalities of the mammary region comprise absence of the glands, supernumerary glands, absence of teats, supernumerary teats, and imperforate teats.

Absence of the Mammary Glands is exceedingly rare, and only occurs in cases of hermaphrodism.

Supernumerary Glands.—It is only in multiparous animals that the number of mammæ varies.

Absence of Teats is extremely rare, but isolated cases in which the teats were only represented by slight eminences have been met with.

Supernumerary Teats.—It is not uncommon to find one or two supernumerary teats in the cow. The extra teat may be alongside a normal teat or in the form of an outgrowth therefrom. It may interfere with the ordinary process of milking, or when the normal teat is being drawn milk may escape outside the pail from the accessory one.

TREATMENT consists in excising the supernumerary teat before the gland becomes active, and suturing the wound. The operation should not be done during lactation, owing to the risk of infection of the udder supervening and the difficulty or impossibility of obtaining healing of the wound on account of the milk constantly passing through it.

Imperforate Teats.—Imperforation of one or more of the teats is occasionally met with in the cow. As a rule, only one teat is involved. The obstruction is usually at the lower extremity of the duct, but it may be in the form of a membrane between its upper part and the galactophorous sinus.

SYMPTOMS.—When it is the lower orifice of the duct that is imperforate, the condition is revealed after the first parturition by the affected teat being abnormally distended, shining, and sensitive on palpation, and by pressure thereon failing to express the milk. On examination of its tip the orifice is found to be absent. When the obstruction is at the origin of the duct, the teat is undistended and feels more or less solid.

TREATMENT.—The obstruction of the orifice may be cleared by the insertion of a milk siphon or, if this is insufficient, of a suitable trocar and canula, the latter being left in position for some time. When the occlusion is due to a membrane traversing the upper part of the duct, it may also be punctured by a trocar and canula. In either case Morier's special curette may be employed (see Obstruction of Teats). It will be necessary to pass the milk siphon occasionally or to leave a wax bougie in position in the intervals between milking to prevent cicatricial contraction and stenosis. The strictest aseptic precautions are essential to prevent infection of the gland. The siphon should always be boiled immediately before use.

Contusions of the Udder

When the udder is distended or pendulous, it is subject to contusions from various causes. In the cow it may be trodden upon by a neighbour during recumbency. It may also be injured by the head of the suckling. In all animals the pendulous udder is apt to be struck against projecting objects.

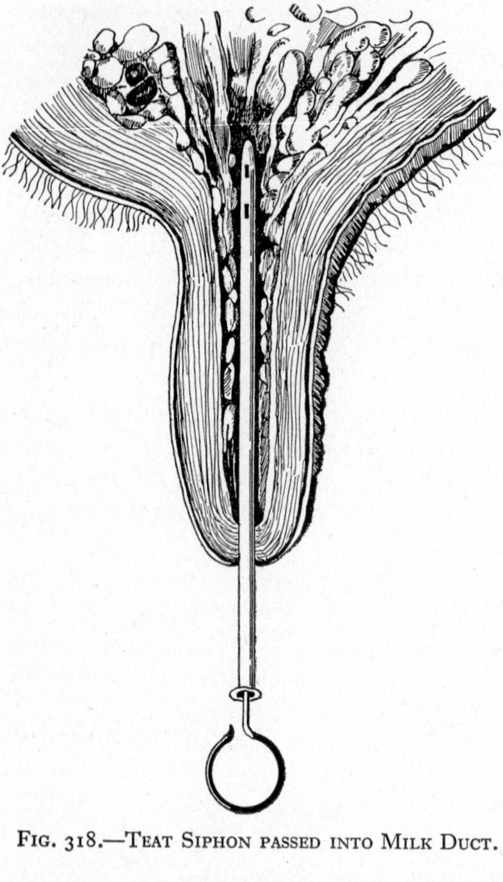

SYMPTOMS are as usual for a contusion — viz., local inflammation and more or less extravasation of blood. There may be a subcutaneous hæmatoma or hæmorrhage into the substance of the gland, characterised by the presence of blood in the milk. When the bruise is severe, gangrene may supervene. The injured part is prone to become infected, resulting in mastitis of the quarter affected or the formation of an abscess.

TREATMENT.—In slight cases the extravasated blood becomes absorbed, and the inflammation soon undergoes resolution. Cold applications are indicated immediately after the occurrence, to be followed by hot applications later. A thick layer of hot antiphlogistine, covered by a layer of cotton-wool kept in position by a suspensory bandage, is very beneficial. Antiseptic agents must be used to ward off infection through abrasions on the injured region. It is advisable to milk the affected quarter at frequent intervals. Massage, aided by the use of a stimulating liniment, will promote absorption of exudate and extravasate.

FIG. 318.—TEAT SIPHON PASSED INTO MILK DUCT.

Open Wounds of the Mammary Gland

The large distended udder of the cow is very exposed to injury, and is apt to be wounded by coming in contact with sharp or pointed bodies. Barbed wire is a frequent cause of lacerated wounds of the teat and gland, which may also be bitten by dogs, while goring by the horn of another beast also occasionally occurs. Even superficial wounds are serious when the organ is active, owing to the risk of the glandular tissue becoming infected therefrom, while deep wounds of the parenchyma are almost invariably followed by mastitis, and when accompanied by much contusion, give rise to gangrene. The escape of milk through open milk ducts retards or prevents healing, a milk fistula usually persisting when a large duct, especially that of the teat, has been penetrated. Very narrow punctured wounds of the teat duct only give exit to milk during milking. Wounds of the gland, when it is not secreting, are of no more consequence than those of ordinary tissue, except in so far as some of the parenchyma is replaced by a cicatrix.

TREATMENT.—Superficial wounds of the gland and teat are treated on general principles. Perforating incised wounds should be sutured and sealed with collodion, with a view to obtaining primary healing, but those accompanied by bruising must be left open and frequently irrigated with an antiseptic solution in the hope of securing healing without infection of the quarter, not forgetting the virtues of penicillin against gram positive bacteria. For perforating wounds of the teat two series of sutures are indicated (see Milk Fistula). When the lesion is on the teat, milking may be performed by compressing the teat with the finger and thumb without touching the wound ; if not, the milk must be drawn off with a milk siphon under the strictest aseptic precautions. The application of cocained vaseline on the teat may enable it to be milked without resentment by the patient.

Milk Fistula

A milk fistula may originate as follows : (1) Rarely it is congenital when it is usually found on the postero-internal aspect of a hindquarter, where a supernumerary teat is commonly found ; (2) it may be due to excision by the owner of a supernumerary teat in a calf without suturing the wound ; (3) the most common cause of the condition is a perforating wound of the gland or teat during lactation.

PROGNOSIS.—A fistula in the gland involving some of the small ducts usually heals spontaneously, but a fistula on the teat is exceedingly difficult to close during lactation, owing to the large amount of milk constantly passing through it. The chief gravity of the condition is that it favours mastitis by (1) leaving a way open for infection of the gland, and (2) keeping the organ and the floor of the shed wet and dirty through the constant escape of milk, when the opening is large. If the fistulous orifice in the teat is very small, milk will only escape when the gland is fully distended or during process of milking. In the latter case it is generally impossible to direct the two streams of milk into the pail.

TREATMENT comprises one of the following methods : (1) The application of a blister round the orifice ; (2) cauterisation of the edges of the opening by the actual cautery or a potential caustic ; (3) suturing the borders of the fistula after freshening them, if necessary, taking care not to include the mucous membrane in the suture, which would prevent union of the cutaneous edges. Nos. (1) and (2) may be said to be useless for a fistula on the teat, and even No. (3) usually fails in this case.

The following method of operation, recommended by Moussu, may prove successful : (1) Having injected a local anæsthetic, pare

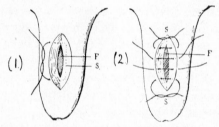

FIG. 319.—Milk fistula. (1) deep suture—schema showing the course of the suture ; F, base of the fistula; S, suture ; (2) superficial interrupted suture.

away the callous surface of the fistula : (2) using fine nylon thread insert a Halsted suture through the deep part of the wound, penetrating the skin only on the side of the wound on which the two ends of the thread are tied ; (3) bring the edges of the skin into contact with ordinary interrupted sutures ; (4) seal the wound with collodion ; (5) insert a milk tube and fix it in position by strips of plaster, to allow the milk to escape through the teat orifice instead of entering the fistula. The operation must be performed with strict aseptic precautions. As a rule, however, it is hardly worth while operating until the animal has gone dry. The application of penicillin to the wound, and its introduction into the quarter through the teat duct, are indicated to ward off an attack of mastitis.

Gold (*Vet. Rec.*, Oct. 2nd, 1943) excises the callous borders of the fistula, removing a piece of tissue like the segment of an orange and then sutures as follows, using silkworm gut. The needle and thread is passed through the lips of the wound thus : (1) through the skin $\frac{1}{2}$–1 centimetre from its edge down to but not including the mucous membrane ; (2) the same course reversely on the opposite side ; (3) through the skin on this side 2–3 millimetres from its border ; (4) through the skin on the opposite side 2–3 millimetres from its border thereby everting the skin and ensuring close apposition of the deep and superficial parts of the lips of the wound. He removes the sutures in 10–14 days, the wound having been left intact in the meantime.

Fissures or Cracks in the Teats

Fissures or cracks in the teats are common in bovines, young cows and fine-skinned animals being particularly liable to them.

ETIOLOGY.—When the teat is very distended in the newly calved cow its epithelium is apt to crack, especially when the skin is left wet after milking or sucking, and exposed to the effects of cold, frosty weather. The friction caused by the hands of the milker or the mouth of the suckling aggravates the condition, and the cracks become deeper and very sore.

SYMPTOMS.—The cracks appear parallel to the circumference of the teats, and vary in width and depth according to the length of time they are in existence. Their borders may be thickened, raised, and callous, and their depth is of a greyish or red colour, and contains a certain amount of whitish, greasy material. The lesions are very painful, and the animal becomes fidgety and restless when they are touched. She will not allow the teat to be milked or sucked. The milk consequently accumulates in the quarter, which becomes uncomfortably distended, and acute mastitis may thus be a sequel of the condition. When the tip of the teat is involved, the inflammatory exudate may seal its orifice and prevent the flow of milk.

TREATMENT.—Preventative treatment comprises drying the teats when they are wet, and protecting the animal from inclement weather. Smearing a little glycerine, lard, or a mixture of lard and glycerine on the teat after drying it has a protective effect. When cracks are present, the teat should be immersed in an antiseptic bath for a while, then carefully dried and smeared with boric or ichthyol ointment, or with one of the following preparations : Liquor plumbi subacet. ℥iii. and glycerine or olive oil ℥xvi., or carbolic acid ℥i. and glycerine O.i. Deep indolent cracks require to be cauterised with the silver nitrate stick. It is usually necessary to draw off the milk with the siphon, as milking by the hand prevents healing of the cracks, and will not be tolerated by the patient. For the same reason the suckling must be weaned or put on a foster-mother. When the point of the teat is covered by a scab or exfoliated epithelium, the latter should be softened with a little glycerine or vaseline to favour its removal. A wax bougie should be inserted to keep the opening patent.

Obstruction of the Teats

Acquired obstruction of the teats may be complete or incomplete. It is most common in milch cows. The obstruction may arise from : (1) Inflammation and thickening of the mucous lining of the duct ; (2) a polypus or polypi in its interior ; (3) a partition across the duct ; and (4) milk calculi more or less occluding its lumen. When there is complete occlusion of the duct, the galactophorous sinus and the teat above the point of obstruction are distended with milk, which cannot be made to flow by the act of milking. If the occlusion is partial the milk can be forced out in a thin stream, and the cow is difficult and tiresome to milk. The additional force required to expel the milk may irritate the mucous membrane and promote the formation of new fibrous tissue, which further diminishes the lumen of the duct. In this way contraction or spasm of the sphincter may be followed by fibrous thickening and increased obstruction to the flow of milk.

Papillomata, or polypi, occupy a variable position inside the teat. A small wart may protrude through the meatus and coexist with other warts on the skin of the teat. When higher up the duct, it can be felt as a nodosity or kernel between the finger and thumb. Inflammatory thickening with obstruction of the teat canal also varies in its situation and extent. It may be in the form of a circumscribed nodule or a cord-like structure involving the greater part of the duct. The former is usually in the middle part of the teat, and feels like a pea, which can be displaced somewhat upwards and downwards. More than one teat may be affected in this way. The latter is cylindrical in shape and rigid on palpation. When recent it is sensitive or painful on pressure, but when chronic it is painless. These lesions would appear to be of bacterial origin.

Obstruction by a partition or septum between the sinus and the canal is produced during the period when the gland is inactive, towards the end of gestation, affecting teats which up to that time were easy to milk. It appears to be due to hypertrophy of and adhesion between the folds of mucous membrane developed at the region mentioned. When the occlusion is complete, the sinus is distended and the teat is flaccid ; but if there is a slight orifice, milk will pass drop by drop into the duct and escape in a normal jet when the teat is milked, after which the duct will be slow to fill again.

Treatment.—The following are methods of dealing with obstruction of the teats :

1. When the duct is merely constricted at a point, it may be dilated by the repeated insertion of a metallic sound or bougie, and by keeping an antiseptic wax bougie in position in the meantime. Even when this is done with aseptic precautions, there is a risk of the quarter becoming infected and acute mammitis ensuing.

2. When dilatation is insufficient, the stricture may be incised by a special knife introduced into the duct, an antiseptic bougie being left *in situ* in the intervals between milking. A very narrow-bladed tenotome may be used to make the incision, or Guilbert's teat knife may be employed for the purpose (Fig. 320). This procedure is even more risky than No. 1, owing to the greater tendency of mammitis to ensue from infection of the operation wound. Moreover, the cicatricial contraction which follows the healing of the incision usually increases the stricture, despite the use of dilating bougies. When the constriction is confined to the tip of the teat, Stinson's method of operating by a crucial incision proves almost invariably successful (see p. 487).

Fig. 320.— Guilbert's Teat Knife.

3. When the obstruction is in the form of a partition between the sinus and the duct, it may be recognised as a circular thickening at the base of the teat. If a small opening still remains, it may be dilated as in No. 1 ; but if this is not sufficient, multiple incisions may be made in the thickened tissue by means of a *bistouri caché* made for the purpose. Good results have been reported after the use of this instrument. Nevertheless, the sequelæ mentioned are to be feared. Operation by Hudson's method has proved very successful for this condition (see p. 488).

4. Fibrous callosities and polypi on the mucous membrane of the milk duct may be pierced by a trocar and canula, or removed. Removal may be effected by a cone-shaped instrument pushed up and down the duct (Fig. 321), or by a knife after making an incision into the duct at the level of the lesion. The special instrument referred to is composed of a metal rod about $\frac{1}{12}$ inch in diameter, terminated at one end by a ring and at the other by a hollow cone with a sharp-edged periphery, by means of which the excision is performed. Different sized cones may be screwed on to the handle. When the knife has been employed, the wound is sutured by the method described for closing a milk fistula.

5. When the foregoing methods have failed and the stricture occurs in the lower part of the teat, but too high for Stinson's method, the teat may be amputated above the affected part. The operation is facilitated by grasping the teat by Kühn's special forceps. The resulting hæmorrhage is slight. The escape of milk is prevented by the application of a rubber band on the stump, exerting moderate pressure. After a few weeks a new sphincter will have developed, when the milk will again be retained or only allowed to escape in drops. The band is then dispensed with, and the teat is milked in the ordinary way.

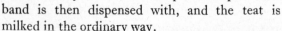

6. When the induration of the duct is recent, it may possibly be cured by ceasing to milk the quarter by " stripping " the teat, using the milk siphon instead, and by gently massaging the teat three or four times a day after smearing it with a little belladonna ointment. When the condition is chronic, the case is incurable.

Notwithstanding the occasional success of the above forms of treatment, it is a wise rule to follow the example of many experienced practitioners and refrain from adopting them on account of the serious risks involved. It is better to allow complete occlusion of the duct to supervene, when the pressure of the milk in the affected quarter will bring about atrophy of its secreting structure, and cause the quarter to go dry, without endangering the health of the animal. A certain amount of compensatory hypertrophy will ensue in the normal quarters. The introduction of penicillin into the teat after operation should materially help to prevent the development of gram positive bacteria in the gland.

FIG. 321.—INSTRUMENT FOR REMOVAL OF POLYPI FROM THE MILK DUCT.

7. Milk calculi are not common. They are composed of 60 per cent. organic matter and 40 per cent. inorganic matter, chiefly phosphate of lime. They vary in size from a pea to a nut. As a rule, only one calculus is present, but there may be several. They may be situated in the small ducts of the gland or in the teat canal. It may be possible to force the calculus down as far as the teat orifice by compression with the fingers and thumbs, as in the act of milking, and it may then be extracted by a fine forceps, or it may be possible to expel it through the opening when the latter is kept dilated by an assistant.

Eruptions on the Gland and Teats

A vesicular and pustular eruption appears on the gland and teats during attacks of foot and mouth disease, cow-pox, gangrenous coryza, and cattle plague, but it may also be the result of local infection by common organisms. The vesicles of foot and mouth disease have distinctive features, being greyish in colour, and containing a clear liquid. They occur simultaneously in the mouth and on the feet, and are accompanied by febrile symptoms. The pustules of cow-pox form chiefly on the teats, are of a pale yellow colour, and are umbilicated. The buccal cavity is not affected, and there is no general disturbance. Three or four pustules are commonly found on each teat, and on bursting leave ulcers which are slow to heal. Malignant catarrh and cattle plague are readily recognised by their characteristic symptoms. A moist eczematous condition or a dermatitis of the skin of the udder, where it comes in contact with the inside of the thighs, is fairly common in newly calved cows, especially those with very large glands. It is due apparently to the constant contact of the two cutaneous surfaces, and of the friction between them during movement. The condition is excited by excessive exercise and by the parts becoming soiled by dirt or grit. When the inflammation is well marked, it is revealed by the animal being disinclined to move, by a straddling gait, and by the appearance of an offensive blood-stained discharge in the affected region. The cow is apt to remain in the recumbent position.

TREATMENT of the foregoing conditions is on general principles, The contagious diseases must be dealt with as such. The eruptions on the teats are treated with mild, warm antiseptic lotions and emollient ointments. Prophylactic measures are essential to prevent the spread of the disease to other members of the herd. The inflamed surface in the region of the groin must be cleaned with a mild, warm antiseptic solution (boracic acid), dried with gauze, and then smeared with zinc ointment or dusted with a mixture of boric acid and starch.

Congestion of the Gland

Congestion of the mammary gland is observed chiefly in the cow sheep, and goat immediately before or just after parturition.

SYMPTOMS.—The gland is abnormally distended, hot, and slightly painful, due to vascular congestion. There is no evidence of constitutional disturbance. The milk withdrawn from the organ is not altered except that it may have a pink or reddish tint, due to the presence of blood from ruptured capillaries. Rarely pure blood drips from the teat. The congestion usually disappears in the course of a few days, but it may be followed by mastitis, which is favoured by the distended condition of the gland.

TREATMENT.—Frequent milking of the gland is indicated, and is generally sufficient. Cold and astringent applications are useful. Bleeding from the jugular may be performed, but is rarely indicated. Leeches may be applied to the gland in small animals to relieve congestion.

Mammitis

Inflammation of the mammary gland (mammitis or mastitis) is observed in all animals, and is very common in the cow and sheep, particularly the former. It is popularly known in these animals in various districts as sore elder, garget, blast or flagging of the udder, udder clap, and downfall of the udder.

CLASSIFICATION.—Mammitis may be classified in various ways, as follows :

1. Acute, subacute, and chronic mastitis.

2. Parenchymatous, catarrhal (confined to the milk ducts), interstitial, and paramammitis. All three, however, are usually present, owing to the rapidity with which the disease spreads from one part of the organ to the other.

3. Purulent and gangrenous mastitis.

4. According to the method of infection—viz., *hæmatogenous*, by the blood stream ; *lymphogenous*, by the lymph stream : *galactophorous*, by the milk ducts.

For clinical purposes, the classification of acute, subacute, and chronic mammitis is the most suitable.

ETIOLOGY.—The cause of mammitis is the entrance of pathogenic organisms into the gland. These may be streptococci, staphylococci, most frequently, or bacilli. The infection may be monomicrobic or polymicrobic. The acuteness of the attack depends on the virulence of the organism or organisms present. The variety of the sources of infection accounts for the different degrees of gravity of the disease. Anything which favours the entrance into or development of bacteria in the organ is a contributory cause—for example :

1. *Secretory activity of the gland*, the disease being practically confined to the organ in the state of lactation, and being most common soon after parturition, when milk secretion is at its height. Even when the disease appears in a heifer it is usually associated with an abnormal secretion of milk.

2. *Retention of milk in the gland.* This is a fruitful source of trouble. Bacteria entering by the teat orifice find the accumulated milk in the duct and sinus a suitable medium for development, and consequently multiply there, and thence invade the rest of the gland and set up their pathogenic effects. Mere retention is not sufficient to cause the disease, as is proved by the fact that it does not ensue when a teat is blind after parturition, although the quarter is greatly distended with milk.

3. *Open wounds and eruptions on the gland and teats,* from which infection is very apt to spread into the interior of the organ.

4. *Retention of the fœtal membranes,* causing a septic discharge from the vagina which may contaminate the gland.

5. *Bad hygiene,* including dirty bedding and insufficient ventilation.

6. *Want of cleanliness on the part of the milkers,* milking the cows with dirty hands or contaminated with the discharge from an infected gland, and the careless use of teat siphons.

7. *Exposure to cold and wet, over-driving, and general maltreatment* after calving, lowering the animal's powers of defence, and allowing bacteria already present in the gland and ordinarily harmless to assume virulent characters.

8. *Moist warm atmosphere,* which favours the development of bacteria.

In veterinary patients, infection nearly always occurs by way of the teat duct. Hæmatogenous and lymphogenous infection are rare, especially the former. The latter may occur directly from septic lesions on the surface of the organ. The fact that the milk is in practically every case altered at the very onset of the disease indicates that the bacterial invasion took place through the galactophorous ducts.

SYMPTOMS.—Acute mammitis is always sudden in onset. The constitutional disturbance may be the first to attract attention, the animal being found shivering, straddling, and restless, with a staring coat, an anxious expression, quick, short respirations, suspended appetite and rumination, and a temperature which may attain 106° or 107° F. There is usually constipation, and sometimes gastric tympany. The secretion of milk is diminished or almost arrested in the healthy quarters of the gland.

The local symptoms are those of intensely acute inflammation. The affected quarter or quarters, including the teats, are enormously swollen, hot, hard, painful, and red in colour. The teat stands out prominently, hard and shining. The least interference with the affected region causes pain, and is resented by the patient. On drawing the diseased quarter, a yellowish or reddish-yellow serosity escapes. This is after-wards mixed with clots of casein, and becomes more or less purulent and fœtid. There may be subcutaneous œdema in front of and behind the gland.

When gangrene supervenes, the teat and affected part of the quarter become cold and insensitive, and purple or green in colour. If the teat is not obstructed, stripping it will cause the discharge of a port-wine-coloured putrid liquid. Crepitation may be detected on mani-pulation, due to the presence of gas. In many cases death ensues from septic intoxication, but sometimes the patient withstands the attack until sloughing of the dead part has occurred, when recovery rapidly ensues, although a considerable time will elapse before the animal regains the condition which it lost in fighting the disease. The first indications of recovery are the cow becoming brighter and commencing to feed.

Abscess formation in the gland is more frequent than gangrene, and of course much less serious. Although it is destructive of the gland tissue, it represents successful defence of the part against general infection. However, when several quarters are affected with diffuse suppuration, the patient is apt to succumb from the accompanying toxæmia.

When mammitis arises from infection through the lymphatic system on the surface of the gland, the constitutional symptoms are much the same as those described, but the local changes are confined for a while to the perimammary and interstitial tissue, the secretion showing little or no alteration. The parenchymatous tissue soon becomes involved, and then the secretion is profoundly affected. The most marked local symptom at first in this case is a painful œdematous swelling of the gland extending anteriorly and posteriorly well beyond the limits of the organ.

Suppurative mammitis may be accompanied in its later stages with synovitis, affecting chiefly the hock and fetlock joints, and characterised by stiffness, lameness, and local inflammation.

Cows that have been put dry in the late spring and put on to rich grass during the summer often become attacked with acute mastitis of one or more quarters during July or August. The hind-limbs become so stiff in some of these cases that the beasts are hardly able to rise. In all cases of acute mammitis the patient rapidly loses condition.

PROGNOSIS.—Acute mastitis is always serious, because the best that can be hoped for is that the animal will recover from the general effects of the disease, the affected quarter or quarters being lost for the production of milk.   There is a constant risk of infection of the healthy quarters from the affected one.   During subsequent lactation there may be a certain amount of compensatory hypertrophy of the quarters that were not affected.   Although evidence of infection has left a diseased quarter and it has undergone atrophy, organisms may remain latent therein during the period when the cow is dry and become active again after the next parturition, setting up a fresh attack of acute mammitis.   Gangrenous mastitis is more frequently followed by death than by recovery.

PREVENTION consists in avoiding as far as possible the causes of the trouble.   Mr. F. T. Harvey, F.R.C.V.S., and others, following his example, have succeeded in preventing "summer mastitis," occurring during the period when the cow is put dry prior to the next parturition, by injecting into the galactophorous sinuses and teat ducts a mixture of bismuth subnitrate and liquid paraffin, with due aseptic precautions. It prevents the entrance of infection through the teats, remaining *in situ* until milked out after the next parturition.

TREATMENT is very unsatisfactory, as little can be done to counteract the effects of the bacteria hidden in the small ducts and acini of the gland.   The ideal treatment would be to remove, destroy, or inhibit the growth of the causal organisms, but this is impossible.   The clinician must be contented with palliative rather than curative measures, including those indicated for febrile disturbance and local inflammation as follows :

1. *Internal treatment* comprises the administration of :

(1) *A purgative* to promote the elimination of toxins.   The more promptly it acts the better, and for this reason some prescribe eserine or arecoline, but magnesium sulphate is most commonly employed.

(2) *Laxative medicine* in repeated small doses when the patient is too weak for purgation, or after the effects of the latter have passed off. Magnesium sulphate combined with potassium nitrate as a diuretic is usually prescribed.

(3) *A diffusible stimulant*, indicated when the beast is shivering.

(4) *An internal antiseptic*, the best being sulphanilamide powder administered in the usual way with large commencing and gradually diminishing doses for a period of 5 or 6 days at 3 or 4 hourly intervals. (See p. 222.)   It has a more or less bacteriostatic effect on certain strains of staphylococci which are commonly the cause of acute mastitis.   Other drugs that have been used are quinine, salicylate of soda, and formalin, the last mentioned appearing to be the most efficacious in daily drachm doses well diluted with water.   It is believed to have some local effect

in being excreted by the gland. The other agents have a general febrifuge effect. Salicylate of soda is particularly indicated when synovitis is present.

(5) *Antitoxic serum or vaccine.* A polyvalent serum might be useful, but a vaccine would probably cause an insupportable reaction in a patient already profoundly affected by the disease. Serum and vaccine treatment have, however, so far proved disappointing. The latter is more useful for chronic forms of mammitis. A serum and vaccine employed simultaneously should be more efficacious than either alone.

2. *Local treatment* includes :

(1) *Frequent stripping of the affected quarter* to remove as much as possible of the septic contents. This is an important indication.

(2) *The injection of an antiseptic solution*, which is only of benefit when the quarter has been well evacuated, and even then its effects are very disappointing. Acriflavin (1–1000), boric acid (4 per cent.) and hydrogen peroxide (1 to 4 or 5) are suitable for the purpose. The solution is diffused as far as possible through the quarter by gentle massage before being withdrawn. The inefficacy of the treatment is doubtless due to the solution's failure to reach the small tubes and acini of the gland. Even the infusion into the organ of a solution of penicillin is of no avail in this form of mastitis. If it is not carried out with strict aseptic precautions, it may aggravate rather than improve the condition. Schmidt, of Denmark, claimed good results from the infusion into the quarter of 4 ounces each of alcohol and glycerine, the preparation being left *in situ* for three days before being milked out. If more than one quarter is affected, only one quarter is dealt with at a time. A little normal saline solution may be added to the liquid.

A preparation known as Aureomycin Hydrochloride Ointment issued by the American Cyanamide Company, New York, has been found to be an effective bacteriostat against many gram positive and gram negative organisms invading the mammary gland of the cow. The ointment is infused from a tube with strict aseptic precautions after milking out the quarter. One infusion with the entire contents of the tube has been found to be sufficient to clear up an infected quarter. If not a repetition of the infusion on two subsequent occasions at 48 hours interval had the desired effect. The author has seen it used in one case of sub-acute staphylococcic mastitis with striking effect, the milk becoming normal and sterile after two infusions at 48 hours interval.

(3) *Hot fomentation of the gland* at least two or three times daily, accompanied by gentle kneading of the organ. This has a somewhat soothing effect, and seems to favour resolution.

(4) *Hot poultices* of bran, spent hops, or marsh-mallows, which constitute a favourite popular remedy, having much the same effect as No. (3).

(5) *A cataplasm of glycerine and kaolin* or " antiphlogistine " applied in a thick layer over the udder and covered by cotton-wool or flannel kept in position by a bandage tied over the loins, openings being left for the teats to enable them to be drawn out at frequent intervals. The dressing should be renewed every twelve hours. It seems to afford relief to the patient. The support given by the suspensory bandage has a comforting effect if it does not become displaced.

(6) *The application of an anodyne ointment or liniment*, such as green extract of belladonna, camphor, and glycerine, or belladonna liniment rubbed in with gentle massage after fomenting.

(7) *The use of a counter-irritant* in the form of a stimulating liniment or blister rubbed into the quarter, but kept clear of the teat, which should be protected by smearing it with vaseline. If an abscess is forming, its maturation will be accelerated and the pus will be brought nearer to the surface. Ammonia liniment, tincture of iodine, and biniodide of mercury ointment are the agents usually used. This treatment is only adopted, as a rule, after the very acute stage of the inflammation has passed.

(8) *Massage*, which is always associated with the application of ointments and liniments, and believed by many to account for the apparent good effects of these applications. It is condemned by some practitioners on the ground that it breaks down granulation tissue in the gland, thereby weakening its defence and facilitating the bacteria in extending their invasion of the organ. It should be practised lightly and superficially.

(9) *Opening of an abscess*. When deep-seated, the method described for opening a deep-seated abscess in a vascular region should be adopted ; otherwise profuse hæmorrhage may ensue. An alternative procedure is to use a pointed hot iron for the purpose. Exploratory puncture with a trocar and canula may be necessary to verify the presence or location of an abscess. A sinus may persist after the bursting of a chronic abscess for want of a dependent orifice or due to a callous lining in the cavity. When there is no systemic disturbance it is not advisable to operate to provide a counter opening or excise the callous tissue because the open wound thus produced may lead to acute or gangrenous mastitis, probably the death of the patient. This however may now be prevented by the administration of penicillin.

(10) *Amputation of the teat at its base or incision of its duct from top to bottom* to provide constant drainage for the septic material in the

50

gland. This is the most rational, and probably the most effective
remedy.   In a case of gangrene extending beyond the base of the teat,
it is always indicated, to allow the putrid liquid to escape.

(11) *Scarification*, indicated in cases of diffuse purulent mastitis to
allow the escape of pus from suppurating centres.   It may also be employed for a gangrenous lesion to provide exits for the toxic liquid, but
there is a risk in its use here of simultaneously wounding the living
tissue and opening the way for inoculation thereof by the putrefactive
bacteria.

(12) *Pyropuncture*, which may be adopted for gangrenous mastitis
or the interstitial form of the disease, the affected region being penetrated here and there by a hot iron to make openings for the escape of
septic liquid.   Moussu claims good results from it in cases of interstitial mastitis.   He punctures the œdematous area in the postero-
superior region of the organ.

(13) *Amputation of the gland* (see p. 432).

Subacute Mammitis

Subacute mammitis is a mild form of the disease due to the presence
of bacteria of feeble virulence, which only cause slight changes in the
gland structure.   The mode of infection is usually by way of the
galactophorous ducts, and it is the latter which are chiefly involved,
being affected with a catarrhal inflammation, causing desquamation of
their lining.   In well-developed cases the parenchyma of the gland is
affected to a varying degree.

SYMPTOMS.—There is not much constitutional disturbance, and the
function of the gland is only slightly impaired.   If the condition arises
on the surface of the gland, there is merely redness of the skin accompanied by a little œdema, and the milk is quite unaltered.   When there
is catarrh of the ducts, there is slight swelling of the teat and of the
quarter at the base of the latter, with more or less tenderness on manipulation.   At first the milk does not appear to be altered, but after a
while it loses its whiteness, and consists of yellowish serum and clots
of casein mixed with cast epithelial cells.   With suitable treatment the
inflammatory symptoms disappear, and the milk gradually returns to
the normal.   A considerable time should be allowed to elapse after
cure of the condition before making use of the milk for dairy purposes.
Although it appears normal it turns more quickly than usual, and may
spoil good milk if mixed with it.   The reduction in milk-secreting
capacity depends on the number of secreting cells that have been
destroyed by the disease.   There is always a certain amount of

atrophy and consequent loss of milk production subsequent to an attack.

TREATMENT is carried out on the principles laid down for acute mammitis.

Chronic Mammitis

Chronic mammitis arises independently or follows the acute form. Infection usually occurs by the secretory ducts, rarely by way of the blood or lymph stream.

SYMPTOMS.—Nodular hardness or diffuse induration is detected in the gland, slightly painful or painless on pressure. On milking the affected quarter, a serous liquid mixed with clots of casein is expelled. Occasionally an abscess or abscesses form in the affected region, and may burst externally or into the milk ducts.

DIAGNOSIS is easy when there is an abnormal secretion from the gland. Otherwise the condition might be confounded with a tumour.

PROGNOSIS.—The disease may undergo resolution, leaving a certain amount of induration in the organ, or it may continue to extend with increased sclerosis and additional destruction of parenchymatous tissue. The life of the animal is not endangered, but when more than one quarter is involved she is useless for dairy purposes, and is often difficult to fatten for the butcher.

TREATMENT is purely local, and consists in the application of iodine ointment or a biniodide of mercury blister. Antiseptic injections through the teat are not of much value, and if carried out carelessly may do more harm than good by setting up acute mastitis. When an abscess is detected, it is opened and evacuated. A vaccine is indicated when the case is persistent.

Contagious Mammitis.—There are various forms of chronic mammitis of a contagious nature affecting the cow due to streptococci of different degrees of virulence. One form studied in France by Nocard and Mollereau responds to prophylactic measures, including the injection of a warm 4 per cent. boric solution into the affected quarter, after milking, at intervals of a week. After three or four injections the disease is arrested. The injection of " Entozon," a Bayer preparation, nto the udder has given good results in the treatment of chronic streptococcal mastitis in cattle.

This disease may be present without causing clinical symptoms and without apparent alteration of the milk except when examined by the fore milk container (strip cup). Diagnosis may be verified by laboratory methods. The other measures are those usually adopted to prevent conveyance of the virus from one animal to another.

Two other forms occurring in Switzerland have been investigated by Tschokke, one being caused by a streptococcus in long chains, defying treatment, and the other by a streptococcus in short chains, quite amenable to treatment.

The commonest form of contagious mammitis in dairy cows is that due to the streptococcus agalactiæ, and this and certain other forms of streptococcic mammitis are promptly cured by the introduction into the affected quarter or quarters of penicillin either as an aqueous solution or incorporated in a non-irritant base of arachis oil with 4·5 per cent. white beeswax in single-dose tubes of 100,000 units of penicillin, the latter securing a steady and prolonged action of the drug in the udder. It is now generally agreed that a single dose of 100,000 units into each affected quarter is sufficient to effect a cure. The advantages of the tube method are that it is safe, simple, and convenient, the trouble of preparing the solution and the provision and sterilisation of teat-tubes being eliminated. Each tube is provided with a nozzle which fits into the teat duct and it is only necessary to have this and the teat sterilised to ensure that no infection is carried into the quarter during the procedure. There is, however, a certain amount of doubt with some practitioners as to whether this method is as efficacious as the injection of the aqueous solution. The writer has found the tube method quite successful. When the aqueous solution is employed meticulous care must be observed as to aseptic precautions, a different sterilised teat siphon being used for each quarter.

Bacillary mammitis, caused by a pyogenic bacillus, has been seen as an enzootic in dairy herds, assuming the catarrhal, parenchymatous, and interstitial forms of the disease, the two last mentioned being characterised by the presence of multiple purulent foci in the gland, destroying its function.

Tuberculous mammitis is usually of a chronic nature, causing induration of the gland. It can only be diagnosed by laboratory methods. According to Bang, about 3 per cent. of tuberculous cows have lesions in the udder. The supramammary gland may or may not be enlarged.

Actinomycosis of the mammary gland has been seen in the cow and sow, and *botriomycosis* in that of the mare. The lesions are of a chronic nature, and are diagnosed by microscopic examination of their discharges. Amputation is the most effective remedy.

Mammitis in the Sheep

Mammitis in the sheep is similar in most respects to that in the cow, but the gangrenous form in this animal deserves special mention. It is ushered in by hyperacute inflammation. The gland becomes voluminous, hard, hot, and painful, and bluish-red in colour, simulating erysipelas, and death of the organ soon supervenes. The swelling extends rapidly along the abdominal wall into the groin and upwards in the perineal region. Death of the patient may occur in the course of twenty-four to forty-eight hours. The disease is due to a specific micrococcus which is found in the interstitial as well as in the parenchymatous tissue of the gland, so that antiseptic liquid introduced into the ducts is powerless in counteracting its effects. The disease is not transmissible to the cow or goat by inoculation.

TREATMENT.—Notwithstanding the rapidly fatal nature of the disease, cure is reported to have followed the injection into the gland of ½ per cent. solution of carbolic acid throughout the periphery of the gangrenous area. The best treatment, however, is prompt extirpation of the gland (see p. 433).

Prophylactic measures are essential to prevent the disease spreading through a flock. Bridré has carried out successful vaccination with an attenuated culture of the micrococcus, and found that the serum of hyperimmunised sheep possessed protective properties.

Mammitis in Goats

There are two recognised forms of mammitis in goats—viz., purulent and gangrenous.

1. **Purulent mastitis** is characterised by acute inflammation and abscess formation. It is usually seen soon after parturition, and is believed to be due to a diplococcus.

2. **Gangrenous mastitis** is almost identical with that described in the sheep, but due to a different organism.

Prophylaxis and treatment are carried out on the usual lines.

Mammitis in the Mare

Mammitis is not common in the mare. The gland is comparatively small, far from the ground, and not so exposed to contamination as that of the cow. The disease may occur prior to parturition, or even to pregnancy, but as a rule it appears during lactation.

ETIOLOGY.—The etiology is infection of the gland, the causal organism being usually a streptococcus. Early weaning of the foal when the organ is in full activity is a predisposing cause. Septic discharges about the mouth and muzzle of the foal may cause the disease, as in a case of strangles or stomatitis in the young animal.

DIAGNOSIS is easy, the symptoms being similar to those described in the cow.   The condition frequently terminates in abscess formation and induration.   Gangrene occurs occasionally.   The disease often becomes chronic when a large amount of fibrous tissue is formed giving the lesion the appearance of a neoplasm or of botriomycosis.

PROGNOSIS.—When gangrene occurs, the mare usually dies.   The gland is always lost as a secretory organ, and the mare will not be able to rear a foal.

PREVENTION consists in avoiding as far as possible the predisposing and exciting causes of the disease.   If the mare is long separated from the foal, as during working, some of the milk should be drawn off with the hand.   It may be necessary to do this at weaning time, if the gland is very full of milk.   Purgation and the local application of vinegar or extract of belladonna or alum favour drying of the organ.

TREATMENT is on the same lines as in the cow.   When the gland becomes enlarged and fibrous, with pus in its centre, amputation is indicated (see p. 433).

Mammitis in the Bitch

Mammitis is occasionally met with in the bitch, in which it is caused in the same way as in other animals, and characterised by the same systemic disturbance and local phenomena.   The disease may affect one or more glands.   In diffuse virulent forms of the affection, death usually ensues.   A chronic mastitis may follow the acute forms recognised by enlargement and hardening of two or more glands, resembling mammary tumours.

PREVENTION consists in observing hygienic measures in kennels, and weaning the pups gradually.

TREATMENT is on the principles laid down for the cow, the local measures to be adopted comprising *hot bathing*, having the patient standing in a bath for the purpose ; *cataplasms* of " antiphlogistine " ; *stripping affected glands*, *removing the offspring*, and milking the healthy glands ; *gentle massage* with an anodyne ointment or liniment ; opening of abscesses when present ; and the excision of fibrous enlargements in chronic forms of the disease.

General treatment consists in administering a purgative, a sulphonamide preparation or penicillin together with good nursing.

Mammitis in the Sow

Mammitis is rare in sows that are well cared for.   It occurs in those exposed to hardship and living in dirty surroundings or in places where the gland may come in contact with projecting objects—

sticks, stones, barbed wire, etc. In snowy weather it may become frost-bitten from contact with the snow, and infection may spread from the surface lesions into the gland. The disease is very similar to that occurring in the bitch, and is dealt with accordingly.

Tumours of the Mammary Gland

Tumours of the mammary gland are rare in the mare. Papillomata are extremely common on the teats in cows, but, apart from these, the bovine mammary gland is seldom the seat of a neoplasm. Pigs and sheep are singularly free from mammary growths, but the bitch is very subject to them.

The following varieties of tumours have been found in the mammary gland in the domesticated animals : papillomata, fibromata, myxomata, lipomata, sarcomata, carcinomata, and adenomata.

Papillomata on the Teats

Papillomata, or warts, occur frequently on the teats of cows of all ages, but most commonly on those of young cows. They may be isolated or multiple, and are usually in the form of small papillary processes. Rare cases have been seen where the warts attained a length of 2 to 4 inches, and were so numerous over the teats and glands that they gave to the organ a cauliflower-like appearance. Sometimes the warts in clusters ulcerate and assume an angry appearance. Occasionally, also, the warts become cracked at their base. Warts may be present on the teats without causing any trouble during milking, being non-inflammatory and causing no pain when compressed by the hand ; but if they are ulcerated or cracked, they are very painful on pressure, and the patient will not tolerate drawing of the affected teats.

TREATMENT.—Warts should be removed at such a time before parturition that the wounds will be healed when milking or sucking is commenced. They can be readily snipped off with a scissors after controlling the cow in the standing or cast position, according to the nature of the case. If present during the milking period, and ulcerated or cracked, antiseptic precautions must be taken to prevent mammitis, and the milk must be drawn off with the teat siphon until the warts are removed and the resulting wounds healed. Touching isolated warts with nitric acid without burning the surrounding skin is an effective way of enucleating them without making a fresh open wound. The repeated application of an ointment made with salicylic acid and vaseline may cause them to separate and fall off. As there is evidence of warts being contagious, affected cows should be isolated.

Mammary Tumours in the Bitch

These comprise all those mentioned already. Chondromata, fibromata, and carcinomata are probably the most common forms met with. In some cases the apparent tumour would appear to be the result of a chronic mastitis.

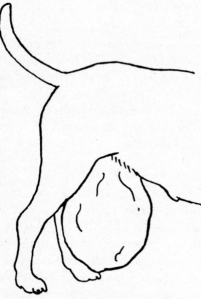

SYMPTOMS. — The tumour varies in size from a walnut to a man's head. The large growth is pendulous, and may almost reach to the ground. The chondroma sometimes becomes ossified. Frequently the tumour, although non-malignant, has a necrotic centre, leading to the formation of a sinus. A tumour in the groin may conceal an inguinal hernia or appear alongside it.

FIG. 322.—LARGE MAMMARY TUMOUR IN THE BITCH.

TREATMENT consists in complete excision of the tumour, taking care to look out for a hernia when the inguinal region is involved. Although the operation wound may be very extensive, cicatrisation is rapid, and complete recovery ensues provided that the growth was not malignant.

AFFECTIONS OF THE TAIL

Open Wounds of the Tail

OPEN wounds of the tail are caused by direct violence (blows, crushing, etc.), rubbing the appendage against fixed objects in pruritic affections of the region (mange, oxyuridæ, and bots in the rectum and anus), and by friction or pressure of the crupper.

TREATMENT consists in removing the cause, if still operating, and applying antiseptic preparations to the wounds.

Rupture of the tail is occasionally met with in the ox, due to the appendage getting caught between two rigid objects and the animal pulling violently to release it, the separation usually taking place near its base. When the wound is irregular, it should be made even and then dressed antiseptically. It may be necessary to remove the remnant of a fractured vertebra.

Fractures of the Sacrum and the Tail

Fracture of the sacrum is rare. It most commonly occurs in the ox, due chiefly to its prominent position. It is usually caused by falling over an embankment.

SYMPTOMS.—When the anterior region of the bone is broken, with laceration of the spinal cord, paraplegia ensues. When the lesion is posteriorly situated, the tail is limp and powerless. In most cases there is deformity, characterised by a prominence or a depression. On rectal examination crepitation can be detected, and if there is depression of a fragment it can be felt as a swelling inside the rectum. There may be injury to pelvic organs (the rectum, bladder, vagina) or to important bloodvessels.

TREATMENT.—If paraplegia is present, the case is hopeless; otherwise treatment comprises reduction and retention. The former may be effected by means of the hand *per rectum* or by the aid of a lever protected by a pad inserted through the anus and supported on an upright post behind the patient to serve as a fulcrum. A charge placed over the sacrum will help to immobilise the seat of fracture. Supporting the tail by a crupper with a well-padded dock may prove useful in keeping the fragments in position. The deformity resulting from this fracture in the female may cause difficulty in parturition.

Fracture of the Tail

The tail, by virtue of its flexibility, is seldom fractured, but one of the first coccygeal vertebræ may be broken by direct violence. The lower part of the appendage may be fractured by crushing, especially in the dog. In the horse, the accident may occur through the tail being caught between the two cross-bars of a tip-cart.

SYMPTOMS comprise abnormal mobility, deformity, and crepitation. When the base is fractured, the tail is paralysed.

TREATMENT.—The padded crupper referred to above is suitable for a fracture at the base. Lower down an adhesive bandage answers the purpose. It must include the tip of the tail, otherwise necrosis of the latter may supervene. A plaster-of-Paris bandage may be applied over it, if necessary, in a large animal. In the dog, a leather sheath enclosing the tail will help a dressing to immobilise the seat of fracture. It is fixed forwards by a strap along the spine attached to a strap round the body and to one round the neck. When several vertebræ are crushed, amputation is indicated. This operation is also advisable in cases that have been neglected, and in which healing has occurred with the tail deviated from its normal direction. In the greyhound, every effort should be made to conserve the tail. When crooked after formation of the callus, it may be refractured and set straight.

Dislocation may accompany fracture. It is dealt with on similar lines. When the fracture is compound, it is treated on general principles.

Tumours of the Tail

The tail is not a common seat of tumours. Fibromata, sarcomata, and carcinomata have been seen affecting it in the horse. In grey horses, melanotic growths sometimes appear on the tail, involving it to a variable extent. They usually ulcerate and give rise to a blackish fœtid discharge.

TREATMENT.—If the tumour or tumours are benign and not interfering with the usefulness of the animal, it is generally better to leave them alone, as operation usually necessitates a large wound, encroaching on the vertebræ, which is slow to heal. If malignant, or ulcerated, or a source of pain to the animal, amputation should be performed.

Botriomycosis occasionally affects the tail in the horse. If not encroaching on the sacral region, the best treatment is amputation. If the latter is involved to a considerable extent the prognosis is grave, and all that can be done is to administer potassium iodide internally and use tincture of iodine locally, with little hope of success.

Dermatitis of the Tail

The horse's tail may be affected with dermatitis consequent on rubbing it against some fixed object when suffering from a pruritic affection, as mentioned in connection with open wounds. The injured part is devoid of hair, and more or less inflamed.

TREATMENT consists in dealing with the cause of the trouble.

The ox also may suffer from cracks or fissures in the skin of the tail as the result of symbiotic mange, whose treatment is indicated.

The dog is frequently affected with eczema of the tail, and the irritation which it produces causes the dog repeatedly to bite the part, aggravating and perpetuating the condition, so that it assumes the nature of an ulcer. The chief treatment consists in preventing the dog from biting the tail. The best way to effect this is by applying the tail guard mentioned (see p. 794) or the steel tubular device advised by Longley (see p. 438). It may be necessary to amputate the ulcerated part.

AFFECTIONS OF THE LIMBS

Lameness

DEFINITION.—Percival's definition of lameness is generally accepted as applicable to most cases—viz., " lameness is the manifestation in the act of progression by one or more limbs of pain, disease, weakness, deformity, or impediment." It may be maintained, however, that an animal evinces lameness when at rest by holding up a limb or allowing it to bear only a portion of its normal weight.

ETIOLOGY.—The etiology is manifest from the definition, and several examples of exciting causes of the condition will be dealt with in the succeeding pages.

DIAGNOSIS.—In many cases the diagnosis of the seat of lameness in a limb is obvious, but in others it is exceedingly difficult. It requires careful and prolonged observation of sound and lame horses in motion to become expert in locating the cause of obscure lameness. The novice may have difficulty in deciding whether a horse is sound or lame, or which limb is affected. To arrive at a diagnosis in a case of lameness it is necessary to ascertain (1) which limb is lame, (2) the seat of the lameness, and (3) the nature of the lesion.

1. *The Lame Limb*.—In order to recognise the affected limb, the animal should be examined at rest and in motion. When the lameness is well marked, the limb is held in an abnormal position during rest. The fore-limb is carried forward or partly flexed at the knee or fetlock. When the foot is kept in an advanced or backward position, it is said to be " pointed." In certain cases the limb is adducted or abducted.

The horse is in the habit of resting the normal hind-limbs alternately when standing by taking the weight off one hind-limb and holding the fetlock semi-flexed, but he never does this with the fore-limb except it is suffering from some painful condition. Frequent lifting of a hind- or fore-limb is an indication of lameness. Repeated shifting of the weight from one foot to the other is a sign of lameness in both limbs. When a lame horse is made to come over in a stall he treads lightly on the lame limb, and in a case of stringhalt or shivering lifts it spasmodically or in an awkward manner.

The subject, having been observed at rest, is then exercised at the walk and at the trot. When the lameness is pronounced it is detected at the walk, but when slight it can only be seen at the trot. Rarely a horse walks lame and trots apparently sound. It is advisable to watch the horse carefully when first trotted out, as ephemeral lameness may pass off with exercise. To facilitate the observer as much as possible, the horse should be trotted slowly in hand, without excitement, on level hard ground, pavement for preference, and in a halter or snaffle bridle, the rein being held about 18 inches from the cheek, so that the head will be free to oscillate with the movement of the limbs and yet be under control. There should be no trappings or clothing on the horse. A rider on the animal would impede the observer and interfere with the head movements of the subject. When the lameness is doubtful, it is advisable to have the horse ridden to increase the weight on the limbs, and thereby intensify the pain and make the lameness more evident when the horse is again trotted in hand. It may be necessary to gallop a horse, then rest him in the stable for upwards of half an hour, and trot him again in hand to bring out a latent or intermittent form of lameness, which becomes marked after rest following severe exercise.

The sound of the shod feet on pavement is a guide as to the presence of lameness, the lame limb being put down more lightly than the others, the sound caused when it comes to the ground is not so loud as that caused by the normal limbs. When the lameness is confined to one fore- or one hind-limb, there is a striking contrast between the sound of the lame limb and that of its fellow.

In fore-limb lameness, the movement of the head is an important indication as to the limb affected. When the lame limb bears weight the head is raised, and when the sound limb comes to the ground the head drops or " nods."

In hind-limb lameness, the movement of the head is not so noticeable. It is raised when the affected hind-limb bears weight. When a horse very lame in a hind-limb is walked, the head falls when the corresponding fore-limb reaches the ground.

The movements of the croup and haunch are also affected by lameness. In hind-leg lameness, at the trot, the croup is raised when the lame limb bears weight and lowered when the weight is transferred to the sound limb. In cases of severe fore-limb lameness, the croup is lowered during the trot when the hind-limb of the opposite side bears weight. At the walk it is different ; the lowering referred to occurs when the corresponding hind-limb is in support. The difference is explained by the limbs moving diagonally at the trot, while at the walk each fore-limb bears weight at the same time as the corresponding hind-limb. Therefore, to recognise lameness in front, the observer should watch the horse carefully when being trotted towards him, while for lameness behind he should pay particular attention to the animal's quarters as he is being trotted away from him.

Lameness is frequently accentuated on turning, owing to the extra pressure put on the lame limb when being used as a pivot in the turning movement. For this reason the horse should always be turned fairly sharply and observed closely when doing so. Stringhalt, shivering, and spavin lameness are most apparent at this time. It is also desirable to have the horse trotted past the observer, so that he may have a side view of the movement of the limbs.

Exercise up or down a gradient is better for revealing certain forms of lameness than exercise on the level. An uneven surface will aggravate swinging leg lameness (difficulty in taking the limb forward), owing to the impediment it offers to forward movement of the limb. Backing the animal is indicated to examine for shivering.

When both fore-limbs are suffering equally from some painful condition, the horse goes level and appears sound to the inexperienced observer. His gait is, however, "pottering," short strides being taken and the feet being placed on the ground in a stilty fashion. The patient appears stiff rather than lame. This is well shown in navicular disease affecting both fore-limbs. In double hind-leg lameness, both limbs are moved stiffly and the gait is suggestive of injury to the loins, particularly in well-marked cases, when the animal assumes a crouching gait. Backing is difficult in this case.

Diagnosis may be difficult when there is a combination of hind- and fore-leg lameness. Lameness in two legs of the same side causes an up-and-down movement of the head and quarters, due to the jerking up of the head as the affected fore-limb reaches the ground and dropping of the quarter as the sound hind-limb touches the ground. This, of course, does not apply to pacers. If the latter are lame in both legs of the same side, the body drops when the sound limbs bear weight and rises when the lame limbs come to the ground.

In a case of diagonal lameness—say near fore and off hind—the body rises as the lame limbs are put on the ground, and the head and quarter drop as the off fore and near hind reach the ground. Ordinarily, a horse lame in a hind-limb appears at first sight to be lame in the opposite fore-limb, and *vice versa* when trotted, due to both limbs contacting with the ground at the same time. This is spoken of as cross-lameness. To avoid an error, it is necessary to watch the fore and hind extremities separately, especially when lame in both places.   It is well to watch the way each limb is brought to the ground, and then it will be seen that the lame limb is put down with less force than the sound one of the other side, for in slight cases of lameness the movement of the head is hardly perceptible.   It is interesting to remark that a horse may be quite lame at the walk and sound at the trot. Griffin (Curragh, Kildare) had three such cases (two in the same place), in each of which the seat of lameness was obscure.

Peculiarities of gait such as the following must not be mistaken for lameness :

(1) *Bridle lameness*—that is, the horse appearing to be lame on the side from which he is led, especially when trotted in a circle with the leading leg inside.   When it is suspected, the animal should be led from the other side or trotted in a halter instead of a bridle.

(2) *Rolling gait*, seen in wide-breasted cart-horses, the horse rolling from side to side in the trot.

(3) *Dishing*—that is, winding outwards of the fore-feet after flexing the knees during the trot.

2. *The Seat of Lameness.*—When the seat of lameness is not obvious, a systematic procedure is necessary in order to locate it, as follows :

(1) Ascertain the history of the case and question the owner on all points that may assist diagnosis.

(2) Have the horse standing square if possible, and walk round him at a distance of a few paces, so as to inspect the limb from every angle. Compare corresponding parts of the sound and lame limbs.   Note the attitude of the limb at rest, and look out for peculiarities of gait at the trot and during turning and backing, which may help to reveal the affected part.

(3) Palpate the limb methodically in front, laterally, and behind from the withers or croup to the foot several times, examining different individual structures on each occasion, paying particular attention to the tendons and ligaments, and examining specially all the common seats of lameness.   In applying compression for the detection of pain, do the same on both limbs, lest when the animal winces he may do so from being naturally irritable.   Complete reliance is not to be placed on apparent flinching, in every case.

(4) Make a special and thorough examination of the foot, despite the fact that there may be some other obvious inflammatory lesion in the limb.

(5) Try passive movements of various parts to ascertain if they cause pain of certain structures, including extension, flexion, adduction, abduction, and rotation of joints.   When suspicious of inflammation

in a joint, flex it forcibly for a couple of minutes and then send the horse on at a trot, when the lameness will be intensified if the joint is affected. This is called the " spavin test " when applied to the hock.

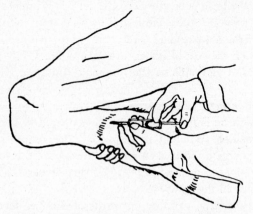

FIG. 323.—BLOCKING THE PLANTAR NERVE.

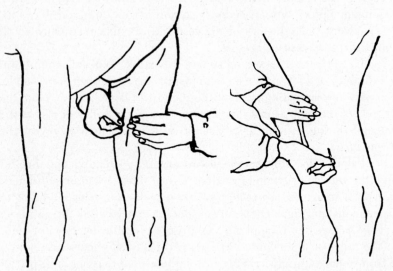

FIG. 324.—BLOCKING THE MEDIAN NERVE.   FIG. 325.—BLOCKING THE ANTERIOR TIBIAL NERVE.

The results obtained from passive movements are often doubtful. It is not always easy to say whether the animal resents them or whether his apparent resentment is due to pain or to his disposition. The same movements should be practised on the sound limb.

(6) If the foregoing examination fails to disclose the seat of lameness,

resort to the injection of a local anæsthetic over certain nerves, so as to arrive at a diagnosis by a process of exclusion thus :

FORE-LIMB.—(*a*) Inject a solution of cocaine hydrochloride, stovaine, novocaine or other local anæsthetic, over each plantar nerve and wait for ten to thirty minutes for its effect to be produced (Fig. 323). If the horse goes sound the seat of lameness is below the point of injection, and if he remains lame it is above this point.

(*b*) Inject the solution over the median (Fig. 324) and ulnar nerves, and interpret the result in the same way.

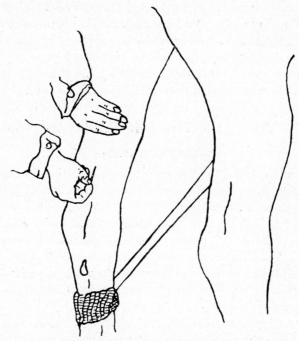

FIG. 326.—BLOCKING THE POSTERIOR TIBIAL NERVE.

It must be remarked that the injection of cocaine may possibly have a misleading effect by exciting the horse and causing him to forget about his lameness, irrespective of its seat.

HIND-LIMB.—Proceed similarly, injecting the anæsthetic over the anterior (Fig. 325) and posterior tibial (Fig. 326) nerves after the plantar.

(7) Radiography may be adopted to reveal obscure lesions below the elbow and stifle in large animals which are capable of being shown on a skiagraph, such as fractures, bony deposits, or foreign bodies lodged in the tissues.

51

(8) Examination *per rectum* must not be forgotten for hind-limb lameness (see p. 690).

3. *The Nature of the Lesion.*—Consideration of the lesions causing lameness will be dealt with in the following pages, but it may be stated here that lameness may be due primarily to the injudicious fitting of shoes on abnormal feet—*i.e.*, not adapting the shoe to the form of the particular foot, but rather endeavouring to alter the latter by paring it to make it approach the normal, thus interfering with the natural balance of the foot and predisposing to sprain of the lower joints of the limb. Lieut.-Colonel H. T. Ryan (Cork) has drawn attention to this, and maintains that he has cured and prevented the recurrence of lameness due to this cause by having the horses exercised barefooted on the road prior to reshoeing, to allow the overgrowth of horn to be naturally worn to the required level, thus permitting the foot to preserve its natural balance when reshod (*Veterinary Record*, Vol. 10).

AFFECTIONS OF THE SHOULDER AND ARM

Shoulder Lameness

" Shoulder lameness " is caused by various affections of the regions of the shoulder and arm. The main features of shoulder lameness are common to them all, and depend chiefly on the difficulty of taking the limb forward. The position of the limb at rest varies according to the nature of the lesion. In many cases it is normal. During motion the following peculiarities are more or less noticeable :

1. Marked lifting of the head when the limb is being advanced.

2. Imperfect extension of the limb, the foot being lifted only slightly clear of the ground.

3. Shortened stride, a short step being taken by the affected limb.

4. Stumbling due to the limb being insufficiently raised to clear slight obstacles.

5. Fixation of the scapula and humerus, recognised by their being held stiffly during progression, with restricted movement of the shoulder-joint.

6. Increased lameness on rough or uneven ground and uphill.

7. Indifference as to the hardness of the ground, provided that it is level. Soft ground is more likely to impede movement, as its surface is apt to be irregular.

8. Circumduction of the limb in the effort to overcome the difficulty in advancing it.

Passive movement of the upper part of the limb causes the animal to evince pain, care being taken that the limb is grasped above the knee, and that the movement is practically confined to the shoulder region. Compression and palpation of the latter may reveal evidence of inflammation. Comparison of the two shoulders may lead to the recognition of an abnormality. Atrophy of the shoulder muscles does not necessarily indicate shoulder lameness. Causes of shoulder lameness will now be dealt with.

Contusions of the Shoulder

Contusions of the shoulder answer to the description of contusions in general. It is only those that are deep-seated which give rise to lameness.

Sprain and Rupture of the Muscles and Tendons of the Shoulder

ETIOLOGY.—The muscles of the shoulder or their tendons may be sprained or more or less completely ruptured by accidents which cause over-stretching of the structures, such as slipping or unexpected movements when jumping or galloping, or during heavy draft, or from falling on the shoulder. Exaggerated muscular effort may also give rise to the lesions. Severe contusions may cause these ruptures directly.

SYMPTOMS.—Generally speaking, the symptoms are those of acute local inflammation and shoulder lameness. When a bundle of muscle fibres or an entire muscle is ruptured, a gap is formed between the ends, and blood accumulates there to form a hæmatoma.

TREATMENT.—The treatment is that described for inflammation, and comprises rest, cold and astringents followed by hot applications, massage with liniments, and, in the later stages, counter-irritation. When weight cannot be borne by the limb, slings are indicated. Should a hæmatoma persist after the prolonged use of absorbent topics, it will be necessary to open and evacuate it, and treat its lining with tincture of iodine or other stimulating antiseptic solution.

Sprain and Rupture of Individual Muscles : The Biceps— (Coraco-radialis, flexor brachii) Bursitis Intertubercularis

This muscle contains much tendinous tissue throughout its length, and is subject to sprain like a tendon from slipping backwards, over-stretching the muscle, or from violent efforts to extricate the limb when fixed. Rarely it is completely ruptured. Local inflammation and shoulder lameness characterise the condition. When the muscle is ruptured, evidence thereof is observed, and there is complete inability to take the limb forward, the toe being dragged along the ground during progression.

Probably the commonest seat of injury in connection with this muscle is its bursa over the bicipital groove in the humerus. Inflammation of this bursa is known as *bursitis intertubercularis*. It is associated with sprain of the muscle, and is manifested by typical shoulder lameness. It is an exceedingly painful lesion, which prevents

FIG. 327.—LAMENESS FROM BURSITIS INTERTUBERCULARIS.
The horse is being led.

any weight being borne by the limb, and completely inhibits its forward movement. During rest, the foot is placed behind its neighbour. There are marked local inflammatory symptoms just below the level of the shoulder-joint. The acute condition may become chronic, with abrasion of the cartilage, the formation of exostoses on the humerus, and even ossification of the muscle, as recorded by Williams and Dieterich. The gliding surface of the biceps is often roughened from friction against the ulcerated bicipital groove.

The local SYMPTOMS are not very obvious at first, but usually some deformity is noticed, such as a diffuse swelling on one or both sides of the tendon, or muscular atrophy. A chronic bursitis (which may be bilateral) has been seen in tramway and omnibus horses, caused by half-falls or slipping in rapid driving. The disease may be of toxic origin, occurring as a sequel to some infectious disease. When both limbs are involved, the animal seems " tied at the shoulder." Atrophy of the shoulder muscles ensues from the prolonged lameness.

PROGNOSIS of sprain of the biceps depends on its severity. When slight, recovery ensues within six weeks ; otherwise it may take months, and chronic bursitis is incurable.

TREATMENT is that already described for sprains in general.

Purulent Bursitis

Purulent bursitis following an open wound and infection of the bursa causes intense lameness, and may be associated with ulceration of the bicipital groove, when cure is impossible.

TREATMENT is on general principles.

The Pectorals

The pectoral muscles may be sprained or ruptured from slipping outwards or violent abduction of the limb, causing the usual local inflammatory symptoms and lameness, characterised by marked abduction of the shoulder, whose point is widely separated from the thorax.

Rupture or Sprain of the Anterior and Posterior Spinati Muscles—Suprascapular Paralysis—" Shoulder Slip "

One or both muscles may be involved. In case of rupture of the anterior spinatus, the scapulo-humeral joint is abnormally flexed ; during the walk, lifting of the limb is difficult or impossible, the toe trailing on the ground. On local examination, a transverse depression is felt a little above the level of the joint. Similar symptoms are observed when the posterior spinatus is affected. Many cases that were formerly described as sprain of these muscles were probably due to paralysis thereof resulting from injury to the suprascapular nerve, which will now be dealt with under the heading

Suprascapular Paralysis

ETIOLOGY.—The nerve may be directly injured as it comes round the point of the shoulder as the result of impact against a fixed object, such as a tree or a vehicle, or it may be over-stretched and rendered functionless by the limb being forcibly pushed backwards when off the ground, as Möller has known to occur during collisions in cavalry charges. Williams described a condition in young horses first put to plough which seemed almost identical with suprascapular paralysis, but which he ascribed to pathological changes in the spinati muscles, affecting chiefly the bursa of the post-spinatus. He believed it was caused by awkward turning of the horses at the headlands. He called the condition " shoulder slip."

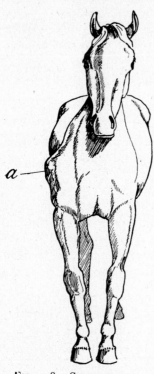

SYMPTOMS.—The symptoms are due to loss of power in the muscles, which is characterised by difficulty in extending the shoulder-joint, and by a marked bulging outwards of the articulation when weight is placed on the limb for want of the binding effect of the muscles. The shoulder-joint appears to slip outwards at each step, thus accounting for the term " shoulder slip." This is best seen when the horse is coming towards the observer. Atrophy of the muscles is well marked when the condition has been in existence for some weeks, causing the spine of the scapula to become very prominent. The anterior spinatus may show more atrophy than the posterior.

PROGNOSIS must be guarded. Recovery may ensue within six weeks or the paralysis may persist for months or become permanent, depending on the nature of the injury to the nerve. Rapid atrophy of the muscles is an unfavourable symptom. In some cases, although the horse eventually goes sound, the muscles never regain their

FIG. 328.—SUPRASCAPULAR PARALYSIS.

a, The bulging shoulder-joint.

normal volume. Although animals affected may not become quite sound, they may be able to do slow work in a breast collar.

TREATMENT is that given for paralysis in general. Electrotherapy is indicated. The local hypodermic injection of veratrine (1 grain of the insoluble form in 75 minims of water) may have a good effect also in preventing atrophy. Strychnine injected beneath the skin in the affected region and repeated daily for several days has given good results. The most common treatment is the application of a blister over the affected muscles and the administration of nux vomica and potassium iodide internally, the latter being discontinued for a while if symptoms of iodism appear. A prolonged course of arsenic or its preparations is an alternative treatment which may have a good effect. Exercise is indicated during convalescence.

Inflammation of the Tendon of the Postero-Spinatus Muscle and of its Bursa

This may be caused by contusion or by strain of the tendon. When horses with narrow chests and closely placed fore-legs are used for fast-trotting work, this tendon may become strained on account of increased abduction of the shoulder necessitated by the special conformation.

SYMPTOMS.—There is abduction of the entire limb, with supporting leg lameness. The foot is placed outwards to relieve tension on the inflamed tendon. Local inflammation is detected on palpation, pain being evinced on pressure, and crepitation (tendo-vaginitis crepitans) may be felt by the hand.

PROGNOSIS.—Recovery is the rule after four to eight weeks' rest.

TREATMENT is as usual for acute or chronic inflammation, as the case may be. The writer had a case in which subcutaneous section of the tendon was followed by disappearance of the lameness which, however, reappeared when reunion of the ends occurred, but the pony eventually went sound after needle-point firing.

The Subscapularis

Slipping outwards has caused rupture of this muscle. Lameness is characterised by deviation outwards of the upper part of the limb. It may be accompanied by rupture of the pectorals and serratus magnus.

The Serratus Magnus (Serratus Ventralis)

Rupture of the serratus magnus has been recorded. When it is present, the trunk is lowered between the two shoulders, the withers being some inches below the level of the croup, while the upper part of the shoulder surpasses the summit of the dorsal spines. The lower margin of the sternum may reach as low as the chestnut. If the trapezius is also ruptured, the anterior part of the cartilage of prolongation of the scapula bulges the skin upwards. The shoulder on the other side is directed obliquely forwards and outwards. Walking is painful, and the animal is reluctant to move. Local inflammatory symptoms are evident.

PROGNOSIS of complete rupture is bad, as perfect recovery is not likely to ensue.

The Mastoido-Humeralis (Brachiocephalicus, Levator Humeri)

This muscle is more subject to contusion or direct injury than to sprain. It is usually caused by the collar when the horse is engaged at heavy draft, and is brought about by some unexpected obstacle to the load which stops the animal and causes the collar to be jerked against the muscle. It may occur in this way during ploughing from the plough being stopped by a root or large stone. Pain is evinced on manipulation of the affected part, and if the horse is put to work he refuses the draft.

The Triceps Extensor Cubiti (Triceps Brachii)

This extensor of the elbow may be sprained or ruptured from violent slipping forward of the fore-limb. Sprain is revealed by difficulty in extending the elbow and by local inflammatory symptoms. During progression, the horse is apt to knuckle forward at the knee. If completely ruptured, the space between the ends will be detected. The tendons may be torn from the bone, or a portion of the latter may be separated.

PROGNOSIS.—Ordinary sprain responds to treatment, but complete rupture causes permanent lameness and may necessitate slaughter. Osteo-periostitis and the formation of exostoses at the seat of rupture on the bone are always to be feared.

TREATMENT in all the foregoing cases is on the same lines, and comprises the measures mentioned under the headings of " Inflammation " and " Contusions."

Shoulder Rheumatism

Muscular rheumatism of the shoulder region is not infrequent in the horse and ox. It is favoured by prolonged exposure to cold and wet.

SYMPTOMS comprise shoulder lameness and more or less evidence of pain on manipulation of the affected muscles. The spinati muscles seem to be the most frequently affected. When the condition is chronic, muscular atrophy may be noticed as well as some diminution of electric contractility. During the walk, the limb is held stiffly and lifted with difficulty. The lameness varies in intensity, and usually diminishes with exercise as the horse becomes " warmed up " or sweats, to reappear after a few minutes' rest. The lameness is often intermittent, and may pass from one limb to the other. If both limbs are affected at the same time, the horse is " tied in " at the shoulders.

When the mastoido-humeralis is the seat of the disease, it becomes swollen, tense, and painful, the neck is curved towards the affected side, and during progression there is marked difficulty in taking the limb forward and the head is more or less lowered. Backing is difficult.

DIAGNOSIS is often doubtful. The diagnostic features are the intermittency and fugitive and shifting nature of the lameness, and its diminution on exercise, associated with the absence of other evidence to account for the condition. When both limbs are involved, the affection may be confounded with laminitis and navicular disease. Young horses, when first put to work, may suffer from simple myositis resembling rheumatism. It is the result of fatigue.

PROGNOSIS varies with the intensity and duration of the lameness. Recent cases receiving appropriate treatment often recover in a few days. Sometimes, however, weeks, and even months, elapse before lameness disappears. There is always the fear of the condition recurring.

TREATMENT.—The treatment is that for inflammation and rheumatism. In recent cases, local applications comprise moist heat, anodyne and stimulating liniments, associated with massage. In chronic lesions, counter-irritation is indicated. Internal treatment includes the administration of sodium salicylate, antipyrine, and iodide of potassium. Success has been claimed for subcutaneous injection of either (1) morphia 4 grains, atropine $\frac{1}{2}$ grain, and water $\frac{1}{2}$ ounce ; or (2) a solution of strychnine in doses of $\frac{1}{2}$ to 1 grain repeated daily for five or six days. This treatment may be renewed several times if necessary.

In obstinate cases other special treatments may be tried, including :

1. *Hypodermic injection of veratrine*, which may be repeated daily for a while if the reaction is not too severe. The dose is about 1 grain in $1\frac{1}{4}$ drachms of water (a suspension) or alcohol (solution).

2. *Subcutaneous injection of a saturated solution of common salt* in five places round the point of the shoulder, 5 c.c. of the solution being used for each injection. It causes great inflammation, and may lead to abscess formation or sloughing.

3. *Subcutaneous injection of the essence of turpentine*, 15 minims of the liquid being injected in four different places equidistant from the point of the shoulder. It causes intense inflammation with diffuse swelling, which increases for some days until it extends as far as the knee, after which it gradually disappears. Some remarkable cures of chronic cases have been claimed for this treatment.

4. *Luchow's treatment.* Ammonia, turpentine, and soap liniment is rubbed into the shoulder, producing a lather. The animal is clothed in a sheet and hood and exercised in the ring with the lame leg outside

until the body is bathed in sweat. He is returned to the stable, and cold compresses are applied to the affected part and renewed every two hours. The last compress put on at night is left in position until the next morning. On the following days the horse is exercised at the walk for half an hour. Cure may be effected in the course of three or four weeks. Two Continental authorities, Hertwig and Delwort, have reported success with this treatment, which, however, is rarely practised.

Radial Paralysis (Dropped Elbow)

The radial or musculo-spiral nerve is the largest branch of the brachial plexus. It supplies the extensors of the forearm, the extensors and external flexor of the metacarpus, and the extensor pedis and extensor suffraginis. Radial paralysis has been frequently seen in the horse, ox, and dog, but most commonly in the horse.

ETIOLOGY.—The usual cause of the condition is some traumatic injury to the nerve whereby it becomes functionless. It has occurred in the following ways :

1. From casting the horse on hard ground, the underneath limb being affected. When Möller practised casting horses on a mattress, the accident ceased to occur.

2. From fixing the under fore-limb to the upper hind in the cast position, thus compressing the nerve between the shoulder and the thorax, or overstretching it. It has often occurred in this way following operations on the foot.

FIG. 329.—FRACTURE OF THE FIRST RIB, IN WHICH THE UNION WAS FIBROUS (HUNTING'S CASE OF RADIAL PARALYSIS).

3. Accompanying fracture of the first rib, the nerve being lacerated by the fragments of the bone or being compressed by the extravasation or inflammatory exudate associated with the fracture. Willis, Rogers, Hunting, and others have drawn attention to the frequency with which it occurred in this way. Hunting has proved its occurrence in this manner in horses working in double harness, the fracture ensuing in one of the horses as the result of plunging forward into the collar when starting while the other horse hesitates. Post-mortem examination of cases which he followed up confirmed his diagnosis (Fig. 329).

Two interesting cases came to the notice of the writer recently resulting from a head-on collision between two thoroughbred yearlings galloping in a field in opposite directions. At the moment of contact the two animals fell and rose with difficulty showing the characteristics of radial paralysis in the off fore limbs which failed to respond to fairly prolonged treatment. Post-mortem examination of one of them revealed fracture of the first rib, that of the other was not reported.

4. Suddenly during a journey, without any apparent exciting cause.

SYMPTOMS.—Owing to the paralysis of the extensor muscles mentioned there is flexion of the elbow and all the joints beneath it, and the animal is unable to extend the limb. The scapulo-humeral angle is very open, the triceps is flaccid and less in relief, and the elbow is

FIG. 330.—RADIAL PARALYSIS IN THE DOG.

dropped. The leg appears too long for the body. The toe or front wall of the hoof is in contact with the ground and placed a little in front of or behind the perpendicular line. The animal moves forward with difficulty, and drags the toe in doing so, but backs with comparative ease. If the knee is firmly supported in front, weight can be borne by the limb.

The foregoing symptoms are those of complete paralysis. In some cases the paralysis is not complete. Then the affected limb can bear weight, but the caput muscles may show tremors. During progression the limb is taken forward in a semi-flexed condition, and if the pace is accelerated the animal stumbles and may fall. Möller met with a number of cases of radial paralysis in 1887 which seemed to be of specific origin, occurring suddenly without any obvious exciting cause. In many of these the paralysis was partial, the caput medium and muscles in front of the forearm being unaffected.   When weight was placed on the foot, these contracted in the ordinary way, giving rise to a peculiar gait characterised by a jerking forward of the shoulder during pro-gression.

When the radial nerve is over-stretched, the twigs supplying the caput medium and parvum and extensors of the digit may escape injury because they are longer and less subject to tension than those supplying

FIG. 331.—COMPLETE PARALYSIS OF THE RADIAL NERVE.

the other muscles.   This accounts for some of the cases of incomplete paralysis.   Loss of sensation does not always accompany paralysis. Muscular atrophy invariably ensues when the condition has been in existence for a considerable time.

DIAGNOSIS presents no difficulty to an observer conversant with the symptoms of the condition.   It is easily distinguished from rupture of the extensor pedis and fracture of the olecranon, which would give rise to somewhat similar symptoms, the local lesion being obvious in each case.

PROGNOSIS.—In some cases occurring after casting, the paralysis is of a very temporary nature, disappearing suddenly in a few minutes, a few hours, or after three or four days, but in the majority of cases it lasts five or six weeks, when recovery gradually ensues. Certain severe cases, possibly due to fractured first rib, persist for six to nine months when the patient is allowed to live so long. Uncertainty of movement sometimes remains after disappearance of the lameness, but disappears in time. In exceptional cases there is no sign of improvement after the lapse of six or more weeks, and by this time the muscular atrophy is very marked. Except the horse is very valuable, it is seldom considered worth while to pursue the treatment further.

TREATMENT is that for paralysis in general. Slings are advisable for the horse when the paralysis is complete, except it is a light animal which can lie and rise on three legs. When they are not employed, short bedding like peat moss should be provided. The measures mentioned for suprascapular paralysis may be adopted. Frequent massage of the muscles is always indicated. The routine procedure, when the case does not respond to the use of liniments and massage, is to apply a blister on the affected muscles and give potassium iodide and nux vomica internally or strychnine hypodermically. When the use of the limb is being regained, exercise should be prescribed (see Suprascapular Paralysis, p. 805).

Fracture of the Scapula

On account of its position and slight mobility, the scapula is comparatively seldom fractured in the domesticated animals.

ETIOLOGY.—The usual cause is direct violence, the result of a blow, collision, kick, tread, or fall. It may also be due to violent slipping outwards of the fore-limb. The neck of the bone has been fractured from forcibly reining-up animals.

SITES comprise the acromion process, one of the superior angles of the body, the neck, and the articular cavity.

1. *The Acromion Process.*—Fracture of this is characterised by an inflammatory swelling at its level. Crepitation may be detected and the loose bone may be felt.

2. *The Superior Angles.*—The muscular attachment at the angles causes displacement of the fragments, which can be felt in a new situation.

3. *The Body, Neck, and Articular Cavity.*—These are the commonest sites of fracture, the direction of which may be longitudinal, transverse, or oblique. There is acute local inflammation, and crepitation may be detected by placing the hand on the scapula and moving the limb in different directions. When the neck is broken, abnormal mobility

may be discovered on manipulating the olecranon, which can usually be pushed farther outwards than normally.

There is severe lameness in each case, but it is most marked in No. 3, in which the animal walks on three legs.

DIAGNOSIS.—Sometimes it is difficult to elicit crepitus, and then diagnosis is uncertain, and can only be suspected from the history of the case and the great lameness.

PROGNOSIS.—In No. 1 complete recovery ensues. When compound, there may be trouble from infection giving rise to necrosis or caries of the bone, or necrosis of the fascia in the region. In No. 2 fibrous union takes place between the fragment and the main bone, but the subject eventually goes sound. In No. 3 the case is serious in large animals, and the nearer the fracture to the lower end of the bone the graver the condition, there being less displacement of the fragments in the upper part. Destruction of the horse is usually necessary.

Exceptional instances of perfect recovery from such fractures in large animals have been recorded. As a rule, treatment is only attempted in valuable subjects. When the articular cavity is involved, arthritis and anchylosis are the usual sequelæ. Cattle sometimes make a good recovery even without treatment. In small animals treatment is always successful, except when the joint is involved and anchylosis supervenes. When sepsis ensues in compound fracture, extensive necrosis of the bone may follow.

TREATMENT is carried out on general principles. Having reduced the fracture as far as possible, an attempt may be made to immobilise the seat of fracture by making use of :

1. *Slings*, which are always indicated in the horse if the patient will tolerate them.

2. *A special apparatus* in the form of an iron band riding across the withers and compressing, by means of a plate and pad at either extremity, the scapular region.

3. *A pitch bandage* enveloping the shoulder, forearm, base of the neck, and girth. Continental veterinarians had several successes in the horse by such a dressing, even without the aid of slings. It is difficult, however, to apply it satisfactorily in the large animals. In the small animals its application is easy, and in these it is advisable to include the paw, for fear of the possibility of the circulation being arrested therein if omitted.

In light cattle a charge is sufficient while the animal is left at liberty. Compound fracture is treated on general lines.

Fracture of the Humerus

Fracture of the humerus in large and small animals is usually due to direct violence, but rarely it occurs from muscular contraction. The inner or outer condyle may be broken by a violent rotary movement at the elbow-joint. The condyles are the commonest seat of fracture in the dog and cat. Falling or jumping from a height is a common cause of the condition in these animals.

SYMPTOMS.—The symptoms are as usual for a fractured bone.

DIAGNOSIS is generally easy, as displacement and crepitation can usually be detected.

PROGNOSIS of complete fracture in the large animals is bad, as it is usually oblique in direction and accompanied by marked displacement, rendering accurate reduction and retention impossible. When displacement is slight or absent, recovery may ensue, as recorded by Meredith, Warnecke, etc. In stud animals, recovery with deformity and mechanical lameness may be sufficient. In small animals cure is the rule, although when the fracture involves the articular surface of the bone anchylosis of the joint may follow.

TREATMENT is on general principles, and on the same lines as those advised for fracture of the scapula. It should be attempted in valuable horses, especially those of the light breeds and of docile temperament. Light cattle are generally good subjects for treatment, the application of a charge usually having the desired effect. When union has taken place, exercise and massage are important indications. Months may elapse in large subjects before lameness disappears.

Dislocation or Luxation of the Shoulder-Joint

Luxation of the shoulder-joint is more rare in animals than in man, due to the joint being more firmly braced by muscles in the former than in the latter. Yet numerous cases of the condition have been recorded by veterinarians as occurring in the horse, ox, and dog. Luxation can generally be ascribed to excessive flexion of the joint. The humerus is then always thrust forwards and upwards, the head of the bone being discovered in front of and above the glenoid cavity of the scapula. As the biceps antagonises this movement, displacement can only occur when this muscle is partially relaxed, as it would be, for instance, during simultaneous flexion of the elbow-joint. For this reason luxation of the shoulder-joint results most frequently from falls in jumping. A sudden check to the movement of the lower portions of the leg may also bring it about. Excessive abduction may result in the head of the humerus being displaced inwards beyond the glenoid cavity. Luxation in other directions is seldom met with.

SYMPTOMS comprise sudden and severe shoulder lameness ; difficulty in passive flexion and extension of the joint, while abduction and adduction are abnormally easy ; shortening of the leg ; and local deformity, associated with inflammation.

POSSIBLE COMPLICATIONS include fracture of the scapula and humerus, most commonly the border of the glenoid cavity, and rupture of vessels and nerves in the axillary region.

PROGNOSIS.—The results of many observations seem to indicate that even complete luxation, if early reduced, can be cured in two to three weeks. Reduction and retention are sometimes impossible, and permanent lameness may ensue from irreparable injury to the articular ends of the bones. In working horses, if there is no improvement within about fourteen days after reduction the case is hopeless. Reduction is easier in small animals.

TREATMENT is carried out in the manner described (see Dislocations, p. 136). In large, quiet animals, reduction may be attempted in the standing position thus : Let one man hold the animal's head, another draw the leg forward, and a third press on the knee-joint to extend it whilst the operator tries to press the head of the humerus into position. It is generally necessary to cast and anæsthetise the patient, and then perform extension and counter-extension by means of ropes applied on the pastern and round the girth, and pulled in opposite directions parallel to the long axis of the limb by assistants, while the operator endeavours by means of the hands and knees, or by standing on the shoulder, to replace the head of the bone. Successful reduction is indicated by a ioud click, and by restoration of the free movement of the limb. When dislocation is lateral, abduction or adduction of the limb is necessary to lever the head of the humerus into place. When the head of the humerus lies in front of the glenoid cavity, strongly flexing the elbow-joint helps reduction, and this should be tried when the method mentioned above fails.

AFTER-TREATMENT consists in keeping the joint at absolute rest to avoid recurrence until the articular ends are safely fixed in position. Bandaging is not necessary, and would be of little use. A charge is sometimes used. A blister may have some good effect in bracing up the shoulder muscles. Eventually, exercise is essential to promote mobility of the joint and prevent stiffness therein.

AFFECTIONS OF THE ELBOW AND FOREARM

Fracture of the Ulna

In the large animals, the usual site of fracture is the olecranon process commonly between its beak and the upper extremity of the radius, or at the level of the radio-ulnar arch. The usual cause is direct violence, such as a kick, but it may be the result of muscular contraction. In the dog, the shaft is often fractured along with that of the radius.

SYMPTOMS.—In transverse fracture of the olecranon, the fragment is drawn upwards by the triceps, causing a gap between the broken ends. The elbow is dropped, as in radial paralysis. The fore-arm assumes an oblique direction downwards and forwards, while the metacarpus is in a vertical position. When the fracture is at the level of the radio-ulnar arch, the ends of the fragments are in apposition. Crepitation can be detected when the fragments are in contact, and abnormal mobility is revealed on manipulating the olecranon.

PROGNOSIS in the large animals is unfavourable, as it is impossible in most cases to keep the fragments in apposition. In small animals, recovery is the rule. When arthritis of the elbow-joint supervenes, the gravity of the case is increased. Fibrous union of the fragments is a good enough result in cattle intended for the butcher and in brood mares, as it enables them to bear weight on the limb and to get about.

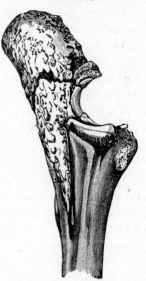

FIG. 332.—FRACTURE OF THE ULNA IN A HORSE.

TREATMENT is on general principles. In transverse fracture of the olecranon, it is generally impossible to immobilise it in the proper position. When the fragments are in apposition, rest in slings may be sufficient to ensure healing. An effective dressing is impracticable in the region of the olecranon, although the bandage recommended for fracture of the scapula may be tried. In the pig, dog, and cat, the ulna, apart from the radius, may be fractured. In this case the radius acts as a splint to keep the fragments of the ulna in position, and allows union to occur even without a dressing.

Fracture of the Radius

The radius in the horse is often fractured by direct violence, such as a fall or a kick, and rarely by muscular violence. The fracture may be in the form of a fissure, which may or may not be followed by displacement later (deferred fracture). In the dog, the fracture is frequently the result of being run over, and is usually accompanied by that of the ulna.

SYMPTOMS.—The cardinal symptoms of fracture are usually observed rendering diagnosis easy.

PROGNOSIS is that given for fractures of the limbs in general. Cure can be effected with satisfactory results in the large animals when there is no displacement, but in case of the latter, permanent lameness generally ensues even after callous formation has occurred. Even compound comminuted fracture of the radius and ulna in both limbs is usually curable in the dog and cat.

TREATMENT is on general principles. When the fracture is transversely through the upper extremity of the bone, it is difficult to apply an effective dressing. If there is no displacement, it will be sufficient to keep the horse at rest in slings. In other situations the best dressing is a pitch bandage from the foot to the elbow, with which splints may be associated. When the fracture is in the vicinity of the elbow, a dressing similar to that used for fractured humerus is indicated. Moussu recommends plaster-of-Paris splints in the ox, leaving a narrow strip of skin uncovered on the inner aspect of the forearm at the level of the median vein. Auchterlonie has reported successful treatment of fracture with displacement of the lower third of the radius in a six-years-old Dutch funeral horse by the use of slings and of splints and bandages (*Vet. Rec.*, **49**, No. 49).

Luxation of the Elbow

Luxation of the elbow-joint is rare. To enable it to occur, there must be rupture of one or both lateral ligaments. The author has seen it occur in a hackney horse from falling on the side with the affected limb bent inwards beneath the body. The force of several assistants applying extension and counter-extension with ropes, with the patient anæsthetised, failed to dislodge the bones from their displaced position. It may also be caused by violence in the dog, but it is more commonly congenital in this animal.

PROGNOSIS.—The case is usually hopeless in the horse, but may be treated successfully in the dog except it is congenital, when it is impossible to keep the bones in apposition.

TREATMENT is carried out on general principles.

Inflammation of the Elbow-Joint

The elbow-joint is particularly prone to traumatic septic arthritis, owing to its exposed and superficial situation. The sheath of the flexor metacarpi externus communicates with the synovial capsule of the joint, and when it is wounded and infected, the infection frequently spreads into the joint. A wound has often been inflicted in this region by kicks, falls, and prods of forks. The bone is apt to be involved in the primary injury, aggravating the prognosis. Even careful antiseptic treatment often fails to exclude infection from the joint, and then septic arthritis usually supervenes, necessitating destruction of the animal.

The SYMPTOMS are as usual for synovitis or arthritis.

TREATMENT is that described for joints in general.

Capped Elbow—Hygroma of the Elbow—Shoe Boil

Under this heading there will be discussed all inflammatory conditions of the elbow involving the subcutaneous bursa and its vicinity at the supero-posterior aspect of the olecranon—viz. : (1) Acute bursitis and parabursitis ; (2) chronic bursitis and parabursitis ; (3) purulent bursitis or abscess formation in the elbow region ; (4) a sinus or fistula of the elbow.

ETIOLOGY.—1. *Acute Bursitis and Parabursitis* are usually the result of direct injury, which may be caused in various ways as mentioned below in connection with No. 2. Occasionally it is of toxic origin, occurring as a complication of an infectious disease like influenza or strangles.

2. *Chronic Bursitis and Parabursitis.*—This constitutes the typical capped elbow, and is brought about by repeated slight injury of the elbow, which may be caused as follows by :

(1) *The heel of the shoe* repeatedly coming in contact with the elbow when the horse is lying. This is more likely to happen when the animal goes down on the knees, like a cow, or when the heels of the shoe are very long. Cart-horses shod with long-heeled shoes provided with calkins are most liable to injury in this way, and are the most frequent sufferers from capped elbow. It is difficult to explain, however, why individual horses are so subject to this injury. Ordinarily the heels of the foot are not in contact with the elbow during recumbency. The relative lengths of the forearm and the

metacarpophalangeal regions may have something to do with it, or it may be a habit acquired by the horse.

(2) *The elbow frequently coming in contact with the bare floor.* The horse, when rising in the ordinary way, sometimes slips or purposely drops back on his elbows, and when this occurs on hard ground they are more or less contused thereby. Horses with prominent elbows are most likely to get them capped in this way. With this conformation the olecranon processes may reach the ground before the sternum, and bear weight during recumbency.

Large dogs sometimes show bursal distensions on their elbows as the result of dropping on them when assuming a recumbent position. When this is done repeatedly, the enlargements take the form of callosities.

(3) *The heel of the shoe or hoof of the corresponding foot during galloping.* Cagny, a French veterinarian, has stated that he has known it to occur in this way in race-horses, the injury giving rise to lameness, which appears after a race and lasts for some hours.

SYMPTOMS.—The symptoms vary according to the nature of the lesion, being those associated with acute or chronic bursitis, or an abscess or fistula, as the case may be. In a case of acute inflammation there is lameness. The typical capped elbow is a chronic lesion unaccompanied by pain or lameness. The enlargement in this case is mostly fibrous, due to the walls of the bursa becoming thickened by new fibrous tissue. When fairly recent the condition is cystic, being in the form of a fluctuating painless swelling. In cases of long standing it is practically a fibroma behind the point of the olecranon. Occasionally the chronic swelling becomes infected, an abscess forming and bursting, and refusing to heal owing to the cavity having a smooth or callous vegetating lining, and thus giving rise to a purulent bursal fistula. Sometimes the liquid contents of the cystic form become absorbed, leaving an empty cutaneous sac hanging below the point of the elbow.

PROGNOSIS.—The condition is not serious, but is often difficult to get rid of owing to the cause persisting.

PREVENTION.—Preventative measures comprise :

1. *Using tan for litter*, which experience has shown to have the desired effect in some cases where the condition was due to the elbow coming in contact with the bare floor.

2. *Applying a pad* over the heel of the foot to prevent the heels of the shoe injuring the elbow.

3. *Fixing a sheaf of straw* longitudinally on the limb below the knee,

preventing the heel of the foot reaching the elbow when the horse is lying.

4. *The use of a special pad*, which adapts itself to the elbow in the standing and recumbent positions. It is obtainable from veterinary instrument makers.

TREATMENT is that for the various forms of acute or chronic bursitis. When the case is acute, measures include cold and astringent applications, followed by hot fomentations and absorbent topics. Iodine preparations usually prove effective in dispelling inflammatory swelling, provided it is not fibrous. Biniodide of mercury ointment (1 in 8) rubbed into a chronic enlargement may reduce it considerably. When the condition is cystic, the best treatment is to incise the bursa, evacuate its contents, and treat its lining with tincture of iodine or other irritant preparation, which will set up inflammation followed by granulation and obliteration of the cavity. When the lining is callous or vegetative it is best to dissect it out, although searing it with a hot iron is an alternative procedure. Inserting a seton through the cyst from above to below is another procedure which acts as in " capped knee." When the lesion is in the form of an abscess, it is treated as such ; and if in that of a tumour, it must be extirpated.

Extirpation may be performed by means of the knife or by ligation. When the knife is employed, the tumour must be dissected out without cutting into its structure or exposing the bone. The cutaneous incision should encircle a considerable piece of skin, to be removed with the tumour, so that the edges of the wound will meet evenly when brought together afterwards. Although primary healing need not be expected, suturing has the advantage of bringing the lips of the wound into contact and hastening cicatrisation. When the wound is extensive and there is much bleeding, a plug of wool or gauze or tow kept in position by sutures is indicated. The plug is removed the next day, and the wound then left open or drawn together by fresh sutures. The horse should be tied up short until the wound is permanently cicatrised, as the movement of lying and rising causes it to gape and retards the healing process. Some veterinarians use slings, but they are not necessary.

The use of the ligature is preferred by many, even for large wide-based tumours. A piece of good quality catapult rubber is passed round the base of the swelling and drawn as tight as possible after cutting the hair and disinfecting the skin. The ends of the ligature are tied together with string. In four to ten days the tumour is sloughed off, leaving a granulating wound which soon closes in. It is a simpler method than excision, and quite as effective. Sometimes the rubber breaks and has to be replaced by cord. When the tumour is large, it may be necessary to remove and reapply the ligature after three or four days. During the process of separation, a disinfectant should be applied daily to the affected region, potassium permanganate being very suitable on account of its deodorant qualities. No form of treatment will be satisfactory if preventative measures are neglected.

Treatment in the dog is on similar lines. When the bursa is cystic and the lesion is not very chronic, aspiration of its contents and the injection of tincture of iodine sometimes effects a cure in a short time. When the enlargement is callous, it must be removed surgically. The wound should be protected with an antiseptic pad and bandage, the latter being carried round the body and base of the neck to keep it in position. Primary healing may be obtained when the operation is carefully performed.

Contusions and Open Wounds of the Forearm

Contusions present no special features except that when inflicted on the inner aspect of the forearm, where the bone is superficial, cutaneous ostitis may supervene or a fissured fracture may be produced. They are dealt with on general principles. Open wounds transverse to the long axis of the limb gape considerably, but nevertheless heal in due course. When infected and involving the aponeurosis, pus may burrow beneath the latter, necessitating a counter-opening and the insertion of a seton to keep the passage patent until discharge has ceased. When the bone is implicated, necrosis or caries thereof may ensue, setting up a sinus, which will not heal until the sequestrum has been taken away, or the diseased surface has been removed with a curette.

Hygroma, or Distension (Hydarthrosis) of the Elbow-Joint

Distension of the synovial capsule of the elbow-joint is rarely observed, yet several cases of it have been recorded.

The ETIOLOGY is not always apparent. There may be little or no inflammation accompanying the condition, but the distension causes a certain amount of mechanical stiffness which impedes free movement of the limb. The abnormality is recognised by the presence of a bilobed swelling at the lower border of the triceps at the level of the tendon of origin of the flexor metacarpi externus, with its long axis directed obliquely downwards and forwards. Its inferior lobe is in front of the tendon mentioned, while the other lobe is behind it.

The surest TREATMENT is aspiration of the swelling and the injection into the cavity of tincture of iodine (pure or diluted with one to two parts of sterilised water), associated with needle-point firing and the light application of a biniodide of mercury blister. Several weeks may elapse before the desired effect is obtained. Strict asepsis must be observed. (See Synovitis, p. 79.)

AFFECTIONS OF THE KNEE

Contusions of the Knee

Contusions of the knee are common in the horse and ox, and are most frequently situated on its anterior aspect, where they are generally caused by falls or by striking the knee against fixed objects. The horse may injure the front of the knee in the stable by going down and getting up on the knees like the ox. The inner aspect of the joint may be bruised by " speedy-cutting "—that is, by striking this region with the inner branch of the shoe of the opposite foot during progression. Cattle injure the front of the knee from constantly lying on bare floors and from striking it against the trough when rising.

SYMPTOMS.—The symptoms, generally speaking, are those of acute traumatic inflammation. Bursitis of the subcutaneous bursa in front of the knee or synovitis of the extensor sheaths in this region may supervene.

TREATMENT is as usual for contusions. Bursal and synovial distensions will be dealt with separately.

Capped Knee—Hygroma, or Distension of the Subcutaneous Bursa in Front of the Knee

This condition is fairly common in the horse, but is most frequently met with in the ox.

ETIOLOGY.—It may be a sequel to a sudden direct injury, as mentioned in the previous section, but it is most frequently the result of repeated contact of the part with the floor, wall, or manger in the shed or stable. It is very common in housed cattle provided with little or no bedding. Horses sometimes lie down and rise like an ox and suffer in consequence. It may also be caused in the ox by the animal repeatedly striking the knee against the trough when rising, and in the horse it may be the result of hitting the manger with the knee when pawing during feeding.

SYMPTOMS.—*In the horse* the lesion is in the form of a diffuse, usually indolent swelling, extending over the whole anterior face of the knee, which is œdematous, fluctuating, or indurated according to the stage of its development. When it is of long standing, its walls become thickened and indurated. It may become infected, and then show the symptoms of an abscess. Its diffuse character distinguishes it from other synovial distensions.

In the ox the hygroma may be in the form of (1) *an acute bursitis*, which is not common ; (2) *a chronic serous bursitis* or typical hygroma ;

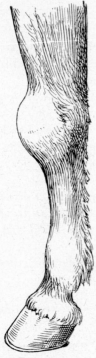

(3) *a suppurating swelling*, due to infection of the injured part ; (4) *a diffuse fibrous enlargement*.

Rarely the lesion is due to botriomycosis or tuberculosis. The swelling may assume enormous dimensions and contain upwards of 10 pints of liquid. The skin over the part may be more or less excoriated. In old-standing cases the whole mass becomes indurated with a thick horny covering, and rarely ossification occurs in its substance.

TREATMENT is that described for bursitis in general, the measures to be adopted comprising :

1. *Removal of the cause* as far as possible.

2. *Antiphlogistic applications* when the condition is recent.

3. *Counter-irritation* with a liniment or blister, which may have the desired effect when the swelling is small.

4. *Puncture* with a trocar and canula to remove the liquid, followed by an injection of tincture of iodine, which is diffused through the cavity and then withdrawn as far as possible, although leaving it in the bursa is harmless. This method is only useful when the enlargement is purely serous, and even then it may require repetition and prove tedious in its results (see p. 84).

FIG. 333.—
HYGROMA OF THE
KNEE RESULTING
FROM BRUISING.

5. *A seton* passed vertically through the swelling, thus providing for the escape of the liquid contents. An antiseptic lotion is injected into the cavity through one of the openings. This is a good method of treatment when the lower opening has been made sufficiently large to allow of the evacuation of riziform bodies. Cicatrisation occurs round the seton, which is removed after a few days.

6. *Incision* of the swelling in a dependent part, complete evacuation of its contents, and the injection of tincture of iodine or other stimulating antiseptic solution. Turpentine or turpentine liniment is a suitable agent to apply to the lining of the cavity. In a case of considerable

standing the bursa contains a lot of loose fibrous tissue, which must be dissected out with the knife. It is generally advisable to plug the cavity with gauze, wool, or fine tow saturated with the antiseptic solution, and leave it in position for twenty-four hours, after which the lesion is treated as an open granulating wound. This is undoubtedly the best treatment for a typical chronic capped knee in the ox.

7. *Needle-point firing*, which may be found efficacious in the horse, provided that much fibrous thickening is not present.

8. *Extirpation*, which is indicated

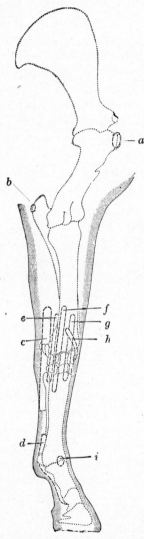

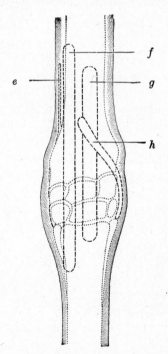

Fig. 334.—Schema of the More Important Tendon Sheaths and Bursæ of the Fore-Limb, seen from in Front and Without.

Fig. 335.—The Same, as seen from the Front.

a, Bursa intertubercularis ; *b*, bursa olecrani ; *c*, upper tendon sheath of the flexor pedis muscles (carpal sheath) ; *d*, lower tendon sheaths of the flexor pedis muscles (metacarpo-phalangeal or great sesamoid sheath) ; *e*, sheath of the flexor metacarpi externus ; *f*, upper sheath of extensor pedis ; *g*, sheath of extensor metacarpi magnus ; *h*, sheath of extensor metacarpi obliquus ; *i*, bursa of extensor pedis.

when the condition is in the form of a small fibroma and incapable of being reduced by other methods. If the enlargement is diffuse the operation is rather drastic, causing an extensive wound that will take a long time to heal and leave a large scar. It is therefore usual not to interfere with an old chronic fibrous thickening in front of the knee in the horse.

Capped knee in the ox is often neglected until it assumes enormous dimensions or becomes septic and inflamed and causes lameness. Instead of completely extirpating a large tumour, a central wedge-shaped piece may be taken out of it and the interior of the remaining halves of the swelling then dissected away as far as possible. Excision of a horny swelling on the front of the knee in the ox is not practicable or advisable. A small fibrous thickening in front of the knee in the horse may be treated by the autoplastic operation advised for broken knees (Cherry's operation, p. 456).

Synovitis and Distension of the Tendon Sheaths in the Region of the Knee

Acute synovitis of the above tendon sheaths may occur from the causes mentioned in the section on acute synovitis. Its symptoms are fairly obvious, and are most marked in connection with the large flexor sheaths, in which it is often associated with sprain of the tendons or of the superior or inferior carpal ligaments.

Purulent synovitis is the result of an open wound and infection of the sheath, or occasionally a complication of an infectious disease like strangles or pyæmia.

TREATMENT is carried out on the general principles already laid down. It may be repeated that purulent synovitis of a large flexor sheath is a very serious condition, and often proves incurable. The pain and lameness accompanying ordinary non-purulent synovitis may disappear, while distension of the sheath persists as a dropsical condition.

Chronic synovitis may be a sequel to the acute form, or occur independently from constant hard work. It is characterised chiefly by distension of the affected sheath. It may be associated with a certain amount of pain and a corresponding degree of lameness. Its prognosis and treatment have been dealt with (p. 79).

Distension or Dropsy of the Carpal Sheath

This is characterised by the presence of three swellings, two above the knee, oblong in shape, one of which is on the outside and the other on the inside of the limb between the back of the radius and the flexor muscles, the former being usually more voluminous than the latter and

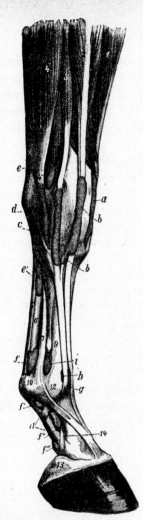

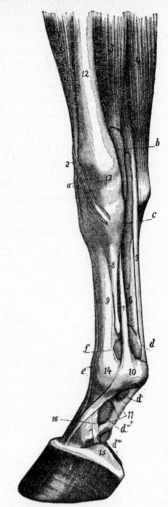

FIG. 336.—OUTER SURFACE OF THE FORE-LIMB, TO SHOW SYNOVIAL SHEATHS.

a, Tendon sheath of extensor metacarpi magnus (extensor carpi radialis dorsalis); b, tendon sheath of extensor pedis (extensor digitalis Communis, anterior extensor of the phalanges; c, tendon sheath of extensor suffraginis (extensor digitalis lateralis, lateral digital extensor); d, tendon sheath of flexor metacarpi externus (extensor carpi ulnaris, ulnaris lateralis); e, e′, superior and inferior pouches of the synovial membrane of the carpal sheath; f, f′, f″, and f‴, superior, middle, and inferior pouches of the synovial membrane of the metacarpo-phalangeal sheath; g, bursa beneath the extensor pedis tendon; h, bursa beneath the extensor suffraginis tendon; i, protrusion of the synovial capsule of the fetlock-joint.

FIG. 337.—INNER SURFACE OF THE FORE-LIMB, TO SHOW SYNOVIAL SHEATHS.

a, Tendon sheath of the extensor metacarpi obliquus; b, tendon sheath of flexor metacarpi internus (flexor carpi radialis, radialis volaris); c, carpal sheath; d, d′, d″, d‴, superior, middle, and inferior pouches of the metacarpo-phalangeal (great sesamoid) sheath; e, bursa beneath the extensor pedis tendon in front of the fetlock; f, distended synovial capsule of the fetlock-joint.

more diffuse than the swellings due to distension of the synovial capsule of the radio-carpal joint or of the sheath of the flexor metacarpi externus, which appear in the same situation ; and a third below the knee, cylindrical in shape, surrounding the tendons, and extending almost half-way down the metacarpal region. A subcutaneous acquired bursal enlargement has been seen on the inside of the limb in the radio-metacarpal region simulating distension of the carpal sheath, but distinguished therefrom by the absence of the other swellings mentioned. The author had a case of this kind in a hunter. The swelling was of long standing and extended for 3 inches above and below the knee. It was opened at the lower part and serum and solid particles escaped and there was a calcareous deposit on its walls. It showed no tendency to heal after repeated irrigation with tincture of iodine, but healed rapidly after the adoption of the Bier hyperæmia treatment.

Distension of the Sheath of the Flexor Metacarpi Externus

This is indicated by a swelling on the outer aspect of the knee and the lower part of the forearm above the pisiform bone. It is usually rounded or ovoid in form, and varies in size from a nut to a hen's egg. It is tense when the limb is bearing weight. The sheath may be in communication with the carpal sheath or the synovial membrane of the radio-carpal joint. In exceptional cases the enlargement may be as big as a fist. As a rule it does not interfere with function, but if very large, or indurated, or calcified, it impedes flexion of the knee, and thus causes lameness.

Distension of the Extensor Sheaths

This is recognised by the presence of elongated swellings on the courses of the extensor tendons in front of the knee. Sometimes the swelling is bilobed, with a lobe on either side of the tendon. They are very distinct from one another when of small dimensions, but, when large, they seem almost confluent. Their form and depth distinguish them from distension of the subcutaneous bursa, while anterior dilatations of the synovial membrane of the knee-joint are hemispherical in outline.

PROGNOSIS.—Mere distension, even of the carpal sheath, not being a painful affection, does not cause lameness. Mechanical stiffness may ensue from a dilated carpal sheath or flexor metacarpi sheath interfering with free movement of the joint. Distension of the extensor sheaths has not this effect.

TREATMENT to get rid of the unsightly swellings is that described in connection with chronic synovitis (p. 79). Care must be exercised with the carpal sheath to avoid infection thereof if puncturing or needle-point firing is adopted, and on no account should a knife be inserted therein.

 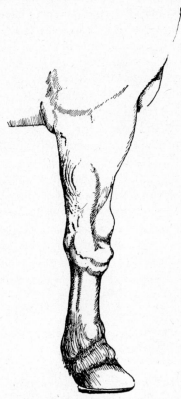

FIG. 338.—DISTENSION OF THE SHEATH OF THE FLEXOR METACARPI EXTERNUS.

FIG. 339.—DISTENSION OF THE EXTENSOR TENDON SHEATHS IN FRONT OF THE KNEE.

Fractures of the Carpus

Fracture of the carpus is rare, and is usually confined to one or two bones, but occasionally all the bones of one of the rows is involved, and more rarely most of the bones of both rows are broken.

ETIOLOGY.—The fracture may be simple or compound. The former is due to concussion of the bones when a false unexpected step is made during jumping, and is consequently most common in hunters and chasers. The latter results from falling on the knee, and is usually complicated with open joint. The pisiform is generally fractured by muscular contraction during jumping or galloping, or as the result of slipping forwards.

SYMPTOMS.—There is sudden and severe lameness, no weight being borne by the affected limb, and the joint is incapable of flexion or extension. Crepitation can generally be detected. Acute inflammatory swelling supervenes later. In fracture of the pisiform, the fragments are usually separated by muscular contraction. Intense lameness and local inflammation supervene, as in the case of the other bones.

PROGNOSIS is always grave, destruction of the horse being usually necessary. The best result obtainable is an anchylosed joint, which is comparatively satisfactory in an animal suitable for the stud. When the fracture is compound, septic arthritis commonly supervenes, rendering the case hopeless. Occasionally complete cure is obtained in fracture of the pisiform when the fragments are not displaced. Even when the union between them is only of a fibrous nature, recovery may ensue, the animal going sound in some cases. Of course, in small animals a stiff joint is not of such importance as in the horse.

TREATMENT is seldom undertaken in large animals. It consists in applying an immobilising dressing and keeping the patient at perfect rest. When an open joint is present, the treatment therefore is indicated. Lameness persisting after healing of a fractured pisiform may be dispelled by needle-point firing.

Sprain of the Knee

Sprain of the knee-joint is rare. It may result from jumping, falling, or slipping.

SYMPTOMS are those of inflammation associated with more or less severe lameness. Passive movement of the joint causes pain. Weight may only be borne by the toe of the foot.

TREATMENT is as usual for inflammation. Recovery ensues after prolonged rest.

Dislocation of the Knee-Joint

Dislocation of the knee-joint is a rare occurrence, and is usually incomplete. It is caused in the same way as sprain.

SYMPTOMS.—In complete luxation the animal goes on three legs, and there is marked deformity and inflammation in the affected joint, which is also abnormally mobile, as a rule, especially when fracture is present, which is not infrequently the case. When the dislocation is incomplete, the lower part of the limb is deviated from the normal, and there is a concavity on the inner or outer aspect of the knee according as the deviation is inwards or outwards. Some of the carpal bones may be felt displaced from their normal position.

PROGNOSIS.—Complete dislocation is hopeless. Partial dislocation may be followed by recovery, as in the case recorded by Flynn in the *American Veterinary Review*. When there is an open wound, the case is still more grave.

TREATMENT consists in reduction and retention and, in the case of the horse, rest in slings.

Synovitis—Arthritis—Distension of the Synovial Capsule of the Joint

Inflammation of the joint may be confined to the serous membrane (*synovitis*) or affect the articular ends of the bones as well (*arthritis*). The causes of synovitis and arthritis have been mentioned in the sections in general surgery dealing therewith. They are often rheumatoid in the dog.

The SYMPTOMS are those of inflammation in the joint and lameness varying in degree according to the acuteness of the affection. At rest the limb is held in an advanced position with the knee semi-flexed. During progression the joint is held stiffly. Dry arthritis affecting this joint was first described by Cherry in 1845, who spoke of it as " chest founder," from the horse giving the sensation of foundering under the rider, and also as " knee spavin." He ascribed the condition to constant hard work, violent exertion, and slipping.

Horses with narrow, imperfectly formed knees, short forearms, and upright shoulders appear most predisposed to the condition, possibly on account of the peculiarly exaggerated movement of the knee-joint which such formation favours. Russian trotters with this form and action often suffer from chronic carpitis. Not infrequently the disease is bilateral ; it is certainly more common in coarse than in well-bred animals. The knee becomes swollen, and the swelling is usually hard, consisting principally of new connective tissue and, later, of exostoses. Free movement of the joint is interfered with. At rest the animals lean forward, and during progression move stiffly. Passive flexion of the knee causes pain and intensifies the lameness, and reveals a varying degree of anchylosis in the joint. Lameness is characterised by the limb being advanced slowly and the stride shortened, whilst the knee-oint is imperfectly flexed and the limb abducted when weight is placed upon it.

Chronic carpitis is incurable. Sometimes a horse has a stiff knee from the development of periarticular fibrous tissue, and is capable of doing moderately hard work.

TREATMENT is useless when the joint is diseased, but when the inflammation is only periarticular, counter-irritation may have a good effect. Median neurectomy may be tried as a last resort. Möller had several successes after this operation.

Distension of the Radio-Carpal Joint

This is characterised by (1) a swelling confined to the upper part of the front of the knee beneath the extensor tendons, and sometimes by (2) a round, firm swelling, varying in size from a walnut to a fist, situated on the outer aspect of the knee above the pisiform bone between the posterior face of the radius and the flexor metacarpi externus, the bulging taking place in the space between the posterior common ligament of the carpus and the carpo-metacarpal ligament. It is sometimes confounded with distension of the sheath of the flexor metacarpi externus. The latter is practically irreducible, while the distension of the joint is compressible, and, when pressed upon, increases the tension of the pericarpal swelling.

Distension of the Intercarpal Joint

This is revealed by the presence of two or three small hemispherical swellings on the middle region of the anterior aspect of the knee. These are tense and hard when weight is placed on the limb, and soft and fluctuating when the latter is lifted, except in very chronic cases, when the walls of the swelling may be indurated or calcified. The carpo-metacarpal joint cannot become distended owing to the close union of the bones by ligaments.

The DIAGNOSIS of the various synovial enlargements of the region of the knee is easy when the characteristics of each are remembered. Ordinary articular distensions, unaccompanied by inflammation, do not cause lameness, but may produce a certain amount of mechanical stiffness of the joint varying in degree according to the size of the swelling and the induration in its walls.

TREATMENT, when required, is that described for chronic synovitis.

An exostosis on the pisiform bone associated with more or less ossification of the tendons which are inserted into it is sometimes seen in race-horses, resulting, as a rule, from a partial rupture of the tendons at their points of insertion or more rarely from fracture of the bone. It gives rise to prolonged or permanent lameness. Needle-point firing and blistering are indicated, and if this treatment fails, the only resort is median neurectomy.

Broken Knee—Open Knee-Joint—Traumatic Arthritis

The front of the knee is a common seat of wounds caused chiefly by falls. They may involve the skin only or extend into the joint, and be associated with fracture of some of the carpal bones. All wounds, superficial and deep, on the front of the knees are spoken of as " broken knees." Once a knee is deeply " broken," the horse is generally prone to fall on it again, owing to the cicatrix diminishing the freedom of movement in the joint, and probably to the animal's knee action being naturally defective. The posterior aspect of the carpus is sometimes wounded by the horse getting the limb over the tying-up chain and making efforts to release it.

Superficial wounds on the front of the knee do not cause severe lameness, but those on its posterior aspect cause much pain during movement, being more affected by flexion and extension of the joint. Synovial discharge from the wound may be due to a tendon sheath or the joint being opened. Probing should not be practised to ascertain the antero-posterior depth of the wound.

PROGNOSIS depends on the nature of the wound. When the joint is open, there is always danger of a fatal septic arthritis supervening. When the bones are damaged, exostoses may be formed, causing anchylosis of the joint. Penetrating wounds of the posterior aspect of the carpus are generally more serious than those in front, due to the complex anatomy of the back of the carpus, comprising tendons and ligaments, wounds of which are slow to heal. Nevertheless recovery may eventually ensue.

TREATMENT is carried out on general principles. There is frequently a " pocket " beneath the skin requiring a counter-opening. Suturing is seldom indicated, but it may sometimes be useful to keep a displaced flap in position. When it is employed it is necessary to apply a gutter splint, with padding beneath, at the back of the knee ; otherwise, the movement of the joint will soon cause the sutures to cut through the skin. It is generally best to leave the wound open and uncovered, having it repeatedly irrigated with an antiseptic solution until it is uniformly granulating, when a dry astringent dressing should be applied.

It must be remembered that when the front of the knee is wounded as the result of a fall, the deep tissues that came in contact with the ground become hidden by the skin when the animal is standing, the cutaneous wound being displaced upwards owing to the skin reverting to the situation it occupied before flexion occurred. It is for this

53

reason that there is usually a pocket beneath the skin containing bruised tissue and foreign matter in its depth necessitating perhaps the making of a counter opening to ensure draining and cleansing of the wound. The same applies to a wound on the outside of the hock caused by contact with a sharp object on the ground in the recumbent position —the cutaneous part of the wound being at a higher level than that in the deep tissues when the standing position is resumed.

When the joint is open, some of the remedies recommended for that condition are indicated. When the synovial fistula is slow to heal, the application of a blister of biniodide of mercury often hastens its closure. Should the articulation become septic, the case is generally incurable. If the infection has not gone beyond the synovial membrane, there is a possibility of recovery ensuing under the influence of the Bier treatment, penicillin, and antisepsis. The blemish caused by a large cicatrix in front of the knee may be removed by an autoplastic operation (see p. 456).

Bent Knees

The knees may be overflexed as the result of contraction of the tendons of the flexor metacarpi muscles, chiefly the externus and medius. The condition may be congenital, or acquired soon after birth, or later in life, apparently as the result of constant hard work. When the deformity is so marked as to interfere with function, tenotomy is indicated (see p. 454).

AFFECTIONS OF THE METACARPUS

Supernumerary Digit—Fissured Digit

Occasionally a foal is born with a supernumerary digit on a hind- or fore-limb corresponding to the index digit of the human limb, and situated to the inner aspect of the normal digit. It is always smaller than the latter, and rarely assists in bearing weight. The plantar aspect of its hoof looks towards the ground, or backwards or upwards It results from abnormal development of the inner splint bone, which becomes furnished with three phalanges and two sesamoids. Rudimentary extensor and flexor tendons detached from those on the normal digit may also be present. It is endowed with very limited movement, and its vascular system is feebly developed.

Another form of congenital deformity sometimes met with is fissure of a digit, involving as a rule the terminal phalanx and os corona.

TREATMENT.—A supernumerary digit has often been successfully removed. The operation consists in making a longitudinal (cutaneous) incision from the upper to the lower extremity of the abnormal metacarpal or metatarsal along its mesial free surface, dissecting back the skin from the bone, separating the latter from the normal bone, removing it, and suturing the skin over the wound, which is then protected by an antiseptic pad and bandage. The union between the lower parts of the bones is fibrous, and can be divided with the knife; but in the upper part the bones are fused, and can only be separated by the use of a fine saw. Healing by first or second intention usually occurs without complication, the wound being completely cicatrised within two or three weeks.

The foregoing procedure involves making a large wound in the main bone, which may consequently become rarefied and fracture subsequently, as in a case recorded by the writer, after apparent complete cure. To avoid this, it is better to remove only the lower third or half of the abnormal metacarpus. This is done by cutting the bone obliquely downwards and inwards with the saw, and then resecting the distal portion by means of a bone forceps or a chisel and mallet.

Supernumerary digits in small animals are dealt with on similar lines.

Traumatic and Inflammatory Lesions of the Metacarpal Region—Section of the Tendons

The above lesions of the metacarpal regions are in accordance with those dealt with in general surgery. Open wounds penetrating the flexor synovial sheaths or the joints are serious, as stated in the sections devoted to these structures. Those involving the tendons are apt to be followed by necrosis thereof, and when it is a flexor tendon that is affected the case may prove incurable. When the bone is wounded a sinus may ensue, due to necrosis or caries of the osseous tissue.

TREATMENT is carried out on general principles for ordinary wounds, open synovial sheaths or joints, or a sinus, as the case may be.

Section of the Tendons

Section of the tendons deserves special mention. Complete division of the tendons gives rise to well-marked symptoms. When it is the extensors of the phalanges that are divided, extension of the digit is impossible, and during progression the front of the wall of the hoof trails on the ground, but weight can be borne on the foot as usual. When the flexors are involved, it may be the perforatus or perforans, or the suspensory ligament, or a combination of these structures that is severed.

The accident is most common in the hind-limbs, where it is often caused by kicking the limb against a sharp object or by the horse backing against the blade of a mowing machine. One or both tendons may be partly or completely divided by an " overreach," or by being struck by the shoe of a following horse during a race. The deformity resulting from these accidents is characterised by more or less descent of the fetlock and abnormal extension of the phalanges, depending on the structures affected. When the perforatus only is severed, there is noticeable lowering of the fetlock, and this is more marked when the suspensory is divided. When the perforans is cut across, there is excessive extension of the interphalangeal joints, causing the toe of the hoof to be turned upwards and its plantar aspect to look forwards. If there is complete section of all the structures, the fetlock pad is down on the ground and the pastern is horizontal.

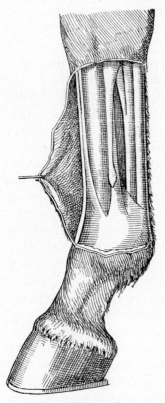

FIG. 340.—SHOWING RELATIVE POSITIONS OF TENDONS, ETC., IN THE METACARPAL REGION.

Immediately behind the metacarpus lies the suspensory or superior sesamoid ligament ; the short band extending from behind the knee half-way down the metacarpus is the check ligament ; behind it lies the perforans tendon to which it is connected ; the hindmost of the tendons shown is that of the flexor pedis perforatus muscle.

PROGNOSIS.—Section of the extensor tendons is much less serious than that of the flexors, and, of course, section of two or all of the latter structures is more grave than that of one only. In all cases there is the danger of necrosis and its consequences supervening, and when one of the flexor sheaths is opened, there is grave fear of purulent synovitis ensuing. Apart from these complications, healing may be imperfect, being followed by elongation of the tendons, and consequent deformity and interference with function. Many cases of complete recovery from division of the flexor tendons and of the suspensory ligament have been recorded. Divided extensors generally heal without difficulty.

TREATMENT comprises antisepsis of the wound and immobilisation

of the limb in such a position that the ends of the divided structure or structures are brought as close together as possible. In small
animals suturing the tendon and the application of an antiseptic
pad and bandage are sufficient. In the horse suturing may also be
practised, and in addition to bandaging support by a special contrivance is necessary, such as the swan-necked shoe, or Defoy's
apparatus, or that of Brogniez, each of which acts as a prop beneath

FIG. 341.—RUPTURE OF THE FLEXOR PEDIS PERFORANS AND PERFORATUS TENDONS.

the fetlock. Slings are also indicated to keep the horse stationary
if of a docile disposition. Healing usually occurs within four weeks
when the case takes a favourable course. After it has taken place in
the horse, a shoe with thick heels or calkins is advisable in many cases
to take the strain off the cicatricial tissue and prevent elongation of the
tendon. After about two months the patient is able to put weight
on the affected limb. The fetlock may be abnormally low for a
considerable time, but eventually cicatricial contraction usually raises
it to its normal level.

Rupture of the Extensors of the Phalanges

Rupture of the extensor tendons is rare. It has been seen as a congenital condition in the foal. Rarely it is caused in the adult horse by a false step during galloping. There is inability to extend the

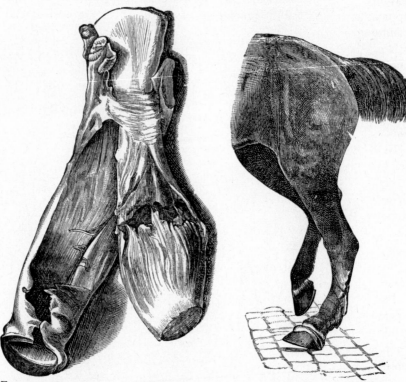

FIG. 342.—RUPTURE OF THE FLEXOR PEDIS PERFORANS BEHIND THE FETLOCK IN CONSEQUENCE OF SUPPURATION IN THE TENDON SHEATH.

FIG. 343.—RUPTURE OF THE FLEXOR PEDIS PERFORANS TENDON.
(From a photograph.)

phalanges and the gap between the ends of the ruptured tendon can be felt. Immobilisation of the part associated with antiphlogistic remedies effects a cure when the tendon is healthy. When of congenital origin there is no effective remedy.

Rupture of the Tendons of the Perforatus and Perforans
(see p. 77)

This condition has been frequently observed. The rupture may be primary or secondary and partial or complete. Primary rupture occurs as the result of violent stretching of the healthy tendon, as may occur during galloping or jumping. It is predisposed to by a period of idleness or a debilitating disease. When the muscles become tired during severe or prolonged exertion they cease to afford active support, and then extra passive strain is thrown on the tendons, which may give way in consequence. Secondary rupture is a sequel to degeneration or necrosis of the tendons. It is fairly common, following double plantar neurectomy. In a case of severe lameness in one limb, whereby it is unable to bear weight, the other limb may suffer from rupture of one or both flexor tendons from the constant unremitting strain thrown upon them, especially when the patient is debilitated or showing signs of lack of nutrition. Mares and cows affected with puerperal metritis have been known to suffer from complete rupture of the flexor tendons. A common seat of rupture is at the level of the fetlock.

SYMPTOMS.—The deformity caused by rupture of the tendons is the same as that resulting from section thereof, being characterised by hyperextension of the fetlock or phalangeal joints, as already described. When the accident is recent, the empty space between the ends of the divided tendon may be felt ; but at a later period it is filled by extravasated blood, and then the local evidence of rupture is not so clear. The subcarpal or subtarsal ligament may be ruptured and evince symptoms of severe strain, so that diagnosis of the exact nature of the lesion is difficult.

PROGNOSIS.—When the ruptured tendon has been the seat of disease or degeneration the case is hopeless. Complete rupture of a healthy tendon or tendons may be followed by recovery. When rupture is confined to one tendon, the prognosis is more favourable than when both are involved. Incomplete rupture of the perforatus and perforans or of their check ligaments is not uncommon, and varies in degree in different cases. It is characterised by marked inflammatory symptoms and severe lameness. Its diagnosis may be difficult.

TREATMENT.—Incomplete rupture is treated as a severe sprain. Immobilisation with a bandage is the chief indication. Complete rupture is dealt with on the same principles as those adopted for section of the tendons. Healing in the case of a healthy tendon occurs in the course of about six weeks if the ends are not too far apart. Two or three months at least will elapse before the animal is fit for use.

Ruptured tendons are more easily treated in small than in large animals. Suturing the ends of the tendon may be practised in the former, in which there is more chance of operating aseptically than in the latter. It is better not to attempt the operation in large animals, on account of the risk of infection and necrosis supervening.

Inflammatory New Growths on the Metacarpus and Metatarsus

Occasionally an open wound in these regions becomes the seat of a chronic inflammatory enlargement, an enormous amount of fibrous tissue being developed, presenting the appearances of a fibroma. It may be wide-based or fungiform in shape.

TREATMENT consists in excising the enlargement level with the surrounding parts and checking the recurrence of excessive granulation by the use of caustic and astringent dressings, formalin (1 in 40) having an excellent effect in this respect.

Rupture of the Suspensory Ligament

The suspensory ligament may be ruptured in much the same way as the flexor tendons. It is usually the result of violent effort in jumping and galloping, and is commonest in racehorses, in which it most frequently occurs towards the end of a race, when the muscles are more or less exhausted and an extra passive strain is thrown on the ligament as well as on the tendons.

SYMPTOMS.—The horse goes suddenly lame, stopping, as a rule, and holding up the affected limb. When weight is momentarily placed on the limb the fetlock comes down to the ground. Local examination reveals a solution of continuity in the ligament, usually just above its bifurcation. This is generally the condition in the racehorse when he is said to have " broken down." It may be accompanied by rupture of one or both flexor tendons or by fracture of the sesamoids. In some instances only one of the branches is ruptured, most frequently the inner one.

PROGNOSIS.—If the rupture occurs in two limbs or is complicated by that of other structures the case may be looked upon as incurable. As a rule treatment is not undertaken for complete rupture except it is unilateral and affecting a very valuable animal. The case is not quite so serious in a hind- as in a fore-limb.

TREATMENT is carried out on the same lines as those laid down for rupture of the flexor tendons, comprising immobilisation of the affected region with a plaster bandage and support of the fetlock by one of the devices mentioned. Several months, amounting often to a year or more, must elapse before work is possible.

Sprain of the Flexor Tendons—Tendinitis

The term " sprained tendons," or " sprain of the flexor tendons," includes sprain of the perforatus and perforans tendons and their check ligaments and of the suspensory ligament. The condition is much more common in the fore- than in the hind-limbs, due undoubtedly to the fact that in all classes of animals the former bear the greater part of the body-weight and in saddle-horses the greater proportion of the weight of the rider. The lesion is particularly common in hunters and chasers, the nature of whose work exposes most of the structures in question to over-distension. The mechanism of sprain has been explained by Barrier and Siedamgrotzky by the aid of instantaneous photography of the various phases of movement of the limbs. Working independently, they arrived at the same conclusions. They found that the moment the foot is placed on the ground there is flexion of the corono-pedal joint, and also, but to a less extent, of the suffragino-coronal joint, whereby the distances between the points of origin and insertion of the perforans and perforatus tendons are diminished, thus relaxing these tendons and leaving all the strain at this moment to be borne by the suspensory ligament, which stretches, allowing the fetlock to descend. After this descent has gone a certain distance the perforatus is put on the stretch, and helps the suspensory ligament to support the bodyweight. It follows from this that if the foot is brought to the ground with great violence the suspensory and the perforatus are liable to be sprained, thus explaining why sprain of these structures is most common in horses doing fast work. They also found that just prior to the foot leaving the ground there is extension of the corono-pedal joint, increasing the distance between the points of origin and insertion of the perforans ; so that if an unusual effort is made at this time, its tendon and check ligament are apt to be sprained. The above findings are in accordance with experience in practice, the facts being that sprain of the perforatus and its check or supracarpal ligament and of the suspensory ligament is most common in galloping and fast-trotting horses, while that of the perforans and the subcarpal ligament is most frequent in draft-horses, in which the greatest effort is made just before the foot is lifted from the ground.

ETIOLOGY.—The etiology of sprained tendons comprises predisposing and exciting causes, which may be taken together as follows :

1. *Unfit Condition*, sprain being much more likely to occur in horses put to severe exertion after a term of rest or idleness than in those kept at regular work.

2. *Conformation.*—Any conformation which puts the " tendons " at a disadvantage favours sprain thereof, such as long sloping pasterns, a very oblique hoof, or one whose toe is long or heels very low, which increase the resistance to the action of the flexors. Also the more slender the fetlock when viewed from the side, the greater the mechanical disadvantage to which the tendons are placed. Horses with " tied-in " knees generally have this type of fetlock. The greater the muscular development of the hind-quarters, the greater the shock produced on the tendons in the fore-limbs by the violence with which the weight of the body is thrown forward on to them. In a horse with " calf-knees," the back tendons are at a disadvantage and predisposed to strain. A heavy body compared with the limbs also favours the condition.

3. *Temperament.*—When a horse is very high-spirited, he is more apt to over-exert his tendons than when of a phlegmatic temperament.

4. *Fast Work.*—Tendons are obviously more likely to be strained during fast work, like galloping, jumping, and fast trotting, than during slow work.

5. *Heavy Draft,* which, as already explained, predisposes to sprain of the perforans and the subcarpal ligament in the cart-horse.

6. *The Nature of the Ground.*—A slippery surface leads to slipping and unexpected movements, which often involve strain of ligaments and tendons, while irregular or yielding ground has the same effect, and in the case of cart-horses makes draft more difficult and irregular and necessitates occasional extraordinary efforts to overcome obstacles.

7. *Muscular Fatigue,* which occurs towards the end of a race or a tiring journey, is a fruitful source of strain, whose occurrence under such circumstances is well known. The muscles, being exhausted, cease to act, with the result that an increased passive strain is thrown on the tendons.

8. *The Quality of the Tendons.*—Soft " gummy " tendons are easily sprained, while " fine " hard tendons are able to withstand prolonged and violent exertion without ill-effects.

Tendinitis, apart from sprain, is caused by contusion and by the toxins of bacterial diseases like influenza and pneumonia, being accompanied in the latter case by synovitis. Invasion of the suspensory ligament by the *Filaria reticulata* occurs in Austria, Russia, and the South of France. It excavates galleries, which are afterwards represented by nodular enlargements. The ligament is predisposed to injury. The perforatus is less frequently affected.

SYMPTOMS.—The symptoms of sprained tendons vary according to the extent and acuteness of the lesions. In a recent case there is evidence of acute inflammation at the seat of sprain. The swelling may be very marked and diffuse, extending over the entire metacarpal region, or circumscribed, confined to a portion of the tendon or to one of the check ligaments, or to the suspensory ligament or one of its branches. The swelling may not be pronounced until two or three days after the accident. Palpation reveals the swelling and the abnormal heat, and pressure with the fingers causes the patient to evince pain. The latter is most marked in the early stage of the condition. Later it is not always in accordance with the gravity of the lesion, which may be very persistent, although the pain and lameness are not very pronounced. Lameness is always severe after the onset of acute tendinitis. It is most intense when the lesion is in the region of the knee or fetlock, or at the back of the pastern. At rest the horse may hold the fetlock flexed.

In cases of chronic sprain the lameness is comparatively slight, and may be intermittent. In some instances the mass of tendons is voluminous and indurated, the chief cause of enlargement often being a thickening of the aponeurosis ensheathing the tendons. In others the lesion is confined to one of the tendons or its ligament, or to the suspensory ligament, or to a part of one of these structures. Individual exploration of the latter reveals any abnormality that may be present. Sometimes the tendinitis is gradual in its development, commencing with stiffness or intermittent lameness, and becoming acute when the horse is put to severe exertion. When sprain occurs at the level of one of the sheaths it is accompanied by synovitis. As regards the incidence of sprain in each of the structures in question, the following chief sites may be mentioned :

1. *The perforatus*, the level of the superior carpal ligament, the upper and middle parts of the tendon, and its branches of insertion. A fairly common lesion is a thickening of the peritendineum in the middle part of the metacarpus resulting from slight and repeated strain. It gives the tendon a bowed appearance, and is known as " bowed tendon."

2. *The perforans*, the level of the check ligament, the middle part of the tendon, and the back of the pastern.

3. *The suspensory ligament*, one of its branches, just above its bifurca- tion, and the middle part of the body of the ligament.

DIAGNOSIS.—In an acute case in which the swelling is diffuse the diagnosis of the exact structure or part thereof involved may be difficult. The region in which most pain is evinced on compression with the fingers and thumb generally represents the chief seat of

sprain.   Each structure is best examined with the knee flexed.
Filariasis of the ligament is characterised by a nodular, diffuse, painless
swelling in the body of the structure, which persists in spite of rest and
treatment.

PROGNOSIS.—" Sprained tendons " is always a more or less serious
condition, because the injured part never completely regains its normal
condition and is predisposed to recurrence of the affection.   The
prognosis varies with the situation, extent, and intensity of the lesion.
Perforatus and suspensory sprains are less serious than those of the
perforans and check ligament.   When both the latter are affected at
the same time, the case is more grave than when one only is involved.
In any particular case the gravity of the lesion is in accordance with the
degree of injury to the structure—that is, with the number of fibres
ruptured or distended.   Severe sprains suddenly produced are of a
more serious nature than those occurring gradually, and may prove
incurable, while the latter usually respond to appropriate treatment.
Repair of ruptured fibres is brought about by the organisation of granulation tissue, and torn peritendineum and interfascicular fibrous tissue
are repaired in the same way.   The contraction of the new fibrous
tissue shortens the tendon involved, and may be so great as to cause
excessive flexion of the fetlock or interphalangeal joints, and consequent
" knuckling over."   When the sprain is chronic this is more likely to
ensue, owing to the greater amount of new fibrous tissue formation.
The prognosis is rendered more grave by the presence of complications,
such as chronic synovitis of the great sesamoidean or carpal sheath, or
ostitis of the phalanges, which is not an uncommon accompaniment of
the lesion.

TREATMENT.—In a general way preventative treatment consists in
avoiding as far as possible the predisposing causes mentioned.   Cold
bathing, massage, and bandaging, combined with regular exercise, tend
to keep the tendons in good condition.   Careful shoeing, ensuring equal
distribution of the weight on the foot and preserving the normal slope of
the digit, is an important point in protecting the tendons from sprain.

Curative treatment, generally speaking, consists in adopting the
measures described for the treatment of acute or chronic inflammation,
as the case may be.   The usual routine of treatment is as follows :

1. *Rest* is the first essential, to give Nature an opportunity of healing
the injured part ; without it other measures are useless.   It should be
prolonged even after the horse has become sound, as the damaged
part of the tendon remains weak and predisposed to sprain until the
new tissue is well developed.   Under this heading may be included

the application of a plaster bandage to immobilise the fetlock and pastern, a method of treatment, however, not often adopted. The patten or skate shoe with high calkins joined by a bar at their free extremities has been recommended to rest the tendons by preventing the limb bearing weight. It raises the foot 3 or 4 inches from the ground, and is in contact with the latter on a skate-like edge, rendering the foot unstable and unfitted to bear weight. It is of very doubtful advantage, and is rarely employed. Raising the heels of an ordinary shoe relaxes the tendons and relieves tension thereon, and on this ground may be justifiable ; but it has the objection when its use is continued for a considerable time of favouring contraction of the tendons. When it is the suspensory ligament that is affected a shoe with low heels is indicated, as it relieves the strain upon it and throws more on to the tendons.

2. *Cold and Astringent Applications* in the form of constant cold irrigation, cold baths, or cold compresses, and the usual cooling lotions have a very beneficial effect in the early stages of the condition, when the pain is severe and the swelling well marked.

3. *Hot Moist Applications* may be employed at once, but usually after No. 2, to promote absorption of inflammatory exudate and prevent thickening in the part. They must be frequently repeated. Hot moist compresses applied over the tendons and renewed every half-hour have an excellent effect. A hot poultice of kaolin or antiphlogistine applied over the inflamed region to a depth of about $\frac{1}{2}$ inch, and covered by a layer of cotton-wool and a bandage exerting slight pressure, is considered by many to be the best form of hot application. It retains the heat for a long time and is certainly very efficacious.

4. *Massage* is always indicated after the acute stage has passed. Its good effects are incontestable. It should be practised for five to ten minutes twice daily in the manner described (see Massage, p. 263).

5. *Compression* by wadding or cotton-wool and bandage is good to promote the reduction of inflammatory swelling, and is always indicated after massage. The late Mr. Wm. Hunting advised the use of cotton-wool and a linen bandage during the day and of a woollen bandage alone during the night. In chronic cases support and compression may be effected with plaster bandages such as Burgess's plaster bandages or those made by spreading roboreous plaster liquefied by heat over strips of calico. These are left in position for six to eight weeks, provided no complication ensues in the form of inflammation of the skin caused by the bandage.

6. *Counter-irritation* by liniments, blisters, or the actual cautery is

frequently resorted to in subacute and chronic forms of sprains. The massage associated with the application of a liniment or mercurial ointment probably accounts for the greater part of its beneficent action. Blistering, or firing and blistering, often has the desired effect, but some chronic cases are met with which defy all kinds of treatment. Superficial firing in the form of transverse lines or of the herring-bone pattern is usually adopted. Deep needle-point firing is the most efficacious, but has the objection that the deep-seated cicatrices to which it gives rise predispose somewhat to shortening of the tendons. (See Objections to Firing, p. 258.)

Other special forms of treatment comprise :

1. *The Insufflation of Air* into the subcutaneous connective tissue of the region, introduced by Joly. A rubber tourniquet is applied above the knee. The air is slowly pumped in through several layers of iodoform wool, which acts as a filter, sufficient being injected to distend the skin moderately over the tendons. The puncture made by the needle is dressed with tincture of iodine, and the tourniquet is removed. The horse is left loose in a box. The insufflated air spreads to the forearm. On the following days cold douches and massage are employed. This treatment is said to be particularly useful for peritendinous thickening. A couple of weeks after its adoption the affected tissues become supple, painless, and free from peritendinous induration. It has been claimed for this treatment that it has cured cases in which firing had failed.

2. *Subcutaneous Injection of the Essence of Turpentine*, as recommended by Cagny, a French veterinarian. One gramme of the preparation is injected on the inner and outer aspect of the limb, below the knee, between the suspensory ligament and the tendons. On the following days a large inflammatory swelling forms at the seat of injection. It is a very severe form of treatment which most practitioners would hesitate to adopt.

3. *Use of Radio-active Muds.*—These are described as having antiphlogistic, analgesic, tonic, and stimulating properties, and have been recommended for tendon sprains in the form of baths, plasters, and dressings. To form the bath, 7 or 8 ounces of radio-active mud are added to 2 or 3 gallons of water at a temperature of 113° to 122° F. It is used once daily for one hour after morning exercise. Slight massage is practised at the same time. After the bath a poultice of the radio-active mud is applied in a thick layer extending beyond the affected part, and covered with a layer of cotton-wool and bandage without pressure. This treatment is to be continued for weeks, when

gradual progressive improvement will be noticed. Cases in which firing followed by prolonged rest at grass had failed were much improved in ten days and cured in six weeks after the commencement of the radio-active treatment. Even a case which had resisted ordinary measures for two years is said to have been cured in fifteen days by this method, the swelling and lameness having disappeared.

As soon as lameness has disappeared, regular daily walking exercise is to be prescribed, if the horse is not at grass. When the animal is put to work the shoeing must be carefully attended to, lest the affected tendon be placed at a disadvantage by an unsuitable shoe.

When all forms of treatment have been exhausted and lameness persists, the only resort is median neurectomy for the fore-limb and posterior tibial for the hind one (see pp. 440 and 451).

Knuckling at the Fetlocks—Contracted Flexor Tendons

Knuckling at the fetlock is due to retraction or contraction or shortening of the flexor tendons. There may be said to be three degrees of the condition :

1. The phalanges are almost vertical.

2. A perpendicular let fall from the front of the fetlock strikes the front of the hoof.

3. The perpendicular referred to in No. 2 reaches the ground in front of the hoof.

This deformity must be considered separately in (1) young animals, and in (2) aged or adult subjects.

, 1. **Young Animals.**—In these it is most frequently congenital, but may be acquired within the first three or four years of age, usually during the first year.

The CAUSE of the condition is not very clear. The fact that recovery frequently ensues spontaneously would go to show that it is generally due to mere shortness or tension of the tendons. It has, however, been ascribed to insufficient nutrition of the dam, to muscular debility induced by confinement in the stable, especially when it is cold and damp, to insufficient food, to digestive troubles, to muscular rheumatism, and to rickets. In cases of muscular weakness the patient seeks to relieve the muscles by " standing over " on the joints. Foals, calves, and lambs suffer from the abnormality, and except for it they may be perfectly developed and in normal health. Among foals it is the coarser breeds which most frequently suffer. Usually both fore-limbs are involved. Less frequently the knuckling is in the hind-limbs.

SYMPTOMS.—The young animal shows one of the degrees of knuckling mentioned or complete flexion of the affected joint or joints, the front of which is on the ground bearing weight. In the latter case an open wound is soon produced, which may extend into the joint and lead to septic arthritis. In the other cases the animals are apt to stumble when trotted. On palpation the tendons seem normal.

FIG. 344.—DOUBLE-SIDED " KNUCKLING " IN A TWO-YEAR-OLD COLT.
(From a photograph.)

PROGNOSIS.—When the condition is congenital or appears a few days after birth and is attended to before complicated by open joint, recovery is the rule ; but when the deformity is acquired later it is more likely to be due to some systemic defect, and the case is not so hopeful.

TREATMENT.—When the condition is congenital the tendency is for the normal position to be assumed, and it is brought about spontaneously if weight can be borne on the foot. The aim of treatment is to get the toe of the foot, at least, to bear weight. Splints or a plaster-of-Paris bandage may be required to maintain the foot in this position, care being taken not to damage the tender skin with the hard dressing.

The young animal is inclined to lie down when the dressing is applied, defeating its object. Slings often succeed in such cases in keeping the animal standing for a sufficient time to obtain the desired effect. At a later period, when the foal's or young horse's foot is capable of being shod, a special shoe may be applied which tends to throw the fetlock back into position. In slight cases it is sufficient to lower the heels and put on a shoe with the toe thickened and projecting in front. In more pronounced cases Friebel's apparatus (Fig. 345) or that of Brogniez is indicated. If these measures fail, tenotomy is necessary ; but then the case is not very promising. Occasionally a case is met with in which the fetlock remains fixed in the flexed position after cutting the tendons.

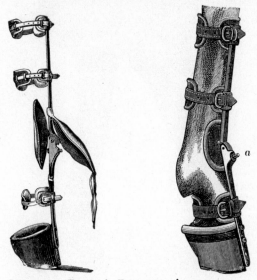

FIG. 345.—FRIEBEL'S EXTENSION APPARATUS.

2. **Adult Subjects.**—Excessive volar flexion in adults may be due to cicatricial contraction of the tendons following chronic tendinitis, or shortening of these structures may be secondary to other lesions, such as ringbone or diffuse osteo-periostitis of the pastern, chronic synovitis, dry arthritis of an interphalangeal joint, corns, or contracted foot. All these conditions interfere more or less with the normal support of weight on the limb, causing the fetlock to assume a permanent degree of flexion, so that the flexors, being no longer subjected to the antagonism which they experience under normal conditions, contract gradually, causing the pastern to become upright or directed slightly downwards and backwards, and the fetlock-joint to project forward.

54

Symptoms.—The deformity, varying in degree, as stated, is very obvious, and local examination reveals the cause of the trouble—viz., one of the lesions mentioned above. The lameness or interference with gait is in accordance with the nature of the affection. When the contraction is very marked and confined to the perforatus tendon the fetlock-joint only shows excessive flexion, the foot remaining flat on the ground ; but when the perforans is much contracted, the fetlock and interphalangeal joints are over-flexed and the heel of the foot

Fig. 346.—Excessive " Knuckling " in a Horse.
(From a photograph.)

cannot be placed on the ground, and weight may be borne by the front of the wall. When the knuckling is less marked, the lameness is characterised chiefly by a tendency to stumble. When the abnormality is of the first degree, the affected fetlock becomes straightened or normal in appearance when forced to bear weight by lifting the other limb ; but in the more advanced degrees of flexion the latter is aggravated when the weight on the limb is increased.

Prognosis is always more or less grave, its degree of gravity depending on the nature of the lesion with which the condition is associated. The only case likely to be improved by treatment is that due to cicatricial contraction of the tendons.

TREATMENT consists in adopting measures appropriate to the cause, but is not likely to be successful except for mere contraction of the tendons, for which tenotomy may have the desired effect (see p. 454). Horses which are " knuckled " if worked slowly and on soft ground may be made useful for a long time by applying a long-toed shoe, though this will not cure or even improve the original disease.

Fracture of the Metacarpus and Metatarsus

The metacarpus or metatarsus may be fractured by direct violence, such as a kick or by bending of the bone, as when the horse puts the foot in a hole during galloping. Occasionally the fracture occurs mysteriously when the horse is cantering on level ground.

SYMPTOMS AND DIAGNOSIS.—The symptoms are as usual for complete fracture, and the diagnosis is always easy except for a fissured fracture, which is not common. Fracture of one of the splint-bones alone may result from direct injury, and is characterised by acute inflammation, which may be hard to distinguish from osteo-periostitis if crepitation cannot be detected.

PROGNOSIS.—In light animals of the large type there is a good chance of recovery, especially if of a docile disposition. But in heavy horses a cure is not likely to be effected, and treatment is seldom undertaken. Cure is the rule in cattle, and almost invariably ensues in small animals.

TREATMENT is carried out on general principles already described, and consists in accurately replacing the fragments in their normal position and maintaining them there by an immobilising dressing extending from the knee (exclusive) to the foot. Plaster-of-Paris bandages form a very convenient and suitable dressing applied over an even layer of padding. Carefully adjusted splints will also have the desired effect. Light horses do not require slings, but they are essential for heavy subjects. As regards dogs and cats, nothing need be added to what has been said in connection with fractures in general. Many cases of cure of fracture of the large metacarpal bone in the horse have been recorded. In a valuable animal treatment should always be undertaken. Fracture of the splint bone is dealt with as a contusion or open wound as the case may be.

Splints

The typical splint is an exostosis situated on or contiguous to one of the splint-bones, but the term splint is often applied to an exostosis on the large metacarpal or metatarsal bone quite clear of the splint-bone. The commonest site of splint is the inner aspect of the fore-limb.

When splint appears in the hind-limb it is usually on its outer aspect. The upper and middle thirds of the cannon region are the usual levels of the exostosis.

Varieties of Splint.—The recognised forms of splint are :

1. *Simple splint*, a simple exostosis at the usual seat of splint.

2. *Knee splint*, in which the exostosis involves the head of the splint-bone or actually encroaches on the knee-joint.

3. *Rod or peg splint*, an exostosis on either side of the cannon-bone connected by an abnormal ridge of bone beneath the suspensory ligament.

4. *Chain splint*, consisting of several small bony excrescences arranged in a row along the course of the small splint-bone.

ETIOLOGY.—The etiology of splint may be discussed under the following headings :

1. *Heredity.*—There is undoubtedly a hereditary predisposition to splints, and they may appear in this way in young unbroken horses without any apparent exciting cause, not being accompanied by pain or lameness. It may be a predisposing conformation which is inherited, such as small knee-joints or bad quality of bone which nature endeavours to strengthen by a new osseous deposit, or an abnormal shape of the limb whereby the weight is unequally distributed, causing a strain of the carpal or interosseous ligaments which may lead to osteo-periostitis and the formation of an exostosis.

2. *Sprain of the Interosseous Ligament.*—Splint usually makes its appearance in a horse under five years of age when first put to work, and is due in many cases to sprain of the interosseous ligament which has not yet become ossified. This occurs more frequently on the inner aspect of the fore-limb, due probably to the fact that the lower surface of the trapezoid articulates almost entirely with the small metacarpal bone, thus transmitting to the latter most of the weight which it bears, whereas the unciform articulates chiefly with the large metacarpus, so that little strain is put on the interosseous ligament on the outer aspect of the limb. The periosteum and the bone become involved in the inflammation, osteoperiostitis and the formation of an exostosis ensuing. Sprain of this ligament affords the most satisfactory explanation of splint of inflammatory origin occurring in young horses first put to work.

3. *Sprain of the Carpal Sheath.*—Traction of this sheath on the periosteum, where it is attached, may give rise to an exostosis at the usual seat of splint, or at the back of the large metacarpus.

4. *Sprain of the Suspensory Ligament* at its origin may be the cause of splint at the back of the metacarpus below the knee.

5. *Concussion* of the bone itself by fast work on hard ground may be sufficient to cause osteo-periostitis and a consequent exostosis.

6. *Traumatic Injury.*—An exostosis on the inner side of the meta-carpal bone below the knee may be caused by the horse striking the part by the other foot during progression, as in " speedy-cutting." On the other hand, an exostosis may appear first from some other cause, and owing to its prominence it may be struck as mentioned.

A blow of any kind on the metacarpus may give rise to an exostosis at the injured part. Such an enlargement clear of the splint-bones is commonly called a " bump " rather than a splint.

SYMPTOMS.—When a splint appears without prior inflammation, the only symptom is the presence of the exostosis. When it is of inflam-matory origin, there are local symptoms of acute inflammation and lameness. Before the exostosis is formed, the inflammation is marked chiefly by pain on pressure and abnormal heat in the affected part. The swelling is at first of an œdematous nature. When the splint is developed, it can be easily felt as a bony enlargement varying in size generally from a pea to a walnut. The following are methods of examining the limb for splints (say the near fore) :

1. Stand on the near side of the horse, looking in the same direction ; pass the fingers of the right hand down the inner aspect of the limb from the knee to the fetlock along the course of the splint-bone and its junction with the large metacarpus.

2. Stand looking in the opposite direction, lift the foot and flex the knee, hold the pastern in the right hand, pass the left thumb over the inner splint-bone from its upper to its lower extremity, pushing the tendons aside at the same time. To search for a splint at the back of the bone, examine deeply in front of the tendons to ascertain if the sus-pensory ligament is bulged backwards by an exostosis. To examine the outside of the limb reverse the hands.

3. Stand as in No. 1, but lift the foot and flex the knee, and examine the limb inside and outside as in No. 2, taking care to avoid being hit should the horse strike backwards with the lifted foot.

Splint lameness presents the following features :

1. There is a striking contrast between the degree of lameness at the walk and at the trot ; the horse may walk practically sound, but trots decidedly lame.

2. The lameness is more marked on hard than on soft ground, and is worse down-hill than on the level.

3. There may be imperfect flexion of the knee and the limb may be abducted in its forward movement.

4. The lameness does not improve with exercise ; it rather becomes more marked.

DIAGNOSIS.—The diagnosis of splint lameness depends on (a) the age of the horse, it being rarely present in a horse over five years old ; (b) the local symptoms of acute or subacute inflammation ; and (c) the features of the lameness mentioned above.   Cases of doubt of course arise, which may necessitate the use of local anæsthesia to aid in arriving at a diagnosis (see Lameness, p. 796).

PROGNOSIS.—A splint devoid of inflammation is of no consequence, except it is so large that it is liable to be struck by the other foot during progression.   Then it is serious, as the horse may fall when he strikes it.   When the acute inflammation associated with the development of a splint has run its course, the pain and lameness disappear and the exostosis remains as a harmless blemish, except it is very large.   Splint involving the knee-joint may be called knee spavin, and is an incurable lesion.   If it is quite close to the articulation, but not interfering with its articular surface, it is serious on account of the possibility of its encroaching thereon.   A peg splint often causes persistent lameness, which may be ascribed to the pressure of the suspensory ligament on the exostosis or to the latter causing distension of the ligament. Exostoses of a longish form occurring on the small metacarpus in young horses are apt to be troublesome.   The chance of recovery is less if in consequence of defective formation of the limb the affected region is likely to be struck by the other foot.   In exceptional instances even a simple splint causes prolonged lameness in spite of treatment.   In rare cases the exostosis disappears, being apparently removed by the osteoclasts.

TREATMENT.—The treatment of splint is on the same lines as that for all inflammatory conditions, and comprises :

1. *Rest*, which is the great essential when the lesion is acute.

2. *Cold and astringent applications*, as advised for inflammation in general.   They are continued until the acute inflammation has subsided.

3. *The application of a blister* to the affected region, biniodide of mercury 1 in 8 being the most effective.   Perchloride of mercury 1 to 4 or 8 of spirit carefully rubbed in with a burnt cork or a tooth-brush is recommended by some veterinarians, but its action may be too severe. This method is indicated after No. 2 has had its effect.

4. *Needle-point firing*, which is the most effective form of treatment for chronic splint lameness, the points being inserted into the exostosis.

5. *Pressure* with a piece of flat lead or of leather, associated with repeated massage, which has been recommended for the purpose of

causing absorption of the exostosis. It may require to be practised for months before its effect is shown, or it may fail entirely.

6. *Periosteotomy* performed over the splint in the same manner as described for spavin (see p. 458). This may be done, however, before the exostosis appears, and may prevent its production by releasing the exudate beneath the periosteum and promoting its absorption before it undergoes ossification. Its practice has not given better results than No. 4.

When after point firing and repeated blistering along with rest extending over months or a year lameness continues, median neurectomy is indicated. When the splint is very large and being struck by the other limb during exercise, the only remedy is removal of the exostosis as follows : Cast and anæsthetise the horse, prepare the site in the usual way, apply a tourniquet on the upper and lower extremities of the cannon-bone, surround the limb with a calico cloth with an opening opposite the exostosis, and make an incision through the skin and periosteum parallel to the long axis of the tumour. Reflect the periosteum or remove it over the exostosis. By means of a sharp chisel and mallet excise the latter level with the bones. Suture the wound and apply an antiseptic pad and bandage. Strict asepsis is essential to avoid the risk of infection and necrosis of the bone. The operation should not be lightly undertaken, owing to the risk mentioned.

In a case of persistent chronic splint lameness cure of the latter has been obtained by repeated fast exercise on the road. It is the opinion of some experienced horse owners that forced exercise is better than rest for persistent splint lameness, the concussion of the bone thus produced apparently acting as a counter-irritant intensifying the local inflammation which on subsequent rest is followed by resolution and consequent recovery from the lameness.

" Sore Shins "

The term " sore shins " is applied to an inflammatory condition of the metacarpal and less frequently of the metatarsal regions, commonly met with in young racehorses in training. It is particularly common in horses from one year and a half to two years old. It seldom affects three-year-olds, and is rare in aged animals.

ETIOLOGY.—The predisposing cause apparently is the immature condition of the animals, while the exciting cause is concussion, the affection being very prevalent when the " going " is hard, although it may also occur when the going is soft. The nature of the lesion has been disputed, but there is no doubt that the commonest source of the trouble is an osteo-periostitis of the cannon-bone, affecting chiefly its lower third.   In some cases the inflammation is confined to the extensor tendons and the peritendinous tissue, constituting *pseudo-sore shins*.

SYMPTOMS.—The first symptom observed is lameness, usually in both fore-limbs, although it may be more pronounced in one than in the other.   There is a diffuse painful swelling on the anterior aspect of the cannon-bone.   Eventually the bone becomes thickened and assumes a more convex shape in front.   In aggravated cases the ligaments of the fetlock become ossified, causing anchylosis of the joint.

PROGNOSIS.—The prognosis is favourable when the horse is rested on the first appearance of lameness, but if work is continued the case may become incurable, owing to the formation of exostoses involving the fetlock-joint.

TREATMENT comprises rest and the usual antiphlogistic applications.   Iodine ointment has been found useful.   Massage is always advisable when the acute symptoms have subsided.   Later blistering is indicated.   Firing is seldom necessary.   Periosteotomy has been advised, but it is better not to practise it on account of the risk of infection and necrosis of the bone.

Rheumatoid Ostitis

Sometimes an intermittent form of lameness is met with, due apparently to a rheumatoid ostitis of the large metacarpus, characterised by pain on pressure in certain regions of the bone, most commonly in its upper part and chiefly below and behind the carpus.

The TREATMENT is that for rheumatism.

AFFECTIONS OF THE FETLOCK AND DIGIT

The fetlock and digit, owing to their situation, are much exposed to traumatic lesions, which vary in gravity from excoriation of the skin to deep wounds involving the bone or tendons or ligaments, or penetrating into the great or small sesamoidean sheath or into the fetlock or one of the interphalangeal joints.   They present symptoms in accordance with their nature, and the prognosis depends on the character of the lesion.   The only dangerous conditions are open wounds of the flexor synovial sheaths and of the joints.

TREATMENT is carried out on general principles.

Special mention may be made of lesions on the inner aspect of the fetlock caused by striking it with the other foot during progression. They vary in character, including excoriation, contusion with subcutaneous extravasation of blood and serum, an abscess, an area of necrosis, and an open wound. The front of the fetlock may be excoriated or contused as the result of knuckling over when asleep in the standing position.

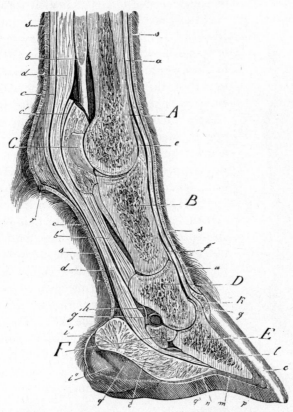

Fig. 347.—Perpendicular Mesial Section of Right Fore-Foot (the Position of the Lower Bones is shown rather too Upright).

A, Lower end of great metacarpus ; *B,* suffraginis or first phalanx ; *C,* inner sesamoid bone (to render the bone visible, a portion of the intersesamoid ligament has been removed) ; *D,* coronet bone ; *E,* pedal bone ; *F,* navicular bone ; *a,* extensor pedis tendon ; *b,* superior sesamoid or suspensory ligament ; *b′,* inferior sesamoid ligament ; *c,* flexor pedis perforatus tendon ; *c′,* great sesamoid sheath ; *d,* flexor pedis perforans tendon ; *e,* capsular ligament of the fetlock-joint ; *f,* capsular ligament of pastern-joint ; *g* and *g′,* capsular ligament of coffin-joint ; *h,* bursa of flexor pedis perforans ; *i,* plantar cushion ; *i′,* portion of plantar cushion forming the bulbs of the heel ; *k,* coronary band ; *l,* sensitive wall ; *m,* sensitive sole ; *n,* sensitive frog ; *o,* horny wall ; *p,* horny sole ; *q,* horny frog ; *r,* ergot at base of fetlock ; *s,* skin.

Treatment of these lesions is preventative and curative. Brushing may be prevented by appropriate shoeing, and the part subjected to injury may be protected by a boot.

The worst injuries to the coronet are caused by treads, and when

produced by sharpened calkins during frosty weather they may penetrate deeply into the tissues, involving the lateral cartilage and even the
synovial capsule of the corono-pedal joint. These wounds are often
complicated with moist gangrene due to contamination with freezing
mud. The sloughing may only involve the skin or extend into a joint.

In such cases the patient often shows symptoms
of toxæmia, which in some instances is sufficient
to cause death. Quittor may be a sequel to deep
injury of the coronet. The thick skin in the
coronary region may be underrun with pus, which
escapes through openings here and there, simulating purulent arthritis of the pedal-joint, from
which, however, it is distinguished by the
absence of synovia and by the symptoms of pain
being less acute than in the latter condition.

The TREATMENT of these open lesions is best
carried out by immersing the foot in a warm
antiseptic bath during the day, and covering
the lesions with an antiseptic compress during
the night. When the inflammatory region extends beneath the horn the pain is particularly
intense, and relief is afforded by thinning the
horn over the part with the rasp. This is always
indicated when there is a painful wound on the
coronet. If quittor or necrosis of the plantar
aponeurosis supervenes, it is dealt with as described under these headings.

FIG. 348.— ENLARGE-
MENT OF THE BURSA OF
THE EXTENSOR PEDIS
TENDON.

See also Figs. 336 and
337.

Capped Fetlock—Distension or Hygroma of the Subcutaneous Bursa in Front of the Fetlock

This condition is equivalent to capped knee,
and occurs in the same way from repeated injury.
It has been seen in cavalry stables as the result
of horses knuckling over on bare flagged floors.
The bursa may become distended suddenly from a contusion, and
then show acute inflammation, otherwise it is of a chronic nature
and devoid of inflammation. It is not a serious affection, but forms
a blemish that may be difficult to get rid of.

TREATMENT is the same as that for hygroma in front of the knee.
Needle-point firing gives the best results in the chronic cystic

condition, but when the walls of the bursa are fibrous a permanent thickening remains.

Synovitis and Distension of the Sheath of the Extensor Pedis Tendon in Front of the Fetlock

Acute synovitis supervenes from the usual causes, but is not common. Chronic synovitis or mere distension of the sheath is more frequently met with, and its cause is not always apparent. It is characterised by a soft, fluctuating, painless swelling, occupying the antero-lateral aspects of the fetlock and inferior part of the cannon region. When large it is very markedly bilobed, being divided into two halves by the extensor pedis tendon, which can be felt on palpation. The condition is much more common in the hind- than in the fore-limb. It is devoid of inflammatory symptoms, and does not cause lameness, but is difficult to remove.

The TREATMENT is as usual for chronic synovitis. Incision should not be resorted to, on account of the risk of infection of the joint with whose synovial sac the sheath sometimes communicates.

Acute and Chronic Synovitis of the Great Sesamoidean Sheath—Windgalls

Acute closed synovitis of the sheath arises from the causes given for synovitis in general. It accompanies tendinitis in this region. Purulent synovitis is common here as the result of septic penetrating wounds of the sheath, and requires no further description than that given in general surgery. Lifting of the limb, as in chronic gonitis, is characteristic of this condition. The limb is carried further forwards than in chronic gonitis.

Chronic synovitis here is also in accordance with the condition as dealt with generally. It is sometimes associated with sesamoiditis, or sprain of the sesamoid ligaments or of the flexor tendons, and its prognosis depends largely on these lesions. A simple chronic synovitis will respond to treatment.

Occasionally a case of subacute synovitis of the great sesamoidean sheath is met with, characterised by an extremely tense distension of the sheath and by severe lameness. The sheath may burst through the skin under the great tension of the liquid, giving rise to a synovial fistula. When this occurs at the upper part of the sheath the fistula closes after a while, to be followed, perhaps, by another at a lower level, and so on until the lowest part of the sheath is reached, the swelling continuing to subside gradually and eventually

disappearing, when the animal usually goes sound.   The application of
a blister of biniodide of mercury is generally effective in promoting
resolution and dispelling the lameness in the course of six to eight
weeks.   Suppuration of the sheath rarely ensues in such cases.

Windgalls are mere distensions of the great sesamoidean sheath.
They appear just above the sesamoids at the level of the inferior
third of the tendons in the form of two roundish or ovoid swellings,
one on either side, between the tendons and the suspensory ligament.

Fig. 349.—Position of the Limb in Suppurative Inflammation of the
Great Sesamoidean Sheath.
(From a photograph.)

They are described as tendinous windgalls, to distinguish them from
articular windgalls, which are due to distension of the synovial
membrane of the fetlock-joint, and appear one on either side just above
the fetlock between the suspensory ligament and the back of the cannon-
bone.   The tendinous windgalls vary in size in different cases, but the
inner and outer swellings are usually of the same dimensions.

The CAUSE of windgalls is not very clear.   They may be a sequel
to chronic synovitis, but most frequently they arise spontaneously
as a dropsical condition of the sheath.   They may appear as such in

young horses that have never worked, especially of the draft type, but they are most common in aged horses, most of which are affected to some degree. The ordinary windgall found in the working horse is devoid of inflammatory symptoms, does not cause lameness, and is of no practical significance. Sometimes the windgall continues to increase in size, and when of long standing its walls may become much thickened and even calcareous. In this case the action of the tendons may be interfered with, causing the horse to be stiff in action and go on the toes.

TREATMENT of windgalls is seldom indicated. In young horses their disappearance is desirable, as they deteriorate their value. Constant bandaging reduces or dispels them. Plaster-of-Paris bandages are the most effective. If it is wished to reduce or get rid of old tense wind-galls, they may be treated as chronic synovitis by aspiration and in-injection or by needle-point firing, or by a combination of the two methods.

Sprain of the Fetlock-Joint

The fetlock is said to be sprained when the flexor tendons or sus-pensory ligament at its level or its own lateral ligaments have been over-distended. When the joint is moved beyond its physiological limits some of these structures are over-stretched or sprained. The situation of the sprain may be anterior or posterior and external or internal. Anterior sprain ensues when the body-weight is thrown on the fetlock in the flexed position, which may occur when the foot slips backwards ; while posterior strain is caused by over-extension of the joint, as may supervene during heavy draft or fast exercise. Lateral sprains are due to a false step or inward or outward slipping.

SYMPTOMS.—In a recent sprain there is more or less intense lame-ness and acute local inflammation. At rest the fore-limb is held forward with the fetlock partly flexed, while the hind-limb rests only on the toe. During the walk and the trot the weight is only supported by the toe of the affected limb, and is quickly transferred to the other limb. The inflammation is characterised by heat, pain, and swelling. Pain is evinced on compression and on passive movement of the joint. To examine the joint the limb is held flexed by an assistant, who grasps the lower end of the cannon-bone while the surgeon catches the pastern in his hand and moves the joint in different directions.

Chronic sprain may succeed the acute form or appear gradually. At rest the fetlock is very upright or slightly " knuckled " over in front, although the back tendons are not contracted. There is a variable amount of thickening in the vicinity of the joint. During trotting the fetlock remains upright or partly knuckled.   Anterior and posterior sprains are common, but lateral sprains are rare.

PROGNOSIS depends on the severity of the sprain.   It is not favourable in a chronic case with " overshot " fetlock—that is, with the joint in a state of semi-flexion (" knuckling ").

TREATMENT is that for acute or chronic inflammation.   In an acute case it comprises complete rest, cold and hot applications (antiphlogistine) in the order mentioned, followed by massage and compression. Massage is very important, as it is effective in reducing subacute inflammatory swellings.   The same applies to compression.   Firm pressure by a lead plaster bandage or a Burgess's plaster bandage has given excellent results, due to its supporting and immobilising effects. In chronic cases counter-irritation by blistering or firing, or both, is indicated, and if this fails median or posterior tibial neurectomy must be resorted to.

Sprain of the Corono-Pedal Joint

Sprain of the corono-pedal joint is a common condition.   It is the result of slipping or making a false step or of violent effort.   Irregularity of tread may cause it, or it may be a consequence of faulty shoeing interfering with the normal distribution of the weight on the foot.

SYMPTOMS.—There is a variable degree of lameness depending on the severity of the injury to the ligaments. Its characteristics are similar to those of fetlock lameness.   It may come on suddenly during work or be first noticed when the horse is going out in the morning.

The local symptoms include heat, pain, and swelling in the region of the coronet.   Pain is evinced on pressure over the coronet and on passive movement of the joint, especially rotation.   The horse may be fidgety when being shod, owing to the pain caused by the movement of the joint.

TREATMENT is the same as for all sprains or inflammatory lesions, and as mentioned for sprains of the fetlock.   When the case is incurable, median or posterior tibial neurectomy is indicated.

Sprain of the Inferior Sesamoidean Ligaments

Sprain of these ligaments ensues on hyperextension of the first interphalangeal articulation, as may result from slipping or a violent effort during heavy draft or when jumping.   Sloping pasterns and long toes or low heels predispose to the condition.   The degree of injury may be slight or severe.   The sprain is more common in the fore- than in the hind-limbs. Only a few or most of the ligamentous fibres may be involved.

SYMPTOMS.—When the lesion is suddenly produced, there is severe lameness and pronounced local inflammation, characterised by swelling

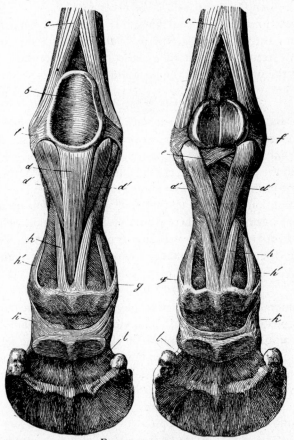

FIGS. 350 AND 351.

a External lateral ligament of pastern-joint; *b*, intersesamoidean ligament; *c*, superior sesamoidean ligament; *d*, middle limb of inferior sesamoidean ligament; *d'*, lateral limb of inferior sesamoidean ligament; *e*, cruciate ligament; *f*, lateral sesamoidean ligament; *g*, outer lateral ligament of the coronary-joint; *h* and *h'*, posterior corono-suffraginal ligaments; *i*, outer lateral ligament of pedal-joint; *k*, postero-lateral ligaments of navicular bone; *l*, fibrous sheath of synovial membrane of coffin-joint.

and by pain on pressure and on movement of the phalanges. The condition, however, may be slow and insidious in onset, with little or no local manifestations. The lameness in this case is slight, and may not be very noticeable until the horse goes on hard ground or is made to bear extra weight on the limb. In all cases there is a tendency to go on the toe.   When the lesion is chronic, exostoses may eventually form at the insertion of the ligaments, constituting posterior ringbone. It may also be accompanied by distension of the great sesamoidean sheath.   At rest the animal often places the heel of the foot of the affected limb on the front wall of the other foot.

TREATMENT is on the usual lines.   If permanent lameness supervenes from osteo-periostitis and periarticular ringbone, neurectomy is the only resort.   Preventative measures are important, in superintending the preparation of the hoof and the way it is shod.

Sprain of the Digits in the Ox

Sprain of the digits occasionally occurs in the ox, especially in working cattle.   One of the claws only is involved, as a rule, the corono-pedal or the suffragino-coronal joint being affected.   If the lesion is in the inner claw the animal adducts the limb during progression, and if in the outer claw he abducts it.

The condition responds to the usual treatment for sprains.   The interdigital ligament, which prevents undue separation of the digits, may be over-stretched or partially ruptured.   Pain is evinced on separating the claws.   A bandage binding the two digits favours recovery.

Dislocation of the Fetlock

Dislocation of the fetlock may be complete or incomplete, and anterior, posterior, or lateral, and simple or compound.   Several cases of complete anterior or posterior dislocation of the fetlock, with little or no injury to the flexor tendons and suspensory ligament, have been recorded.   Incomplete dislocations are usually lateral.   Many cases, however, of complete dislocation are compound, with the metacarpus or metatarsus protruding through the skin.

The DIAGNOSIS is obvious.

PROGNOSIS is always more or less grave, although surprising cases of perfect recovery after simple complete dislocation have been recorded.

TREATMENT consists in reduction and retention (see Dislocations, p. 134).   A special apparatus may be employed to support the joint.

Inflammation of the Fetlock-Joint

Acute synovitis usually results from a sprain of the articulation, but it may be due to some bacterial disease.   It is characterised by acute local inflammation, with distension of the culs-de-sac of the synovial membrane, as in articular windgalls, and by lameness.

TREATMENT is on the principles prescribed for inflammation and for sprains in general.

Dry arthritis is occasionally met with in aged horses, apparently as the result of constant hard work, although it may be rheumatoid. It is associated with ossific deposits round the joint, and sometimes with distensions of its synovial capsule. It causes chronic lameness, for which the only relief is neurectomy. " Cab-horse disease," or " bobba bone," is sometimes associated with arthritis of this joint.

Articular Windgalls

These have already been alluded to as resulting from distension of the synovial capsule of the fetlock-joint, appearing on either side above the sesamoids between the suspensory ligament and the back of the cannon-bone. They are tense when the limb is bearing weight, and soft and fluctuating when it is lifted. There has been observed in racehorses a distension of this capsule appearing below the fetlock on either side of the pastern and extending down almost to the first interphalangeal joint. The swelling here may reveal abnormal heat on palpation, and be more or less painful on pressure. This form of distension is serious. It may disappear with rest, but reappears when the horse is put to work and gives rise to lameness. The ordinary synovial enlargement above the fetlock is usually of a chronic nature, and does not cause lameness as a rule.

TREATMENT is that prescribed for chronic synovitis.

Inflammation of the Interphalangeal Joints

This is rarely observed except as a chronic arthritis in conjunction with ringbone, under which it is dealt with.

Open Wounds of the Fetlock-Joint

The fetlock-joint is very exposed to open wounds, especially in its lateral aspects, at the points where the distensions of its synovial membrane appear, and in front, where its capsule is only supported at the level of the extensor pedis and, in the fore-limb, that of the extensor suffraginis. The articulation may be injured in various ways : by prods of forks, kicks, falls, barbed wire, by the blade of a mowing machine, and by other means. When the synovial membrane has been penetrated there is a copious discharge of synovia, which is increased by movement of the joint. The situation of the fistula distinguishes it from that of the great sesamoidean sheath.

The PROGNOSIS is always guarded, on account of the risk of infection

55

and septic arthritis supervening ; but when severe infection is excluded recovery is the rule. Many cases of cure of open fetlock-joint have been recorded.

TREATMENT is carried out on the principles mentioned in the section on " Open Joint." Suturing is indicated when the wound is comparatively extensive. Bier's hyperæmic treatment is always advisable to help to control infection and promote rapid healing.

Fractures of the Phalanges—Split Pastern

Fractures of the pastern are common in the horse, the os suffraginis being the bone most frequently affected. The fracture may be complete, with more or less displacement, or in the form of a fissure or crack in the bone. Fissured fracture occurs mostly in the first phalanx, and is known as " split pastern." The fissure usually commences in the depression on its upper articular surface, and extends straight through the length of the bone or takes an oblique course towards its lateral aspect, terminating at its lower articular extremity or at a variable distance above this point. Sometimes the fracture is comminuted. Fracture of the os corona is usually vertical in direction and often comminuted.

ETIOLOGY.—The most common cause of fractured pastern is concussion, the accident occurring during galloping or jumping. It also results from violent slips and sudden turns. It seems to take place with little provocation on some occasions—for example, during the trot or canter. Some of these cases are accounted for by the bone being affected with a rarefying ostitis or osteomalacia. Neurectomy is a well-known predisposing cause. Direct violence is the cause in exceptional instances—for example, a heavy cart-wheel passing over the coronet, fracturing the os corona or os pedis. Several cases have been recorded of simultaneous fracture of both fore-pasterns during ordinary fast exercise on level ground. The accident occurs in fore- and hind-limbs, but more frequently in the former. The pedal bone may be fractured by the penetration of a sharp hard object through the sole.

SYMPTOMS.—The first symptom is sudden and severe lameness during work or fast exercise, causing the horse to stop and hold up the affected limb or rest it only on the toe. Inflammatory swelling appears quickly when the fracture is complete, but is slow in onset when it is a fissure. When displacement is present, mobility and crepitus are easily recognised, especially in the first phalanx. They are not always so apparent in the second phalanx, and in the os pedis they cannot be detected.

In fissured fracture the chief local symptom is evidence of pain on pressure with the finger over the front of the bone, especially on the line of fracture. A local periostitis would be detected in the same way,

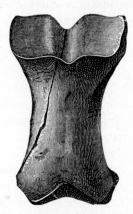

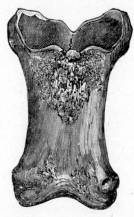

FIG. 352.—FRACTURE OF OS SUFFRAGINIS.

FIG. 353.—FRACTURE OF OS SUFFRAGINIS WITH FORMATION OF EXOSTOSIS.

but the history of the case and the more marked and more prolonged nature of the lameness in the case of fracture generally enable a correct diagnosis to be made. The X-rays may be used to confirm the diagnosis

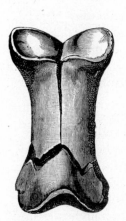

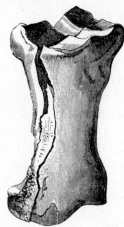

FIG. 354.—TRANSVERSE FRACTURE OF OS SUFFRAGINIS.

FIG. 355.—DOUBLE FRACTURE OF UPPER END OF OS SUFFRAGINIS.

FIG. 356.—LONGITUDINAL FRACTURE OF OS SUFFRAGINIS.

TREATMENT.—Treatment of fracture with displacement is seldom indicated. Although union of the fragments ensues, a deformity in the shape of a large exostosis is produced, which generally causes permanent lameness, for which the only remedy is neurectomy. When there is little or no displacement, as in the case of split pastern, recovery is the rule.   In such cases rest in slings or in a box is generally sufficient to effect a cure, but it is always advisable to apply a plaster-of-Paris bandage from the hoof half-way up the cannon-bone after filling up the hollow at the back of the pastern with padding.   Care must be exercised to avoid undue pressure with the hard dressing, lest necrosis of the skin supervene.   Weight may be borne on the limb within a fortnight after the fracture has occurred, but six to eight weeks usually intervene before the horse goes sound.   Recovery from split pastern has been many times verified on post-mortem examination months or years afterwards.   Compound fracture is hopeless.

Fracture of the phalanges in the dog is readily diagnosed, and is amenable to treatment even when compound.   In the latter case, however, the fragments may become septic and require to be removed, leaving the patient short of one or more digits which is of no consequence except for a racing dog, and even the latter can dispense with one digit without material impairment of its speed.

Fracture of the Sesamoids

Fracture of the sesamoids has been frequently recorded.   It generally occurs during fast exercise, and may be the result of a slip or fall, or an unexpected movement of the fetlock.   The fracture is usually transverse through the middle of the bones.   Several cases have been reported of the fracture occurring in both limbs simultaneously. The writer has seen the condition occur at the end of a race accompanied by fracture of the inner articular half of the lower extremity of the metacarpus.   Crepitation due to the latter fracture was manifested on manipulation of the part.

SYMPTOMS.—The animal stops suddenly and ceases to bear weight on the affected limb.   Local examination reveals inflammatory swelling.   When the case is very recent, the space between the fragments may be felt.   When both limbs are involved, the animal stands with both fetlocks lowered, as in rupture of the suspensory ligament. The foot is flat on the ground when weight is borne by the limb.

TREATMENT is rarely undertaken, as it is generally useless.   If adopted, it is on general principles.

Sesamoiditis

The sesamoids in the horse may be affected with acute or chronic inflammation, associated with ulceration of their anterior or posterior surface, usually the latter.

ETIOLOGY.—The condition may arise from the same causes as those producing sprain of the flexor tendons. It is predisposed to by long, sloping pasterns, especially under a heavy body. It is commonest in " weedy " hacks and hunters, and in draft-horses, affecting chiefly the fore-limbs. It may be the result of jumping, especially from a height, or from suddenly reining-up. In this case the disease may set in with acute inflammation, but as a rule it develops slowly, the flexor sheath being often simultaneously affected at a point close to the fetlock-joint.

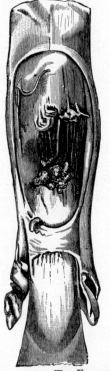

FIG. 357.—THE FLEXOR PEDIS PERFORANS TENDON IN A CASE OF SESAMOID LAMENESS.

At the point where it passes over the sesamoid bones the perforans tendon is fibrillated.

(After Brauell.)

SYMPTOMS comprise lameness and local inflammation. Pain is most marked when weight is placed on the limb. Lameness decreases, and may disappear, with exercise. It is decreased by long rest and increased by work, is more marked on rough hard ground than on sand or grass, and is sometimes so slight as only to be detected by carefully watching the animal whilst trotting, though in severe cases it is apparent at a walk. Pain may be evinced on local manipulation. After some time the sesamoid bones become enlarged and the fetlock assumes a square appearance when viewed from behind. If it is the anterior surface of the sesamoids that is ulcerated, the enlargement is close to the metacarpus—i.e., at the side of the joint; in disease of the posterior surface it is farther back on the volar aspect of the joint. After a further variable period the flexor tendons become swollen in the neighbourhood of the sesamoid bones, though such swelling may occasionally appear before the other symptoms. The acute form is distinguished by local heat, etc., which is absent in chronic cases. During the later stages there is knuckling at the fetlock-joint from thickening of the tendons. Movement of the fetlock-joint is often distinctly limited. Crepitation can rarely be detected. The course is chronic, the inflammation seldom subsiding, so that cure is usually out of the question.

DIAGNOSIS is based on the symptoms mentioned. It may be doubtful until enlargement of the sesamoid bones is evident, but it must be said that exostoses sometimes occur on the sesamoid bones, particularly on their lateral surfaces, without causing lameness.

TREATMENT is that for acute or chronic inflammation. It is of no avail in established chronic cases, in which median neurectomy is indicated.

Ringbone—Phalangeal Exostoses

The term ringbone is the popular name for bony enlargements on the pastern or phalangeal bones. It has been classified as follows :

1. **True ringbone,** in which the exostosis occurs at the level of one of the interphalangeal joints.

2. **False ringbone,** in which the exostosis is quite clear of the interphalangeal joints.

TRUE RINGBONE is subdivided into (1) ARTICULAR RINGBONE, in which the bony deposit is associated with an arthritis of the joint at whose level it is situated ; and (2) PERIARTICULAR RINGBONE, in which there is merely a bony deposit at some part of the periphery of the joint, whose articular surfaces are intact.

There is some confusion about the terms true and false ringbone. Some authorities confine the term " true ringbone," or even " ringbone," to that form of the disease associated with arthritis. Some discard the term false ringbone, while others include periarticular ringbone under this heading.

Another classification is the following :

1. **High true ringbone,** at the level of the suffragino-coronal articulation.

2. **Low true ringbone,** at the level of the corono-pedal articulation.

3. **High false ringbone,** affecting the os suffraginis.

4. **Low false ringbone,** affecting the os corona.

The tendency in practice is to make use only of the term " ringbone " for any phalangeal exostosis, and explain its significance according to its situation. The foregoing classifications, however, are useful for descriptive purposes.

ETIOLOGY.—*False ringbone* is the result of osteo-periostitis, which is usually of traumatic origin, such as a blow or a knock, but it may be due to concussion. The inflammatory exudate becomes ossified to form the exostosis.

Articular ringbone is a form of dry arthritis whose cause is often obscure. It has been ascribed to concussion without any definite reason. If due to this cause, it should be more prevalent. There may be an hereditary predisposition to the condition. The exciting cause may be rheumatism, or it might possibly be a remote sequel to navel infection. The lesion may ensue from sprain of the joint, but this is more likely to give rise to periarticular ringbone.

Periarticular ringbone most commonly occurs at the lateral aspects of the suffragino-coronal joint, where it arises in many cases from sprain of the lateral ligaments. Therefore, anything favouring sprain of these structures predisposes to the condition, such as malconformation of the limbs, unequal distribution of the weight on the foot, and uneven footing. Improper shoeing, interfering with the normal

FIG. 358.—ARTICULAR RINGBONE.   FIG. 359.—PERIARTICULAR RINGBONE.

slope of the digit or the balance of weight on the foot, causes a strain on the ligaments of the interphalangeal joints, and favours the production of ringbone. The prevalence of this form of the disease in heavy draft-horses has been ascribed to the fact that they are usually shod with calkins and work on roads sloping from the centre towards the sides, a combination of circumstances which predisposes to sprain of the lateral ligaments of the first interphalangeal joint. The condition may occur, however, without any history of local inflammation or lameness and is then probably due to a hereditary tendency to the formation of exostoses in this class of horses. Appearing in young unbroken horses, periarticular ringbone may be of rachitic origin, the lower end of the os suffraginis and upper end of the os corona becoming enlarged without any evidence of inflammation.

The low variety of this ringbone is usually due to direct injury, such as may be caused by a weight falling on the coronet or a cart-wheel passing over it. Sometimes a phalangeal exostosis is the result of a fissured fracture of the os suffraginis or os corona. Hard work in young horses, before the bones are mature, predisposes to ostitis and periostitis and the formation of ringbone.

SYMPTOMS.—*False ringbone* may appear mysteriously without any evidence or history of inflammation, but it usually commences as an osteo-periostitis with lameness and local symptoms of acute inflam-mation. When the exostosis is completely developed, the local inflammation and lameness disappear and the horse remains sound.

Should the enlargement be on the inner aspect of the pastern, it may be struck by the other foot during progression and be a constant cause of lameness. The exostosis varies in size in different cases; it may be hardly perceptible or very pro-minent.

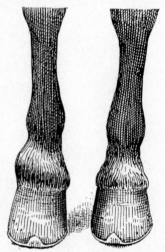

Articular ringbone causes permanent lameness, which is often present before the exostosis appears, being due to the inflammation in the joint. The bony de-posit may form on any aspect of the joint or all round it (hence the term " ring-bone "), but most commonly in front. It may be so small that it is hardly percept-ible, or it may be quite obvious to sight and touch. An enlargement in front is best seen by standing at the side, and one at the side by standing in front.

FIG. 360.—THE OUTSIDE OF THE RIGHT CORONET SHOWS RING-BONE FORMATION; THE LEFT IS NORMAL.

There is supporting leg lameness. Pain is evinced on passive move-ment of the joint. Anchylosis of the joint may supervene from fusion of the articular surfaces, and then the absence of movement can be detected on manipulation.

Periarticular ringbone may or may not be accompanied by lameness. Lameness is present during the acute inflammatory stage of the condi-tion following sprain of the ligaments and the osteo-periostitis which results therefrom. The lameness may persist after the complete de-velopment of the exostosis, but it usually disappears when this stage is reached. The most common site of the ringbone is on the lateral aspects of the first interphalangeal joint, where it is best seen by standing in front. When well marked or confined to one side of the joint or to one limb, it is easily detected by comparison with the normal joint. When the joints of both limbs are unusually large and of the same size, it is difficult to decide whether the condition is normal or abnormal. These joints may be normally very prominent in the draft-horse, and must not then be condemned as being affected with ringbone.

The exostosis in this form of ringbone is sometimes enormous, and may extend all round the pastern, and even then the horse may go sound. Anchylosis may ensue from fusion of the ossific deposits on the os suffraginis and os corona, causing mechanical lameness, which may not be very noticeable. The writer has seen a case in which the exostosis formed a sheath for the perforans tendon, and yet the horse was working sound. The nature of the condition was seen on post-mortem examination. The rachitic form of the disease in young horses is not accompanied by lameness, and may disappear as the animal grows. Low ringbone, whether articular or periarticular, is characterised by the presence of a hard bony swelling at the level of the coronet, and in either case causes lameness, the pressure of the horn on the exostosis being sufficient to cause pain apart from the presence of an arthritis.

DIAGNOSIS of ringbone is difficult in its incipient stages, before the exostosis appears, and sometimes the latter is so small that it is difficult to detect. When lameness is present it is impossible to say whether true ringbone is articular or periarticular, but when lameness is absent it is certainly not articular.

, PROGNOSIS.—False ringbone is of no consequence when the inflammatory stage has passed, except it is large and situated internally, when it may be struck by the other foot during progression. The same is true, as a rule, of periarticular ringbone, but exceptionally it causes more or less anchylosis of the joint, as mentioned. Articular ringbone is incurable. Low ringbone is always more serious, owing to its being partly beneath the wall of the hoof.

TREATMENT.—During the acute inflammatory stage of the condition the treatment is that for acute inflammation, the chief indication being rest. When the ringbone is developed and lameness is present, the treatment consists in blistering or firing the enlargement, needle-point firing being undoubtedly the best. No form of treatment will have any good effect on articular ringbone, and the only thing to be done in such a case is double plantar neurectomy. Should persistent lameness ensue from false or periarticular ringbone, median neurectomy should first be tried, and if it proves insufficient, external plantar neurectomy should then be performed.

Bobba Bone—Cab-Horse Disease

Lameness due to osteo-periostitis, and a consequent exostosis affecting the supero-antero-internal aspect of the os suffraginis in the fore-limb, is fairly common in horses doing fast work in cities. Its frequency in cab-horses in London accounts for the condition being spoken of as cab-horse disease. It is of the same nature as ringbone, but is usually described as a separate condition. It is often accompanied by a dry arthritis of the fetlock-joint.

ETIOLOGY.—The lesion is apparently brought about by concussion resulting from rapid work on paved streets.

SYMPTOMS.—The affection is insidious in origin. The late Mr. William Hunting was very familiar with the disease. He said that its first indication was intermittent lameness. The horse would be noticed lame one day, but the next morning would be sound and continue so while going on the macadamised road, but when brought on to the pavement lameness would reappear. Eventually lameness is constant. At first there is no local evidence of the lesion, which does not appear until lameness has been in existence for some time. The enlargement is not preceded by obvious local inflammation, thus rendering early diagnosis difficult.

When the exostosis is present it can be seen and felt. It is recognised by standing in front of the horse and comparing the two fetlocks. It is situated as mentioned, and is on a level with the tuberosity which can be easily felt on the supero-postero-lateral aspect of the os suffraginis.

PROGNOSIS.—The lesion, being usually associated with arthritis of the fetlock-joint, is incurable in most cases. That this is not invariably the case, however, is proved in some instances by the horse going sound after treatment.

TREATMENT.—Needle-point firing and blistering should be tried, and if it has not the desired effect median neurectomy is indicated.

Sprain of the First Interphalangeal Joint in the Dog

Sprain of the first interphalangeal joint is common in track greyhounds characterised by lameness and by inflammatory swelling at the level of the articulation. The degree of injury to the periarticular structures varies in different cases. Some acute cases respond to antiphlogistic remedies followed by prolonged rest to prevent recurrence of the condition. Many cases, however, assume a chronic character with a fibrous thickening round the joint and enlargement of the articular ends of the phalanges and usually defy treatment, although an occasional case is cured by counter-irritation in the form of repeated rubbing in of tincture of iodine or an iodine ointment or a blister of biniodide of mercury or line or needle-point firing, followed by a long period of rest. In a typical case of this kind, it is best to excise the affected joint or remove the second and third phalanges (see p. 476).

This chronic form of the lesion is popularly known as " Sprung toe."

Arthritis of this joint is not uncommonly met with causing permanent lameness and characterised by crepitation on manipulation of the affected phalanges and which renders diagnosis from fracture difficult without the use of X-rays. Excision of the joint or amputation of the two terminal phalanges is the only effective remedy (see p. 475).

Dislocation of the Phalanges in the Dog

Dislocation of the phalangeal articulations is very rare in large animals, but is common in sporting dogs, especially track greyhounds.

It is usually accompanied by rupture of the ligaments of the joint, and although reduction is easy in such cases, recovery seldom supervenes, the condition recurring under fast exercise. Sometimes although the articular ends of the bones are in apposition, the joint appears lax from stretching or rupture of its ligaments. In both cases it is usually necessary to amputate the second and third phalanges or excise the affected joint (see p. 476).

The terminal phalangeal joint is often deformed in the greyhound as the result of rupture or stretching of the flexor tendon at its insertion into the third phalanx. The nail projects beyond the level of those on either side and the joint cannot function properly, the displaced nail being an impediment and source of discomfort during fast paces. This condition is also referred to as " knocked-up toe." Amputation of the terminal phalanx enables the dog to race to his usual form.

Dislocation of the First Interphalangeal Joint in the Dog

TREATMENT.—When the joint is loose owing to rupture of its lateral ligaments the bones can be kept in apposition by means of wire. The procedure as demonstrated by Formston (London Veterinary College) at the Congress of the National Veterinary Medical Association at Bournemouth, 1937, consists in incising the skin so as to expose the ends of the two phalanges on each lateral aspect of the joint, drilling a hole transversely through each bone, passing a piece of German silver wire through the holes and twisting its two ends round each other by means of two artery forceps, one for each end of the wire. Grasping both ends

with one forceps is apt to result in the wire breaking before it is sufficiently twisted. Having made the wire taut, flatten the twisted end
against the lateral aspect of the bone, suture the skin with silkworm
gut and apply a protective dressing of gauze, cotton-wool and bandage.

The wound usually heals by first intention and the desired effect is
obtained, the dog going sound and being fit to race in the course of
five or six weeks.

AFFECTIONS OF THE HIND-LIMB

Hip Lameness

HIP lameness is due to various affections of the hip region, including those of the coxo-femoral and sacro-iliac joints, the bones, muscles, tendons, nerves, and bloodvessels, which are dealt with under special headings.

SYMPTOMS.—Although the various forms of hip lameness, being due to different causes, exhibit important peculiarities in their symptoms, yet taken as a whole they show certain features of general agreement. Thus in all there is difficulty in advancing the limb (swinging leg lameness), retardation of movement, and shortening of the forward stride, and in many cases a tendency to stiffen the limb during movement and to drag the toe. When the hip-joint itself is diseased there is supporting leg lameness, and the animal tries to avoid throwing weight on the affected side—symptoms which are usually absent in the purely muscular forms. Lameness is marked when turning and backing, and appears in an aggravated form after severe exertion. Sometimes it is most distinct when commencing work and gradually decreases ; sometimes the reverse. Though rheumatic lameness usually wears off with exercise, the continuance or aggravation of lameness under such circumstances by no means points to a traumatic origin. Mechanical lameness is a much more common cause of lameness than rheumatism. Sometimes anatomical changes, such as muscular atrophy, swelling, and increased warmth, which can be detected, assist diagnosis and render it approximately exact. The more thorough and complete the examination, the less common will be the diagnosis " hip lameness." The injection of a local anæsthetic over the anterior and posterior tibial nerves will serve to eliminate the hock and the parts below in arriving at a diagnosis.

AFFECTIONS OF THE QUARTER

Traumatic Lesions

1. **Contusions** of the hip, thigh, and leg are common in the horse, caused by falls, blows, and kicks, and by getting the leg over a bar. The nature of the lesion depends on the violence with which the injury is inflicted. The symptoms are those described for contusions in

general. A superficial or deep hæmatoma may be produced, or a collection of serum may be formed beneath the skin or between muscles. When the inside of the leg and thigh are injured by being caught over a beam or board, the skin is severely abraded and a diffuse hæmatoma is frequently produced.

The angle of the haunch is frequently contused by falls and by striking against door-posts, and in cattle it is often injured by repeatedly knocking against the sides of wagons in long train journeys. In many cases of direct injury fracture of the bone results. Should infection gain entrance to any of the bruised parts alluded to, an abscess will ensue and must be dealt with accordingly. When the angle of the ilium or tuber ischii is involved necrosis of the bone may supervene, giving rise to a sinus which will persist until the sequestrum is removed.

2. **An abscess** of obscure origin or due to strangles sometimes forms in the psoas magnus, accompanied by febrile disturbance and causing severe lameness, characterised by stiffness of the joints in the corresponding limb and by arching of the loins. The abscess may point in the groin or in the hollow of the flank, or at the level of the transverse processes of the lumbar vertebræ. Rectal examination will reveal the true seat of the abscess. The latter may burst internally, causing the death of the patient, or externally and be followed by recovery. An abscess (in the same situation) sometimes occurs in the ox,

3. **Open wounds** of the regions mentioned are frequently met with, and are treated as described in general surgery. Pus may burrow deeply beneath the fascia, necessitating a counter-opening and the insertion of a seton to ensure drainage. When bone is involved a sinus may ensue, due to necrosis thereof, and will require to be treated as such. A foreign body may be embedded in the tissues of the quarter, and necessitate incision to remove it.

4. **Bed-sores** in the form of dry gangrene may form over the angle of the haunch and the great trochanter of the femur as the result of prolonged decubitus. Prevention of these lesions should be aimed at by supplying plenty of litter and keeping it dry, as moisture favours their occurrence.

TREATMENT of the foregoing conditions is on general principles as described under the respective headings in General Surgery.

Bursal Enlargements

A hygroma may form over the external angle of the ilium in the horse and ox from repeated slight injury. It is more common in the latter animal, which is more subject to knocks passing through doorways. Prolonged decubitus is a fruitful source of the condition. It is of the same nature as a collection of serum. A hygroma may also appear over the great trochanter of the femur, due to distension of the gluteal bursa following direct injury. The tuber ischii is occasionally the seat of a bursal enlargement. It is probably most common in the large breed of dogs, especially deer-hounds and wolf-hounds, as the result of contact with hard ground.

TREATMENT is that given under the heading of " Bursitis." Removal of the cause is always indicated as far as possible. Aspiration and injection should be tried in the dog before resorting to the knife, as there may be difficulty in obtaining healing of the wound caused by the latter. A biniodide of mercury blister has succeeded in healing a callous bursal wound on the tuber ischii in the dog after other applications had failed.

Sprain and Rupture of Muscles

The muscles of the croup, hip, and thigh may be sprained or ruptured in various ways : slipping, jumping, falling, violent effort.

Sprain and Rupture of the Psoas Muscles.—The psoas muscles may be sprained or ruptured from over-stretching as the result of the hind-limbs slipping backwards—for example, into a ditch, which the animal has failed to clear in jumping, or of violent struggling when cast, or of forcible extension backwards of the hind-limbs.

SYMPTOMS.—The condition is spoken of as sprain of the loins. There is stiffness of the dorso-lumbar region and difficulty in moving the hind-limbs, especially in the act of backing. The gait is straddling, and there is a tendency to drag the toes and to knuckle at the fetlocks. The horse finds it difficult to assume the position for stalling. There may be blood in the urine, due to over-stretching of the ureters and rupture of capillaries therein. Pain is evinced on pressure over the muscles *per rectum*. When the horse is lying he may have difficulty in rising. The severity of the symptoms, however, depends on the degree of injury. When it is slight they are not very noticeable, but when there is complete muscular rupture the above well-marked symptoms are observed, and even death may ensue from hæmorrhage or peritonitis.

PROGNOSIS.—Complete recovery seldom follows rupture of these muscles. An abscess has been seen, apparently as a sequel of the condition, pointing in the groin under Poupart's ligament some weeks after the accident to the muscles, recovery ensuing rapidly after bursting of the abscess. Repair is brought about by fibrous tissue, whereby the muscle loses much of its power.

The Gluteal Muscles may be ruptured in the region of the hip-joint, causing local symptoms of inflammation and hip lameness, characterised by a shortened stride and by dragging the toe. There may be adduction of the limb during its forward movement.

Rupture of the Biceps Femoris.—This muscle may be ruptured as the result of violent contraction, as may occur when a horse struggles vigorously in hobbles, or during heavy draft. The rupture usually occurs at its upper attachment, where it causes a well-marked, slightly painful swelling. Lameness is characterised by difficulty in taking the limb forward, and by a movement of circumduction when attempting to do so.

Rupture of the Tensor Vaginæ Femoris has been seen near its origin from the external angle of the ilium. It is manifested by a swelling a little below the latter point, and by a depression between the bone and the enlargement. The hip is lowered, and the limb is carried somewhat diagonally towards the opposite fore-limb. When bearing weight, the limb is not completely extended. The horse may have difficulty in rising from the recumbent position.

Rupture of the Adductor Muscles Inside the Thigh.— Rupture of some of these muscles, most frequently the semi-membranosus and semitendinosus, occurs occasionally from excessive contraction when struggling in the cast position, or more rarely when galloping. The accident is apt to occur in vigorous thoroughbred stallions when cast for operation. The author had such a case in an aged thoroughbred stallion cast for castration.

SYMPTOMS.—A hot, painful swelling forms at the seat of injury, due to extravasation of blood, and severe lameness supervenes. Both limbs may be affected, and then the horse is almost powerless in the hind-limbs. When the animal is able to walk or stand the limb is abducted. If there is only partial rupture of one or two superficial muscles, the extravasation of blood is slight and becomes absorbed after some time, leaving a depression corresponding to the space between the divided fibres.

PROGNOSIS of complete rupture is bad, a perfect recovery seldom or never ensuing.

Rupture of the Quadriceps rarely occurs. It is characterised by the usual local symptoms of inflammation and extravasation. Lameness is manifested by inability to extend the stifle-joint, and it, as well as the hock, is held in a state of flexion, as in crural paralysis.

A partial rupture of the muscles may occur, characterised by lameness, which is more or less severe according to the nature of the lesion. The local symptoms in this case may not be very obvious.

TREATMENT of all the foregoing lesions is carried out on general principles as laid down for inflammation and contusions. In cases of complete rupture, when the case is worth treating, slings are necessary to support the patient and to keep him at rest. The danger of rupture of the thigh muscles should be considered when about to cast a " blood " horse, and to prevent the accident chloroform should be administered in the standing position.

Displacement of the Biceps Femoris

In cattle the biceps femoris or longus vastus muscle glides on the great trochanter of the femur by means of a large serous bursa, and its anterior border is firmly embraced by the double laminæ of the fascia lata. This fascia may become fissured, allowing the muscle to slip backwards off the trochanter, which passes into the fissure, and flexion of the femur is then impossible. The accident happens particularly in emaciated animals with prominent trochanters and in mountain cattle with sloping quarters, and is caused by slipping with the limb extended backwards in the cowshed, at work, or during coitus.

SYMPTOMS.—The condition is usually confined to one leg. Immediately the muscle becomes fixed behind the trochanter, flexion of the thigh is impossible and lameness is at once developed. The limb is fixed in an extended position, similar to that in upward displacement of the patella, or is thrust outwards and forwards with a kind of mowing movement, the claws scraping the ground. On local examination, the trochanter appears very prominent and situated directly above a rigid cord, which extends parallel with the anterior margin of the luxated muscle. The limb is not so firmly fixed in the extended position as in luxation of the patella. Sometimes the dislocation is only momentary, the muscle immediately returning to its normal position, so that the animal goes sound for a few steps, but soon falls lame again. When the muscle becomes fixed in the abnormal position it appears tense and its outline is more distinct, whilst a depression appears in front of the trochanter.

COURSE AND PROGNOSIS.—Spontaneous recovery is never permanent, and, unless operation be resorted to, habitual luxation results—i.e., the lameness continually recurs or becomes lasting. Prognosis is only grave in working animals. The accident is now less common than formerly, probably because cattle are better fed and better managed.

56

TREATMENT.—When the displacement is due to stretching of the fascia, rest and good feeding favour the deposition of fat, and soon alter the conditions responsible for the accident.   Counter-irritation may be employed with advantage in cases where spontaneous reduction occurs.   If, however, the fascia lata is ruptured and the " trochanter " firmly fixed in the fissure, operation becomes necessary to release the trochanter and restore the function of the limb.   To operate, proceed thus : At a point about 3 inches below and in front of the trochanter,

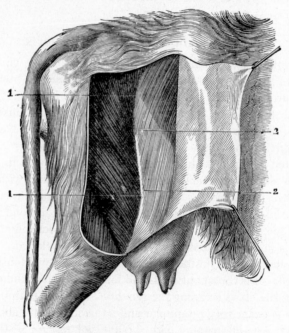

FIG. 361.—BICEPS FEMORIS MUSCLE.
1, Anterior margin of muscle ; 2, fascia lata.

in the direction of the muscle, make an incision about 2 inches long through the skin and aponeurosis, separate the anterior border of the muscle from the subjacent tissues by using a spatula, pass a director transversely beneath it, and divide it from within outwards.   It may be necessary to plug the wound to arrest the hæmorrhage.   The wound usually heals in ten to eighteen days.   The condition is rare in the horse, in which the displaced muscle passes in front of the trochanter.   In fracture of the ischium the tuber ischii may be displaced by the pull of this muscle, resulting in deformity of the buttock.

Ossification of the Aponeurosis of the Hip or Thigh

This lesion is rarely met with. It may occur without any apparent cause, or be the result of direct injury. Its most common site is the outer aspect of the hip.

SYMPTOMS.—There is slight lameness or mere stiffness in the limb. Locally a hard painless swelling is detected, regular or irregular in outline.

TREATMENT consists in excision of the ossified tissue, the resulting wound being sutured in its upper part. Complete cure is usually effected.

Inflammation of the Gluteal Bursa

Inflammation of the gluteal bursa, which facilitates the gliding of the gluteal tendon over the convexity of the great trochanter, is occasionally met with, associated with more or less inflammation of the tendon itself.

ETIOLOGY.—The tendo-synovitis is the result of violent contraction of the gluteal muscles, or of stretching of their tendons when the horse falls with the limb underneath the body. It might be of toxic origin occurring during the course of an infectious disease like rheumatism, influenza, or strangles.

SYMPTOMS.—There is hip lameness, characterised by a crooked or oblique configuration of the quarter, the body being slightly curved inwards, with the convexity on the lame side. A short step is taken by the affected limb. At rest the latter is held flexed and in a state of adduction, with its foot in advance of that of the other limb. During the trot there is marked lowering of the affected hip. These features of the lameness are not of themselves diagnostic of the condition, but when associated with local inflammatory symptoms there can be little hesitation about the nature of the lesion.

The local symptoms consist of a swelling, which is at first hot and painful, but afterwards cold and indolent, when crepitation, due to synovitis, may be detected on passive movement of the limb. Eventually atrophy of the muscles ensues.

TREATMENT is that for acute or chronic inflammation according to the age of the lesion. When there is marked atrophy of the muscle, there is little chance of recovery. The condition may be complicated with periostitis of the great trochanter, and the consequent production of exostoses, causing permanent incurable lameness.

Fractures of the Pelvis

The site of fracture may be the ilium, pubis, ischium, or cotyloid cavity, and several of these bones may be involved at once.

Fractures of the Ilium

The External Angle—ETIOLOGY.—The fracture is due to direct violence, such as falling on the haunch or striking it violently against a post or corner of a wall. In young animals it is believed that

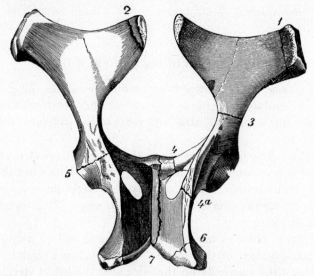

FIG. 362.—SCHEMA ILLUSTRATING FRACTURES OF THE PELVIS IN THE HORSE.

Fracture of : 1, external iliac angle ; 2, internal iliac angle ; 3, shaft of the ilium 4, transverse portion of the os pubis ; 4a, external portion of the ischium 5, cotyloid cavity ; 6, tuber ischii ; 7, symphysis pubis.

the angle may be detached by muscular exertion, especially in two-year-old racehorses. Occasionally only one of the tuberosities of the angle is fractured, and usually remains attached to the bone, causing little or no deformity, but capable of being diagnosed by slight crepitation on manipulation. As a rule, however, the whole angle is fractured, and the fragment is pulled downwards by contraction of the tensor vaginæ femoris, causing marked deformity.

SYMPTOMS.—The deformity is readily detected on standing behind the animal and comparing the two hips. Locally there is evidence of a contusion, and the displaced fragment can be felt as a hard substance in the hollow of the flank below its normal situation.

When the fracture is compound the broken bone can be seen and felt, and a hollow wound is observed at the seat of the lesion. Crepitation is absent, owing to the space between the fractured surfaces. The animal affected is said to be " hipped " or " down of its hip." There is distinct lameness at first, but when the local inflammation subsides it disappears, and the only bad result of the accident is the blemish caused by the deformity. When there is an open wound there may be trouble, due to infection, causing necrosis or caries of the bone. Apart from this, however, the horse is usually fit to return to work in three or four weeks.

The Body.—Sometimes the fracture involves the body of the bone, extending from its anterior to its lower border. In this case there is not so much displacement, and crepitation can be detected. Fracture of the angle and of the body may occur at the same time. The lameness is more marked and the sinking of the quarter more pronounced when the body of the bone is broken, while the width of the two sides remains the same. The lameness is very marked, little or no weight being borne, and great difficulty being evinced in taking the limb forward. Crepitation may be heard when the animal moves, and is usually easily detected on external and rectal manipulation. It is generally more easily felt than heard by placing the hand flat on the hip while the patient is made to walk, or by grasping the external angle of the ilium in one hand and the tuber ischii in the other, and pushing the animal gently from side to side. It is recognised *per rectum* during movement of the patient or passive movement of the limb. Rectal examination reveals the swelling and deformity caused by the lesion, and confirms the diagnosis.

FIG. 363.—FRACTURE OF THE EXTERNAL ANGLE OF THE ILIUM.

The PROGNOSIS is more serious, for if union of the fragments does not occur, permanent lameness ensues. A possible complication of both fractures is the penetration of spicules into the peritoneal cavity, resulting in the case of compound fracture in peritonitis and death.

The Internal Angle of the Ilium is rarely fractured. It is generally caused by falling over an embankment and landing on the croup. Crepitation may be detected on external and rectal palpation.

The Shaft of the Ilium—ETIOLOGY.—The fracture is usually caused by falling on the hip, but cases of its occurring during exercise, without any obvious exciting cause, have been recorded. Rarely the fracture is bilateral.

SYMPTOMS.—On comparing the quarters from behind, the absence of symmetry is at once observed, the whole of the gluteal region on the affected side being gradually lowered from the middle line towards the external angle of the ilium. Crepitation can be detected as in fracture of the body. Sometimes displacement of the fragments is deferred, and the diagnosis is difficult at first. The history of the case and the sudden and severe lameness are aids to diagnosis, although the degree of lameness is not always in proportion to the gravity of the lesion.

PROGNOSIS.—The prognosis must be guarded. It depends largely on the amount of displacement and the quietude of the patient. Complete recovery, except for a varying degree of persisting deformity, ensues in some cases, while in others union of the fragments fails to occur. The resulting constriction of the pelvis after healing of the fracture may render the mare unfit for breeding, but even marked deformity of the hip does not interfere with the animal's utility for work. Death may rapidly supervene from internal hæmorrhage, due to laceration of an iliac artery or vein by one of the fragments.

Fracture through the Cotyloid Cavity results from direct violence, usually from falling on the great trochanter of the femur, the force being transmitted to the head of the latter, and thence to the bones forming the cavity. It may be associated with fracture of the head of the femur.

SYMPTOMS.—There is sudden and severe lameness, and the patient evinces pain on the least movement of the affected region. Crepitation can usually be detected. There is not much deformity of the quarter. On palpation *per rectum*, the inflammatory swelling caused by the lesion is not always evident. Crepitation may be perceptible when the animal is made to walk or the limb is passively moved. Occasionally diagnosis of the exact condition is only confirmed on post-mortem examination, owing to the absence of characteristic symptoms during life.

PROGNOSIS.—The case is incurable.

Fracture of the Floor of the Pelvis

ETIOLOGY.—Fracture of the pelvic floor is caused by falls and by slipping outwards of the hind-limb or limbs. It usually occurs through the obturator foramen, and generally involves the pubis and ischium.

SYMPTOMS.—The animal goes suddenly lame. When the accident results from falling, the patient may be unable to rise without assistance. The lameness is characterised by stiffness in the hind-quarters, and by circumduction of the limb on the affected side. There is no deformity of the quarters, but in a recent case there is swelling at the level of the tuber ischii and œdema may be noticed in the perineal region. In the mare ecchymosis may be observed in the mucous membrane of the vagina. Crepitation can be detected by placing the hand firmly against the tuber ischii while the patient is being slowly walked. Rectal, or in the mare vaginal, examination reveals deformity, crepitation, and mobility in the region of the fracture, rendering diagnosis easy. The fracture may be overlooked at first, the lameness in some cases being apparently not sufficiently well marked to warrant the existence of a fracture. In all cases of marked hind-leg lameness the pelvis should be carefully examined before giving a definite opinion as to the seat of lameness.

When the condition has been in existence for some time, atrophy of the muscles of the hip and thigh is observed, and paralysis of the adductors of the thigh may ensue from a callus pressing on or overstretching the obturator nerve, giving rise to symptoms of " obturator lameness." Death may result from hæmorrhage, due to rupture of the obturator vessels by one of the fragments. The callus may be so large that it causes pelvic constriction, precluding the use of the female for breeding. This, however, is seldom the case.

PROGNOSIS.—The prognosis must be guarded. It depends on the degree of displacement and the amount of mobility of the fragments. In many cases complete recovery is obtained.

TREATMENT of the foregoing pelvic fractures is carried out on general principles. In simple fracture of the external angle of the ilium rest and antiphlogistic applications are sufficient. In the course of a few weeks the animal will go sound. When the body of the bone or its shaft is fractured, it is generally advisable to put the horse in slings to restrict movement and prevent the patient lying and rising. They do not always have the desired effect in these respects, as the horse may sit on the slings and thus disturb the seat of fracture more so than by ordinary movements. In all cases the stall should be made narrow to prevent side-to-side movements. A charge over the affected quarter is usually applied to diminish mobility there. A fair percentage of recoveries occurs, but the issue is always in doubt. The deformity persists after healing of the fracture, but even when it is marked it does not interfere with the utility of the animal for work.

For fracture of the pelvic floor treatment is on the same lines. Strapping the two hind-limbs together above the hocks helps to keep the fragments in apposition, but it may not be tolerated by every patient. A charge over both quarters may also be used with advantage. Some cases make good recoveries, while others prove incurable. Mares have been known to breed successfully after healing of the fracture. Fracture of the tuber ischii is dealt with in the same way as that of the external angle. In each case fibrous union occurs between the detached fragment and the bone.

Separation through the symphysis pubis and ischii occurs in cattle from violent slipping outwards of the hind-limbs and from powerful traction on a large fœtus during parturition. The animal goes down in the spread-eagle position, and is unable to rise. Vaginal examination reveals the space where separation has taken place. The case is incurable.

Fractures of the Pelvis in Small Animals

Fractures of the pelvis in the dog and cat result from falling from a height and from being run over by vehicles. Diagnosis is easy, crepitation and mobility being readily detected. Digital examination *per rectum* reveals the exact seat of the lesion and the degree of displacement. Peritonitis and death may ensue from perforation of the anterior part of the rectum, or fatal hæmorrhage may supervene from laceration of the iliac vessels. Otherwise recovery is the rule, provided that the displacement of the fragments is not very marked.

TREATMENT consists chiefly in keeping the patient confined in a small kennel, so as to restrict movement as much as possible. Further immobilisation, however, may be effected by a pitch plaster over the quarters. When there is great displacement of the fragments bone-pinning will be necessary to bring about their alignment and immobilisation (see p. 120).

Fracture of the Femur

ETIOLOGY.—The fracture may be caused by external or muscular violence. It is comparatively rare in large animals, but is very common in the dog. In the former it results from falling on the hip, and from struggling when cast and fixed with ropes, or when a back strap is used after casting with hobbles. In the latter it is caused by falling from a height, by kicks, and by being run over.

SITES.—The site of fracture may be the shaft, the lower epiphysis the neck, the head, or one of the trochanters. The commonest site is the shaft, particularly its lower third. Fracture of the neck is probably more common in the dog than in the horse.

SYMPTOMS.—When the shaft is involved, the characteristic symptoms of fracture are observed—viz., abnormal mobility, crepitation, inability to bear weight, and local inflammation and deformity. The limb can be bent outwards almost at right angles to the body. Some hours after the occurrence of the fracture a large swelling may be formed, due to extravasation of blood. When the line of fracture is very long and oblique, abnormal mobility is not so evident. Fracture at the level of the condyles is indicated by similar symptoms, and on careful manipulation crepitus can always be detected.

When the lesion is in the head or neck of the bone, diagnosis may be difficult, the symptoms being similar to those due to dislocation. Sharp crepitation is a distinguishing feature, as is also the greater mobility of the limb in the case of fracture. When fracture of the neck has been in existence for some weeks, considerable weight may be borne on the affected limb, and in this case there is marked prominence of the great trochanter, which is displaced upwards, and a rude noise rather than a crepitation is produced by rubbing of the femur against the ilium, the head of the femur remaining in the cotyloid cavity. Separation of the articular head of the femur has been observed in colts (males) under three years old that have been running at grass, resulting from slipping or from muscular effort when first put to work, with symptoms similar to those just described. It has been reported as fairly common in Belgium.

Fracture of the great trochanter is characterised by local acute inflammatory swelling, crepitation, and severe lameness. The fragment may be movable on manipulation. Little weight is borne on the limb, which is held in a state of abduction, and during progression it is taken forward with difficulty and directed somewhat outwards. When there is an open wound communicating with the broken bone, necrosis of the latter may ensue, causing a fistula, which persists until the diseased tissue is removed. When the third trochanter is fractured, similar local symptoms are observed, but the lameness is not so severe.

In many cases of complete fracture of the femur in the horse and ox the animal is lying and unable to rise when the veterinarian arrives, and it is necessary for him to have the animal turned over to make a diagnosis when it is the under side that is affected.

PROGNOSIS of complete fracture of the femur in the large animals is grave, and slaughter is usually advised for the horse and large bovine. In light cattle and sheep spontaneous recovery may ensue, and cure is helped by treatment. Even a false joint in these animals does not prevent their getting about and being prepared for the butcher. In dogs and cats fracture of the shaft and condyles almost invariably heals under suitable treatment, but that involving the head and neck or lower articular surface is incurable. Fatal hæmorrhage is a possible complication in all animals from laceration of the femoral artery.

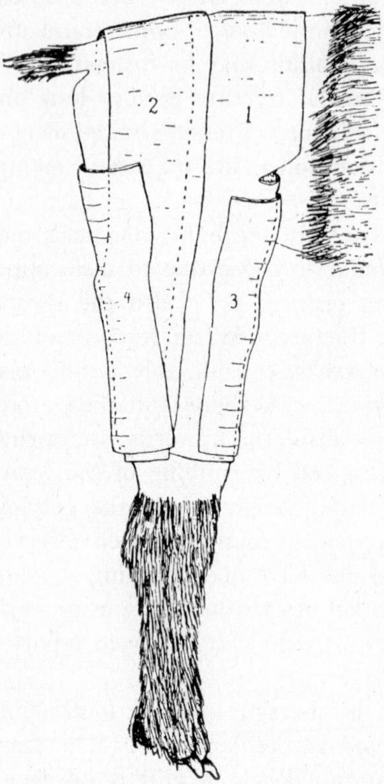

TREATMENT.—As indicated, treatment in the large animals is unsatisfactory, as reduction and immobilisation cannot be properly effected, and even if healing were obtained in the horse, the deformity resulting from defective reduction would render the animal useless except for the stud, when suitable for breeding. Treatment in all classes of patients is on the usual lines for complete fracture. In the small animals a pitch bandage applied from the foot to the croup always has the desired effect for fracture of the shaft and of the condyles. It immobilises the whole limb. The ordinary calico or tarlatan bandage is commenced on the lower part of the limb and carried up to the croup, where it is made to adhere by means of pitch. It is then folded in different directions over the outer aspect of the thigh and hip, and made to encircle the former, with a layer of pitch between each fold and turn of the bandage, the skin on the inside of the thigh being protected by a layer of cotton-wool. A single turn is brought down over the lower part of the limb, to which it is made adherent by a layer of pitch. The patient is kept in a cool place, and if it attempts to bite the dressing an Elizabethan collar is applied. Portions of the dressing may become separated now and again, but can be readjusted by a fresh application

[Vet. Rec.

FIG. 364.—PLASTER CAST APPLIED FOR FRACTURE OF THE FEMUR IN THE DOG. Shaft and lower third femur.

of pitch. Burgess's plaster bandage is very suitable for the purpose, and for small dogs an ordinary adhesive bandage has the desired effect. This treatment has been followed by complete recovery even when both femurs were fractured. Unpadded plaster splints have also proved very suitable for immobilising the seat of fracture (Fig. 364) (see p. 123). Keeping the patient confined in a small kennel would probably effect a cure in the majority of cases, but if the animal is allowed to move about without a dressing a false joint is very likely to result. In the event of this happening, a cure may be obtained by cutting down on the seat of fracture, scraping the ends of the fragments, and uniting them with plates and screws, or applying an external rigid dressing. The Stadar Splint is the best means of reducing and immobilising the fragments.

Dislocation of the Ilio-Sacral Joint

This is a rare condition, and occurs more frequently in the bovine than in the horse. It may be complete or incomplete, and is usually observed in the cow as the result of a difficult parturition, being due to the forcible extraction of a fœtus which offers unusual resistance to delivery.

SYMPTOMS.—There is difficulty in moving, but weight can usually be borne on the affected limb. When the beast is down, she has great difficulty is rising. The ilio-sacral region is swollen, hard, and slightly painful. When the dislocation is complete there is marked deformity, the sacrum being depressed and the internal angles of the ilia being abnormally prominent. The depression of the sacrum is confirmed on rectal examination. In this case the patient is down and unable to rise, and the condition is apt to be confounded with post-partum paralysis.

PROGNOSIS.—Complete dislocation is incurable.

TREATMENT.—If the symptoms warrant treatment, the horse should be rested in slings and the bovine left at liberty, a charge being applied over the croup in each case.

Dislocation of the Hip-Joint

Dislocation of the coxo-femoral articulation is fairly common in the dog and ox, less frequent in the sheep and goat, and rare in the horse. It may be complete or incomplete. The former is distinguished as follows : (1) Anterior or precotyloid ; (2) posterior or postcotyloid or ischiatic ; (3) internal pubic or obturatoral ; and (4) outward or supracotyloid. Experience has shown that the accident can occur without fracture, although the latter is a common complication. The comparative frequence of the condition in the ox and the small animals is due to the absence of the pubo-femoral ligament in these animals.

ETIOLOGY.—The dislocation is due to violent movement of the joint beyond its physiological limits, as may result from a fall or from slipping outwards. In the dog it is commonly the result of a severe contusion, caused by a kick, blow, or fall from a height or the passage of a wheel of a vehicle over the region. Spontaneous luxation as a sequel to chronic arthritis is rare, as is also that due to tubercular arthritis. Bilateral dislocation may occur in the ox from both hind-limbs slipping outwards. The surrounding muscles are more or less ruptured.

SYMPTOMS.—Severe lameness follows the accident. The toe of the foot only may be in contact with the ground, or some weight may be borne on the whole plantar aspect. During progression the affected limb is deviated outwards and is taken forward stiffly, without flexion of its joints, by a movement of circumduction. The great trochanter becomes very prominent in outward dislocation, whereas when the latter is inwards the tuberosity can hardly be recognised. The length of the limb is diminished or increased according as the head of the femur is displaced upwards or downwards. In the former case the projecting upper extremity of the bone moves backwards and forwards during progression, and the movement can be felt by placing the hand on the prominence. When the head of the bone occupies the obturator foramen, it can be felt there on rectal examination. A rocking noise may be heard during progression, due to the displaced femur rubbing against the ischium.

DIAGNOSIS is based on the differences between fracture and disloca-tion described in General Surgery. The condition may be confounded with fracture of the neck of the femur, as mentioned when dealing with that condition.

PROGNOSIS.—The obturator or sciatic nerve may be compressed or crushed by the displaced bone, causing temporary or permanent paralysis. Reduction of the dislocation in the large animals is often impossible, and when it is effected, even in small patients, retention may be impossible on account of the damage done to the surrounding tissues, including rupture of the round and capsular ligaments. In bovines the veterinarian is generally satisfied with the formation of a false joint, which is sufficient to enable the animal to bear weight on the limb while being prepared for the butcher or being used as a milker or for breeding.   In the dog the false joint may be so well formed that lameness is hardly noticeable.

TREATMENT is carried out on the lines mentioned in General Surgery. Extension and counter-extension and local manipulation are practised under general anæsthesia, the lower portion of the limb being used to lever the head of the femur into its socket.   In the large animals a rope passed through the groin and its two ends attached to a fixed point will serve as a fulcrum.   A large cylindrical object placed between the limbs in the perineal region also answers this purpose.   After reduction, the horse should be put in slings and kept there for some weeks.   A pitch plaster over the joint may have some immobilising effect, but some practitioners prefer the application of a blister on the ground that it stimulates the process of repair.

Inflammation of the Hip-Joint

ETIOLOGY.—Inflammation of the hip-joint is a rare occurrence in all animals.   It is caused in the following ways : By—

1. *Direct injury* following heavy falls on rough, hard ground.

2. *Excessive movement* of the joint, spraining its ligaments or even causing its dislocation.

3. *Rheumatism,* which is most common in cattle and may cause chronic arthritis.

4. *Joint-ill* in young animals.

The chronic inflammation termed malum coxæ senile, so common in men, is not met with in veterinary practice.

SYMPTOMS.—Lameness is more or less severe, depending on the degree of inflammation.   In cattle the diseased limb is extended with the toe turned outwards.   The gait is of a rolling character, the limb being directed outwards and carried forward in a semicircle.   It is apt to collapse under the animal, especially when turning on the diseased side.   In the horse the symptoms are similar.   As a rule the quarter is tilted and atrophied, the animal moves diagonally or away from the lame side, the limb is abducted, and in harness work the leg and shaft on the sound side show marks of friction.   Suppuration is notified by great increase of lameness and by cellulitis in the region of the joint.

PROGNOSIS.—Simple traumatic synovitis of the joint responds to treatment, but arthritis is incurable.

TREATMENT comprises rest and the use of the usual antiphlogistic agents or that for rheumatism or joint-ill if due to one of these affections. Counter-irritation by blistering, firing, or the insertion of a seton is indicated in chronic cases.

Paralysis of the Obturator Nerve

ETIOLOGY.—The paralysis may be due to :

1. *Laceration of the nerve* by a fragment of a fractured pubic bone.
2. *A callus*, following fracture of the pubis, compressing the nerve.
3. *The pressure of a fœtus* during delivery in a case of fœtal dystokia.
4. *A tumour* on the course of the nerve, compressing it, such as a melanotic tumour in a grey horse.

SYMPTOMS.—The characteristic feature of the condition is marked abduction of the limb during progression, due to loss of power in the adductor muscles supplied by the obturator nerve—viz., the adductors parvus and magnus, the pectineus, and the gracilis. The abduction is accompanied by more or less difficulty in taking the leg forward. The limb is lifted as in stringhalt. Gradual atrophy of the affected muscles supervenes, although it is not so noticeable as in other forms of paralysis.

PROGNOSIS.—When the condition is due to extravasation or effusion following temporary compression of the nerves, it disappears when they become reabsorbed. But when caused by a tumour, or by rupture of the nerve, it is incurable. When a callus decreases in size, diminishing the tension on the nerve, the function of the latter may return.

TREATMENT is of no avail when the cause cannot be removed. When due to a temporary condition, recovery is favoured by the administration of potassium iodide and nux vomica, and by regular exercise.

Crural Paralysis

Crural paralysis is indicated by loss of power in the quadriceps extensor cruri muscles—viz., the vastus externus, the vastus internus, the rectus femoris, and rectus parvus—situated in front of the femur.

ETIOLOGY.—The cause may be :

1. *Over-stretching* of the nerve, as may ensue from slipping backwards of the hind-limb or from violently kicking backwards, or from a great effort during heavy draft.
2. *Hæmoglobinuria*, in which the muscles supplied by this nerve as well as other muscles of the hind-quarters may become powerless and rapidly undergo atrophy.
3. An *abscess*, *tumour*, or *exostosis* compressing the nerve, or *toxic neuritis*.

No. 1 is the commonest cause of simple crural paralysis.

SYMPTOMS.—During rest the limb is held with the stifle and the joints below it in a semi-flexed position. Extension of the stifle is impossible. Consequently, when the horse attempts to put weight on the limb there is sudden flexion of the stifle and hock. There is marked dropping of the stifle, simulating dropped elbow in the fore-limb. If the condition persists for some time, gradual atrophy of the quadriceps supervenes. At first sight the limb appears to be fractured on account of its loose, powerless appearance.

FIG. 365.—PARALYSIS OF THE ANTERIOR CRURAL NERVE.

DIAGNOSIS is easy from the characteristic symptoms mentioned. It can only be confounded with rupture of the muscles concerned, a rare condition accompanied by local inflammatory symptoms.

PROGNOSIS.—In most cases the injury to the nerve is of a temporary nature, and recovery ensues within six weeks, occasionally in a few days, but exceptionally months elapse before cure is effected. Resulting from hæmoglobinuria, the prognosis is unfavourable.

TREATMENT is that described for paralysis in general. Counter-irritation over the muscles affected and the administration of potassium iodide alone or along with nux vomica or strychnine hypodermically constitute the chief curative measures. When power returns to the muscles, gradually increasing exercise is indicated. The other methods of treating paralysis may also be employed. In a valuable subject hope should not be abandoned until at least six months have elapsed since the accident.

Sciatic Paralysis

The sciatic nerve is not much exposed to injury, being well protected by the overlying muscles, yet several cases of paralysis of the muscles supplied by it have been reported in the horse, ox, and dog.

ETIOLOGY.—The condition may be caused by :

1. *Excessive extension* of the hind-limb from slipping or from its being fixed in this position when the animal is cast.

2. *Falling* on the corresponding quarter.

3. *Toxœmia*, following strangles, pneumonia, or purpura, or distemper in the dog.

4. *Compression* by a tumour.

SYMPTOMS.—There is paralysis of all the muscles of the hind-limb, except those supplied by the crural nerve—viz., the quadriceps. During progression the patient is powerless to lift the affected limb forward, and it is dragged with the front of the foot in contact with the ground. The stifle is jerked forward by the action of its extensor muscles. Backing is difficult.

In the dog the skin on the anterior part of the paw becomes excoriated from friction against the ground, and in the horse and ox the front of the fetlock may be similarly affected. If by manipulation the limb is placed in its normal position, it is able to sustain weight in the usual way, because the extensors of the stifle fix that joint, and with it the other joints of the limb. Anæsthesia of the skin of the lower part of the limb accompanies this condition.

TREATMENT is as usual for paralysis. When the result of direct injury, antiphlogistic remedies are indicated, and if due to a tumour the latter must be removed. Slings are advisable for the horse until the muscles regain some power, when exercise should be prescribed.

Paralysis of the External Popliteal Nerve

This belongs rather to the region of the leg, but may be conveniently dealt with here in company with the other forms of paralysis affecting the hind-limb.

ETIOLOGY.—The cause of the paralysis may be :

1. *Direct injury*, such as may ensue from a fall, a blow, or a kick inflicted over the nerve where it passes downwards and forwards over the supero-external aspect of the tibial region. This is the usual cause of the condition.

2. *Toxic*, ensuing in the course of an infectious disease like strangles or purpura. It very rarely occurs, however, in this way.

SYMPTOMS.—When the paralysis is complete, there is total loss of power in the extensor pedis and the flexor metatarsi muscles, which are innervated by this nerve. At rest, the limb may appear normal, bearing weight with the foot resting naturally, or the stifle may be dropped, the hock extended, and the fetlock and front of the pastern

FIG. 366.—PARALYSIS OF THE EXTERNAL POPLITEAL NERVE.

resting on the ground. In advancing, the limb appears to dwell, becoming rigidly extended backwards, and then dragged forwards, renewing contact with the ground by the flexed fetlock or the plantar surface of the foot. In backing, at first the fetlock is straightened and the heels come to the ground, then the foot is drawn stiffly backwards, the fetlock is suddenly shot forwards, and the heels are raised from the ground. At liberty in a field the patient can canter, trailing the defective limb, which touches the ground by the front of the fetlock and the toe-wall of the foot.

PROGNOSIS.—Recovery is the rule in a few days or a few weeks when the lesion is the result of injury.

TREATMENT is the same as that described for the other forms of paralysis.

Internal Popliteal Paralysis

The muscles at the back of the tibia are affected.

SYMPTOMS.—The hock cannot be extended nor the foot flexed, but as flexion of the hock causes automatic flexion of the interphalangeal joints, these joints remain in a state of flexion. The limb can bear weight because the Achilles tendon fixes the hock. The limb is advanced with all the joints excessively flexed, the foot being lifted very high and set down with a hesitating (" tapping ") movement, the action, as a whole, bearing some resemblance to stringhalt. The gastrocnemii are unable to extend the hock while the flexor metatarsi is passive, and only affects movement through the medium of the peculiar tendinous apparatus. Trotting is impossible. The muscles affected, especially the gastrocnemii and flexor pedis perforans, are relaxed, and afterwards become atrophied. The nerve would appear to be affected in its course between the gastrocnemii muscles.

TREATMENT.—As usual for paralysis.

FIG. 367.—PARALYSIS OF THE INTERNAL POPLITEAL NERVE.

Thrombosis of the Posterior Aorta and of its Branches

Arterial thrombosis and its consequences have been dealt with under the heading of Affections of Arteries. The commonest seat of the disease, giving rise to clinical symptoms, is the termination of the posterior aorta, the vessel itself or one or more of the iliac vessels being involved.

ETIOLOGY.—The etiology is sometimes obscure, but in a general way it may be said that the condition arises from an arteritis which roughens the intima of the vessel, on whose lining a thrombus then forms. The commonest cause of this in the horse is the presence of sclerostomes in the blood stream, which become arrested at the double bifurcation of the posterior aorta. The thrombosis may also be due to an embolus arrested here after separation from a thrombus in an aneurism of the anterior mesenteric artery, which is almost invariably present as the result of sclerostomes located there. Bacteria in the circulation may have the same effect. The condition has also been ascribed to over-stretching of the affected vessels from slipping backwards of the hind-limbs, as may possibly occur in a stallion during vigorous service.

SYMPTOMS AND DIAGNOSIS.—The symptoms and diagnostic features of the disease may be briefly stated as follows :

1. The patient is perfectly normal at rest and at walking exercise, or perhaps during light work.

2. When the animal is made to trot, functional disturbance ensues after the lapse of about five to fifteen minutes, affecting one or both hind-limbs.

3. The lameness is characterised by gradually increasing powerlessness of the limb or limbs, which are carried stiffly with little or no flexion of the hocks. If the exercise is continued when both limbs are affected, the patient will fall as if affected with paraplegia.

4. The affected limb or limbs are cold compared with the rest of the body, and when the latter is bathed in sweat they remain dry.

5. When the lameness appears, the animal evinces signs of pain, which become intensified as the exercise continues. The expression is anxious and the respirations hurried, and the animal stops, if not forced to go on. Sweating occurs over the body, except in the affected region. The patient sometimes behaves as if affected with colic for some time after forced exercise.

6. After a period of rest, the normal appearance of the animal is restored.

7. On rectal examination the thrombus may be detected, and the feeble pulsation or entire absence thereof may be recognised on the distal side of the thrombus, or a vibratory tremor may be felt, due to the blood percolating through the stenosed vessel.

When the thrombus is small no functional disturbance may ensue. Stallions are sometimes unable to serve mares. Möller saw one in which erections occurred, but were not followed by ejection of semen. The post-mortem of such animals shows emphysema of the lungs and dilatation of the heart. The pain caused by the condition during exercise is comparable to that occurring in man during temporary obstruction of an artery in a limb from pressure—viz., a feeling of painful stiffness and severe burning (" pins and needles ").

PROGNOSIS depends on the degree of interference with movement, but the tendency is towards aggravation of the symptoms, and only in slight cases can the development of an efficient collateral circulation and recovery be looked for. Sometimes, however, the stallion improves sufficiently to be fit for service.

TREATMENT is unsatisfactory. The administration of potassium iodide and alkaline carbonates, formerly recommended, is of little value. Massage *per rectum* is dangerous. It has led to increased thrombosis and death. The only treatment likely to have some good effect consists in exciting collateral circulation by regular work. The animal is exercised until the first symptoms of lameness appear, and then rested, or it may be put to continued light work. The increased blood circulation thus excited favours development of collateral circulation, but too much is not to be expected from this treatment. The writer had a case in a racehorse which recovered sufficiently to be used successfully at the stud.

Tumours

The hind-quarters may be the seat of various kinds of tumours, including papillomata (common on the inside of the thighs in the horse and ox), fibromata, botriomycomata (affecting the croup and tail), sarcomata, melanomata round the anus and extending into the pelvis in grey horses, osteomata in the aponeurosis already mentioned (see p. 883), and cutaneous epitheliomata (fairly common in dogs). The inguinal lymphatic glands may be affected with primary or secondary malignant growths. Chondromata and osteosarcomata of the femur have been reported in the dog.

TREATMENT is as described for tumours in general.

AFFECTIONS OF THE STIFLE AND OF THE LEG

Contusions and open wounds of these regions do not require description except to mention some special features as follows :

1. **Hæmatoma or Collection of Serum,** which is a common condition in the regions of the stifle and lower part of the buttock, being situated inside or outside the former, or in both or in all three situations. It is usually the result of a fall, and forms almost immediately. It presents the characteristic symptoms already described in Part I.

TREATMENT is that given when dealing with the lesion in general.

2. **Sinus abutting on the Tibia.**—Occasionally, as the result of an open wound of the tibia following a blow or a kick, the bone undergoes necrosis and gives rise to a sinus, which persists until the sequestrum is removed.

3. **Fissure of the Tibia.**—When violence, as from a kick, is inflicted on the tibia where it is subcutaneous, it may be fissured without displacement.

The SYMPTOMS are those of acute local inflammation due to osteo-periostitis and well-marked lameness.

The DIAGNOSIS can only be conjectured from the history and severe local inflammation and lameness, except radiography is resorted to. Displacement of the fragments is prevented by the periosteum and by the strong fascia in the region.

TREATMENT is that for acute inflammation associated with complete rest of the patient to avoid disturbance of the seat of fracture. Slings are indicated for this purpose. Some veterinarians advise the application of a blister to effect hyperæmia, limit movement of the limb, and enforce general rest. Or a charge or pitch plaster bandage may be applied to immobilise the part. If the patient is exercised or put to work before union has had time to take place, displacement of the fragments will ensue, giving rise to a " deferred fracture," which has often occurred in this way.

Distension of the Subcutaneous Bursa in Front of the Patella

The subcutaneous bursa in front of the patella may become affected with an acute or chronic bursitis as the result of injury, and display the usual symptoms of either of these conditions. Lameness is present in an acute case, but may be absent when the lesion is chronic. The swelling may be confounded with distension of the femoro-tibial articulation, which, however, is situated beneath the patella, while the bursal enlargement is in front. Both conditions might coexist. The lesion in the joint is more serious, and is always associated with lameness.

TREATMENT comprises the measures described for bursitis in general. In an obstinate chronic case the best method to adopt is to incise the bursa, evacuate its contents, and irrigate its lining with tincture of iodine or other irritant antiseptic solution.

Sprain of the Flexor Metatarsi

This was first described by M. V. Robin and M. G. Lesbouyries (*Revue Générale de Médecine Vétérinaire*, Vol. xxxvi, No. 430). They had seen it several times in heavy horses.

ETIOLOGY.—The history of the case never gives reliable information as to its cause, but simply indicates that the lameness appeared suddenly during work. It must be due to some movement which puts an extra strain on the muscle without being sufficient to rupture it.

SYMPTOMS.—During rest weight is borne normally by the limb, and at the walk nothing unusual is observed. During the trot, however, the characters of the lameness are well shown as follows : (1) The length of the stride is the same for both limbs ; (2) the foot is placed flat on the ground without flexion of the joints ; (3) there is difficulty in lifting the foot clear of the ground, owing to imperfect flexion of the hock, the toe striking its surface during the movement, and in a case of protracted lameness causing excessive wear of the front of the shoe, especially when the trot is hurried ; (4) backing is difficult, the plantar aspect of the foot being trailed on the ground during the act ; (5) turning the animal sharply with the affected limb inside aggravates the lameness.

In all the affected subjects pressure exerted on the anterior aspect of the inferior part of the tibial region caused the animal to wince, and in one case the antero-external aspect of the stifle-joint at the level of the outer straight ligament of the patella was the seat of pain and slight swelling. Forced extension of the hock before trotting does not exaggerate the lameness, doubtless because it is difficult to perform this extension without opening at the same time the angle of the stifle-joint. The lameness is continuous, being neither diminished nor increased during work.

DIAGNOSIS.—Diagnostic features are : (1) Imperfect flexion of the hock ; (2) pain on pressure above the angle of flexion of the joint ; and (3) the pathognomonic symptoms of rupture of the muscle being absent. The lameness may be confounded with that of spavin, especially when the latter is occult ; but in sprain of the muscle the lameness is not intermittent, and is not affected by passive flexion of the hock. The symptoms also simulate those of external popliteal paralysis, but in the latter the phalangeal joints cannot be extended, the front of the pastern may be in contact with the ground, and during backing the foot is more decidedly dragged over its surface.

PROGNOSIS.—Complete recovery is the rule. The intensity of the clinical symptoms is no guide to the time required for recovery. It usually takes weeks, but may take months.

TREATMENT consists in prolonged rest, accompanied by the use of antiphlogistic applications and massage on the anterior aspect of the leg. Blistering or firing may be necessary, taking care to avoid the angle of flexion of the hock

Rupture of the Tendinous Portion of the Flexor Metatarsi Muscle

This condition has been frequently observed in the horse, and less frequently in the ox. Rupture of the tendon, which extends from the internal surface of the tibia to the bones of the tarsus (in the dog), has been recorded.

FIG. 368.—RUPTURE OF THE FLEXOR METATARSI.

ETIOLOGY.—Rupture of the tendon results from over-extension of the hock, due to the animal kicking violently or struggling in hobbles, or to the limb slipping or being violently drawn backwards, as in shoeing in the trevis, or drawn upwards by means of a cord passed through a ring, especially if the animal fall while thus fixed. Efforts to withdraw the foot when fixed in railway points or in soft ground and getting the limb over a bale may also give rise to it. It seldom follows external violence, but rupture of the corresponding tendon in the dog may be caused in this way. It is rarely bilateral.

SYMPTOMS.—There is lameness, characterised by marked flexion of the stifle-joint and excessive extension of the hock-joint. As the fibrous band stretching between the external condyle of the femur and the metatarsus is no longer able to transmit the movements of the femur to the metatarsus, and as the flexor metatarsi muscle itself is powerless to make up for the deficiency, the cannon-bone is no longer flexed on the limb, but hangs inertly, and all the lower joints of the limb follow suit or are slightly flexed. That portion of the limb below the hock is not properly advanced, while the relaxation of the tendon favours excessive flexion of the stifle-joint. The want of harmony in the function of both joints produces an uncertain movement of the limb, which may give the impression of a broken bone, which is disproved, however, by the fact that the limb still supports weight. At rest nothing unusual is observed, but

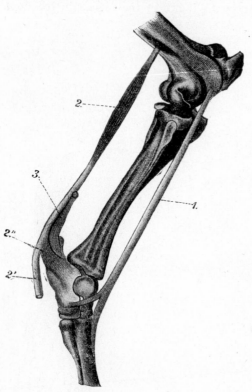

FIG. 369.—SHOWING THE MECHANISM OF THE HOCK AND STIFLE JOINTS.

The tendons of the flexor metatarsi and gastrocnemius muscles unite the bones forming the joints in such a way that they are unable to move independently. 1, Tendinous division of the flexor metatarsi muscle; 2, 2′, and 2″, flexor perforatus; 3, gastrocnemius tendon.

during movement the diagnostic features of the condition are very evident. When the foot is lifted off the ground, the absence of the antagonism of the tendon of the flexor metatarsi is revealed by relaxation of the tendo Achillis, which becomes flaccid and thrown into a fold, constituting a pathognomonic symptom of the lesion. This relaxation is very marked when the limb is taken backwards, as in the

act of shoeing. As a rule, nothing is observed in the front of the limb
to indicate the exact site of the rupture.

PROGNOSIS.—Recovery is the rule within a period of four to eight
weeks, but occasionally it is delayed for three or four months
and in rare cases does not ensue at all. When the tendon is
divided in the bursa at its origin, or is torn away from this point,
recovery is less assured, because formation of new tissue remains
incomplete, the paratendineum essential to union being absent from the
tendon sheath and bursa. When cure supervenes in this case, it takes

FIG. 370.—RUPTURE OF FLEXOR METATARSI MUSCLE.
(From a photograph.)

months before it is complete. Insufficient rest militates against
recovery. If the horse is put to work too soon, the newly-formed
cicatricial tissue gradually becomes strained and the tendon lengthened,
necessarily causing permanent lameness.

TREATMENT consists in keeping the patient perfectly quiet for four
to six weeks. Recovery is favoured by keeping the limb in a forward
position by means of a rope attached to a hobble on the pastern, or
better to a ring in the toe of the shoe and fixed round the neck. A
blister applied over the level of the affected muscle will not have much
effect, except to enforce rest. It is, however, a measure which is usually

adopted. When the lameness disappears the horse may be gradually put to work.

" Track-Leg " in the Greyhound

The term " track-leg " in the greyhound is applied to an inflammatory swelling on the inner aspect of the left tibial region and a little below its midway point, at about the level of the insertion of the tendon of the semimembranosis. The condition is evidently due to a strain of the structures of the affected region, with vascular rupture and extravasation of blood and the formation of an inflammatory exudate. The symptoms are those of acute inflammation with a well marked swelling which may or may not fluctuate according as it contains much or little fluid exudate or extravasate. The treatment is that for acute or chronic inflammation, as the case may be. When the case is slow to respond to hot stuping and the use of absorbent topics, and the enlargement is distinctly fluctuating incision is advisable to permit of the escape of the fluid and thus hasten recovery, careful antiseptic precautions being taken and the wound being protected by a pad and bandage. When the lesion is in the form of a fibrous thickening causing persistent lameness line or needle-point firing is indicated, followed by prolonged rest and gradual return of the dog to fast exercise. Recovery is the rule.

Rupture of the Tendo Achillis

Rupture of the gastrocnemius muscles or of the Achilles tendon is oftenest seen in cows, and sometimes in both limbs at once. Rupture generally occurs at the lower point of insertion of the tendon, a portion of the os calcis being at the same time torn away. It also takes place where the muscle becomes continuous with the tendon. Rupture of the muscle itself has been seen in horses and cattle.

ETIOLOGY.—Rupture results from excessive strain thrown on the tendon, as may ensue from cattle jumping on one another. In horses it may occur during jumping or during heavy draft. External violence may produce the lesion. In dogs it has been caused by the animal being caught in a door. In exceptional cases the rupture is secondary to necrosis or suppuration of the tendon, and it has been reported by Uhlic as a sequel to influenza.

SYMPTOMS.—There is inability to bear weight on the affected limb and flexion of all the joints. The hock and stifle joints can no longer be fixed to support the body-weight, and there is consequent collapse of the limb, allowing the back of the hock to approach or come in contact with the ground. The excessive flexion of the hock increases the distance between the points of origin and insertion of the flexor pedis, and the phalanges take up a position of excessive plantar flexion. As a rule, a depression can be noted in the course of the tendon or swelling in the gastrocnemii muscles; the tendon appears relaxed even when the limb touches the ground.

PROGNOSIS depends almost entirely on whether the uninjured leg

FIG. 371.—RUPTURE OF THE TENDO ACHILLIS.

can sustain weight until union occurs. Small animals like dogs and cats almost always do well, but larger animals are less favourably circumstanced. They sometimes succumb to the continued standing or lying, for union takes from four to six weeks, and under some circumstances may be protracted for several months. Oxen do best lying, but as horses are obliged to stand, it becomes a question whether laminitis may not supervene in the other foot. Nevertheless, a considerable number of recoveries have been recorded in the horse. The hind-foot is more subject to laminitis from bearing undue weight than

the fore-foot.   As a rule, the more marked the degree of flexion, the
slighter the chance of recovery, which is often protracted by elongation
of the tendon and consequent lameness.

TREATMENT consists in keeping the hock in a state of extension, so as
to have the ends of the ruptured tendon as close together as possible,
and thus favour their union.   This can be effected by a plaster bandage
in small animals.   The horse is generally put in slings, while the hock
is kept in extension by an immobilising dressing, which may be in the
form of two wooden splints applied laterally from the region of the

FIG. 372.—RUPTURE OF THE TENDO ACHILLIS.   (AFTER STOCKFLETH.)

stifle to the foot and shaped to correspond exactly to the normal conformation of the limb.   Ample padding is applied beneath the splints,
which are fixed by straps and buckles above and below the hock.   In
the dog, suturing the ruptured tendon has been successfully performed.
The dressing advised for fracture of the os calcis in the dog is
indicated here (see p. 926).

Section of the Gastrocnemius and Perforatus Tendons

This has been seen in the horse, ox, pig, and dog as the result of
cuts by sharp bodies.   It has often been done maliciously, when the
animals are said to have been "hamstrung." The nature of the
condition is obvious, and it renders the limb quite powerless.   Recovery is not likely to ensue in the large animals.   It may be obtained
in small patients by suturing the severed tendons and immobilising the
limb with the hock fully extended.

Fracture of the Tibia

In the horse, fracture of the tibia ranks next in point of frequency with that of the pelvis.

ETIOLOGY.—The cause may be :

1. *Direct violence*, usually a kick from another horse, inflicted on the internal face of the lower fourth of the tibia, which lies directly under the skin. In many cases the bone is at first only fissured, separation taking place later during such acts as rising, lying down, or passing urine or fæces. It is seldom postponed more than a week or ten days from the date of original injury, although cases have occurred where separation did not take place until four or five weeks afterwards. Displacement at first is prevented by the periosteum and fascia, which are intact. When they become softened and weakened by inflammation, displacement occurs more readily. The injury to the bone may only cause ostitis at first. This produces rarefaction of the bone, which may then fracture during severe exertion. The fracture may also be caused by a fall or a collision.

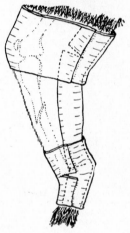

2. *Muscular violence*, most commonly when struggling in hobbles, but also as the result of slipping.

The accident is very common in dogs, due to kicks, blows, and being run over. Parrots and canaries are not uncommon sufferers from

FIG. 373.—PLASTER CAST ON MID-SHAFT OF THE TIBIA WITH WINDOW. (*Veterinary Record.*)

fracture of the tibia. Fenimore describes a case of fracture of the tibia in a fœtus ; the fracture had been caused by a kick received by the mother (a cow) whilst pregnant, and when the calf was born the fracture was healed.

SYMPTOMS.—The symptoms of complete fracture are typical, and cannot be mistaken. Fissured fracture can only be guessed at from the history of the case and the seat of the inflammation. The more severe the latter and the greater the lameness, the more likely is fracture present. X-rays will reveal the fissure.

PROGNOSIS.—The prognosis in large animals is grave, recovery seldom supervening. There is always the risk of laminitis affecting the other foot from the constant excessive weight thereon. In light horses, ponies, and foals, especially the latter, there is a good chance of obtaining a cure by the usual methods of treatment. In dogs and cats complete cure is almost invariably effected. When the seat of fracture is in the lower part of the bone, the prognosis is more favourable than when it is higher up. In France a number of cases are reported where complete fracture of the tibia in horses has been treated successfully, but they extend over many years, and must be regarded as exceptional.

TREATMENT.—As already stated, all serious injuries of the tibia should be regarded as possible fractures, and dealt with as such, the

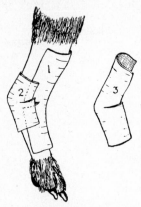

horse being rested for at least four weeks to enable a fissured fracture to heal, and to prevent displacement. The horse should be placed in slings or tied up short in order to restrict movement as much as possible. Complete fracture is treated on general principles. An immobilising dressing from the foot to the stifle is necessary. A pitch bandage, which can be made adherent to the skin in the stifle region, is the most suitable; it may be associated with splints, with padding beneath to prevent wounding of the soft tissues by the latter. A charge or

FIG. 374.—PLASTER CAST FOR FRACTURE OF THE TARSUS AND DISTAL END OF THE TIBIA.

pitch dressing is commonly applied in cattle. Light beasts often recover without treatment of any kind. The dressings recommended for fracture of the femur in the dog are very suitable for fractured tibia, also the unpadded plaster cast described on p. 124.

Fracture of the fibula usually accompanies that of the tibia. Rarely it occurs alone, and then usually at its upper part. It is not a serious lesion, and heals under ordinary antiphlogistic treatment.

Fracture of the Patella

Fracture of the patella is rare, and up to the present has only been seen in horses.

ETIOLOGY.—Kicks, collisions, and falls with the stifle-joint strongly flexed are the principal causes, especially of vertical fractures. Those horizontal in direction may be caused by violent muscular contraction.

SYMPTOMS.—There is inability to bear weight on the limb, and intense inflammation at the seat of injury. When the fracture is vertical there is no evidence of displacement, which is prevented by the fibrous covering on the anterior aspect of the bone, but when it is horizontal a portion of the bone may be drawn upwards by the muscles attached thereto. Diagnosis is confirmed when crepitation and mobility of the fragments can be recognised. The limb is usually held in a state of flexion, and may be pendulous. Crepitation resembling that of fracture may occur in a case of arthritis affecting the trochlea of the femur, but in this case weight can be borne by the limb and acute local inflammation is absent.

PROGNOSIS is grave. Even when union of the fragments occurs permanent lameness is apt to ensue. When the fracture is comminuted or compound, exposing the joint, the case is hopeless.

TREATMENT, from what has been said, is not likely to be successful. It is carried out on general principles, slings being necessary for the horse. The joint should be kept as far as possible in a state of extension. Removal of the fractured bone is indicated in the dog after dissecting back its periosteum, which is afterwards sutured. A slight limp will remain, which is preferable to stiffness and pain in action (Craven, N. S., N. Amer. Vet., **19**, 12, 55).

Contusion and Sprain of the Stifle-Joint—Acute Gonitis

ETIOLOGY.—Contusion is caused by external violence. Sprain is not common. It is more often met with in working oxen than in horses. It is fairly common in greyhounds, as the result of over-exertion of the joint in some particular direction when racing or coursing, especially in the act of turning shortly. In any animal it may be due to violent slipping when the joint is extended.

SYMPTOMS.—The symptoms are those of acute synovitis and periarthritis. There is well-marked local acute inflammation, and the lameness is very pronounced and characterised by stiffness of the stifle-joint, and consequent shortening of the stride, the animal going on the toe.

TREATMENT is as usual for a sprained joint or for a contusion. If more than one patellar ligament is ruptured, there is little chance of recovery. When the sprain has been severe, recovery may be very protracted. A chronic synovitis may succeed the acute form. A long rest is always necessary before returning the animal to work or racing.

Open wounds of the stifle-joint are of the same nature as those of joints in general. When septic arthritis supervenes it is incurable.

Chronic Inflammation of the Stifle-Joint—Chronic Gonitis

This condition is most common in heavy draft-horses, but is also seen in other breeds, and in the ass and mule as well as in the ox. The typical arthritis is not common in the dog, but it is occasionally met with in the larger coursing and working breeds. The disease may be bilateral in the horse.

ETIOLOGY.—The etiology of the lesion is obscure. Heavy haulage appears to be a predisposing factor, as the disease is certainly most common in horses doing heavy draft work. Shunters are particularly liable to it, and farm-horses are often affected. It may be rheumatoid. It is sometimes present in young unbroken horses, and may then be looked upon as of toxic origin, following navel infection.

FIG. 375.—LEFT-SIDED CHRONIC INFLAM-MATION OF THE STIFLE-JOINT (GONITIS CHRONICA).

FIG. 376.—BILATERAL CHRONIC INFLAM-MATION OF THE STIFLE-JOINT (GONITIS CHRONICA BILATERALIS).

(From a photograph.)

SYMPTOMS.—At the outset the lameness is slight or intermittent, and where the disease is bilateral may for a long time be overlooked. Well-known features of the disease may be briefly stated as follows :

1. The lesion is of a chronic nature, defying treatment.

2. During rest the horse repeatedly flexes the stifle and hock, and holds the limb suspended for a while. On exercise at a walk the animal shows well-marked lameness, and may go on the toe or put the foot flat on the ground. When made to trot he keeps the joint

extended, and may go on three legs with the joint locked in this position.

3. The stifle-joint is enlarged, due to periarticular fibrous thickening and the deposit of osteophytes round the articular ends of the femur and tibia, as well as to synovial distension of its capsule. The synovial distension is recognised as a boggy swelling behind and between the anterior straight ligaments of the patella.

4. Pain is usually evinced on pushing the fingers deeply into the

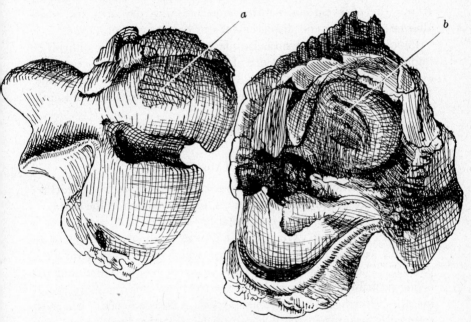

FIG. 377.—CHRONIC ARTHRITIS OF THE FEMORO-TIBIAL JOINT.
a and *b,* Eroded surfaces on the tibia and femur.

boggy swelling and on passive forcible movement of the joint, and sometimes from compressing it laterally.

5. Crepitation is sometimes heard on flexion and extension of the joint, due to friction between the eroded articular surfaces.

DIAGNOSIS is easy when the disease is well established, but in its early stages it may be hesitating.

PROGNOSIS.—The condition is incurable.

TREATMENT is useless, but firing and blistering are sometimes practised when the diagnostic features are not pronounced, in the hope that the condition is curable. The fact of their having no good effect confirms the diagnosis when it is doubtful.

58

Post-mortem examination reveals the typical lesions of a chronic arthritis. Erosion of the articular surfaces is most marked around the tibial spine and the inferior surface of the condyles.

Dislocation of Femoro-tibial Articulation

This is a rare occurrence. It is most common in the dog, especially the racing varieties, and is brought about by over-exertion of the joint. It has taken place during galloping. The condition is easily recognised. It may be of a chronic nature associated with dry arthritis, when alternate reduction and displacement can be passively produced.

PROGNOSIS.—The prognosis is unfavourable, as it may be difficult or impossible to prevent recurrence of the dislocation after reduction, and even when retention is effected permanent lameness may ensue. Recovery is likely to ensue in the dog when the luxation is promptly reduced.

TREATMENT is on general principles.

Dislocation of the Patella

True dislocation of the patella over one of the lips of the trochlea is a rare condition in the large animals, but is common in the dog.

ETIOLOGY.—It is often congenital in the dog, and may affect a whole litter of pups. Otherwise it is due to direct violence, or to powerful contraction of the muscles which are inserted into the patella. The dislocation is usually outwards in the horse and ox, owing probably to the inner lip of the trochlea being the more prominent. Nevertheless it also occurs inwards in these animals. It is most frequently inwards in the dog. In order that the displacement may take place there must be elongation or rupture of one of the femoro-patellar ligaments. In the dog it results from a fall or a jump, or a blow inflicted in the stifle region. A chronic form of the condition has been seen in young coarse bred horses, apparently due to chronic arthritis, the patella slipping in and out with a clicking noise during progression.

SYMPTOMS.—In the case of outward dislocation the stifle is in a semi-flexed position, and appears deviated outwards with the toe only touching the ground. The nature of the condition is ascertained on palpation : the patella is felt in an abnormal situation, and the patellar ligaments are found directed upwards and outwards. During progression the limb is carried stiffly, the stride is shortened, and the movements of the patella are observed.

When the dislocation is inwards the stifle can be neither flexed nor extended, and the straight ligaments and the quadriceps are directed inwards. In all cases the vacant trochlea of the femur may be recognised. In the dog it is generally easy to replace the patella, but it immediately becomes displaced again. In some instances the luxation is associated with a chronic arthritis.

PROGNOSIS is generally unfavourable, as it is often impossible to retain the patella in its normal position after reduction. Congenital cases and those due to chronic arthritis are hopeless.

TREATMENT comprises reduction and retention. To effect reduction, apply a rope to the pastern of the affected limb, let assistants pull the limb forwards by means of the rope, and at the same time push the patella into its normal position. To prevent recurrence of the condition, tie the horse up short and apply a blister over the patellar region. When the luxation occurs suddenly in the dog, without rupture of the lateral patellar ligaments, and is promptly reduced, it may not recur. If reduction prove difficult in the horse in the standing position, he may be cast and chloroform may be administered to overcome muscular resistance.

Bénard claims to have cured congenital cases in the ox as follows : Take a linen bandage about 6 inches wide and long enough to go four times round the stifle, make a hole in its centre sufficiently large to accommodate the patella, and 4 to 6 inches from this make a transverse slit in the bandage. Arrange the bandage so that the patella is lodged in the central opening, pass one of the ends through the other opening, and pull it tightly. Cross the two ends first above and then below the patella, and tie them. It is usually impossible to keep the patella in position in the dog after reduction. Section of the tendons of insertion of the vasti muscles relieves the tension on the patella and improves somewhat the animal's gait. It is easily done subcutaneously.

Fixation of the Patella above the Trochlea

This has been described as upward dislocation of the patella, but it hardly deserves this name, as the patella is not out of line with the trochlea, and the condition is not associated with rupture or severe injury of the ligaments which keep the bone in position. It is much more common in horses and oxen than the true dislocation above described.

ETIOLOGY.—The accident occurs suddenly without any extraordinary effort, in the stable or outside. It sometimes happens when the horse stretches the leg rigidly backwards, thereby fully extending the stifle. It has been seen taking place in this way in the young horse tired after a hard day's ploughing the day before. The condition is favoured by debility and poor condition and consequent absorption of the fat between the straight ligaments and the joint.

SYMPTOMS.—The affected limb is rigidly extended backwards and cannot be flexed. On palpation the straight ligaments are felt to be tensely stretched, the trochlea of the femur is free from the patella, and the latter is found fixed beyond its upper extremity. When the animal is walked, the front of the hoof trails on the ground. During backing the limb is also rigid. The fetlock can be passively flexed, but all attempts at flexion of the hock and stifle are in vain.

Sometimes the symptoms disappear as suddenly as they came. When the animal is made to move on, or more frequently when backed, the patella may be released, and then the limb regains its normal position, the joints being at first spasmodically flexed as in stringhalt, but afterwards flexed normally. A dull sound may be heard when the patella slips back on the trochlea. In many cases, however, the displacement continues for hours or days until it is reduced by manipulation.

TREATMENT.—Reduction may be effected as follows :

1. By local manipulation, pushing the patella forwards while the horse moves on a step or two in the loose box or stall.

2. Make the animal walk forward with the head high, and if he is too slow in his movements flick him with the whip. After a few steps the patella may return to its place.

3. If No. 2 has not the desired effect, forcing the animal to back may succeed.

4. When Nos. 2 and 3 fail, apply a rope to the pastern of the affected limb, have the latter drawn forwards by an assistant pulling on the rope after passing it through a collar on the patient's neck or through a ring in the wall in front of the animal, and at the same time push the patella downwards and inwards.

5. If No. 4 prove difficult, cast the patient and draw the limb forward to the shoulder by means of a side-line. As a rule reduction is easily accomplished, but the displacement may recur after a variable interval. The application of a blister over the joint will cause inflammatory swelling, which will help to prevent recurrence. Giving the animal nutritious diet and moderate work or regular exercise will also aid in this respect.

In many cases the displacement recurs repeatedly after easy reduction, and they seem hopeless, but experience has shown that eventually, in most instances, the normal condition is restored. These cases would appear to be due to loss of tone in the muscles which bind the stifle joint accompanying a sort of general debility following severe work such as racing, and when the normal condition is regained the abnormality disappears. Recovery is undoubtedly favoured by applying a high heeled shoe and by bedding the horse with peat moss or sawdust. The author has knowledge of cases of this nature in race horses in which this procedure has proved successful. Should these measures fail to prevent recurrence the operations for section of the internal straight ligament of the patella is indicated (p. 458).

Henry Taylor, Haywards Heath, published a good article on " Luxation of the Patella," *Vet. Rec.*, May 4th, 1946 ; and the *Indian Veterinary Journal*, July, 1944, contains one on " Luxation in Bovines." Sir Frederick Smith in his *Physiology* states that the condition is usually due to cramp of the muscles attached to the patella, owing to their being affected with maintained contraction known as " contracture."

AFFECTIONS OF THE HOCK

Contusions and Open Wounds of the Hock

The hock, being much exposed to injury, is a common seat of traumatic lesions. Contusions vary in gravity ; they may involve fracture of one or more of the bones of the joint, or cause displacement of the perforatus tendon. When slight and repeated at the level of the os calcis they cause capped hock. Open wounds are of various kinds, the most serious being those penetrating the true hock-joint or one of the gliding articulations.

The SYMPTOMS are in accordance with the nature of the condition, and treatment is carried out on general principles.

A guarded PROGNOSIS must be given in connection with punctured and contused wounds of the hock, when recent, as there is always the risk of the joint or the tarsal sheath being involved, and the results of infection thereof will not be apparent for some days, and all such wounds must be treated with meticulous care on the principles laid down in General Surgery.

Large open wounds in the front of the hock or encroaching thereon from its lateral aspect are often difficult to cure, owing to the persistence of excessive granulations due to the irritation caused by the frequent flexion of the joint. Excision followed by the use of formalin (1 in 40) may have the desired effect.

Capped Hock—Hygroma or Distension of the Superficial Bursa on the Point of the Hock

This is a common condition in the horse, and it varies in character according to the age of the lesion.

ETIOLOGY.—Contusion of the point of the hock will always give rise

FIG. 378.—EXUBERANT GRANULATION IN FRONT OF THE HOCK.

FIG. 379.—CAPPED HOCK (DROPSY OF THE SUBCUTANEOUS BURSA OF THE HOCK).

to a swelling there, which, however, is only temporary when the cause is not renewed. Typical capped hock is caused by repeated injury of the part from kicking in the stable or in harness, or from lying on bare floors. Sudden effort of a horse in rising may cause the point of the hock to be injured against the floor. When a severe injury is inflicted there, the swelling forms quickly. Distension of the bursa may occur during an attack of lymphangitis or purpura hæmorrhagica.

SYMPTOMS.—When the case is recent and the result of a definite contusion, an acute inflammatory swelling appears on the point of the hock. If it become infected an abscess will form. Otherwise, if the injury is not repeated, it will gradually subside and perhaps disappear entirely. Chronic cases resulting from inveterate kicking or frequent friction against the ground or wall of the stable are characterised by the presence of a painless, more or less prominent swelling, due to a chronic bursitis associated with a varying degree of fibrous thickening. Occasionally this becomes acutely inflamed and infected as the result of more severe injury, and when the resulting abscess bursts it may refuse to heal, owing to the presence of a smooth, non-granulating lining. Lameness, even in acute cases, is rarely present.

PROGNOSIS.—The condition in itself is not serious, but it is an unsightly blemish which may be difficult or impossible to get rid of, chiefly due to the fact that the cause cannot be removed.

TREATMENT consists in adopting measures to arrest the cause of the trouble, and applying the usual remedies for acute or chronic bursitis, as the case may be.

Prevention may comprise padding the sides of the stall ; providing an increased amount of litter, peat moss or tan being the most suitable ; the use of a good kicking-strap in harness ; and the application of hock-caps in horses travelling by boat or train.

The details of curative treatment are those described in connection with bursitis in general. Nothing will succeed in dispelling an old fibrous enlargement. The best results are obtained by the repeated application of a slightly stimulating absorbent preparation, such as a combination of iodine, potassium iodide, and Archangel tar, as is found in the proprietary preparation known as " Reducine." Painting the swelling with ordinary gas tar at intervals for a prolonged period is said to be very effective. French veterinarians have great faith in a liniment composed of goudron de Norvège 450 parts, savon vert 450, poudre de tan tamisée 100. It is applied daily with a brush, and is said to remove even a voluminous capped hock in the course of a few weeks. When the condition is cystic, aspiration and the injection of tincture of iodine associated with needle-point firing is a very effective form of treatment. The use of the knife for incision or excision of the swelling is generally contra-indicated, as the resulting wound might be very difficult to heal and cause more trouble than the original lesion, suppuration and increased fibrous thickening ensuing. Lanzillotti, however, reports having operated successfully. To excise a fibrous enlargement, he made a crescentic incision on the inner aspect of the hock, reflected a flap of skin, and after excising the tumour sutured the cutaneous edges and obtained healing by first intention.

Strict asepsis and antisepsis and protection of the wound afterwards from outside interference are essential.

The ox may also be affected with capped hock in the same way as the horse and requires similar treatment.

The dog occasionally shows slight capping of the hocks, especially amongst the larger breeds, from repeated contact with hard ground, the best treatment for which is the application of iodine preparations.

Dislocation of the Perforatus Tendon

Dislocation of the perforatus tendon, from the summit of the os calcis to the outside or inside of the process, is not a common condition, but several cases of it have been recorded in the horse. It is much more rare in other animals. Outer dislocation is the more common.

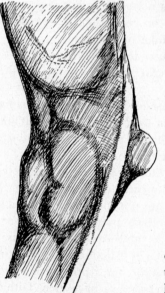

ETIOLOGY.—The cause may be :

1. *External violence,* such as a kick or a severe knock against the point of the hock.

2. *Powerful muscular contraction* when the hock is in a state of flexion.

3. *Rearing and falling on the hock.*

4. *Slipping during a gallop.*

In all cases there must be rupture of one of the lateral ligaments which bind the tendon to the os calcis. The inner ligament is the weaker, and gives way more readily than the outer.

FIG.3 80.—DISLOCATION OF THE PERPORATUS TENDON.

SYMPTOMS.—When the case is recent, there are well-marked lameness and acute local inflammation. The tendon is seen to be displaced from its normal position. When the animal is made to move, the tendon may slip laterally to and from its normal situation, and the slipping is sometimes accompanied by a slight noise. There is excessive flexion of the hock and stifle. The horse may carry the affected limb during progression, or take it forward with difficulty, dragging the foot along the ground.

PROGNOSIS.—Treatment usually fails to keep the tendon in its normal position. Nevertheless, the function of the limb is completely restored in most cases, the tendon operating in a new channel to the side of the os calcis. Occasionally, instead of doing this, the tendon continues to glide on and off the os calcis, causing a permanent interference with gait. As a rule outward is more hopeful than inward luxation.

TREATMENT.—All efforts at keeping the tendon in place on the summit of the os calcis usually fail. Reduction is always easy in a recent case. Section of the tendon at the level of the base of the hock has been advised to permit of its upper part being kept in position on the os calcis. Drouet and others suggest suturing the tendon to the tendo Achillis and calcaneo-metatarsal ligament. It is better, however, to trust in recovery ensuing without these operations. Otherwise the treatment is that for acute or chronic inflammation, according to the age of the lesion. Counter-irritation by blistering or firing, or both, may be practised when

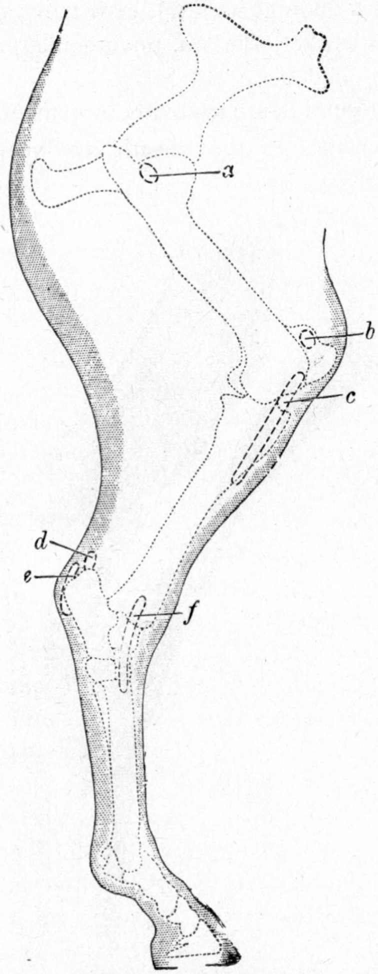

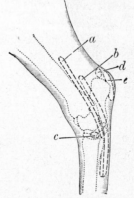

FIG. 381.—TENDON SHEATHS AND BURSÆ OF THE HIND-LIMB OF THE HORSE SEEN FROM WITHOUT (SEMI-DIAGRAMMATIC).

a, Trochanteric bursa ; b, prepatellar bursa ; c, tendon sheath of the extensor pedis ; d, bursa calcanea ; e, tendon sheath of the flexor pedis perforatus tendon ; f, tendon sheath of the peroneus tendon.

FIG. 382.—TENDON SHEATHS AND BURSÆ OF THE HOCK-JOINT SEEN FROM WITHIN (SEMI-DIAGRAMMATIC).

a, Tendon sheath of the flexor accessorius tendon ; b, tendon sheath of the flexor pedis perforans tendon ; c, bursa of the internal division of the flexor metatarsi tendon ; d, bursa calcanea ; e, tendon sheath of the flexor pedis perforatus on the point of the hock.

lameness persists and is apparently due to chronic inflammation in the part.

Synovitis of the Tarsal Sheath

Acute Synovitis of the tarsal sheath may be the result of a contusion or of a sprain of the perforans tendon at its level, or it may be due to the toxin of an infectious disease like influenza, pneumonia, or rheumatism.

SYMPTOMS.—The symptoms are those of acute synovitis in general. The acute inflammation and distension of the sheath are very pronounced, and the lameness is severe.

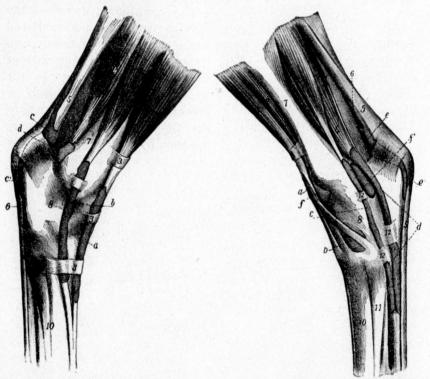

FIG. 383.—EXTERNAL SURFACE OF THE HORSE'S HOCK, TO SHOW SYNOVIAL SHEATHS.

a, Tendon sheath of the extensor pedis muscle ; *b*, tendon sheath of peroneus muscle ; *c*, *c'*, tendon sheath of flexor perforatus and gastrocnemius muscles ; *d*, protrusion of the synovial capsule of the true hock-joint.

FIG. 384.—INTERNAL SURFACE OF THE HORSE'S HOCK, TO SHOW SYNOVIAL SHEATHS.

a, Tendon sheath of flexor metatarsi muscle ; *b*, tendon sheath under inner terminal tendon of flexor metatarsi ; *c*, tendon sheath of flexor accessorius ; *d*, tendon sheath of flexor perforans ; *e*, *e'*, tendon sheath of flexor perforatus and gastroenemius muscles ; *f*, *f'*, distended synovial capsule of the true hock-joint.

TREATMENT.—The treatment is that already described for all cases of acute synovitis.

Purulent Synovitis of this sheath is a dangerous condition. It may be complicated with necrosis of the tendon, and prove incurable. It causes intense pain and lameness.

TREATMENT is on general principles including drainage and antiseptic irrigation of the sheath (see p. 81). It is usually the result of an open wound. More rarely it is due to strangles.

Chronic Synovitis, or Distension of the Sheath—Thoroughpin

Chronic synovitis may follow the acute form, or occur independently as the result of constant hard work. The pain and lameness which arise from it vary according to the degree of chronic inflammation present. It may be very slight or well marked. Distension of the sheath often occurs without any inflammation or lameness. In either case the condition is known as thoroughpin, and is characterised by two swellings above the hock, one on the inside and the other on the outside, filling up the hollows on either side of the tendo Achillis, and sometimes by a third swelling below the hock on the inside at the level of the seat of curb, and spoken of by some authors as soft curb. Mere distension of the sheath occurs without any apparent cause, being

FIG. 385.—DISTENSION OF SHEATH OF FLEXOR PEDIS PERFORANS.
(From a photograph.)

of the nature of a dropsy. It is often present in young horses that have never done any work. Straight hocks favour distension by tending to relax the sheath. It occurs in all breeds of horses, but draft-horses are most subject to it. The swellings vary in size in different cases, and the inner of the two superior ones is generally the larger. Sometimes, however, the outer enlargement is more prominent than the inner. Exceptionally the inner swelling above is so great that it is rubbed by the other limb during progression.

PROGNOSIS.—Where there is merely distension of the sheath lameness is absent, and the condition may disappear as mysteriously as it came without any treatment; but when it is associated with chronic synovitis the lameness may be difficult to get rid of, especially when the inferior swelling is present.

TREATMENT to dispel the swellings is often tedious, and sometimes disappointing. It consists in adopting some of the measures advised for the treatment of chronic synovitis and synovial distensions in general, including the following :

1. *Expectant treatment*, indicated in young horses in which the sheath is merely distended, and there is no evidence of pain or lameness. The swellings often disappear spontaneously in such cases in the course of a few months.

2. *Pressure* constantly applied by several layers of cotton-wool and a bandage, or by means of a thoroughpin truss. The former method is probably the better, as it distributes the pressure more evenly over the hock. The truss cannot be always easily adjusted, and it may not be tolerated by the horse. The rubbing in of a mild liniment is advisable before applying the cotton-wool. The condition may recur when the pressure is discontinued.

3. *Blistering*, which is generally disappointing in its results. It may have some effect in relieving chronic inflammation.

4. *Line firing* and blistering, more effective than No. 3, but often failing to have the desired effect.

5. *Needle-point firing*, which often proves efficacious, but is by no means infallible.

6. *Aspiration of the sheath and the injection of* (*a*) *tincture of iodine*, pure or diluted with one or two parts of boiled water ; or (*b*) of *Dean's preparation* ; or (*c*) of *Collinson's preparation* ; or (*d*) *Cagny's injection of antipyrine* (see p. 84). This is better than any of the foregoing methods of treatment ; (*b*), (*c*), and (*d*) have given excellent results. The operation must be done with strict asepsis. Its beneficial effects are frequently not shown until several weeks or even some months have elapsed after its performance. The sheath remains swollen in the meantime, but eventually the distension gradually subsides until it disappears altogether. It is probably an advantage to repeat the aspiration once or twice when the swelling is slow in its disappearance.

7. *A combination of No. 5 and No.* 6 is better than either alone, and if there is no objection to the slight marks of the iron is the best method of treatment to practise. It may also be slow in producing its good effect.

8. *Synoviotomy*, opening the sheath with the knife, the only efficacious method of removing riziform bodies. It has been done successfully by some veterinarians, including Williams of New York. It is a dangerous procedure, because if very strict asepsis is not

observed purulent infection of the sheath may ensue, with fatal results. When this complication does not occur, cure is said to be obtained in the course of three or four weeks. The ordinary practitioner would be well advised to avoid this method.

To the foregoing may be added the repeated rubbing into the swelling of equal parts of rectified spirits of tar and linseed oil, which the late Mr. James Daly, F.R.C.V.S., of Dublin, claimed as an almost certain cure when patiently persisted in, perhaps for months. The same good result is claimed for " Reducine," a preparation of iodine, potassium iodide, and Archangel tar.

Distension of the Sheath of the Cunean Tendon

This is rarely seen. It is recognised as a small, oval, fluctuating, painless swelling at the level of the tendon. It constitutes a blemish on the inner aspect of the hock, but does not incommode the animal, although when very tense it might cause a little stiffness in flexion of the joint. The surest way to get rid of it is to incise the sheath and treat its lining with tincture of iodine.

Distension of the Perforatus Bursa on the Point of the Hock—Deep-Capped Hock

Distension of this bursa between the perforatus and gastrocnemius tendons at the point of the hock is occasionally met with. Its cause is not always apparent, and it is seldom accompanied by pain and lameness. It appears on either side of the tendons just above the point of the hock.

The best TREATMENT is either needle-point firing and blistering or aspiration and injection, or a combination of these measures. Incision with the knife is contra-indicated, owing to the risk of infection, which might be followed by necrosis of the tendons. It has been called " deep-capped hock."

Distension of the Sheaths of the Extensor Pedis and Peroneus Tendons

The distension is recognised by the presence of a fluctuating cylindrical swelling at the level of the tendon involved. One or both sheaths may be affected, but distension of the peroneal sheath is more common than that of the extensor pedis, and has been noticed most frequently in horses doing fast work. Lameness seldom accompanies the condition in either sheath.

TREATMENT is the same as in the preceding case, but if necessary the sheath may be incised and its interior then treated with tincture of iodine, as there is less risk of complications here.

Fractures of the Tarsal Bones : Fracture of the Os Calcis

ETIOLOGY.—The fracture may be caused by external violence or by muscular contraction. Falls and kicks are common causes in all animals, and in dogs it may be the result of being run over. It is a fairly common accident in racing greyhounds. It has occurred in the horse when jumping.

SYMPTOMS.—There is inability to extend the hock, as in the case of rupture of the tendo Achillis, but the local inflammation is more pain-

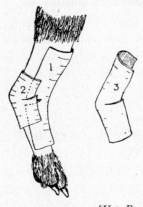

[*Vet. Rec.*

FIG. 386.—UNPADDED PLAS-
TER CAST FOR FRACTURE OF
TARSUS IN THE DOG.

ful in the case of fracture. Abnormal mobility of the os calcis is readily recognised. Crepitation is not evident when the upper fragment is drawn upwards by the action of the gastrocnemius muscle ; but when the line of fracture is inside the ligamentous attachments and the fragments are in contact, it may be heard and felt.

PROGNOSIS.—The condition is practically hopeless in the large animals, although exceptional cases of successful treatment in the ox have been recorded. Cure is more likely to be obtained in small animals like the dog and cat.

TREATMENT consists in immobilising the hock in the state of extension. This may be effected in the small animals by the use of one of the dressings recommended in the chapter on Fractures. A gutter-shaped splint fitted to the anterior aspect of the limb, and reaching from the middle of the metatarsus to the middle of the tibia, with padding beneath, and fixed with straps and buckles above and below the hock, is a suitable contrivance for the horse and ox, should treatment be attempted.

The following method of immobilisation of the seat of fracture (recommended by Elam (Liverpool)) has proved completely successful in the greyhound when applied before displacement of the os calcis has occurred.

Apply a splint at the back of the limb extending from the paw to a point about 4 inches above the summit of the os calcis. Bind the projecting part of the splint to the limb above the hock by several turns of a bandage, thereby keeping the tendo Achillis completely relaxed and taking all strain off the bone into which it is inserted.

If displacement has occurred, this treatment is not likely to succeed, although the os calcis has been replaced into what appears to be its normal position before application of the dressing.

The unpadded plaster dressing (Fig. 386) is suitable for this fracture.

Fracture of the Astragalus

The astragalus is not so exposed to fracture as the os calcis, but the bone has been broken by violent torsion of the hock when the foot was bearing weight and fixed, and also by direct violence.

SYMPTOMS.—There are sudden and severe lameness, with inability to bear weight, and intense local inflammation. The whole hock is swollen and very painful on manipulation. Its synovial capsule is distended, as in acute synovitis. Crepitation may be detected by placing both hands around the joint and moving the lower part of the limb. It may, however, be masked by the great swelling, and then the diagnosis is hesitating until the latter has subsided. Abnormal mobility and deviation of the inferior portion of the limb are generally observable.

TREATMENT.—There is no chance of treating the lesion successfully in the horse. When treatment is undertaken, it is the same as that for the os calcis. When healing ensues a stiff joint is apt to result.

Fractures of the other bones of the hock may be caused by direct violence, such as a kick or from lashing out and striking the hock against a fixed object. The writer saw simple fracture of the scaphoid in a pony from striking the back of the hock against the step of a van to which it was yoked. If the fracture is compound, there is little hope of recovery. Otherwise, and when confined to one bone, it may ensue, but even then permanent lameness may supervene. Sudden and severe lameness, with inability to sustain weight, is observed after the accident. The local symptoms are those of a severe contusion. On careful manipulation, some abnormal mobility and crepitus can generally be detected.

Sprain of the Hock-Joint—Sprung Hock

Sprain of the hock is fairly common as the result of over-exertion of the joint, as may ensue when jumping or during heavy draft, or from slipping at this or some other time. The ligaments may in this way be more or less severely stretched and injured. The surfaces of the bones where they are inserted also become inflamed, and a synovitis of the true hock-joint may also be set up. When the whole hock is thus involved, the condition is spoken of as " sprung hock." Lameness is always well marked. At rest, weight is only placed on the toe of the foot, the hock being in a state of semi-flexion. Pain is evinced on passive movement of the joint. During progression the hock is carried stiffly, little or no weight is borne by the limb, and the toe of the hoof may only touch or be trailed along the ground. The local inflammatory swelling is very obvious, and is most pronounced at the chief seat of sprain. When the hock is " sprung," it is swollen all round.

The SYMPTOMS, of course, vary according to the severity of the sprain.

PROGNOSIS.—Recovery is the rule, but sometimes a chronic inflammation ensues, causing permanent enlargement of the joint and protracted lameness. The horse, however, may go sound, while the hock remains enlarged. Spavin and curb are possible sequels of the accident.

TREATMENT of the acute case comprises rest and the application of the usual remedies for acute inflammation, while the chronic form requires counter-irritation by blistering or firing, or by both. The cautery should be used all round the hock, except in the angle of flexion.

Sprain of the hock is not uncommon in sporting dogs, and must be treated on lines similar to those for the horse. Rubbing in tincture of iodine or iodine ointment often has a good effect on the dog. When the case is chronic, needle-point firing is indicated.

Dislocation of the Hock

Dislocation of the hock has been recorded by various observers as occurring in the horse, ox, sheep, dog, and cat, being produced in most cases by violent contusion or extraordinary muscular effort, as may occur in an endeavour to release the foot when fixed between two objects. The seat of dislocation varies. It may be the tibio-tarsal joint or one of the gliding articulations. It is not infrequently accompanied by rupture of ligaments and fracture or crushing of some of the tarsal bones. The symptoms are those of dislocation and of acute inflammation.

PROGNOSIS.—The prognosis is very grave. Perfect cure is seldom or never obtained, and the rule is to destroy the large animal when affected with the condition. In small animals even imperfect recovery may satisfy the owner.

TREATMENT is carried out on general principles.

The writer had a case of dislocation of the tibio-tarsal joint in a greyhound with overlapping of the bones and found it impossible to reduce the dislocation, under complete nembutal anæsthesia, until he cut the tendo Achillis subcutaneously when reduction was easily effected. The case did well afterwards except that slight thickening remained at the seat of the tenotomy.

Synovitis and Arthritis of the Hock-Joint—Distension of the Tibio-tarsal Articulation—" Bog Spavin "

Synovitis may ensue from a contusion or sprain of the joint, or be a complication of a bacterial affection like influenza.

Purulent Synovitis or Arthritis is usually the result of a penetrating wound, or it might be due to strangles.

SYMPTOMS, PROGNOSIS, and TREATMENT of these conditions are in accordance with what has been said in the general articles thereon.

Bog Spavin, or distension of the synovial capsule of the tibio-tarsal joint, is characterised by the presence of three uniformly fluctuating swellings, one situated antero-internally at the level of the inner lip of the trochlea of the astragalus, and one on either side of the joint posteriorly at the level of the malleolus of the tibia, in the lower part of the hollow of the hock, and above the lateral ligaments. The swellings vary in size in different cases. Those laterally situated are small compared with the one in front, which constitutes the typical bog spavin. The former have been described as *articular thoroughpin.* Pressure on any one of the swellings causes increased distension of the others. One of the lateral distensions may be more prominent than the other. When the swelling in front is not well marked, those at the sides are hardly perceptible. Nevertheless, pressure at their level can be felt going through to the distension in front. Sometimes it is only one of the lateral swellings that is noticeable. Then the condition is not called " bog spavin," but merely " articular thoroughpin."

FIG. 387.—DISTENSION OF THE SYNOVIAL CAPSULE OF THE TRUE HOCK-JOINT.

ETIOLOGY.—The distension may be due to chronic synovitis, or

59

merely to dropsy of the joint, the latter being often present in young unbroken horses, in which it is frequently accompanied by tendinous thoroughpin and windgalls. Bent hocks relaxing the synovial capsule of the joint favour its occurrence. It has been ascribed to constant hard work in aged horses. Aged stallions and breeding mares are frequently affected.

SYMPTOMS.—In the absence of synovitis, the only symptom is the presence of the swellings mentioned. If the distension is very prominent, there may be some mechanical interference with the movement of the hock. When synovitis is more or less severe, there is a corresponding degree of lameness.

PROGNOSIS.—When the horse is not lame the condition does not interfere with its usefulness, but is a blemish and an unsoundness. When lameness is present it may be difficult to get rid of.

TREATMENT must follow general principles. The measures mentioned for thoroughpin may be adopted here, but one hesitates perhaps a little more in this case to perforate the cavity by needle-point firing, or by the trocar and canula, although the operations are quite safe when aseptically performed.

Spavin, Osteo-periostitis, and Chronic Arthritis of the Gliding Articulations of the Hock

Spavin in its widest sense is an exostosis on the hock below the level of the true joint, but in the vast majority of cases it is confined to its inner aspect. The lesion may be merely a superficial osteo-periostitis, with consequent exostosis formation. As a rule, however, this is associated with a chronic arthritis of one or more of the gliding articulations of the joint. The bones most commonly involved in the disease are the large and small metatarsals, the large and small cuneiforms, and the scaphoid, but in rare instances the astragalus and cuboid are involved. Anchylosis of the affected joints frequently ensues, and is a favourable termination, as then the pain caused by movement of the ulcerated bones on one another disappears and the horse goes sound, provided that a chronic ostitis does not persist.

Arthritis may occur without any exostosis, constituting " *occult spavin.*" It may be said that all true cases of spavin are due to a chronic arthritis of some of the gliding articulations of the hock. The terms " dry arthritis " and " arthritis ossificans " are also applied to the condition.

The origin of the disease has often been discussed, and various theories have been put forward with regard to it, but the prevailing belief is that it starts as an ostitis and that the articular and periosteal surfaces become affected subsequently. The idea of Dieckerhoff and others, that the disease begins in the bursa of the cunean branch of the flexor metatarsi, cannot be sustained. It must be mentioned that fusion of the small bones of the hock consequent on anchylosis of the gliding articulations is not uncommon in old horses that have never shown hock lameness. The interosseous ligament may become ossified, while the articular surfaces remain intact. It is possible that permanent lameness may supervene in such cases from chronic ostitis alone, which is favoured by the loss of the articular movements. A bony deposit may occur at the seat of spavin in young horses affected with rickets. In this case there is neither inflammation nor lameness, and the condition is usually accompanied by enlargements on the inferior extremities of the radius and cannon-bone. As the animal grows, these exostoses diminish or disappear.

ETIOLOGY.—The causes are predisposing and exciting.

Predisposing causes comprise :

1. *Heredity.*—Experience has proved that there is an hereditary predisposition to the disease.

2. *Defective conformation*, including *small hocks* ; " *tied-in* " *hocks* in which the joint is not " well let down," but becomes constricted at its base ; *sickle-shaped hocks* ; and " cow hocks." Such conformations constitute weaknesses, rendering the joint liable to inflammation under the stress of work.

3. *Youth.*—A young horse put to hard work is more liable to develop spavin than a mature animal.

4. *Severe exertion* of the hock, as occurs in heavy draft and in galloping and steeple-chasing.

Exciting causes comprise :

1. *Violent movements* of the hock, as may occur in starting or drawing heavy loads, in rearing, jumping, and slipping.

2. *Rheumatism*, setting up a rheumatoid arthritis, as in chronic carpitis and articular ringbone.

3. *Rickets*, giving rise to exostoses or osteophytes at the seat of spavin, apart from osteo-periostitis and arthritis. The enlargement, however, in this case is not true spavin, there being no arthritis present.

In galloping horses the injury caused by exertion is of the nature of concussion, which sets up a central arthritis, while in draft-horses the injury is caused by laceration of the ligaments and gives rise to a marginal osteo-arthritis.

SYMPTOMS.—Under this heading there are to be considered (1) local symptoms, and (2) spavin lameness.

1. *Local Symptoms.*—Spavin may be classified as follows :

(1) *Visible spavin*, in which there is an exostosis as well as an arthritis.

(2) *Occult spavin*, in which there is only an arthritis.

(3) *Anterior spavin*, situated towards the anterior aspect of the joint.

(4) *Posterior spavin*, situated postero-internally.

(5) *High spavin*, located close to the true hock-joint.

FIG. 388.—SPAVIN FORMATION ON LEFT HOCK SEEN FROM IN FRONT.

FIG. 389.—SPAVIN FORMATION ON RIGHT HOCK SEEN FROM BEHIND. A, Spavin.

The popular term " jack spavin " is applied to a very prominent spavin. Visible spavin can be seen and felt. The following are recognised methods of viewing the hocks in an examination for spavin :

(1) Hold the cheek of the bridle standing at an arm's length therefrom, and facing in the opposite direction to that of the horse, and look obliquely at the inner aspect of the hock. If there is an enlargement at the seat of spavin it will catch the eye.

(2) Stand in front of the horse, stoop, and compare the two hocks, looking between the forelegs.

(3) View and compare the two hocks from behind. This is the best way to see a posterior spavin.

The exostosis can be felt by passing the fingers lightly over the small bones of the hock from above downwards. It requires much experience and oft-repeated manipulation of hocks to appreciate the difference in some cases between sound and spavined hocks. When the exostosis is very slight, it is difficult to recognise. It is important to bear in mind the normal prominences on the antero-internal aspect of the joint, and not to mistake them for spavin—viz., the ridge on the large cuneiform and the tuberosity on the supero-antero-internal aspect of the large metatarsus. These prominences are more marked in some horses than in others, and may even differ in size on the two hocks of the same animal.

Coarse Hock.—When these normal enlargements are very pronounced the horse is said to have a coarse hock, and as they are rather a sign of strength than of weakness, such a hock is perfectly sound. It is the tuberosity on the large metatarsus which is most likely to be mistaken for spavin. The coarse hock is most common in the horse under five years old. It becomes finer with age. In the normal hock the following grooves may be made out :

(1) A vertical groove between the large and small metatarsal bones, always very evident.

(2) A vertical groove between the large and small cuneiforms, not so distinct as No. 1, but still appreciable and situated immediately above and slightly in front of No. 1.

(3) A transverse groove between the large metatarsal and the large cuneiform.

(4) A transverse groove between the large cuneiform and the scaphoid.

Therefore, when one or more of these grooves are absent or replaced by an exostosis the hock may be said to have spavin.

2. *Spavin Lameness.*—A spavin may be present without lameness, as in the case where anchylosis has ensued and ostitis is absent. On the other hand, spavin lameness may occur in the absence of an exostosis, as in occult spavin and in cases in which the exostosis has not yet developed. The following features are usually associated with spavin lameness :

(1) *Imperfect Flexion of the Hock.*—During progression the hock is not well flexed, and there is a tendency to drag the toe. In some cases the wall at the toe of the foot is worn in this way.

(2) *Going on the Toe.*—The horse puts most weight on the toe of the foot, especially on starting, with the result that the toe of the shoe is excessively worn.

(3) *Diminution of Lameness on Exercise.*—The lameness is always worse on starting after resting, but gradually diminishes with exercise, and in some cases almost entirely disappears. However, when the lesion is extensive, and in case of occult spavin, the lameness continues.

(4) *Lowering of the Hip.*—When the horse is made to trot, the hip of the affected side is lowered in taking the limb forward.

(5) *Exaggeration of the Lameness on Passive Flexion of the Hock.*— If the hock be forcibly flexed for about one minute and the horse then made to trot on, the lameness is intensified. This has been called the " spavin test." Flexing other joints affected with arthritis would have the same effect. Care must be taken in practising this on aged horses, as it might cause the animal to fall over on the other side.

(6) *Spasmodic Flexion of the Hock.*—In some cases the horse, when at rest, repeatedly flexes the hock in a spasmodic manner. Exceptionally the hock is excessively flexed during exercise. When the horse is made to come over in the stable, the lameness is more marked on moving towards the sound side than towards the affected side. When both limbs are affected, the horse has a peculiar short stiff gait, as if suffering from an injury to the loins.

When a horse affected with spavin lameness is kept at work, atrophy of the gluteal muscles of the lame limb ensues ; whereas if the horse is left idle, the atrophy does not occur. Hunting, of London, explained this phenomenon as follows : When the horse has been working all day he suffers pain at night, and consequently rests the limb all the time, throwing the muscles out of action, and thus leading to atrophy thereof ; while the idle horse suffers no such pain, and hence does not rest the limb.

DIAGNOSIS.—From the symptoms described it is evident that the diagnosis may be easy or difficult. The X-rays might be employed in a case of doubt to locate exostoses, and to ascertain whether prominences are abnormal. Cocaine injected over the tibial nerves may be used when there is indecision as to whether the lameness is in the hock or higher up. In cases of dispute, veterinarians often differ in their opinions as to the existence of spavin.

PROGNOSIS.—It has been estimated that approximately two-thirds of the horses suffering from spavin go sound eventually, owing to anchylosis having taken place in the affected joints and ostitis having disappeared. Occult spavin is not likely to result in anchylosis, and is therefore often incurable. Anterior is more serious than posterior spavin, as it interferes most with movement of the joint and is subjected to more disturbance, which hinders fusion of the affected bones. For the same reason a high is more serious than a low spavin. The longer the horse is kept at work before being treated, the less favourable the prognosis, as anchylosis is not likely to supervene after prolonged exertion of the affected hock. As a rule, when a horse with spavin is sound he remains sound, but lameness from the condition may recur, especially if the animal is put to heavy work.

TREATMENT of spavin aims at bringing about anchylosis in the affected joints. The chief essential for this is complete rest, which usually must extend over a period of six to eight weeks. Other measures favouring this result are :

1. *Blistering*, which has some effect in hastening anchylosis by counter-irritation and in enforcing rest of the joint. Its action, however, is too superficial to be of much benefit.

2. *Line Firing*, which is better than No. 1, but still not deep enough in its action.

3. *Puncture Firing*, inserting a sharp-pointed iron into the exostosis, and only through the skin in its vicinity. If the exostosis is large this procedure is without danger, but if it is small there is a risk of opening the joint and setting up an incurable septic arthritis. When the spavin is small, the iron should only be inserted once into the bone. This method has often proved effective.

4. *Needle-point Firing.*—This is the best form of counter-irritation, being safe and producing a deep-seated inflammation which greatly favours anchylosis. A blister should be applied after firing in each case.

5. *Cunean Tenotomy and Periosteotomy.*—See p. 458.

6. *Anterior and Posterior Tibial Neurectomy,* indicated when all the foregoing measures have failed (see pp. 449 and 451).

Curb

DEFINITION.—Curb is an enlargement at the postero-inferior aspect of the hock, causing a backward curvature of the normal straight line between the point of the hock and the fetlock. It may be hardly perceptible or very distinct.

STRUCTURE INVOLVED.—The structure involved may be either :

1. *The Aponeurosis.*—Post-mortem examination in some cases, in young horses that have not shown lameness, has revealed a thickening confined to the aponeurosis and apparently of no consequence.

2. *The Perforatus Tendon.*

3. *The Perforans Tendon.*

4. *The Check Ligament.*—Nos. 2, 3, and 4 are rarely affected.

5. *The Calcaneo-Cuboid Ligament.*—It is generally accepted that this is the structure usually involved when the curb is inflammatory in origin—that is, the result of sprain following over-distension of the ligament. When the lesion arises in this way it constitutes the

most serious form of the condition, and has been spoken of as true curb, in comparison with the forms due to other causes.

6. *The Head of the Outer Small Metatarsal Bone.*—The head of the outer small metatarsal bone may be so prominent that it answers the definition of curb, but when it can be definitely shown that the enlargement is not pathological, but merely due to well-marked development of the bone, it is not a curb. It must, however, be remembered that the calcaneo-cuboid ligament is partly inserted into this bone, and that the apparent enlargement of the latter may be due to a thickening of the ligament. It is not always easy to say whether the thickening is in the bone or in the ligament.

An exostosis may form on the postero-external aspect of the hock, involving the head of the outer splint-bone, associated with an arthritis of the gliding articulations in the region. When the enlargement encroaches on the straight line referred to in the definition it simulates curb, but the condition is really spavin affecting the outer side of the hock.

The French use the terms *jarde* and *jardon* for enlargements about the seat of curb, but are not unanimous as to the signification of each term. *Jardon* generally means an enlargement on the postero-infero-external aspect of the hock, due as a rule to an enlarged head on the outer splint-bone, and not projecting behind the straight line mentioned ; whereas, when this projection does occur, the term *jarde* is applied. When the swelling is bony it is called *jarde osseuse*, and when fibrous *jarde fibreuse*.

Formerly in France *courbe* had the same signification as the present-day *curb* in English-speaking countries, but it has been replaced by *jarde*, and is now applied to an exostosis on the internal aspect of the lower extremity of the tibia, where it is rarely associated with arthritis of the tibio-astragaloid articulation.

A cutaneous thickening does not constitute a curb.

ETIOLOGY.—The causes of curb are predisposing and exciting. Predisposing causes include :

1. *Mal-conformation of the Hocks*, as is represented by—

(*a*) *Sickle-shaped or curby hocks*, in which the os calcis, instead of being vertical, is inclined slightly forwards, thus favouring sprain of the calcaneo-cuboid ligament by the pull of the gastrocnemius muscle in extension of the hock-joint.

(*b*) *Tied-in hocks*, in which the lower row of tarsal bones and the upper end of the large metatarsal are too slight, putting the ligament at a disadvantage by increasing the strain thereon. Curb, however, is not confined to such hocks, for it may appear in those that are well shaped.

2. *Powerful Quarter Muscles*, whose action during severe exertion is apt to sprain the ligament.

3. *Violent Exertion*, as jumping and heavy uphill draft-work.

4. *Hereditary Predisposition.*—This has been often illustrated in the progeny of certain mares or sires. The predisposition may be in the form of the hock or apart therefrom. In such cases the curb may appear without any apparent exciting cause, arising insidiously in young animals, without inflammation or lameness, and before being put to work.

EXCITING CAUSES comprise movements which result in great exertion of the hock-joint—viz. :

1. *Violent Attempts at Extension* at moments when the limb is flexed and bearing weight, as in jumping, or heavy or uphill draft-work.

2. *Suddenly throwing a Horse on his Haunches.*—When a curb occurs suddenly in either of these ways, with local inflammation and lameness, the horse is said to have sprung a curb.

But a curb may form without any apparent exciting cause, and can then hardly be ascribed to sprain of the ligament, the enlargement in such instances appearing without inflammation or lameness and being probably due to a thickening of the subcutaneous aponeurosis, as was observed by the writer on post-mortem examination of two subjects affected with typical curbs.

SYMPTOMS.—When a curb forms without any local inflammation or lameness, the only symptom is the presence of the curb, which can be seen and felt. In order to recognise a curb, the observer must stand at right angles to the vertical line between the point of the hock and the fetlock. If he stands obliquely, he may mistake the normal outward curvature at the level of the head of the external splint for a curb.

The enlargement is usually bow-shaped, shading off gradually upwards and downwards from its centre, which is about on a level with the chestnut. It must be on the straight line at the back of the hock to answer the definition of curb.

The swelling can be felt by passing the fingers or thumb firmly and horizontally down the back of the limb from the point of the hock towards the fetlock. If it is very small it feels like a button beneath the skin. When the curb has been sprung, its formation is accompanied by acute local inflammation and lameness of varying intensity in different cases. In the hunter it may be first noticed in the morning after a day's hunting.

The lameness is characterised by the horse tending to go on the toe, and to rest the limb with the heel off the ground, so as to relieve tension on the inflamed part. It does not diminish with exercise. These symptoms of pain generally disappear in from one to three weeks, but the swelling persists.

DIAGNOSIS.—The diagnosis is usually easy. Doubt arises when the backward curvature is due to enlargement of the head of the outer small metatarsal, and a careful examination is required to ascertain whether the swelling is entirely bony or partly fibrous.

Distension of the tarsal sheath may cause a swelling to the inner aspect of the seat of curb, and gives to the eye the appearance of the latter, but manipulation will reveal its true nature. Möller has called this condition *soft curb*. Cutaneous thickening can be recognised by its being movable along with the skin.

PROGNOSIS.—When the hock is well formed, curb is not a serious condition, as it rarely causes recurrent lameness, even under severe exertion ; but when its conformation is bad, lameness may repeatedly ensue if the horse is put to hard work. It is a common belief that when the curb has been fired, lameness is less likely to supervene. It is always a blemish, is hereditary, and in every case constitutes, at least, technical unsoundness.

TREATMENT.—When there is acute local inflammation with lameness, treatment comprises :

1. *Rest* of the patient.

2. *Cold and astringent* applications.

3. *The application of a high-heeled shoe*, with a view to relieving tension on the structures at the back of the hock. It is not essential, and is not always employed.

In a chronic case, with or without lameness, treatment includes :

1. *The use of absorbent topics*, rubbed well into the overlying skin, and repeated, if necessary, with a view to promoting resolution of inflammation, when present, and diminishing or removing the enlargement, such as :

(a) *Preparations of iodine*, including a mixture of iodine, potassium iodide, and Archangel tar, as represented by " Reducine," iodine ointment (" Vetiod "), and linimentum iodi. These topics require to be repeated several times, and even then generally prove disappointing.

(b) *A solution of perchloride of mercury in spirit* (1 in 10), rubbed in once with a tooth-brush.

(c) *A blister of biniodide of mercury.*

All the foregoing applications, however, usually fail to diminish or dispel the curb.

2. *Firing* in the form of :

(*a*) *Horizontal, oblique, or vertical lines* covering the curb and extending a little beyond it. When the vertical pattern is adopted, five lines are made, one long centre line and two gradually shorter on either side, thus : | | | | One pattern is just as effective as the other.

(*b*) *Penetrating points.*

(*c*) *Needle points*, which is the most effective and leaves least mark.

(*d*) *A transverse cutaneous incision* in the centre of the curb made with a sharp-edged hot iron, the edge of the iron being directed upwards and forwards. The writer was informed that the late Mr. Bell, M.R.C.V.S. (Clonmel, Ireland), found this procedure very successful in the removal of small curbs. The writer proved its efficacy in one case.

(*e*) Passing a red-hot needle transversely through the curb is also said to have proved effective in some cases.

Occasionally curbs vanish spontaneously from young horses as they become older. Lieut.-Colonel Ryan, in an article on curbs, and referring chiefly to horses four and five years old, says : " If an animal has a good broad hock with a large os calcis, and he is lunged four or five times a week over a low wall or pole, or both, and if the height of the jump be increased each day by 1 inch till it is 3½ or 4 feet high, it is extraordinary how quickly some curbs vanish " (*Veterinary Record*, Vol. 10). A horse with curbs should be put to severe work gradually. If made to do it suddenly, lameness is more likely to ensue.

Stringhalt

Stringhalt is an involuntary spasmodic lifting of one or more of the limbs during progression. It is a common condition in the hind-limbs, but rarely affects a fore-limb. It differs from chorea in that it only occurs when the animal is made to move.

ETIOLOGY.—Temporary or symptomatic stringhalt often appears as the result of some irritation in the lower part of the limb, such as a cracked heel, a sandcrack, a bandage or blister on the hock, or even the straw bed (straw cramp). The exaggerated flexion of the limb in these cases is evidently due to reflex action. It has been noticed that in some cases the stringhalt persisted after the obvious cause had disappeared. In the great majority of cases of stringhalt nothing can be detected to account for the condition, and many theories have been put forward as to its etiology, including the following, ascribing it to :

1. *Articular Lesions of the Hock or Stifle.*—It has been seen accompanying arthritis of the true hock-joint and chronic gonitis, but was probably only a coincidence, as it does not always accompany these lesions. Pastureau looked upon it as a modified form of fixation of the patella above the internal lip of the trochlea, the bone becoming momentarily fixed there, and offering only a temporary resistance to the flexor muscles, which overcome the resistance by a sudden convulsive flexion, causing the limb to be lifted excessively.

2. *Muscular Tendinous and Aponeurotic Lesions.*—Lafosse ascribed it to spasmodic contraction of the muscles which flex the metatarsus, the cause of the contraction being some obscure reflex irritation. Boccar and Brogniez believed the abnormal movement was due to shortening of these muscles or their tendons, particularly the peroneus. Colour is given to this belief by the fact that section of the peroneus tendon, as recommended by Boccar, sometimes cures the condition. The spasmodic lifting of the limb has also been ascribed to shortening of the fascia lata. Cutting the fascia, however, has failed to arrest the abnormal movement.

3. *Nervous Lesions.*—Youatt and Spooner were of the opinion that stringhalt was due to lesions of the great sciatic nerve, causing overstimulation of the flexor muscles, while Percivall attributed it to an affection of the spinal cord or of the nerves of the hind-limb, whereby excessive muscular contraction was produced.

4. *Affections of the Feet.*—Flexion of the hock brings about flexion of the digit by putting its flexors into action. If there is any obstruction to the latter movement, an extra effort will be made to overcome it. Should the resistance disappear suddenly, there will be excessive flexion of the hock, or stringhalt. Hence, any lesion, painful or mechanical, which would retard digital flexion would favour stringhalt. Watrin, Weber, and others have upheld this theory, which is feasible enough in some cases.

SYMPTOMS.—When stringhalt is present it is generally easily recognised. It may be so slight as to be hardly noticeable, or so marked that the hind-foot almost touches the abdomen. It is best seen when the horse is walked after resting, or when turned in short circles. It is often intermittent, disappearing for variable periods. When the horse is worked hard, rested for a while, and then exercised, the stringhalt is aggravated. It is also worse as a rule after a journey by train, and after an attack of influenza. In some cases the foot, after being spasmodically lifted, is brought to the ground with great force, whereas in others it is brought down normally. The former constitutes the more serious form of the affection.

DIAGNOSIS.—The only difficulty about diagnosis is that the string-halt might be absent at the time the horse was being examined, in a case where it was intermittent.

PROGNOSIS.—As a rule stringhalt does not interfere with a horse's usefulness, but occasionally the spasm is so acute or convulsive that it impedes a horse galloping and jumping. A temporary string-halt due to an apparent lesion disappears with the latter, but the ordinary stringhalt, whose cause is obscure, shows no tendency to spontaneous recovery, and is unsatisfactory to treat.

TREATMENT.—The only treatment that has given a fair measure of success is peroneal tenotomy (see p. 486). Section of the tensor vaginæ femoris, of the fascia of the leg, and of the cunean tendon, has been done without success. Anterior and posterior tibial neurectomy have been recommended when the condition appears of nervous origin, but the result of these operations might be worse than the disease.

Shivering

" Shivering " is the name applied to a peculiar neuro-muscular disease, characterised by involuntary spasmodic muscular contraction, with consequent irregular movements, generally affecting one or both hind-limbs and the tail ; sometimes only a fore-limb, or occasionally the limbs, lips, cheeks, eyelids, and neck.

Shivering is often regarded as hereditary, but the cause has not been ascertained. Frequently its occurrence is preceded more or less remotely by an attack of strangles, influenza, or pneumonia ; and this fact has led many observers to suggest that shivering is connected with neuropathic lesions produced by infection, or toxins derived from ante-cedent disease. Shivering is sometimes attributed to accidental injuries, falls, fright, etc.

It occurs at all ages, and while principally affecting draft-horses, it is frequently seen in light harness-horses, hunters, and hacks, and occasionally in thoroughbreds. It is very rare in ponies. It has also been observed in cattle.

SYMPTOMS AND DIAGNOSIS.—Shivering varies very much in degree or manifestation. The symptoms may be constant and easily seen, or intermittent, occasional, or latent, and very difficult to discover. Many shivering horses only exhibit the symptoms when being shod, or when moving over in the stall; others while standing in harness constantly attract attention by frequently raising and abducting the shivering hind-limb. In well-marked bilateral posterior shivering the horse in advancing may give no sign of the disease, or the symptoms may be restricted to the first two or three steps ; but on lifting a hind-foot, or in backing the horse, the limb is suddenly raised, semi-flexed and abducted, shaking or shivering in suspension, the superficial muscles of the thigh and quarter quivering, while the tail is elevated and tremulous. In a few moments the spasms cease, the limb is slowly extended and the foot brought to the ground. In severe cases the horse exhibits symptoms on every occasion he is set back, turned round, or moved from side to side. He may be unable to move backwards or to lie down, and if he should fall, unable to rise without assistance.

Diagnosis of cases in which the symptoms are slight or intermittent usually requires patient observation of the animal in the stable or the forge. Hammering the foot or shoe, allowing the horse to drink from a pail placed on the ground, forcibly backing the horse uphill over rough setts or slippery pavements, or puncturing the pastern with a pin may reveal the symptoms. Repeated testing of the horse at longer or shorter intervals, after prolonged exercise or hard work, or watching the horse rising in the early morning, may be necessary before a positive opinion can be formed in a doubtful case.

In anterior shivering, which seldom interferes with the animal's capacity for work, on attempting to lift the foot the limb is thrust forwards in full extension, the foot barely touching the ground, or the limb with the knee flexed is elevated and abducted, the extensors above the elbow quivering while the spasm lasts or until the foot returns to the ground. When affecting the head, the lips exhibit twitching with spasmodic retraction of the commissure, rapid blinking of the upper eyelid, and sometimes the ear of the same side is in constant motion.

PROGNOSIS.—Usually shivering is a chronic or very slowly progressive affection, but it may develop rapidly under constant hard work, or during an attack of intercurrent debilitating disease. This is particularly noticeable in the intermittent and latent forms, when, owing to the excitement of a railway journey, or the pain produced by wounds, injuries to the feet, or arising from colic, influenza, or other systemic disease, the symptoms become much aggravated. Hunting-horses that are known to be occasional shiverers may hunt and jump for several seasons without hindrance or complaint, but eventually they lose power behind, and, though able to gallop and willing to jump, are unable to clear the obstacle with the hind-feet or to rise sufficiently to jump a moderate fence.   Rest in the stable or on pasture for six or eight weeks will produce considerable modification in the symptoms of most well-marked cases, and it may enable an affected horse successfully to pass an examination as to soundness.   Horses that are slight shiverers, and even those that offer no difficulty in diagnosis, may work satisfactorily for many years, but in time their usefulness becomes greatly impaired ; the spasms increase both in frequency and in severity, the hind-quarters become atrophied, and the limbs more or less stiff or rigid.   Animals so affected sleep standing, and their fore-fetlocks and knees are much bruised and disfigured by frequent half-falls.   There is no curative treatment for shivering.

AFFECTIONS OF THE FEET

Examination of the Foot

As already indicated, the foot should be thoroughly examined in all cases of lameness, even when there is a lesion in some other part of the limb sufficient to account for the lameness.   The procedure usually adopted in the examination of the foot comprises :

1. **Inspection.**—That is, viewing the foot from different aspects, and comparing it with the other foot.   Various abnormalities may be noted in this way.

2. **Palpation,** applying the palmar surface of the fingers and hand over the wall of the hoof to ascertain if the heat of the foot is greater than normal or than that of the other foot, and over the coronet to find out whether it is swollen or abnormally hot.   Lifting the foot and holding the wall resting on the two hands is another method of palpating it.

3. **Percussion** of the hoof with the hammer to ascertain if there is a tender spot indicating the presence there of some inflammatory lesion.   The percussion is performed by smart, but not heavy taps with the hammer, using the foot of the sound limb as a control.   When the horn is thick and the inflammation slight, it is possible for the latter to escape notice, little or no evidence of pain being exhibited by the animal.   The tapping is done all over the hoof from heel to heel on the wall and on the sole, and at the level of the frog.   Pain is shown by the horse attempting to draw the foot away when it is struck.   When in doubt, the other foot should be percussed in the same way to compare the effects.

4. **Compression** with a pincers with large jaws, so that when the foot is grasped between them one can be made to reach the centre

of the sole and the frog. When the inflamed part is squeezed, the horse shows resentment by drawing away the foot. The ordinary farrier's pincers answers the purpose well enough. Compression of the coronet with the fingers will cause pain when it is inflamed.

5. **Paring** the horn in a place where inflammation is suspected to see if its deep layers are discoloured from extravasation of blood, or whether pus is imprisoned beneath it. The junction of the wall and sole is the proper place to search for pus beneath the latter. The deep layers of the horn in this case are yellowish and infiltrated with moisture. When the horn has been thinned, pain is more readily manifested on pressure, and may be evident on compression with the thumb.

6. **Mensuration** by the aid of the calipers or a tape measure to compare the dimensions of two fore- or two hind-feet to ascertain if one has undergone contraction, which might be the cause or the effect of lameness.

Affections of the Horn : Sandcrack—Fissure in the Wall

A sandcrack is a fissure in the wall of the hoof, parallel to the horn tubules, commencing at the coronet and extending a variable distance down the wall, usually to its plantar aspect. It may occur at any part of the wall, and even in the bar, but its commonest situations are the toe of the hind-foot and the inner quarter of the fore-foot. The following varieties of cracks are distinguished :

(1) **Complete,** extending from the coronet to the plantar border of the wall.

(2) **Incomplete,** extending downwards through part of the height of the wall.

(3) **Superficial,** only going through part of the thickness of the wall.

(4) **Deep,** extending as far as the sensitive tissues.

(5) **Straight or sinuous** in direction.

(6) **Recent,** (7) **old,** (8) **simple,** (9) **complicated,** with more or less damage to the sensitive tissues beneath.

ETIOLOGY.—The causes of sandcrack comprise :

1. *Heredity,* an inherent weakness in the horn being transmitted from parent to offspring, rendering it liable to crack.

2. *Alternate moisture and dryness* of the horn, causing it to become brittle and easily cracked.

3. *Thinness of the horn.*

4. *Violent extension* of the corono-pedal joint, whereby the os corona comes to press forcibly against the coronet, causing the horn

to split at its origin in the region of the toe. It has often occurred in this way in the hind-foot of heavy draft-horses in cities and in tramway horses. It is more apt to occur when the animal's hind-foot slips from one pavement block against another. A crack at the quarter is most common in contracted feet, and in those low at the heels. In the case of out-toed or in-toed horses it is the surcharged quarter which is usually affected.

5. *Excessive rasping of the wall,* removing its periople and superficial fibres, and exposing its deeper layers to evaporation, rendering them brittle and easily ruptured.

SYMPTOMS.—The fissure in the wall may be hardly perceptible or well marked. When the crack is simple it is the only local symptom, but when it is complicated there may be an escape of blood when the condition is recent, due to rupture of the laminæ from the violence which caused the fissure or from their being pinched between the lips of the latter, or an oozing of serum or pus when the sensitive tissues are inflamed or suppurating. When the inflammation is severe the coronet is swollen and painful. When necrosis of the laminæ or caries of the os pedis has supervened there is diffuse inflammatory swelling of the digital region.

Lameness is absent when the crack is superficial, but is usually present when it is deep, due either to laceration of the laminæ when the case is recent and the result of violence, or to inflammation of the sensitive structures when the crack has been in existence for some time, and they have undergone repeated irritation from the movement of the lips of the fissure, or have been subjected to injury from the presence of foreign matter and invasion by micro-organisms. When suppuration has supervened the lameness is very marked. Lameness from sandcrack at the toe of the hind-foot is characterised by the horse lifting the foot spasmodically, as in stringhalt, taking it well forward, and putting it carefully on the ground heel first. When the crack is in the quarter, the foot is also lifted smartly. When weight is placed on the foot, the sensitive tissues are compressed by closure of the crack, and relief is obtained by rapidly removing the weight from the foot.

DIAGNOSIS is generally easy, but the crack may be concealed by the presence of mud on the wall, or it may be skilfully filled with wax or gutta-percha. Hence the necessity of washing muddy feet before examining them. Scraping the wall at a suspected point will reveal whether a fissure extends through the horn. A crack in the bar is detected on lifting the foot and paring the horn. It may be difficult to determine the exact nature of complications when present, but the

6c

more pronounced the lameness and the greater the inflammatory swelling the more serious is the lesion.

PROGNOSIS varies according to the nature of the condition. When the crack is simple and properly treated recovery ensues eventually. When it is complicated with necrosis of the sensitive tissue, the case requires special treatment, and is more or less protracted. When the horn is brittle, cracking is apt to recur.

TREATMENT.—1. *Sandcrack at the Toe—Simple Crack without Lameness.*—The indications in this case are to (1) immobilise the lips of the crack, and (2) promote the secretion of new horn to fill the crack at its origin in the coronary band.

(1) *Immobilisation of the Crack* may be effected by :

(a) *A Special Shoe* divided in the inner half of its width at the toe, and provided with quarter clips and with special clips at the heels, one at the inner aspect of the branch on each side fitting into the lateral lacuna. When the shoe has been applied its branches are forcibly separated at the heels by the aid of a sort of vice, thereby bringing the lips of the fissure into contact and maintaining them there. The shoe, however, is not much in vogue.

(b) *Bandages*, either in the form of an ordinary bandage or of a tar rope wound round the hoof from the coronet to its plantar aspect. They really have little or no effect in keeping the edges of the crack in apposition, but are efficacious in preventing the entrance of foreign matter into the fissure.

(c) *Clasps.*—These are inserted by the aid of two instruments made for the purpose, an iron and a forceps. The iron is made red hot and used to form a groove to receive the clasp, which is fixed in position by means of the forceps in much the same way as a ring is inserted into a pig's nose. The uppermost clasp is applied about $\frac{1}{2}$ inch below the coronet, and two others below this about $\frac{3}{4}$ inch apart. It is advisable to fill the crack with gutta-percha or Archangel tar. These clasps look well and are fairly effective, but are apt to become loose or fall out under severe exertion.

(d) *Horseshoe Nails* driven transversely through the lips of the crack sufficiently deeply to get a good hold without compressing the sensitive tissues. A little transverse groove is first made on either side of the fissure with the searcher, or more conveniently with the iron used in connection with the clasps to accommodate the nail, which is then driven carefully through the horn, its point being afterwards cut off and the stump clenched towards the crack. For the sake of appearance the head may also be filed off to enable a second clench to be made. This is the best method of fixing the lips of the crack, but it requires care and skill to carry it out properly without wounding the sensitive laminæ. The insertion of the nail may be facilitated and rendered more safe by first boring a hole in the horn with a drill. A good farrier can drive the nail safely through the horn.

(e) *A Piece of Wood* inserted into the crack. A slot is first made to receive the wood, which is then tapped into position like a lid on a chalk-box. It prevents pinching of the tissues by the edges of the crack, and excludes dirt from the latter. The method was much in favour with Greaves, Pritchard, Sowerby, and other London practitioners. Filling up the crack with gutta-percha 2 parts and gum ammoniac 1 part has also been recommended for the same object, but its chief effect is the exclusion of mud and dust.

(2) *Promotion of the Secretion of New Horn* is effected by counter-irritation of the coronary band by means of a blister or the actual cautery. A common method of using the latter was to make three transverse lines at the level of the crack—one on the coronet, another ½ inch above it, and a third ½ inch below. Another procedure is to make two transverse grooves across the crack in the wall, and a third on the coronet. Those in the wall have the effect of intercepting pressure transmitted to the lips of the crack.

Instead of adopting the above devices for preventing movement of the lips of the crack, the edges of the latter may be thinned for a short distance on either side to prevent pinching of the tissues between them. The shoe should have side toe-clips, or quarter clips instead of a toe-clip, and the wall should be slightly shortened with the rasp in the vicinity of the crack to prevent bearing on the shoe in that region.

2. *Sandcrack accompanied by Lameness.*—The indications here are to remove the shoe and immerse the foot in a warm antiseptic bath for at least half an hour morning and evening. If the horse becomes sound the measures prescribed in No. (1) can be adopted. If the lameness persists after the lapse of a few days it will be necessary to thin the horn on each side of the fissure to relieve the pressure on the inflamed tissues and permit of the escape of inflammatory exudate or pus, if present, and if this procedure fails to have the desired effect an operation will be required to strip off completely the overlying horn, to expose the necrotic tissue which is probably the cause of the trouble, and to enable it to be removed. It may be necessary to curette the os pedis.

3. *Sandcrack at the Quarter.*—When lameness is absent the treatment is on the same lines as those for sandcrack at the toe, except that

clasps or horseshoe nails cannot be employed with safety owing to the comparative thinness of the horn in this region. The usual procedure, which gives satisfactory results, is to make a transverse groove across the crack in its upper third, to put on a flat shoe having no bearing in the vicinity of the crack, and to apply a vesicant on the coronet. When the condition is accompanied by lameness, the measures to be adopted are exactly the same as those advised when it is situated at the toe.

When there is a crack in the bar the surrounding horn should be thinned, and a leather sole with tar and tow applied along with a flat shoe if the horse is sound. If lameness is present, the treatment prescribed for other situations must be adopted.

Transverse Cracks

These may be superficial or deep. They follow injury to the coronet and separation of the horn in this region. As the horn grows down the separation becomes a crack. If they go right through the wall, lameness will ensue from injury of the sensitive laminæ.

TREATMENT consists in paring the lips of the crack to relieve pressure on the subjacent structures, and thus prevent or remove lameness.

Seedy Toe

This is characterised by separation of the wall from the subcorneal tissue, and the formation in the interspace of crumbly pumice-stone-like horn secreted by the sensitive laminæ. This abnormal horn does not completely fill the space beneath the wall, which is consequently more or less hollow.

ETIOLOGY.—The cause is not clear, but the condition would appear to be the result of a chronic local laminitis following traumatic injury, such as might be caused by a too-closely-driven nail, or by the pressure of a large clip. Wide-spreading feet are most subject to it.

SYMPTOMS.—The condition is often first recognised by the farrier when preparing the hoof for shoeing. The foot appears normal when resting on the ground, but if the wall be struck on its outer aspect with a hammer a hollow sound will be emitted opposite the affected part. The extent of the lesion varies in depth and peripheral area. It may occupy any region of the circumference of the wall, and may affect only the lower portion of the latter or extend as far as the coronet. Lameness is absent when the area involved is small, but when there is considerable separation of the horn the sensitive laminæ are insufficiently protected from concussion, and, moreover, foreign matter accumulates in the space, causing pressure on the laminal surface, giving rise to more or less well-marked lameness. The abnormal horn is easily broken down with the knife.

PROGNOSIS depends on the depth and area of the lesion. When circumscribed it is not of much importance, not causing lameness, and allowing the horse to work during treatment. When a large part of the foot is affected to a great depth, causing lameness, months may elapse before the horse is fit to work.

TREATMENT.—Remove the new formation of horn to diminish the pressure on the sensitive structures, pack the cavity with tar and tow, and apply a shoe having no bearing on the affected region and a leather sole to keep the dressing in position. If the disease extend far beneath the wall, it will be necessary to remove a portion of the latter at the level of the lesion in order to expose it and enable the abnormal horn to be pared away. A bar shoe with a breach in the iron opposite the affected part is suitable. A blister on the coronet will promote the growth of normal horn.

Keratoma

Keratoma is a horn tumour growing from the inner aspect of the wall. It varies considerably in volume, form, and extent. Its diameter may be ¼ inch to 1 inch. Its shape may be cylindrical, conical, pyramidal, or irregular, and it may be bifurcated at its upper extremity. It may extend up a portion or the full height of the wall, or even bulge into the cutigeral groove. Exceptionally it is only adherent at its lower part. It may be solid or fistulous, the fistula terminating in the tumour or passing through it to abut on the laminæ, and having its lower orifice at the white line.

ETIOLOGY.—The condition is apparently due to hyperactivity of the laminæ or coronary band, caused by some irritant or injury, whereby an abnormal quantity of horn is secreted. In this way it may result from mechanical injury of the wall or coronet, or from a close-driven nail compressing or penetrating the laminæ, or from dirt gaining entrance through a sandcrack, or a separation between the wall and the sole. There is another and rare form of keratoma which appears independently of inflammation or irritation of the horn-secreting structures. It may be adherent or free, and of similar dimensions to the one just described.

SYMPTOMS.—The tumour may develop insidiously and be present for a considerable time before being detected. Its presence is recognised on examination of the plantar aspect of the foot by the abnormal appearance of the horn at the place corresponding to the lower end of the growth between the wall and the sole, the white line being deviated inwards here. If fistulous, a probe can be passed into it, and the fistula may be discharging pus. The pressure of the tumour on the laminæ and os pedis may cause inflammation and lameness. The former is indicated locally by pain on percussion at the level of the lesion, and by abnormal heat on palpation. The latter varies in degree. The abnormality of gait may be of the nature of stringhalt. The wall may bulge over the tumour. When the sensitive tissues become affected through the fistula, the laminæ may undergo necrosis and the os pedis may become affected with caries. The pressure of the new horn causes atrophy of the laminæ, which eventually disappear, preventing further increase in size of the tumour. The pedal bone may also undergo atrophy and become weakened in consequence, and fracture on slight provocation.

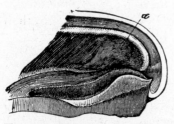

FIG. 390.—PORTION OF THE INNER SURFACE OF THE WALL, SHOWING CHANGES AFTER OLD-STANDING CORN.

a, Horn tumour.

DIAGNOSIS is easy, owing to the characteristic appearance of the horn at the lower end of the tumour or to the presence of the fistula, into which a probe can be passed to abut on the tumour or pass through it as mentioned.

PROGNOSIS, generally speaking, is unfavourable, there being no tendency to spontaneous cure and no means of effecting the latter, except by operation, after which the tumour may recur.

TREATMENT.—If there be neither pain nor lameness, it is sufficient to regulate the shoeing so as to have a minimum amount of bearing on the affected region. When lameness supervenes, palliative or curative measures may be adopted. Palliative treatment comprises rest and antiphlogistic applications, which may cause temporary improvement, and if these fail, paring out the tumour from below with a searcher or boring it with a drill to allow it to collapse on itself, and thus diminish the pressure on the sensitive tissues until the tumour increases in size, when this procedure will require repetition. Curative treatment consists in performing the operation described (see p. 470).

Keratoma on the Sole

A keratoma may be found on the deep face of the sole in flat or convex feet, in which it may arise from circumscribed chronic inflammation resulting from contusion. It is hemispherical in shape, its base being flush with the sole. The velvety tissue becomes atrophied through its pressure, and the os pedis may become excavated from the same cause. It is diagnosed by pain confined to the region affected, revealed on percussion, and by the dry, hard consistence of the horn of the tumour, which retains these characters after deep paring, while that of its periphery, when cut to the same extent, causes wounding of the sensitive tissues. Infection of the lesion rarely occurs.

TREATMENT.—Thin or hollow out the tumour to diminish its pressure or remove it radically. If necrotic tissue is present, excise it. Cover the wound until healed with an antiseptic dressing and a leather or metal sole fixed under the shoe.

Thrush

Thrush is the term applied to an affection of the frog characterised by an offensive greyish discharge from the central lacuna, and sometimes from the lateral lacunæ as well, and associated, as a rule, with more or less disintegration of the horn.

ETIOLOGY.—Constant moisture of the frog favours the condition, which is thus brought about by prolonged standing on dirty wet litter, especially peat moss, or running in a marshy pasture. The moisture softens the horn, which then becomes broken and ragged, and emits the characteristic discharge from the lacunæ. Atrophy of the frog from disuse favours the trouble, and for this reason contracted feet are very subject to it. Hind-feet are more often affected than fore ones, due to the fact that the former are more frequently in contact with wet bedding, and their frogs are more often prevented from bearing weight. Neglecting to pick out the feet regularly naturally favours the onset of the condition.

SYMPTOMS.—The local symptoms are the conditions of the frog, as described. There is no evidence of inflammation or lameness, except the greater portion of the horn has been shed, and the insufficiently protected sensitive tissue suffers from contusion or from the action of a caustic dressing.

DIAGNOSIS.—Thrush is distinguished from canker by the horn being separated from the sensitive tissues in the latter case, and by the ready response of the former to appropriate treatment.

Contusion, Crushing, and Open Wounds of the Foot

Contusion or crushing of the foot is generally caused by direct violence inflicted from above downwards on the upper part of the foot in the region of the toe, quarters, or heels, the offending body being usually the wheel of a heavy vehicle passing over the coronet. The

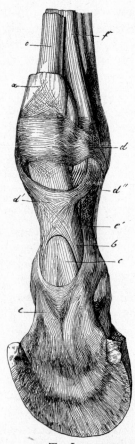

FIG. 391.—TO ILLUSTRATE THE SUPERFICIAL STRUC-
TURES INVOLVED IN SURGICAL INJURIES OF THE
FOOT.

The outer lateral cartilage and the tissues covering
the lower surface of the pedal bone (sensitive frog
and sensitive sole) have been removed. *a*, Plantar
cushion; *a'*, bulbar portion of plantar cushion;
a'', cleft of the frog in which rests the "frog stay";
b, origin of the so-called "suspensory ligament of
the bulbs"; *b'*, small elastic band passing towards
the lateral cartilage; *c*, elastic band arising from
lateral cartilage and becoming inserted into pastern bone—it unites with *b*; *d*, small tendon
which arises from the skin and becomes attached,
in common with *b* and *c*, to the pastern bone;
e, fibro-elastic supporting sheath of flexor pedis
perforans; *f*, fibro-elastic supporting sheath of
flexor pedis perforatus; *g*, flexor pedis perforatus
tendon; *h*, flexor pedis perforans tendon; *i*, suspensory ligament; *k*, lower surface of pedal bone, to
which the flexor pedis perforans tendon is attached.

FIG. 392.—TO ILLUSTRATE THE
DEEPER-SEATED STRUCTURES
INVOLVED IN SURGICAL IN-
JURIES OF THE FOOT.

Right fore-foot seen from behind
and slightly from one side.
a, Flexor pedis perforatus tendon; *b*, two limbs formed by
its bifurcation; *c*, flexor pedis
perforans tendon; *d*, fibrous
reinforcing band of great sesamoid sheath; *d'*, fibrous supporting sheath inserted into
suffraginis bone by four heads;
d'', upper insertions (the lower
not visible in figure); *e*, fibro-
elastic plate covering the lower
surface of flexor pedis perforans and inserted into suffraginis bone at *e'*; *f*, suspensory ligament.

foot may also be crushed between the kerbstone of a footpath and a heavy wheel.

SYMPTOMS.—A slight contusion causes a varying degree of lameness,

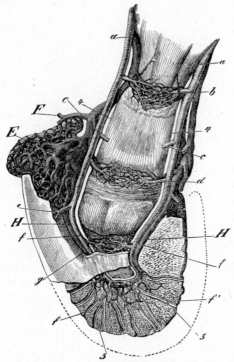

FIG. 393.—TO ILLUSTRATE THE JOINTS AND DEEP-SEATED ARTERIES, VEINS, AND NERVES INVOLVED IN SURGICAL INJURIES OF THE FOOT.

Right fore-foot seen from below, behind, and somewhat from one side. The outer lateral cartilage is removed, together with sufficient of the pedal bone to render visible the vessels, etc., in its interior. The nerves accompanying arteries f' are shown too thick; they should be less than half as broad as figured. a, Digital artery; b, posterior suffraginal artery; c, artery of plantar cushion (cut through); d, posterior artery of coronary circle; f, plantar artery, which anastomoses with its fellow within the pedal bone and gives off twigs f', which pass to the anterior surface of the pedal bone just above its lower edge; g, twigs of plantar artery supplying coffin-joint; E, deep lateral layer of coronary plexus clothing inner surface of lateral cartilage; F, divided ends of superficial part of coronary plexus. From these arise the digital vein (not shown), H, plantar vein; 4, posterior branch of digital nerve accompanying vessels into pedal bone; 5, twigs of posterior branch passing towards sensitive laminæ.

which disappears in the course of a few days. There is slight hæmorrhage or ecchymosis in the bruised tissues. When the contusion is caused by severe violence, or when the foot is actually crushed, the animal becomes extremely lame. If there be no breach in the horn there will be no obvious local symptoms, but in many instances some trace of the accident is left on the horn or the coronet reveals evidence of a contusion, with heat, pain, and swelling. The damage done to the foot varies according to the severity of the injury. Extravasated blood may collect beneath the horn or in the small sesamoidean sheath,

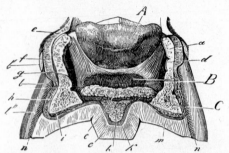

FIG. 394.—VERTICAL CROSS-SECTION OF A FOOT SEEN FROM BEHIND.

To illustrate the structures involved in surgical injuries of the foot. *A*, Coronet bone ; *B*, navicular bone ; *C*, pedal bone ; *a*, lateral cartilage ; *b*, anterior portion of plantar cushion ; *c*, divided part of flexor pedis perforans tendon ; *d*, postero-lateral ligaments of navicular bone ; *l*, horn wall ; *m*, horn sole ; *n*, white line ; *o*, horn frog.

or even in the joint. The tissues may be so disorganised by the contusion that their return to normal is impossible. Exostoses may form as a sequel to the accident, causing low ringbone and permanent lameness. Occasionally the hoof is completely torn off, with little damage to the deep structures of the foot. Should infection gain entrance to the injured region, serious complications may ensue, due to the destructive effects of the bacterial toxins.

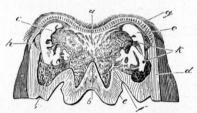

FIG. 395.—VERTICAL CROSS-SECTION OF FOOT SEEN FROM BEHIND (THIS SECTION HAS BEEN MADE NEARER THE HEELS THAN FIG. 394).

To illustrate the structures involved in surgical injuries of the foot. *a*, Posterior part of plantar cushion ; *b*, median ridge of frog ; *c*, lateral cartilage ; *d*, horn wall ; *e*, lateral face of frog ; *f*, point of union between the bars and frog.

When an open wound is present, its seat will be a guide to the parts likely to be involved—lateral cartilage, bones, or joint. Crepitation on manipulation of the foot will reveal fracture, and a synovial discharge from a wound on the coronet will be proof of an open corono-pedal joint.

DIAGNOSIS may be difficult when there is no history to the case and no mark of injury to the hoof. When the horn of the plantar region is pared, ecchymosis may be seen at the white line. These symptoms, associated with severe lameness and the acute pain evinced on percussion or compression, generally lead to a correct conclusion, although

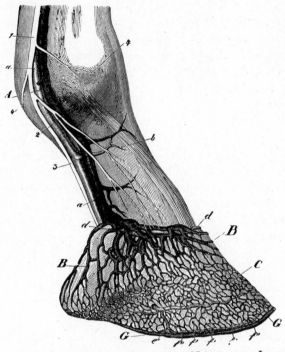

FIG. 396.—LATERAL VIEW OF FORE-FOOT, WITH NERVES AND INJECTED VESSELS, SHOWING SOME OF THE STRUCTURES INVOLVED IN INFLAMMATION OF THE SUB-CORONARY CONNECTIVE TISSUE AND ITS COMPLICATIONS.

a, Digital artery ; *b*, perpendicular artery ; *e'*, preplantar artery ; *f'*, twigs from the plantar artery which escape through the foramina just above the lower margin of the os pedis, and by their anastomosis form *f''*, the circumflex artery of the toe ; *A*, digital vein ; *B*, coronary venous plexus ; *C*, laminal plexus ; *G*, circumflex vein ; 1, digital nerve ; 2, anterior terminal branches of digital nerve ; 3, posterior terminal branches of digital nerve ; 4, cutaneous branches.

it is not always easy to give a definite opinion as to the exact nature of the lesion or the extent of the injury inflicted.

PROGNOSIS.—In cases of moderate contusion cure is effected in a few days, but when the tissues are severely damaged there is always the danger of secondary changes occurring, such as the formation of exostoses, or anchylosis of the pedal-joint, causing incurable lameness. It is important to bear this in mind from the point of view of jurisprudence. These changes may not supervene until months after the accident. Injury to the anterior or middle regions of the foot is more likely to have serious consequences than that confined to the region of the heel. Deep-seated septic conditions are always serious and may defy treatment. Infected open joint is, of course, hopeless, as is also complete compound fracture of the os pedis or navicular bone.

TREATMENT comprises removal of the shoe and the use of anti-phlogistic and antiseptic applications, and when the lameness is very severe, placing the patient in slings. At first immersing the foot in a cold bath or irrigating it with a constant stream of cold water, and afterwards using hot fomentations and compresses, are indicated in cases where there is no open wound. When the latter is present, rigorous cleanliness and antisepsis are essential to prevent septic complications. All foreign matter and destroyed tissue must be removed, the skin of the coronet and pastern in the vicinity should be shaved, the whole foot thoroughly washed and disinfected, and then kept in a warm antiseptic bath for at least half an hour two or three times daily, the wound in the meantime being protected by an antiseptic dressing and the hoof kept clean by being enclosed in a boot. When the wound is uniformly granulating, the baths are to be discontinued and a dry dressing only employed.

Separation or Evulsion of the Hoof

Separation of the hoof may be caused by degeneration of its attachments through the agency of infection, or it may be the result of mechanical violence.

Degeneration may ensue from extensive suppuration beneath the horn, and it is favoured by ordinary poultices, which have no anti-bacterial effect, but rather promote the growth of bacteria. It is, however, most frequently a sequel to neurectomy.

Mechanical violence is a cause when all muscles of the limb are violently contracted in an effort to extricate the foot which has become fixed between two resistant objects, or when the foot is crushed from above downwards by a heavy weight such as a wagon wheel passing over it, and the pain thus caused makes the animal endeavour to snatch it away suddenly.

SYMPTOMS.—The sensitive tissues are all exposed and more or less injured when the result of violence. Evidence of pain is not always marked. It is surprising how slight it is in some cases. Instances are recorded where the horse continued to trot fairly well after losing one or two hooves.

PROGNOSIS.—When the condition is the result of degeneration and sloughing after neurectomy it is hopeless. But if the case be noticed when separation is commencing at the coronet, it may be possible to arrest it by keeping the foot for prolonged periods in an antiseptic bath. When the loss of the hoof is due to mechanical violence, the chances of recovery depend on the amount of injury suffered by the tissues. In every case it will take about nine months for the new hoof to grow down from the coronet. Sometimes the newly formed horn is deformed, and occasionally, although the regenerated hoof is fairly normal in shape, lameness persists from hyperæsthesia in the subcorneal tissues. The hoof, however, may be perfectly reproduced, and even in cases where a piece of bone has been torn away with a portion of the horn-secreting membrane recovery may occur to an extent sufficient to enable the animal to go to work.

TREATMENT comprises the removal of shreds of dead tissue, thoroughly cleaning and disinfecting the foot after clipping or shaving the pastern, and applying a dressing of iodoform or sulphanilamide covered with gauze and several layers of cotton-wool kept in position by a bandage and protected from the dirt of the stable floor by a boot. The frequency of renewal of the dressing will depend on the progress of the case. It should be renewed whenever it becomes moistened from discharge. When the sensitive tissues are covered with horn, it will be sufficient to keep them covered with tar until the new wall is formed. If the hæmorrhage after the accident is severe, a tourniquet should be applied above the fetlock until the foot is enveloped in the compressive dressing.

Chronic Coronitis or Villitis—Chronic Dermatitis of the Perioplic Band and of the Coronary Cushion

ETIOLOGY.—The etiology is often obscure. The condition may accompany skin affections or be associated with a febrile condition. Its typical form often appears without any apparent cause, but it may result from repeated injury or irritation of the coronet. In all cases there may be an hereditary predisposition to the affection, which may be of a rheumatoid nature. It most commonly affects light horses, those engaged in fast work. It is particularly common in the ass and mule. The disease affects chiefly the toe and quarters. The perioplic band appears to become more active, secreting a horny material, disposed in irregular masses, separated by narrow fissures, resembling somewhat the bark of an old tree.

The coronary cushion in the affected part produces thickened abnormal horn of the same appearance as that formed by the perioplic

ring.   The skin in the vicinity may also be covered by a horny formation, fissured in every direction and sometimes discharging from the
cracks a purulent fluid.   In old-standing cases there may be separation
of the horn at the coronet.   The subcutaneous tissue becomes thickened
at the level of the lesion in typical old cases, causing a swelling which
projects over the hoof.   Sometimes an ulcer forms between the swelling
and the horn.   In the subacute form accompanying a febrile disease
or skin affection, the whole of the coronet is involved and reveals slight
symptoms of inflammation, chiefly abnormal heat.   In this case there
is more or less marked lameness, characterised by a shuffling gait
something like that of subacute laminitis.   In the ordinary chronic
form of the disease, with local changes as described, lameness may or
may not be present.   When the new formation of horn on the coronet
is thick or cracked or when the wall is separated from the coronary
band, lameness supervenes.

TREATMENT.—When apparently of constitutional origin, treat the
general affection from which the animal is suffering.   Apply cold
swabs to the coronet to counteract local inflammation.   Afterwards
rub on the coronet an ointment composed of equal parts of Stockholm
tar and mutton suet boiled together, or a preparation consisting of
one part of coal tar and six parts of fish oil, in order to promote the
growth of good horn and to render it supple and elastic.   A blister on
the coronet may have a good effect in an old-standing case.   When
the growth of new horn is thick it should be thinned to a pellicle, and
the weeping cracks therein should be treated with an antiseptic lotion.
Ulceration should be combated by the use of a wound stimulant or
caustic, to excite a healthy reaction and bring about granulation and
cicatrisation.   In all cases the horn beneath the affected part of the
coronet should be made as thin as possible with the rasp to diminish
the pressure and pain in the inflamed part.   Delpérier, a well-known
French authority on the horse's foot, recommends washing and drying
the affected part every five days, and then applying rapidly over its
surface the flat portion of a red-hot iron, and passing its edges into the
fissures.   Slight repeated application of nitric acid more or less dilute,
or of chloride of zinc (5 to 10 per cent.), or of pyrogallic acid, or of picric
acid in saturated aqueous solution or as an ointment (1 to 10 of vaseline) has often had good results.

Gangrenous Coronitis

Gangrenous coronitis, or sloughing of a portion of the coronet or
subcorneal tissues, may result from an open wound and infection by

the bacillus of necrosis or other virulent organism. The condition is fairly common in horses constantly standing in mud, especially during very cold frosty weather, the severe cold diminishing the vitality and resistance of the tissues. The lesion was very prevalent in army horses during the winter months of the First World War.

SYMPTOMS.—There is intense inflammation in the region of the coronet and severe lameness. An extremely painful swelling more or less diffuse is formed ; the skin, if not pigmented, becomes dark red, and serum oozes from its surface, which becomes clammy, owing to the desquamation of the epithelium, which can be scraped off with the nail. The affected part then becomes insensitive, and a line of demarcation is observed between the dead and healthy tissues. If infection has not extended beneath the horn, the lameness attenuates when the eschar is formed. When the subcorneal tissue is involved the pain is more excruciating, owing to compression of the inflamed part by the resistant horn, and it does not subside with separation of the slough, which cannot be cast off on account of being confined beneath the horn, the result being that the bacteria continue to exercise their pathogenic effects, causing further necrosis of the sensitive parts, including the laminæ, or extensor pedis tendon, or the lateral cartilage or pedal bone. A general toxæmia generally ensues which may prove fatal.

TREATMENT.—Thoroughly clean the extremity of the limb, clip or shave the hair in the affected region, thin the horn to a pellicle beneath the lesion, and keep the foot immersed in a warm antiseptic bath, which will have a hyperæmic and softening effect, promoting separation of the slough and facilitating the penetration of the antiseptic solution. When the bath is not being used, envelop the foot in moist antiseptic compresses. When the slough has separated healing ensues rapidly, provided that the joint has not been opened, when the case is incurable.

Fracture of the Os Pedis

ETIOLOGY.—Fracture of the os pedis may be caused by violent concussion, or by crushing of the foot by a heavy object falling on or by the wheel of a heavy vehicle passing over it. Rarefying ostitis of the bone predisposes to the accident. Partial fracture may result from the penetration of a nail or other sharp rigid substance through the sole of the foot.

SYMPTOMS comprise sudden and severe lameness and evidence of severe inflammation in the foot, characterised by pain on palpation of the coronet, percussion of the hoof, as well as on torsion of the terminal phalanx. When there is an open wound with exposure of the bone the fracture may be obvious, but otherwise the diagnosis cannot be certain without the aid of X-rays, although the history of the case is strong evidence in favour of fracture. Crepitation can seldom be detected.

TREATMENT is that for a contusion, comprising rest and antiphlogistic applications. When there is an open wound with partial fracture of the bone, operation is indicated to remove the loose separated portion of bone.

Fracture of the Navicular Bone

Fracture of the navicular bone may be caused also by violent concussion, as may occur in jumping or prancing. Navicular disease is a predisposing cause, rendering the bone more brittle, and when neurectomy has been performed the fracture is still more prone to occur. The bone has often been broken by a nail penetrating it through the plantar aspect of the foot.

SYMPTOMS are on a par with those mentioned for fracture of the os pedis.

DIAGNOSIS can only be guessed from the history of the case. Radiography is the only means of confirming it.

TREATMENT is useless, as a rule. Nothing can be done except to wait and see if recovery will supervene. When associated with a punctured wound of the foot, the case is incurable.

Wounds of the Plantar Aspect of the Foot—Picked-up Nail

ETIOLOGY.—An open wound in the plantar aspect of the foot is usually in the form of a puncture, caused by the penetration of a nail or some other sharp-pointed resistant object, such as a piece of iron, wood, or bone, or the clip of a shoe, or a piece of shrapnel, or a fragment of shell casing. The point of entrance may be in the sole or frog. When the sole is hard, concave, and free from cracks, the offending object may glide from it into the lateral lacuna and enter the foot there. In the frog the commonest seat of puncture is near its point. The bar is seldom penetrated, owing to its obliquity and hardness. The thinner and softer the horn, the greater the risk of sharp bodies passing through it into the sensitive tissues. The direction of the wound depends on the angle at which the foot meets the projecting point, and on the deviation which the latter may undergo by the weight exerted upon it. The lesion is one of the commonest affections of the foot, and is particularly frequent in horses working in places where rubbish of every kind is strewn. In military horses on active service it is the chief cause of foot trouble.

SYMPTOMS.—When the foreign body enters the horn it may not at once penetrate the sensitive tissues. This may occur from repeated force applied to it by the foot striking the ground during progression. Attention is generally first attracted by lameness, and when the foot is examined the cause of the trouble is usually discovered at once by finding the foreign body more or less firmly embedded in its plantar region. It may require a pincers to remove it from the foot. The object may, however, be broken on a level with the horn, when its situation may be recognised by a dark or abnormal spot corresponding to its distal extremity, or it may have become divided at some distance in from the surface of the horn, and require to be searched for with the hoof knife before being discovered. When it is removed the lameness may disappear ; the resulting perforation in the horn may be so small that it is hardly visible. There may be some blood on the object when withdrawn, or a little hæmorrhage may appear at the orifice after its removal. When the wound is slight, it may heal at once without further symptoms. If not, and the condition has existed for some days, infection will have supervened, and there will be a purulent discharge from the wound, blackish or whitish in colour, or mixed with blood. The deep layers of the horn in the affected part will be infiltrated with moisture, yellowish, and separated from the sensitive tissues. There is severe local inflammation, causing great pain and lameness. At a later stage the tissues will be more altered, owing to the prolonged action of the organisms, causing more or less necrosis of the velvety sole or plantar cushion, and the purulent discharge will be more copious, a sinus being present.

When important deep-seated structures are involved in the necrotic or septic lesion, special symptoms are manifested according to the nature of the complication. If the os pedis undergoes necrosis, there will be a profuse escape of blood-stained pus, and a probe passed into the sinus will come in contact with the bone. The plantar aponeurosis may become necrotic, causing a constant purulent discharge until the affected portion is removed. Should the synovial sheath be opened, there will be a purulent synovial discharge and an inflammatory swelling will form in the hollow of the heel at the level of the sheath. The navicular bone may be ulcerated on its tendinous aspect or completely fractured. The interosseous ligament may be destroyed, allowing infection into the joint, setting up arthritis, which becomes evident by a prominent coronary swelling, with perhaps abscesses, which, on

61

bursting, discharge offensive purulent synovia and persist as fistulæ until the horse dies from septicæmia or toxæmia, or is destroyed, the case being hopeless. Lameness is always well marked in connection with these deep-seated complications, which may prevent any weight being borne by the affected limb.

DIAGNOSIS is easy after removing the shoe and paring the foot.

PROGNOSIS depends on the part affected and on the nature of the injury. Taking the plantar region of the foot as being composed of an anterior, middle, and posterior region, the most serious part to be perforated in a more or less upright direction is the middle region, because most of the important structures of the foot are situated directly above it. After it comes the anterior region, in which the os pedis may be injured. The posterior region is made up practically entirely of the plantar cushion, lesions of which are comparatively benign, being always followed by recovery when rationally treated. When the case is seen early, before complications have arisen, the latter may be prevented by careful treatment. All the septic lesions of the foot arising in the manner described respond to treatment, except arthritis, extensive disease of the os pedis, and fracture of the navicular bone. The degree of lameness and the temperature of the patient are guides as to the gravity of the condition. The lameness, however, may be extremely severe, no weight being borne by the affected limb, and yet the case may be amenable to treatment—for example, septic synovitis of the small sesamoidean sheath causes alarming lameness, but when it is properly treated recovery ensues. When arthritis supervenes or when the navicular bone is fractured the case is incurable, but superficial ulceration of the cartilaginous surface of the bone may be treated successfully.

TREATMENT.—An injection of antitetanic serum is indicated at once. The treatment in a recent case, before suppuration has had time to ensue, is that of an ordinary open wound. Having extracted the wounding body, thin the horn round the orifice of the wound over an area of the diameter of half a crown or a crown to facilitate the escape of discharge should it form, to relieve pressure on the injured region, and to allow the antiseptic lotion to come into contact with the wound. It is a good and common practice to pour into the latter a little pure carbolic acid or pure creolin, which ensures the destruction of any bacteria that are present, and causes no ill-effects from the superficial destruction of tissue which it produces. Afterwards protect the wound with an antiseptic dressing of iodoform and cotton-wool, or a moist antiseptic compress kept in position by a bandage and boot, or by strips of hoop-iron or a metal plate inserted between the shoe and the hoof. Remove this dressing the following day, and immerse the foot for at least half an hour in a warm antiseptic bath, after which reapply the dressing. Continue the foot-baths daily until the horse goes sound. Should the wound be fairly large and the sensitive tissues exposed, excessive granulations are likely to form from the irritation caused by the edges of the surrounding horn, and it will be necessary to remove them with the knife, if large, or, if smaller, by the application of a caustic, such as powdered sulphate of zinc, perchloride of mercury, or sulphate of copper, or formalin 1–40. When the wound is cicatrised and covered by horn, put on a dressing of tar and tow covered with a leather or metal sole.

In slight cases where the wound is superficial, one or two applications of an antiseptic dressing are generally sufficient. When the lesion is of some standing and discharging pus, it must be treated as a sinus by adopting measures to provide for drainage, to remove necrotic tissue, and destroy the bacteria which have invaded the affected part. Paring the horn round the seat of injury and removing it entirely where it is underrun, followed by the use of the antiseptic foot-bath once or twice daily and an antiseptic dressing in the meantime, often prove effective in the course of a few days. Should this procedure fail, it may be concluded that there is necrotic tissue in the wound requiring removal. This may be effected by the use of a caustic, or the hot iron, or by surgical interference (see p. 467).

Sprain of the Corono-pedal Joint

Sprain of this joint ensues when its lateral ligaments are distended as the result of a false step, slipping, or falling.

SYMPTOMS.—There is a varying degree of lameness, appearing suddenly after the accident mentioned. During rest the foot is held forward in a state of semi-flexion. To examine the joint, let an assistant lift the foot and hold the pastern firmly and horizontally while the examiner practises torsion of the joint by grasping the hoof in the two hands. In the case of sprain this causes the horse to evince pain, which is also revealed on pressure of the coronet in the region of the quarters. Afterwards abnormal heat can be detected in the foot and at the coronet, and the latter may be more or less swollen. In slight cases the lameness gradually subsides, and recovery may be complete in the course of a month. When the joint is very severely sprained synovitis and the formation of exostoses may ensue.

TREATMENT is as usual for sprains in general.

Osteo-periostitis of the Pedal Bone

This may ensue from a trauma, but a primary form of the condition also occurs affecting chiefly the fore-feet, where it would appear to be the result of repeated concussion, to which they are more subject than the hind-feet. Anything favouring concussion is therefore concerned with its etiology, such as fast work on hard ground, boxy contracted feet, absence of frog pressure, and the use of high-heeled shoes. To these may be added an inherent defect in the bone, whereby it is predisposed to inflammation. It may also occur during the course of an infectious disease. The lesion is characterised at first by the bone becoming rarefied, appearing more porous than normally. Later, the bone may become denser and harder than normal, and little conical excrescences appear on its surface and penetrate the overlying tissues. The most constant change in the bone is rarefaction, affecting chiefly its antero-inferior portion. The phalanx eventually becomes deformed, undergoing atrophy to a varying extent. Its solar aspect may become flat or convex, and its articular surface lowered. Osteo-periostitis involving the pyramidal process is seen chiefly in the hind-foot, and predisposes to fracture of the eminence. It may be associated here with the formation of osteophytes, invading the tendon of the extensor pedis, where they are recognised by the hard swelling to which they give rise.

When the malady is localised at the level of the semilunar crest, the nodosities formed there penetrate the plantar aponeurosis, interfering with its movement, and causing symptoms similar to those of navicular disease, which in some cases is an accompanying lesion Beneath the velvety sole the disease may cause a bony enlargement. The wings of the os pedis are probably the commonest seat of bony deposits, causing increase in size of the basilar and retrosal processes. From these the process of ossification may extend to the lateral cartilages, which then also become enlarged and constitute " *side-bones*." When these osseous excrescences form beneath the heels, they cause compression of the soft tissues between the bone and the horn, producing ecchymotic spots or staining of the horn, which is known in the heel region as a " *corn*." In the same way the parietal horn may be found discoloured on paring into its depth.

SYMPTOMS.—There is lameness, which at first is intermittent, disappearing when the horse is rested, and returning when the animal is put to work on hard ground, being due to compression of the soft tissues between the bone and the hoof. The local symptoms include abnormal heat, pain on percussion, staining of the horn in certain regions as mentioned, and swelling, due to enlargement of the pyramidal process, or of the alæ of the os pedis when those parts are involved. When work is continued, the heels gradually increase in height, the coronet becomes horizontal, and the horse commences to knuckle at the fetlock. Sometimes the hoof becomes elongated antero-posteriorly, as in a case of chronic laminitis. Many cases of obscure lameness are due to the condition under consideration, and its diagnosis is not easy, as the local symptoms are not always obvious or characteristic. Although the use of a local anæsthetic confines the lesion to the foot, it does not distinguish it from navicular disease, with which it has many points in common.

PROGNOSIS.—The disease is generally incurable.

TREATMENT is that for acute or chronic inflammation, according to the duration of the affection. Smith's operation always deserves a trial (see p. 471). Neurectomy is usually necessary.

Navicular Disease

Navicular disease is due to chronic ostitis of the navicular bone, associated usually with chronic synovitis of the navicular bursa and inflammation of the plantar aponeurosis. The condition is practically confined to the fore-feet, affecting both as a rule. The hind-feet are rarely affected. The most noticeable change in the navicular bone is the presence of ulcers on its tendinous aspect, appearing as outcuts in the cartilage thereon. Osteophytes may also form on this surface, especially near its extremities. The articular aspect remains intact. Owing to the rarefaction of the bone, it becomes weak and brittle, and may fracture under the body-weight, especially if the foot is brought violently to the ground. Adhesion may occur between the bone and the tendon as the result of fibrinous synovitis. The tendon sometimes becomes fibrillated from friction against the roughened posterior surface of the bone.

ETIOLOGY.—The real exciting cause of the disease is obscure, but the circumstances under which it most commonly occurs are well known. It is most common in light horses, especially those doing fast work on hard roads, particularly when they are not getting regular exercise, but are subjected to rapid work occasionally after more or less prolonged rest in the stable. Cart-horses are rarely affected. An hereditary tendency to the malady is believed to exist in certain breeds of horses of the roadster type, but it is also common in hunters.

The disease usually attacks the horse when he is in his prime, about seven years old, but it may appear even at the age of two years, before the animal has been put to work. The conformation of the foot has been looked upon as a factor in the production of the disease, which most commonly occurs in narrow, upright, or contracted feet. The cause in this case, however, may be confounded with the effect, for when the disease has been in existence for some time it tends to produce this conformation. The disease is usually gradual in its onset and insidious in its appearance, being generally well established before the symptoms are sufficiently developed to attract the serious attention of the owner. Rarely it appears suddenly as the result of shock on the foot, as may occur during jumping, or prancing in a fresh horse, or from making a false step. The cause might be of a toxic nature, resulting from rheumatism or some infectious disease like strangles or influenza. The absence of frog pressure, preventing the action of the anti-concussion mechanism of the foot, is undoubtedly a contributing cause of the affection. Hence a defective system of shoeing, such as the application of thick-heeled shoes or those furnished with calkins, on horses engaged in fast work on hard ground favours the onset of the condition, as does also a long toe and a sloping pastern by throwing excessive weight on the posterior region of the foot.

SYMPTOMS.—The first symptom, as a rule, to attract attention is the horse pointing his foot when at rest, and as both feet are usually involved he points them alternately. Afterwards the animal is observed to go tender occasionally, but when given a rest for a few days he goes sound again. As time passes the lameness becomes decided, and is characterised by the horse taking a short stride, going on the toe, with a tendency to stumble when the toe strikes the ground. The gait is pottering or groggy, and the seat of lameness appears to be the shoulders, on account of the shortened stride. The lameness is most marked on starting after resting for a while, and diminishes with exercise. It is more pronounced on hard than on soft ground, and is intensified by frog pressure and by the use of thin shoes, which have not the same effect in breaking the shock on the feet as thick shoes. When the disease is well established the lameness is continuous. When the horse is turning, he screws round on his fore-feet instead of lifting them. Hence probably the term " Screw " sometimes applied to such a horse. The local symptoms comprise the alterations in the form of the foot, which becomes " boxy "—that is, contracted and high at the heels, with a very concave sole—deep lateral lacunæ and an atrophied frog, some swelling in the hollow of the heel due to distension of the navicular bursa—not a constant symptom—some pain perhaps, on percussion of the frog, and abnormal heat on palpation, only noticeable, as a rule, after a long journey. The form of the foot is not always altered. It may be perfectly normal in shape.

In rare cases in which the affection is sudden in appearance the lameness is severe from the beginning. When the hind-foot is affected the horse rests it more than usual, and during progression goes on the toe. If both hind-feet are affected, the lameness is characterised by stiffness of the posterior limbs. When the condition has been in existence for some time, the muscles of the shoulder undergo atrophy and the foot becomes more contracted, both changes being due to the prolonged restricted use of the limb.

DIAGNOSIS is made from the case history, the changes in the foot, and the nature of the lameness. It must be remembered, however, that the foot may be perfect in form, and yet affected with navicular disease. Local anæsthesia may be used to locate the seat of lameness.

Pryer and Oxspring in England have done much good work in the use of X-rays in the diagnosis of navicular disease and have demonstrated their reliability in this respect in the hands of an expert. The ordinary practitioner, however, would often have difficulty in deciding whether the shadows depicted on the plate represented lesions of navicular disease or were due to other effects.

PROGNOSIS is bad, because once the disease is established it is incurable, and the best that can be hoped for is that the horse will prove useful for a reasonable time after the performance of neurectomy. Adhesion of the perforans tendon to the navicular bone has been spoken of as a favourable termination to the disease by arresting the movement of the tendon on the roughened surface of the bone. Despite this, however, the lameness persists.

TREATMENT.—Veterinarians of the old school claimed that they cured navicular disease by bleeding from the jugular, by purgation, by applying poultices to the feet, and by giving prolonged rest, especially on a marshy pasture ; also by the insertion of a frog seton passed through the plantar cushion from the hollow of the heel to the point of the frog just behind the plantar aponeurosis, and left in position for about three weeks and cleaned daily, its object being to favour union between the navicular bone and the perforans tendon. Grooving the contracted hooves and applying light shoes are said to have a good effect. The former usually has a palliative effect by relieving pressure on the inflamed region, but the light shoes can only be beneficial in favouring frog pressure and acting as a preventative rather than a curative agent. Many of the so-called cures were cases of temporary improvement or mistaken diagnosis, for it is now universally admitted that in a true case of the disease cure is out of the question, and that the only means of rendering the horse workable is to perform neurectomy. Digital neurectomy is usually sufficient, but sometimes at a variable period afterwards lameness recurs, due apparently to inflammation spreading above the seat of operation, when it is necessary to do either double plantar or median neurectomy. The latter frequently has the desired effect, and should therefore be tried first, as it does not deprive the foot entirely of its innervation (see p. 444).

Canker

Looking upon the integument of the foot as a modified portion of the skin, canker may be defined as a chronic, hypertrophic, moist, eczematous dermatitis, a definition which answers the description of the disease in its most typical form. The condition is not so common now as formerly, owing apparently to the advance of hygiene in connection with the care of horses, for it is generally admitted that the affection is greatly favoured by dirty surroundings, keeping horses in dirty, ill-drained stables with the feet constantly in contact with litter soiled with fæces and saturated with urine, which macerates the horn and exposes the sensitive tissues to injury and infection, which may be a predisposing, if it is not an exciting, cause of the disease. This theory is also borne out by the fact that it is the hind-feet which are most commonly affected. Marshy localities seem to have a determining influence on the malady, as it is certainly more often found there than in upland districts. It is more common in the East Midlands of England than in other parts of the country. It occurs more frequently in coarse-bred, phlegmatic subjects than in the finer breeds.

It is generally believed that there is an hereditary tendency to the disease, and it is looked upon by many as a local manifestation of a constitutional affection, like other skin eruptions. The disease presents features which are suggestive of its being of an infectious nature, but so far no specific organism has been found in connection with it. Spirochætes and various forms of bacteria have been found in the lesions, but the disease could never be set up experimentally by any of them. Canker may remain localised on one foot for a long time, and then attack successively the other feet, and after being apparently cured it may break out again. It begins either as a sort of " grease " or moist eczema in the skin at the back of the pastern or beneath the horn. In the former case the affection gradually encroaches on the subcorneal tissue, whilst in the latter case it commences insidiously, and may remain unsuspected for a long time, until the separated horn is removed with the farrier's knife or is worn by use. It is the middle lacuna of the frog which first shows symptoms of the disease, as a rule, the affection spreading from there with more or less rapidity beneath the branches of the frog to the lateral lacunæ, and thence to the sole, from which it may extend under the wall to the coronet.

SYMPTOMS.—When a considerable area of the foot is involved and the disease is well established, the symptoms are very characteristic. The horn overlying the affected part is separated (under-run), more or less ragged, and sodden with moisture, having the appearance in the case of white horn of having been soaked in oil. In an advanced case the horn is absent and the lesion of the sensitive tissues is exposed. They appear to be affected with chronic inflammation, being covered with a whitish caseous exudation having a very foetid odour, and showing in places vegetations or hypertrophied papillæ or finger-like processes, which in old-standing lesions may be capped with horn, constituting what are known as ergots. The foul-smelling caseous material also forms between the vegetations and ergots. There is evidently no acute inflammation, as a rule, because lameness is frequently absent even in a well-marked case, and when it is present it may be the result of a contusion of the exposed sensitive structures. In bad cases where the os pedis is exposed, either as the result of the disease or injudicious treatment, the lameness is very pronounced, and when the laminæ are involved it may also be well marked.

DIAGNOSIS is generally easy. The appearance of the lesion is diagnostic—viz., the underrun and sodden horn, the discharge, the vegetations, the ergots, and the very penetrating offensive odour. Wherever the horn is adherent the disease is absent.

PROGNOSIS depends on the extent of the disease and the number of feet affected. It has no tendency to undergo spontaneous cure; on the contrary, it is progressive in its course. Except treatment is carried out with great pains and very thorough measures are adopted it will fail to have the desired effect. Sometimes, when it is almost cured, discontinuing the treatment causes it to break out afresh. When all the feet are badly affected, it is hardly worth treating. Nevertheless, when the malady is not too extensive or far gone, does not extend beneath the wall, and the os pedis is not exposed, proper treatment generally effects a cure within an average period of six weeks, and within two or more weeks of this time the horse may be working.

TREATMENT.—The exact cause not being known, the veterinarian is at the disadvantage of not being able to remove it, but he can avail himself of his knowledge of the admitted predisposing causes to avoid them as far as possible in combating the affection. Experience has shown that the principles of treatment which have given the best results are as follows :

1. After removing the loose horn, thoroughly cleansing and disinfecting the affected foot by enveloping it in antiseptic compresses for twenty-four hours, excise the ergots and vegetations, when present.

2. Apply to the affected part a caustic, an astringent, or merely an antiseptic, according to the nature of the lesion.

3. Exert firm pressure on the affected region by means of twisted pledgets of tow firmly compressed by the aid of a metal sole fixed to the shoe or by strips of hoop-iron inserted between the shoe and the hoof.

4. Attend to the general health of the patient and prescribe arsenic or one of its preparations, to be administered daily for a while at intervals until the disease is cured.

5. Removal of the vegetations and ergots is necessary to bring the affected part on a level with the normal tissues. Care must be taken in so doing not to expose the pedal bone, and in operating on the frog to follow its configuration, and not mutilate it unnecessarily. It is also advisable to thin the normal horn for a short distance beyond the periphery of the affected region to facilitate equalising the distribution of pressure, and to prevent irritation of the sensitive tissues by the edges of the horn.

6. Nearly all the common caustic and astringent drugs in the pharmacopœia have been recommended by different authorities for application to the diseased surface. Probably any of these is as efficacious as another, success depending rather upon the method of application than upon the agent employed. The following applications have been lauded by different practitioners : Nitric acid, sulphuric acid, pure or mixed with alum (Plasse's paste), hydrochloric acid, butyr of antimony, carbolic acid, acetate and sulphate of copper, creosote, salicylic acid, formalin, Czerney's solution (arsenic 1, methylated spirit 40, water 40), a mixture of carbide of calcium, iodoform, acetate of copper, and starch, a mixture of the three sulphates of copper, zinc, and iron, and powdered chinosol, etc.

With each of the foregoing topics success has been obtained, while failure has also been recorded, and one can hardly be said to possess more virtues than another. The hot iron is also strongly recommended by many veterinary surgeons as having an excellent effect when its edge is passed lightly over the affected region before applying an astringent dressing, such as the three sulphates as recommended by Malcolm and others. After the diseased surface has been sloughed away apply an antiseptic powder, such as iodoform, or a mixture of it with starch and oxide of zinc, or powdered chinosol. As the cases progress favourably, avoid the frequent use of caustics, and depend chiefly on antiseptic powder associated with pressure.

7. In arranging for pressure, take precautions to have it firm and equally distributed. The pledgets of tow should be in the form of hard cords of assorted sizes for adaptation to the different parts of the foot, care being taken that the lacunæ of the frog are well packed with rolls of corresponding shape and size. Apply a series of large thick pledgets on the outside. Bring pressure on the tow either by means of pieces of hoop-iron bent in the form of a bow to permit of their ends being introduced beneath the foot surface of the shoe, where they are driven in by striking the convexity with a hammer, or by a metal sole driven in from behind between the shoe and the hoof or screwed on to the sole of the shoe. The strips of iron are more satisfactory than a metal sole. To carry out these measures thoroughly it is generally necessary to have the horse fixed in stocks or cast, and when vegetations have to be removed general anæsthesia is advisable. The case should be dressed daily for a while until considerable improvement occurs, when the intervals between the dressings are gradually extended until once per week proves sufficient, the surgeon being guided by the state of the lesion. If lameness be absent it is an advantage to keep the horse working. During the early stages of the treatment, the severity of the dressings and the great pressure exerted on the exposed sensitive tissues may cause some lameness and necessitate keeping the horse idle for a while. Working on dry clay favours recovery, and may be sufficient of itself to effect a cure should it be possible to continue it for a long period.

8. The administration of arsenic has long been known as beneficial in the treatment of the affection, and comparatively recently the late Major Holmes, R.A.V.C., found, when treating surra in India with a course of arsenic, that those animals which happened to be affected with canker at the same time were cured of the latter disease by this treatment. In the United Kingdom, however, it has not proved a specific.

Nairn (Blairgowrie) claims to have got excellent results with the following application in the form of a paste :

Creta Prep. . . . . . . ℥iii.
Plumbi Nit. . . . . . . ℥i.
Formalin . . . . . . ℈ii.
Ol Rapii . . . . . . qs.

He has found cases affecting the perioplic ring causing a " groggy " gait and effected a cure by rasping down the separated horn at the coronet and applying the paste (*Veterinary Record*, Vol. 11, No. 6). He insists that the dressing must be thoroughly carried out.

Corns

A corn is a contusion of the sensitive tissues at the heel in the angle between the wall and the bar, the structure affected being the sensitive tissue of the sole, wall, or bar. The condition is most common in horses working in cities. In an ordinary recent or dry corn there is merely an escape of blood from the injured vessels, causing more or less staining or ecchymosis of the overlying horn in a punctiform, linear, or diffuse manner. If the cause be repeated, the condition becomes aggravated and the inflammation becomes more severe, but remains aseptic so long as there is no breach in the horn to allow the entrance of infection. When the contusion is severe, the horn in the affected part becomes infiltrated with serum or the latter may accumulate beneath the horn, giving rise in either case to a " *moist corn*." When infection ensues through an accidental fissure in the horn, or as the result of excessive paring of it, the lesion suppurates, and a *suppurating* or *festered* corn is produced. The corn is said to be *complicated* when it is accompanied by necrosis of any of the tissues in the vicinity, such as the laminæ, the plantar cushion, the plantar aponeurosis, or the lateral cartilage.

ETIOLOGY.—Corns are very rare in unshod feet. Consequently, shoeing is blamed as the primary cause of the affection. Any defect in shoeing which results in excessive pressure being brought to bear on the seat of corn favours the latter. Fitting the shoe very close on the inside to avoid the risk of brushing may have this effect, and the frequency with which this is done probably accounts for corns being more common in the inner heel. Faulty conformation of the limbs, causing unequal distribution of weight on the foot, is a predisposing cause, and it is for this reason that a corn is more often present in the outer heel when the toe is turned in. Interference with the anti-concussion mechanism, such as is caused by atrophy of the frog, high-heeled shoes preventing the frog reaching the ground, high contracted heels preventing expansion of the posterior region of the foot, upright pasterns causing increased concussion on the bony column of the limb, favours the production of the lesion. Fast work on hard roads, especially in the case of heavy horses, is a fruitful source of contusion of the heels if the shoeing is not carefully attended to

That concussion is a prime factor in producing corns is proved by the fact that they are very rare in the hind-feet, while they are very common in the fore-feet, where concussion is greater. Wide spreading feet with low weak heels are very likely to become affected, owing to the horn affording insufficient protection to the sensitive tissues of the region where the shock is greatest. Leaving the shoes on too long causes them to be drawn forwards by the growing wall, and may thus result in their heels being brought to bear on the seat of corn and to give rise to the affection. A stone accidentally fixed between the heel of the shoe and the frog may cause a bruise in this situation.

SYMPTOMS.—A corn during the acute stage is characterised by local symptoms of a contusion, with more or less acute inflammation, and by a varying degree of lameness. The local phenomena are in accordance with the nature of the lesion. Pain is evinced on percussion and compression of the affected heel. Abnormal heat is revealed on palpation. In the case of a dry corn, paring the horn in the affected region discloses the staining of its deeper layers, varying from a glassy yellowish appearance to a deep red tinge, occupying an area of varying dimensions in different cases. In a moist corn the overlying horn is infiltrated with serum, which makes it moist in its deeper parts, or the liquid may accumulate beneath it and escape when an exit is made with the knife. When suppuration supervenes the inflammation is very intense, and if the pus is not allowed to escape by removing the horn which confines it, it will extend upwards to the coronet and become discharged through the medium of an abscess. The pain is very acute until the pus gets an outlet, when it is greatly relieved. When a sinus persists it is due to necrosis of some of the tissues in the region, caused by the bacteria present, and a probe passed into it will give an idea of the depth of the lesion and of the part affected.

Quittor is a common sequel to suppurating corn, and is very likely to ensue after the pus has reached the coronet, and when it does supervene in this case the orifice of the first abscess between hair and hoof does not constitute the opening of the quittor, which forms at a higher level by the bursting of a secondary abscess after the primary one has healed. The sinus may also abut on the plantar aponeurosis or on the os pedis. The lameness varies in degree, according to the nature of the local lesion. In a well-marked case the horse goes on his toe with the heels clear of the ground, and when standing points the affected foot, resting it only on the toe. When both feet are involved the animal has a pottering gait, and at rest points the two feet alternately. In " suppurating " corn the lameness is extreme until vent is given to the pus. In an old-standing case of corn in which the pain and lameness have disappeared, the only indication of the lesion will be the discoloration revealed on paring the horn.

DIAGNOSIS is easily made out from the symptoms. The changes in the horn at the seat of corn are characteristic.

PROGNOSIS.—A simple contusion is of little or no consequence, lameness being slight or perhaps absent. When the contusion is more severe the case is more serious, causing pronounced lameness, which may persist for a considerable time. Purulent corn is serious on account of the troublesome complications to which it may give rise. Once a corn is established, recurrent lameness is apt to ensue. Hence it is an unsoundness.

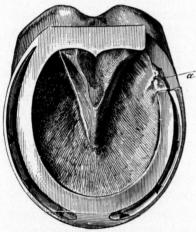 

FIG. 397.—THREE-QUARTER BAR SHOE.
a, Seat of the corn.

FIG. 398.—ORDINARY THREE-QUARTER SHOE.

TREATMENT consists in removing the cause and adopting the usual methods for dealing with inflammation, or an abscess, or a sinus, as the case may be. Removal of the offending shoe may be all that is necessary. Paring the horn over the corn has a decidedly good effect in relieving tension on the affected part, but care must be exercised not to overdo it by wounding the sensitive tissues and causing the risk of infection. When suppuration supervenes, a free exit must be made for the pus by removing the underrun horn, and the foot should be immersed in an antiseptic bath for half an hour to an hour morning and evening until the discharge ceases, the lesion being protected in the meantime by an antiseptic compress or a dry dressing. The wound in the sensitive tissues usually granulates excessively, owing to the irritation caused by the edges of the cut horn. The exuberant granulations must be removed with the knife or caustic, the wound being afterwards treated with an astringent or slight caustic to prevent recurrence. When suppuration has extended upwards beneath the wall, it is advisable to remove a ʌ-shaped portion of the wall to ensure the escape of the pus. Complications must be treated according to their nature, the principles of treatment being those of a sinus. When the wound following a suppurating corn has healed and is covered with horn, and in all cases where the horse is going sound, a shoe having no bearing on the affected region and a leather sole with tar and tow should be applied. An ordinary shoe with the wall shortened so as not to bear on it at the affected heel, or a shoe truncated or excavated on its foot surface, or a bar shoe with the bar resting on the frog, or a three-quarter bar shoe, the iron being omitted opposite the seat of corn, may be used.

Pricks in Shoeing

A prick or wound caused by driving a nail into the sensitive tissues in the act of nailing on a shoe is of two kinds—viz., (1) where the offending nail is withdrawn immediately after being driven, and (2) where it is not withdrawn. Another variety of the lesion similar to the second one is caused by an old stump remaining in the wall since the previous shoeing, being driven into the subcorneal tissues by the force of the newly-driven nail, which comes in contact with it.

ETIOLOGY.—The accident is favoured by several circumstances, such as :

1. *Contraction of the hoof*, rendering the wall less oblique, and thereby making the nail more likely to take an inward course.

2. *Thinness of the horn*, which accounts for pricking being more common in the inner than in the outer quarter of the foot.

3. *Want of skill* on the part of the doorman in failing to drive the nail properly.

4. *Faulty workmanship* in making the shoe, stamping the holes too coarse or too oblique, causing the nails, when driven, to be diverted towards the sensitive laminæ.

5. *Badly-shaped nails*, the malformation making the nail take a wrong course.

6. *Restiveness* of the horse, resulting in the animal violently snatching his foot from the shoer when the nail is only partly driven, and stamping the foot with great force on the ground and forcing the nail into the flesh. The lesion is more common in hind- than in fore-feet, due

probably to the fact that the horn is more upright behind than in front, and that the hind-foot is often more difficult to control than the fore-foot.

During the busy time when horses are being roughed for frost, the hurried way in which shoes are put on after being removed may lead to pricking. The amount of damage done by the nail will, of course, vary according to the depth of the injury and the part affected. The nail may merely touch the sensitive laminæ, or it may wound or even fracture the pedal bone.

SYMPTOMS.—During the process of shoeing it may be recognised that the nail is being wrongly driven by (*a*) the sound of the hammer-ing, which, instead of becoming clearer, becomes duller, due to the nail entering the soft tissues ; (*b*) the nail meeting with less resistance

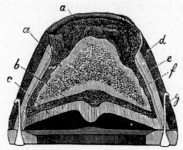

FIG. 399.—CROSS-SECTION OF A SOUND AND WELL-SHOD HOOF, SHOWING THE
PROPER POSITION OF THE NAILS.

a, Pedal bone ; *b*, sensitive sole ; *c*, horny sole ; *d*, horn wall ; *e*, dark-coloured
outer layer of wall ; *f*, laminal sheath ; *g*, nails.

as it penetrates deeply, showing that it is not taking an outward course towards the hard surface of the wall ; (*c*) resentment of the horse, which snatches away the limb suddenly ; (*d*) blood appearing on the nail when it is withdrawn or oozing from the orifice in the horn. The blood, however, may be wiped off the nail in its passage through the horn, and the hole in the latter may close by its walls falling into contact, thus preventing the escape of blood. The flinching of the horse may be prevented by the use of a twitch or ascribed to temperament in a fidgety animal. A simple prick, where the nail is immediately with-drawn and the nail-hole left vacant, is usually of no consequence, but when the nail is left more or less embedded in the soft tissues, lameness supervenes immediately or may be delayed for a day or perhaps several days.

The DIAGNOSIS of the cause of the lameness is easy. The horse having been recently shod, irregularity of the clenches, one or more

being unusually high, and perhaps the absence of a nail, arouse suspicion which is confirmed by examination of the foot revealing
symptoms of inflammation at the seat of injury. Pain is evinced on
percussion, and abnormal heat is felt on palpation. Cutting the clench
of the offending nail and traction on the corresponding branch of the
shoe in removing it are resented by the patient. When the nail which
caused the injury is withdrawn, it is seen to be black from the action
of the sulphur of the horn on the iron. A greyish-whitish or blackish
discharge escapes from the hole in the horn. When the nail-bed is
pared out it is found to be surrounded by soft, blackish horn, infiltrated with the purulent discharge, and more or less separated from
the subcorneal tissue.

PROGNOSIS.—A simple slight prick of the sensitive tissues in which
the nail is at once extracted and omitted is usually of no consequence,
neither pain nor lameness supervening. The other form of prick
caused by the nail being left inserted in the sensitive laminæ may have
serious consequences, such as diffuse inflammation of the foot, or
necrosis of the horn-secreting structures, the os pedis, or the lateral
cartilage.

TREATMENT.—When the prick has been discovered during the
shoeing it is usually sufficient to leave the corresponding nail-hole
vacant, but to prevent the possibility of infection a little antiseptic
solution may be poured into the orifice, or the latter may be closed by
collodion, or a red-hot nail may be passed rapidly into the hole in the
horn and quickly withdrawn to act as a germicide. This is a common
practice with farriers. Should a severe wound be inflicted, the horn
all round the track of the nail should be thinned to favour the exit of
discharge in case any may form as the result of infection of the wound,
which should be prevented as far as possible by antiseptic applications,
such as a little pure or strong solution of carbolic or creolin passed into
the orifice, or the use of a foot-bath. No lameness may ensue ; if it
does, the treatment should be continued, and the horse kept at rest
until it disappears. In the case where inflammation and suppuration
have taken place before the condition is detected, or as a sequel to
infection in the first case, the shoe must be removed, the horn thinned
in the vicinity of the affected region, and the foot immersed in an
antiseptic bath for half an hour to an hour morning and evening until
the discharge ceases and the lameness disappears, the part being protected in the meantime by an antiseptic dressing kept in position by a
boot or poultice bag. When suppuration is extensive beneath the wall,
it is advisable to remove a portion of the latter to provide free drainage

62

and relieve pressure on the inflamed area. There is usually no difficulty with the case when treated on these lines, provided that some of the complications mentioned have not arisen, when special measures may be required according to the case, as described elsewhere. When the horse is sound, a dressing of tar and tow should be applied over the seat of the lesion, and kept in position by a leather sole. The animal is then fit to go to work.

Nail Binding

The condition known as " nail binding " is that caused by driving a nail or nails too close to the sensitive laminæ without wounding them, but causing more or less pain or discomfort by pressure thereon. It most commonly occurs in feet with a thin crust.

SYMPTOMS.—The affection is manifested by cramped action or lameness, which is usually slight, and by symptoms of mild local inflammation—viz., pain on percussion or compression, and some abnormal heat on palpation of the affected part.

TREATMENT.—Removal of the shoe and the application of cold or hot compresses for two or three days have the desired effect. A prick is generally suspected, and if care is not exercised in searching for it the sensitive tissues may be wounded and infected, complicating the condition.

Bruised Sole

Contusion of the sole may be caused by treading heavily on a projecting or loose stone, or by a badly-fitting or displaced shoe. The bearing surface of the hoof on the shoe should be confined to the wall, the white line, and a narrow strip of the sole where it adjoins the wall.

The SYMPTOMS and TREATMENT are similar to those described for " corns."

Contracted Hoof

A contracted hoof is one whose wall has become contracted or shrunken in one or more situations, usually in the regions of the quarter and heel on one or both sides of the foot. The condition is more common in the fore- than in the hind-foot.

ETIOLOGY.—Anything causing dryness or brittleness of the horn, or which prevents expansion of the hoof, favours its contraction—for example :

1. *Injudicious use of the rasp*, filing the outer surface of the wall, and thereby removing the periople, which prevents evaporation and consequent dryness and shrinking of the horn, and also removing some

of the superficial horn fibres, thus exposing the deeper ones to the action of the air, and allowing them to become dry and contracted.

2. *Chronic lameness*, diminishing the activity of the foot, and consequently its expansion.

3. *Excessive paring of the frog*, causing it to become dry and contracted, and preventing its coming in contact with the ground to promote dilatation of the heel region of the foot.

4. *Mutilating the bars*, and in this way removing or weakening the buttresses or stays of the wall, and permitting it to fall inwards at the heels.

5. *Shoeing with calkins* or thick-heeled shoes, absolutely preventing the frog bearing on the ground. This want of frog pressure is probably the chief cause of the abnormality.

SYMPTOMS.—When the foot is on the ground and viewed from in front the deformity is noticed, and when unilateral the contrast between the two sides of the hoof is very striking. When looked at from the plantar aspect, the marked difference in length of the antero-posterior and transverse diameters of the hoof is observed, the former being decidedly in excess of the latter, whereas a normal fore-foot is about as broad mesially as it is long. The narrowness is most noticeable in the posterior part of the quarters and at the heels. The normal length of the hoof is not altered. The bars are less divergent posteriorly than usual, having a tendency to approach each other behind. The frog is always more or less atrophied, and the lateral lacunæ are abnormally deep. Frequently the horn is dry and brittle. Lameness may be present as the result of the contraction alone, or of the disease which gave rise to it.

PREVENTION of the deformity consists in avoiding the causes mentioned, and above all in maintaining frog pressure as far as possible by shoeing with tips or thin-heeled shoes, or by the Charlier system, even temporarily, by leaving the frog intact when preparing the hoof, and by the use of rubber pads, causing bearing on the frog when the latter is insufficiently developed to reach the ground with an ordinary shoe applied.

TREATMENT comprises : (1) Improvement of the method of shoeing, (2) the use of dilating or expanding shoes, and (3) grooving the wall to permit of its expansion.

(1) Improvement in the method of shoeing may be sufficient in slight cases, such as substituting flat shoes for those with calkins, or adopting some of the measures mentioned under the heading of prevention.

(2) The use of mechanical means to cause expansion of a contracted foot is not much in vogue, although several special shoes have been invented for the purpose, especially on the Continent. None of them is of sufficiently proved merit to deserve description. A shoe whose bearing surface, instead of being horizontal, is made to slope downwards and outwards is believed to have some effect in expanding the hoof.

(3) When the hoof is decidedly contracted, and especially if lameness is present, the best treatment is to groove the horn as described (p. 471).

Side-Bones

A side-bone is an ossified lateral cartilage.

ETIOLOGY.—The actual exciting cause of side-bones is not always clear. The ossification of the cartilage may be due to :

1. *Heredity*, as apparently obtains in draft-horses, in which side-bones are very common, without any visible external cause to account for them.

2. *A natural tendency for cartilage continuous with bone to become ossified*, as occurs in the development of bone.

3. *Concussion*, causing shock or inflammation of the bone at the base of the cartilage, stimulating proliferation of the osteoblasts, which then invade the cartilage. The prevalence of side-bones in heavy horses, their comparative rarity in light horses, and the fact that they are seldom associated with inflammation do not support this theory as a common cause of their occurrence. Anything which favours concussion would act as a cause under this heading—*e.g.*, interference with the anti-concussion mechanism of the foot, such as contracted heels and absence of frog pressure. Side-bones being practically confined to the fore-feet is evidence in favour of the concussion theory, as is also the fact that cart-horses are usually shod with calkins in front, which increase the shock on the region of the heels.

4. *Direct violence*, such as a blow, a tread, or a weight falling on the foot. Side-bone has often occurred in this way on the outer side of the inner limb of horses working in pairs.

SYMPTOMS.—When the lateral cartilage becomes ossified it also increases in size, and in some instances assumes enormous proportions. The presence of ossification is revealed by the absence of flexibility in the structure, recognised by compressing the two structures at the same time with the fingers and thumb from above with the foot on the ground and by grasping each with the finger and thumb and trying to bend it with the foot on and off the ground. The entire cartilage is usually involved. In the early stages of the process its upper portion may not be affected. The condition is non-inflammatory, there being no evidence of pain, heat, or exudation. Side-bones *per se* are therefore not likely to be a cause of lameness, although indirectly they may act as such, especially in horses doing fast road work and in those with contracted feet, owing to their favouring concussion by preventing expansion of the posterior part of the foot, and leading to corns or compression and pain of the sensitive tissues beneath the hoof. A side-bone may be present on the inside or outside of the foot, or in both situations, and in one or both fore-limbs. It is rare in a hind-foot.

DIAGNOSIS is easy when the whole cartilage is transformed into bone, but there is sometimes difference of opinion as to whether it is partially ossified or normal, or in the former event whether it should be classified as a side-bone or not. When there is a doubt, one is justified in giving the horse the benefit of it.

PROGNOSIS.—Side-bones in horses with good open feet doing slow work are of no consequence. They are present in a large proportion of cart-horses without causing lameness. In animals intended for fast work on the road and in those with contracted feet they are serious, for the reasons stated.

TREATMENT.—If side-bones are not associated with pain or lameness no treatment is indicated. Nothing can be done to get rid of the side-bone except operation (p. 472), which is seldom desirable, and can have little or no beneficial effect except the removal of an unsightly enlargement when the structure is very prominent. Counter-irritation by blistering or firing, or both, is sometimes done on the assumption that lameness, when present, is due to chronic inflammation in the new bone. When the hoof is contracted, grooving it is indicated to permit of its expansion and relieve pressure on the subcorneal tissues (see p. 471).

Quittor

Quittor is a sinus opening on the coronet at the level of the lateral cartilage, and due to necrosis of this structure.

ETIOLOGY.—The cause of the condition may be :

1. *Injury and infection* of the cartilage, such as may result from a tread on the coronet, causing a contused or punctured open wound, which is more likely to occur when the shoes have calkins, and especially when the latter are sharpened for frost.

2. *Necrosis of the skin* in the affected region from the combined effects

of cold and septic mud, the infection spreading subsequently to the cartilage.

3. *A suppurating corn or sandcrack*, or lesion resulting from *a punctured wound or a picked-up nail*, from which suppuration extends to the cartilage.

The cartilage may be involved in an open wound without undergoing necrosis, but the latter is very likely to ensue owing to the feeble vascularity of the part, making it an easy prey to the organisms invading the wound. Once necrosis begins in the cartilage, it has a great tendency to gradually affect the whole structure on account of its poor blood supply and the close continuity of the dead and healthy parts. Spontaneous separation of the necrotic piece of cartilage may, however, take place, and should it escape with the discharge natural cure will result. This is much more likely to occur posteriorly than anteriorly, because in the former situation the cartilage is more interspersed with fibrous tissue, separating it into islets, which are comparatively easily detached.

SYMPTOMS.—The symptoms are those of a sinus, with a combination of more or less acute and chronic inflammation in its vicinity. The inflammatory swelling varies in size according to the extent of the disease. It may correspond only to a part or the whole of the cartilage. It projects beyond the level of the hoof, and bulges it outwards at the coronet. It generally begins at the heel and spreads thence forwards. It is more or less painful on manipulation, the pain being usually most marked when the antero-inferior extremity of the cartilage is affected, and being always very acute when an abscess is being formed. When the skin is unpigmented the redness due to the inflammation is noticeable, and varies in intensity according to the acuteness of the condition. The sinus has usually only one orifice on the coronet, but rarely it has two or more openings here, and they all communicate with the necrotic centre. The entrance to the sinus may be only large enough to admit a probe, and is often obscured by a mass of granulations, but it may be infundibuliform in shape. It is constantly weeping or discharging a greyish purulent fluid, which may be streaked with blood, due to rupture of some of the capillaries in the granulation tissue of the part. The calibre of the sinus varies in different cases. It may be branched. Its course is usually oblique, a common direction being downwards and forwards, terminating on the wing of the os pedis in well-established cases. When the condition is a complication of a corn or sandcrack, there may be a plantar or parietal sinus respectively, in addition to that of the coronet, or rarely the latter may be absent until the disease has been in existence for a considerable time. There may be one or more cicatrices on the skin over the swelling, representing orifices that have healed after the pus had gained exit in a new situation through the medium of a secondary abscess. Afterwards some horizontal rings or rugæ form on the wall beneath the affected part, due to the latter interfering with the secretory function of the coronary band in this region. By noticing the depth to which these extend and remembering that the horn grows at the rate of $\frac{1}{4}$ to $\frac{3}{8}$ inch per month, one can estimate approximately the duration of the affection. The degree of lameness varies according to the nature of the lesion. When the superior or posterior part of the cartilage is only affected it is slight or absent, but when the disease is in the vicinity of the antero-lateral ligament, or when the latter is involved, it is very marked. If arthritis supervene, its symptoms will be manifested.

COMPLICATIONS.—The complications which may arise are :

1. *Necrosis of the antero-lateral ligament*, which may in consequence become ulcerated, thus exposing the joint to infection.

2. *Septic arthritis* resulting from No. 1 or from perforation of the cul-de-sac of the synovial membrane of the articulation where it comes in contact with the antero-internal aspect of the cartilage, allowing infection of the joint.

3. *Necrosis of the os pedis.* Infection may spread from the cartilage to the os pedis, causing necrosis or caries thereof. If this occur near the articular surface, septic arthritis may supervene.

4. *Necrosis of the sensitive laminæ or plantar cushion*, or *plantar aponeurosis*, the latter being rare. The plantar aponeurosis is more likely to be affected when the quittor results from a suppurating corn than when it arises in some other way.

5. *An abscess*, which forms at the inner side of the cartilage and bursts on the skin.

6. *Gangrene of the skin* over the affected region.

DIAGNOSIS is generally easy on account of the circumscribed swelling at the level of the cartilage and the presence of the sinus. A probe passed into the sinus abuts on the hard cartilage. Wounds of the coronet and abscesses not involving the cartilage heal easily.

PROGNOSIS.—Quittor is an obstinate affection having practically no tendency to spontaneous cure, and often resisting ordinary therapeutic measures for months. The condition is not so serious when confined to the superior or posterior part of the cartilage, as already explained. Operative treatment is nearly always successful. Great depth of the sinus and a copious discharge of pus indicate that treatment other than operation is not likely to succeed. The presence of complications, of course, aggravates the affection. The lesion is perhaps more easily dealt with in the hind- than in the forelimb, because the cartilage is less dense and more vascular in the former.

TREATMENT.—The principles of treatment are those of a sinus, and comprise measures for the removal of the necrotic tissue, the provision of drainage for the pus, and the destruction of bacteria, with the object of causing a healthy granulating wound which will heal and bring about recovery. The method of procedure may be :

1. *The Injection of an Antiseptic Liquid* by means of a syringe with a long narrow nozzle into the depth of the sinus two or three times daily in order to flush out loose necrotic tissue, arrest the development of bacteria, render the lesion sterile, and thus allow healing to take place. This may succeed in a recent case where the sinus is not deep and the necrotic cartilage is near the surface—that is, affecting its upper or posterior border. Otherwise it is generally a failure, the affected part being too deep-seated to be effectively acted upon by the injection or to permit of the escape of necrotic material. To obtain the best result, it is necessary to enlarge the entrance to the sinus in order to facilitate reaching the affected area with the germicidal agent. The patient resents this treatment, and it is generally disappointing in its results.

2. *The Injection of a Caustic Liquid.*—This is more effective than No. 1, the agent being a more powerful germicide and having an escharotic effect, which brings about separation of necrotic tissue and the removal of the lining of the sinus, thereby opening it up and facilitating the escape of necrotic debris and purulent matter. It is carried out in the same way as No. 1, and when thoroughly done it often effects a cure within two or three weeks, the discharge becoming gradually less and the inflammation and lameness disappearing by degrees. It is, however, by no means infallible, and is contra-indicated when the sinus is deep and anteriorly situated, on account of the risk of sloughing the thin layer of tissue protecting the joint in this region and causing arthritis. Various preparations have been used with more or less success, including the following : (*a*) Corrosive sublimate 1 and alcohol 10 ; (*b*) corrosive sublimate 17, methylated spirit 140, hydrochloric acid 2 to 4, acetate of lead 34 ; (*c*) sulphate of zinc 5 to 10 per cent. solution ; (*d*) chloride of zinc 5 to 10 per cent. The result depends not so much on the agent used as the manner in which it is applied to ensure its reaching the affected part. It is a painful procedure which is strongly resented by the patient.

3. *The Use of Solid Caustics*—that is, the introduction into the bottom of the sinus of a caustic in the form of a powder, or pencil, or plug, the one most commonly and successfully employed being corrosive sublimate. To allow of its deep insertion it is necessary to open up the sinus with a knife. The powder may be enveloped in blotting paper to enable it to be passed into the sinus. It has the effect of causing an eschar or slough, which comes away in the course of ten to fifteen days, carrying with it the diseased cartilage in favourable cases, and leaving a gaping granulating wound, which rapidly heals. A second application of the caustic may be necessary in some cases where a portion of the necrotic cartilage remains *in situ* after the separation of the eschar. This procedure is spoken of as the coring treatment, on account of the formation of the eschar or " core." It often fails, owing to the agent employed not " touching the spot." Used in the vicinity of the joint, it may lead to opening of the latter, with fatal consequences.

4. *The Use of the Thermo-Cautery.*—A red-hot iron rapidly plunged into the lowest part of the sinus and rapidly withdrawn has often proved effective in sloughing out its lining, including the necrotic cartilage, while at the same time it acts as a powerful bactericide. Its use is dangerous in the vicinity of the joint, on account of risk of penetrating it with the instrument, which must be inserted more or less blindly without any reliable guide as to its exact course or depth which it reaches. If not inserted deeply, it will not have the desired effect when the sinus is deep.

5. *A Combination of Nos. 3 and 4*, which is often employed, and proves more successful than either alone. All these caustic preparations cause severe inflammation, rendering interference with the part very painful and provocative of resentment on the part of the horse, which may become very restive and difficult to control.

6. *The Use of a Seton* or piece of tape passed into the sinus above and brought out through the wall of the hoof at the level of the bottom of the suppurating tract to ensure drainage through a counter-opening and to enable a caustic applied on the seton to be brought into contact with all parts of the lesion, a method of treatment which has often proved efficacious.

7. *The Bier Treatment* alone or combined with one of the foregoing methods. Very favourable reports have been given of its efficacy. It should always be tried (see p. 260).

8. *Operation to remove the Cartilage.*—See p. 460.

Acute Laminitis

Acute inflammation of the sensitive laminæ may occur in all the feet or in both fore- or both hind-feet, or in one foot, but never in only two diagonal or two lateral feet.

ETIOLOGY.—This comprises (1) predisposing causes, (2) exciting causes.

(1) *Predisposing Causes.*—These include :

(a) *Heavy Body-Weight*, big, heavy horses or those whose bodies seem too heavy for their limbs, like fat ponies and idle heavy stallions, being likely subjects.

(b) *Unfit Condition.*—Horses being left in the stable for days, without or with insufficient exercise, and then made to go a long journey, often become affected at the end of the latter. Young horses put to work for the first time are apt to suffer from the disease if made to do more work than their immature condition is fitted to bear.

(c) *Plethora.*—Plethoric subjects are more susceptible than those in moderate hard condition.

(d) *Hot Weather* favours the onset of the malady.

(e) *Abnormal Conformation of the Feet.*—Flat, spreading feet and narrow, contracted feet are more often attacked than normal feet.

(2) *Exciting Causes.*—The exciting causes may be :

(a) *Errors in Diet*, such as overfeeding, especially on nitrogenous food—for example, oats, rye, barley, wheat, peas and beans—or taking a big feed of any stuff to which the animal is not accustomed. Too much green food may give rise to it, such as lucerne, sainfoin, and vetches. Horses eating too much of the gleanings in the harvest field sometimes become affected.

(b) *Overwork.*—Horses doing long fatiguing journeys by road frequently become affected in consequence of the prolonged concussion on the feet. When (a) and (b) are associated, the condition is still more likely to supervene.

(c) *Exposure to Cold and Damp*, which has been blamed as a cause on the Continent, but in Great Britain and Ireland it does not seem to have a predisposing or exciting effect in producing the disease. When it does appear under these circumstances, it seems to be of a rheumatoid nature.

(d) *Excessive Weight on One Foot*, which, owing to the presence of a painful lesion in the other limb, may cause laminitis in the former.

(e) *Toxæmia*, resulting from an infectious disease, such as purpura, pneumonia, or metritis, or from the absorption of toxins from the alimentary tract following an attack of colic. It is a very common complication of simple metritis in the mare.

SYMPTOMS.—The symptoms vary according as the disease affects one or two or four feet, and according to the acuteness of the attack. They are general and local.

General Symptoms.—The general symptoms are those of pain and fever. Pain is evinced by the attitude and expression of the patient. When the two fore-feet or all the feet are affected, the horse stands with the fore-limbs in front of the body and the hind-limbs well under it, his object being to let most of the weight fall on the heels. If the hind-limbs only are affected, he keeps all the feet under the body to make the fore-feet bear most of the weight, and so that the heels will bear most of the pressure on the hind-feet. The animal stands persistently and is very unwilling to move, and when forced to do so groans. When recumbent, he lies stretched out and is very reluctant to rise, being afraid of the pain caused by putting weight on the feet. During progression the gait is of a peculiar crouching character, the heels being put to the ground first and the feet lifted quickly, as if they were burned by contact with the earth. When only one foot is affected, weight is alternately placed on it and the other foot, which is always suffering from some other painful lesion. The expression is anxious and indicative of suffering. Fever is manifested by the usual symptoms of febrile disturbance. The temperature is 103° to 106° F. ; the pulse is frequent and strong in the early stages of the affection before exhaustion supervenes, when it becomes weak. It may be 70 to 120 per minute. The respirations are accelerated, due chiefly to the pain. The conjunctiva is injected.

The *Local Symptoms* are those of more or less acute inflammation. Abnormal heat is readily detected by placing the hand on the hoof, and throbbing can be felt in the digital arteries. Pain is evinced on the slightest percussion of the foot by the animal snatching it smartly from the ground. In the course of four to twelve days these symptoms usually subside and resolution sets in, the horse gradually regaining its normal condition. Sometimes, however, they become intensified, due to hæmorrhage or exudation taking place beneath the horn. Hæmorrhage is due to rupture of the inflamed and weakened laminæ by the pressure of the body-weight exerted through the os pedis. The blood accumulates between the wall and the os pedis, and its pressure on the sensitive laminæ causes excruciating pain, the patient lying prostrate, groaning and bathed in sweat. Occasionally some of the blood escapes at the coronet through a separation between the horn and the coronary

band.   Death soon follows in a bad case of this kind.   The collection
of inflammatory exudate in the same situation causes similar symptoms,
and some of it may ooze out between hair and hoof.   Gangrene may
supervene in one of the latter conditions, due to infection gaining entrance to the inflamed region.   Its onset is characterised by suppression
of the intense symptoms of inflammation and pain, giving the owner the
impression that the patient is better, but the cold sweat over the body,
the feeble, frequent, or imperceptible pulse, and the cold extremities
indicate that death is approaching.

DIAGNOSIS is generally easy after careful examination of the case,
which prevents the condition being confounded with tetanus, coronitis,
sprained back, or rheumatism.

PROGNOSIS.—The prognosis varies according to the nature of the
attack.   It is more serious when all the feet are affected than when
two or only one foot is involved.   The condition is generally more
grave in horses that have been doing fast work than in those that have
been engaged in slow work, in highly-strung nervous animals than in
those of lymphatic temperament, and in big than in small animals.
If a cure is not obtained within fourteen days, the affection is apt to
become chronic or still more acute and to terminate in death.   When
the symptoms are alarming in the beginning, the prognosis is generally
gloomy.

PREVENTION consists in avoiding the causes mentioned and in
keeping animals under good hygienic conditions.

TREATMENT.—Having put the horse in the roomy loose box with
short bedding (*e.g.* peat-moss) prompt and energetic treatment should
be adopted.   Its general principles are those recommended for fever
and acute local inflammation.

Constitutional Treatment comprises :

1. *Jugular Phlebotomy*, removing 1 to 2 gallons of blood in a sthenic
subject.   This has undoubtedly a good effect when promptly performed soon after the commencement of the attack.   The objection to
it is the risk of phlebitis.

2. *Purgation.*—Prompt purgation is decidedly beneficial.   Consequently the administration of eserine or arecoline or other quick-
acting drug hypodermically is indicated on account of its rapid effect.
Pilocarpine may be combined with the eserine.   Arecoline is particularly
efficacious, and is looked upon by some authorities as a specific, its
action being so frequently followed by immediate amelioration of the
disease.   It is not, however, invariably successful.

3. *The Administration of Febrifuges*, such as tincture of aconite,

salicylate of soda, quinine sulphate, spts. ether. nit., liq. ammon. acet., or sodium hyposulphite. Tincture of aconite is probably the most effective febrifuge in the early stages of an acute attack, but neither it nor any of the others has much influence on the course of the disease.

4. *Counter-irritation.*—On the Continent, counter-irritation of the upper part of the limbs, the chest, and abdominal walls by rubbing in a rubefacient application is done in order to cause a deviation of blood thereto from the feet, so as to relieve the congestion of the laminæ.

5. *Intravenous injection of " Anthisan " (Mepyramine Maleate)* a recently introduced chemo-therapeutic substance described as the most potent and least toxic of the synthetic antihistaminic agents. It is also indicated for other conditions including serum sickness and anaphylactic shock, hoven and lymphangitis. Reports indicate that it is an efficacious remedy for acute laminitis.

Local Treatment comprises :

1. *Cold Applications* in the form of a foot-bath, moist compresses, or constant irrigation. The foot-bath may be provided by a stream or pool, or by digging a hole in a clay floor in the stable or in the open, or by a thick bed of sawdust or sand saturated with cold water, the patient being allowed to stand in the bath for the greater part of the day or constantly. Cold swabs applied round the pastern and overhanging the hooves may be used in the interval between the baths, or instead of them, especially when the patient is recumbent. They should be kept cold by frequent or constant application of cold water. Continuous irrigation through a perforated rubber bracelet round the limb above the fetlocks, communicating with a rubber tube from a tank of water above the level of the horse, is a very effective means of carrying out this method of treatment. Ice-bags applied over the coronets would prove more beneficial than cold water.

2. *Astringent Applications*, to be used alternately with the cold applications, and including the usual refrigerant lotions, such as liquor plumbi subacetatis and white lotion.

3. *Bleeding from the Toe.*—Paring the horn of the sole at the toe and drawing blood from the sensitive tissues in this region has had considerable vogue, and is certainly a good method of relieving congestion in the inflamed part ; but it has the serious objection that it opens the way for infection and its dangerous sequelæ, suppuration and gangrene. When it is done, antiseptic precautions are essential.

4. *Hot Applications.*—Hot poultices or hot, moist compresses are favoured by some practitioners, but they are probably not so useful as the cold treatment.

5. *Hypodermic Injection of Adrenalin.*—The hypodermic injection of adrenalin in a dose of 20 to 30 minims diluted with an equal quantity of normal saline solution over each digital artery may have a marked beneficial effect, causing a rapid fall in the temperature and a decided and prompt improvement in the animal's gait. Nevertheless, it is not an infallible agent for bringing about a cure, and sometimes it is followed by sloughing of the skin at the seat of injection.

6. *Hypodermic Injection of a local anæsthetic* over the plantar nerves, removing sensation for a while from the feet, gives the patient some intervals of ease, allowing him to rest and recover to some extent from the exhaustion caused by suffering, and facilitates exercise, which has a good effect in dispelling the congestion by stimulating the circulation in the foot.

7. *Bier's Treatment*, the explanation of the good effect in this case being that the venous congestion increases phagocytosis, and leads to an outpouring of serum containing antibodies which act beneficially in counteracting the effects of bacteria and their toxins, which may be present at the seat of the lesion.

8. *Grooving the Hoof* at the junction of the wall and the sole at the toe to permit of the escape of inflammatory exudate. This has the same objection as No. 3, otherwise it has the good effect of relieving pain.

9. *Ligation of the Digital Artery.*—See p. 459.

Exercise is an important indication recognised by most practitioners as having a marked effect in favouring resolution. It should be continued for twenty minutes to half an hour twice daily on soft ground. If the hoofs are strong, the horse may go bare-footed or wear ordinary shoes ; but if they have dropped soles, rocking shoes should be applied —that is to say, shoes thin at the toe and heels and thick in the centre, with a wide, well-seated-out web. Exercise is most efficacious when practised early in the attack. When the disease is well established its utility is doubtful. It has been observed during military marches that when affected horses are kept moving slowly behind the column recovery usually ensues, whereas if they are left at a station many cases prove fatal.

Diet.—Soft laxative diet should be prescribed, such as linseed and bran mashes, and grass if in season. A little magnesium sulphate and potassium nitrate in the drinking water has a febrifuge effect, and keeps the excretory organs active. When pain is very severe, a hypodermic injection of morphia may be given.

Chronic Laminitis

Chronic laminitis is a sequel to the acute form or appears spontaneously. It is characterised locally by changes in the form of the foot. It becomes elongated antero-posteriorly, narrow transversely, and somewhat flattened in front. The heels are higher than normal, and the wall approaches the horizontal direction in the region of the lower part of the toe, while in its upper part it is inclined to the vertical direction, so that its centre portion appears depressed or constricted. Rings or rugæ form on the wall parallel to the coronet, comparatively widely spaced behind and almost confluent in front. The sole is convex or flat anteriorly; the lateral lacunæ are abnormally deep, more so than in an ordinary flat-foot. The sole may be perforated in front of the frog, exposing the sensitive tissues, which become inflamed, emitting a serous, sanguinolent, or greyish purulent discharge, and may also undergo necrosis. The wall becomes separated from the laminæ in front, receding from the sole at the white line, the interspace being empty or filled with abnormal horn secreted by the laminæ. The space is widest at the centre of the toe, where it may measure 2 to 3 inches. When the condition follows the acute form, the symptoms of the latter have disappeared, but a certain amount of hypersensitiveness persists in the affected feet. The degree of lameness varies. It may be absent, but the gait is always abnormal, being characterised by the horse going decidedly on the heels. If an antero-posterior section of a chronic laminitic foot be made, the alterations in its conformation will be very evident. The wall is thicker than normal, projected forwards at the toe, and not parallel to the anterior surface of the os pedis, which is more vertical than usual.

Between the wall and the sensitive laminæ in front the space already mentioned is seen filled with homogeneous laminal horn or practically vacant, except for a small deposit of horn covering the laminæ. In a recent case there may be osteophytes on the bone, but in an old case it may show signs of atrophy. The mechanism by which these changes occur is probably as follows : The sensitive laminæ in front rupture, while those at the heels, being much less involved, remain intact, and in consequence the os pedis tends to descend anteriorly under the body-weight, and the perforans muscle, asserting its superiority over its antagonist, the extensor pedis, causes the bone to swing backwards on the horizontal axis formed by the intact laminæ at the sides, thus bringing the anterior plantar border of the bone to press on the sole,

causing it to bulge downwards and become flat or convex. In consequence of this pressure, the sensitive sole undergoes atrophy and ceases
to secrete horn. When the existing horn becomes worn away perforation takes place. The descent of the os pedis causes stretching and
bending of the papillæ on the coronary band, so that the horn formed
by them is more vertical than usual and thicker than normal, on account
of their secretory activity being stimulated by this interference. This
accounts for the prominence and upright direction of the horn near the

FIG. 400.—LONGITUDINAL SECTION OF
HOOF THREE MONTHS AFTER ATTACK.

a, Pathologically modified horn of the
white line ; *b*, distortion of the horn
tubules in consequence of sinking of
the os pedis.

FIG. 401.—LONGITUDINAL SECTION OF
HOOF ONE YEAR AFTER SEVERE ATTACK
OF LAMINITIS.

FIG. 402.—HOOF AFTER LAMINITIS.

coronet. During progression the horse puts most weight on the heels,
thus pushing the separated wall at the toe forwards and making it
approach the horizontal direction.

DIAGNOSIS is usually easy, even when the toe is shortened and the
rings removed by the rasp, the convexity of the sole, the deep lacunæ,
and the space between the wall and sole being characteristic.

PROGNOSIS.—The prognosis is unfavourable, the deformity and
abnormal gait persisting. Recurrent attacks of subacute inflammation
may supervene, especially after a long journey by road. For a long
time the horse affected can only be used at slow work on soft
ground.

TREATMENT comprises dressing of the feet and the application of appropriate shoes thus : Remove the excess of horn at the toe, but spare the horn on the sole quarters and heels. Apply a wide-webbed, well-seated-out shoe, so as to afford protection to the dropped sole without pressing on it. In order to avoid making the shoe very thick and heavy for the purpose of deep seating, a strip of leather may be interposed between the bearing surface of the shoe and the wall, so as to keep the former away from the sole. A leather plate is desirable as a protection to the sole. The horse generally goes best in long-heeled shoes whose heels project well behind those of the hooves, ensuring the posterior part of the foot striking the ground first, thus saving jar to the hypersensitive anterior laminal region. As time goes on the shape of the foot may improve. When the sole is perforated, immerse the foot in an antiseptic bath if inflammation is present, and after it has subsided dress the part with tar and tow and cover the sole with a metal plate fixed between the hoof and the shoe. When a subacute attack recurs, treat as for acute laminitis. Standing the animal in a cold bath for prolonged periods generally dispels the inflammatory symptoms.

Operative Treatment.—Removing the entire separated portion of the wall by means of the rasp has proved effective in promoting a normal growth of horn at the toe and obliterating the subparietal space in this region, and thereby causing the pedal bone to resume its normal position, with the result that the dropped sole disappeared. Mr. Baker, of Bansha (Ireland), has reported successful treatment in this way, and the writer, acting independently, has had a like experience in a racehorse in which the disease was confined to a fore-foot, causing lameness which rendered the animal unfit for racing.

AFFECTIONS OF THE FEET OF THE OX

Affections of the feet are not so common in the ox as in the horse. Even the working ox is less subject to inflammatory affections of the foot than the horse, due probably to the fact that the bovine works at a slower pace and that its digits are more mobile and elastic than those of the equine, the result being that the shock or concussion on the foot is less. Nevertheless, nearly all the diseases of the feet in the horse are met with in the ox.

Sandcrack

Sandcrack is more common in the fore-foot and in the outer aspect of the claw. The chief exciting cause is the force caused by the weight on the foot, especially during heavy draft.

63

TREATMENT is on the same principles as in the horse, but clasps or horseshoe nails cannot be employed, the horn being too thin to bear them. Transverse cracks parallel to the coronet are fairly common in the fore-feet. They may be due to separation of the horn at the coronary band, the separation appearing afterwards as a crack when the new horn has grown down, otherwise it is due to fracture of the horn. If the crack causes trouble, its lips should be thinned as described.

Contusion of the Sole

This is caused by treading on a hard, resistant body, such as a projecting stone. A long journey by road in unshod oxen or those wearing very thin shoes is a common cause of the condition, or it may be

due to the shoe being convex on its upper surface and causing too much pressure on the sole. Fat cattle driven a long distance to shows or fairs are frequent sufferers, their heavy weight being a contributory cause. It is more common in the hind-feet, owing to the horn being thinner there.

FIG. 403.—VERTICAL SECTION OF AN OX'S CLAW.

SYMPTOMS comprise lameness and local inflammation. When the animal is left at rest it lies down almost constantly, and when standing holds the affected limb in front of the other one. On examination of the foot, the seat of the lesion is detected by palpation, percussion, and paring. In a typical case the horn is ecchymosed, and may be softened and moist from infiltration with serum, and more or less separated from the underlying tissue. If the case has been neglected the separation may be extensive, involving the greater part of the sole and perhaps part of the wall, on account of the inflammation spreading and the serum or inflammatory exudate insinuating itself between the horn and the sensitive tissues, whose union is less intimate than in the horse. Should infection gain entrance, suppuration will supervene, and the inflammation will be intensified, and separation of the horn will occur more rapidly, leading in some cases to shedding of the hoof.

TREATMENT.—In slight cases, where the beasts are merely footsore or tender on their feet after walking a long distance by road, rest in the field or on soft litter is sufficient to bring about resolution. Otherwise the treatment is that advised for the same lesion in the horse.

Should necrosis supervene a sinus will develop, and must be treated accordingly by removing the dead tissue, providing drainage, and dressing antiseptically.

Pricks in Shoeing

These are more common in the ox than in the horse, owing to the horn of the hoof being thinner in the former. The lesion is the same as that in the horse.

Picked-up Nail or Open Wound of the Foot

The horn of the hoof being thinner than in the horse, it is more easily penetrated by sharp bodies, such as broken glass, but the commonest seat of injury in the ox is the interdigital space, where a foreign body frequently becomes lodged, such as a stone or a piece of wood.

SYMPTOMS are those of a punctured wound and of inflammation and lameness.

PROGNOSIS depends on the seat and depth of the injury. Complications which may arise are necrosis of the interdigital ligament, the tendon, or bone, and septic arthritis.

TREATMENT is the same as that described for the horse. If arthritis is present, or necrosis of the bone proves difficult to cure. the best treatment is to amputate the affected phalanx or phalanges, when healing will ensue without interruption (p. 472). A foreign body often becomes fixed between the claws, causing pain and lameness without wounding the tissues. Its removal gives immediate relief.

Separation of the Hoof

The hoof may be torn away from the foot in the same circumstances as in the horse. It will take three or four months for the new hoof to grow.

The TREATMENT is the same as in the horse.

Acute Laminitis

The condition is usually the result of walking a long distance by road. It may also be caused by long journeys by rail, the enforced standing and the shaking of the wagons accounting for the inflammation in the feet. Fat beasts, like those prepared for shows, are predisposed to the affection, owing to their great weight. One foot, or two fore- or two hind-feet, or all the feet may be affected. The inflammation may be more marked in the internal digit.

The SYMPTOMS are similar to those in the horse, the same attitude being assumed when standing, but the attack is generally less severe in the bovine. Febrile disturbance is present, with loss of appetite, and the animal loses condition rapidly.

PROGNOSIS.—Resolution is the rule, but in a severe case more or less separation of the horn occurs. Its onset is indicated by diffuse swelling of the digital region, by prominence of the coronet, which becomes dark red, and by symptoms of increased pain. About a week after the commencement of the disease a blood-stained serum escapes between the hoof and the coronet. The separation is generally confined to the posterior region of the foot, but it may extend farther and bring about shedding of the hoof. The disease seldom becomes chronic, although lameness sometimes persists from the flexor tendons becoming contracted, the abnormality being usually confined to the inner claw, with the result that excessive weight is then thrown on the other one, causing, perhaps, sprain of the ligaments of the fetlock and of the interphalangeal articulations, which may lead to periostitis and the formation of exostoses, the condition being then sometimes referred to as " big foot."

TREATMENT is on the same lines as in the horse, comprising jugular phlebotomy, purgation by sulphate of magnesia, or by the injection of arecoline, and local antiphlogistic applications. One should hesitate about bleeding, owing to the risk of phlebitis. The animal should be kept on a thick bed of short litter—peat, moss, or sawdust, or damped chaff. When separation of the horn occurs, antisepsis is necessary to prevent septic complications. When the sensitive tissues are covered by new horn, tar and tow covered by a piece of leather buckled round the pastern should be applied until the new wall is formed. After about a couple of months the animal may be fit to work on soft ground.

Simple Dermatitis of the Interdigital Region, or Scald

This condition is common. It is due to the action of an irritant on the skin, such as dirty wet bedding or mud.

SYMPTOMS.—There is inflammation in the interdigital region, the skin being red and swollen, and well-marked lameness is present.

TREATMENT.—Remove the cause by cleaning the foot and keeping the animal in a clean place, and apply some astringent, such as a 5 per cent. solution of sulphate or chloride of zinc, or sulphate of copper, or an ointment made with the latter, any of which soon effects a cure.

Toxic Dermatitis

This occasionally results from eating brewer's or distiller's grains, and may affect the digits. It is characterised by intense inflammation of the skin, and in some cases by necrosis, occurring in patches, which may extend to the deeper tissues and even involve a joint, causing septic arthritis. Constitutional symptoms of toxæmia may also be present.

TREATMENT.—The first indication is to remove the cause by stopping the grains. The local treatment is that for inflammation or necrosis, antiseptic applications being always necessary to counteract the effects of micro-organisms.

Chronic Vegetative or Verrucose Dermatitis of the Interdigital Space

This is characterised by chronic inflammation of the skin, which becomes thickened, red, and slightly painful. The thickening is noticed as a ridge or prominence appearing in front of the space between the claws. Later, owing to the persistence of the inflammation, granulations or vegetations, wart-like growths, swollen at their summits and arranged in tufts, due to hypertrophy of the papillæ of the skin, are formed. The condition is more common in the hind-than in the fore-feet. It may affect one or both feet. Occasionally both fore- and hind-feet are affected.

ETIOLOGY.—The lesion is apparently due to the constant action of an irritant on the skin of this region, as may result from an animal always standing on dirty wet bedding or in a muddy place, especially in cold weather. Frosty dew on the grass is sometimes blamed for causing the affection in animals on pasture. There is believed to be a predisposition to the malady.

SYMPTOMS.—In the early stages of the inflammation there is slight lameness, but this disappears after a while, when the condition becomes chronic, to reappear later, when acute inflammation is produced by the vegetations becoming pinched and injured between the claws during progression, causing them to ulcerate and suppurate. The digits are pushed apart by the presence of the vegetations.

TREATMENT comprises excision of the vegetations with the knife or scissors, and cauterisation of their bases with a mild caustic such as silver nitrate, or powdered sulphate of zinc, or sulphate of copper. The hot iron lightly applied may also be used ; it is caustic and styptic. It is necessary to have the animal well secured or fixed in the cast position to perform the operation, which must be done with the usual precautions under a local or general anæsthetic. The patient must be kept at rest in a perfectly dry, clean place until the wounds are healed. Astringent lotions, such as sulphate of zinc and acetate of lead, 1 ounce of each to a pint of water, will be necessary during the healing process to prevent the granulations becoming exuberant, which they have a tendency to do owing to the irritation caused by the movement of the claws. When they become excessive, the caustic must be applied to destroy them and make the wound level. A dry dressing of equal parts of zinc oxide and boric acid is indicated when the wound is uniformly granulating. It is astringent and absorbent, and tends to keep the granulations firm and healthy. It is kept in contact with the wound by means of a pledget of cotton-wool or tow, maintained in position by a bandage. Copper sulphate ointment is also a very useful application when a powerful astringent is required.

Foul in the Foot

Foul in the foot in its widest sense means a suppurating lesion in the interdigital region, but according to some authorities the term is confined to a necrotic lesion in this situation. In either case the condition is due to injury causing a breach of surface, and consequent infection of the part. It is often of the nature of a carbuncle or boil, with a necrotic centre or " core."

SYMPTOMS.—The symptoms are those of severe inflammation in the digital region, and of a suppurating wound, or an abscess, or a sinus in the interdigital space, with pronounced lameness and marked loss of condition. The sinus is due to the presence of necrotic tissue. The depth of the necrosis varies in different cases ; it may be confined to the skin, or affect the interdigital ligament, or the tendons, or extend into the joint, causing septic arthritis, which is characterised by extreme lameness and by a fœtid, purulent, synovial discharge. The necrotic centre is recognised by its yellowish-greyish colour, and by being surrounded by an inflammatory suppurating zone, causing a line of demarcation or separation, at the level of which the dead part may be eventually cast off. The death of the tissue is due to the presence of the bacillus of necrosis.

PROGNOSIS.—When the lesion is superficial, affecting only the skin and subcutaneous tissue, it responds promptly to simple treatment ; but when the ligament or tendon undergoes necrosis, resolution is very tedious, the dead tissue being slow to separate, owing to its feeble vascularity, and if the joint be infected, recovery is impossible without amputation of the digit.

TREATMENT is as usual for a septic wound, or abscess, or sinus, as the case may be, its principles being to overcome the action of the microbes by disinfection, by providing drainage for pus, and by the removal of necrotic tissue. When the case is recent, immerse the foot in a warm antiseptic bath and apply antiseptic compresses, as advised for septic foot lesions in the horse. When an abscess is present open it, and if necrosis supervene await the spontaneous separation of the dead part while using the antiseptic applications. If the separation is too slow, operate and excise the necrotic tissue ; or if the latter is very extensive or the joint is diseased, amputate the digit (see p. 472). Since the announcement, however, of C. R. Forman (*J. Amer. Vet. Med. Ass.*, **109**, 176–7, 1946) that he had found that the intravenous injection of 60 grammes of sodium sulphapyridine in 500 c.c. of distilled water is a specific non-toxic treatment for all forms of the disease, and this has been confirmed by other practitioners, the foregoing forms of treatment will not be necessary when this drug is available. By its use marked improvement occurs within 24 hours and complete recovery in from two days to two weeks. One injection is usually sufficient. The dose mentioned may be increased for very large bovines. He found that 90 grammes in 900 c.c. of distilled water caused only slight nervous reaction immediately after injection, but he considers that this is on the border of a toxic dose. In cases of long standing however, this treatment is not always successful.

Contagious Foul

Sometimes the condition just described appears as an enzootic in a herd, and is then believed to be due to contagion, and is consequently spoken of as " contagious foul." In this case the lesion is generally necrotic. Several animals in a field or shed become affected about the same time. No specific organism other than the bacillus of necrosis has been found in connection with the disease, and this is a common saprophytic microbe which may gain entrance to any wound or breach of surface convenient to its habitat.

TREATMENT is the same as for ordinary foul, associated with the usual prophylactic measures for a contagious disease.

Deformity of the Claws

This is due to the hoof becoming overgrown as the result of prolonged housing, preventing wear of the horn.

SYMPTOMS.—The toes become excessively long and are turned inwards or outwards, often overlapping in the former case. The sole becomes convex. When the deformity is well marked and allowed to persist for some time, it causes pain and lameness by preventing equal distribution of weight on the foot, and thereby over-stretching some of the ligaments of the interphalangeal joints. The animal lies more than usual, and when standing is fidgety on its feet.

TREATMENT consists in removing the excessive growth of horn by means of a fine sharp saw or a horn-cutting forceps and finishing off with the rasp. It may be necessary to cast the beast for the operation. If the sole is very prominent, it is advisable to level it to a slight extent with the rasp. Tar should be smeared on the hoof afterwards. Deformity may also result from chronic laminitis, a rare condition, and is then characterised by rings in the wall and by convexity and thinness of the sole. It may improve with time. Little can be done to remedy it.

AFFECTIONS OF THE FEET IN SHEEP

Traumatic Affections

The sheep's foot may be wounded in the same way as in other animals. A common seat of injury is the interdigital space, where infection may give rise to suppuration or necrosis, producing in the latter case a lesion similar to foul in the foot of the ox.

The SYMPTOMS will vary according to the nature of the condition, those of more or less acute inflammation being always present and causing a varying degree of lameness. When necrosis supervenes there is an intensely inflammatory swelling in the digital region, and the animal is unable to put the foot on the ground. The redness of the skin is very noticeable when it is not pigmented, and of course the pain on manipulation is very severe. The patient is feverish, and remains lying almost constantly.

TREATMENT.—Warm, moist antiseptic applications are indicated to overcome the action of the infecting bacteria and to hasten the removal of the slough in a case of necrosis. In the event of complications such as necrosis of the phalanges or arthritis, amputation of the affected part of the digit is necessary.

Inflammation of the Biflex Canal

The biflex canal is a double blind passage which opens on either side of the middle line of the digit about ¼ inch above the entrance to the interdigital space in front, its orifice being marked with a tuft of hair. The canal is not present in the goat.

ETIOLOGY.—Inflammation of the canal is due to irritation caused by foreign matter gaining entrance to it, wounding its lining, and leading to suppuration and necrosis.

SYMPTOMS.—There is inflammation in the affected region, and a fatty fœtid discharge oozes from the canal when it is compressed by the fingers. Gangrene may supervene. Lameness is pronounced, the animal remains lying most of the time, and if both limbs are affected progresses on the knees. Complications may arise in neglected cases from infection extending to the deep-seated tissues.

TREATMENT is on the same lines as for traumatic affections.

Foot Rot

This is a specific infectious disease of the feet in sheep.

ETIOLOGY.—The disease is due to a micro-organism in the soil which gains entrance to the subcorneal tissue and there produces its pathogenic effects. A favourite habitat of the organism is wet or marshy places, especially those soiled with an accumulation of excreta, such as dirty folds. When one case of the disease appears in such a place, it rapidly spreads through the flock if preventative measures are not adopted. The disease is rare in dry, upland districts. Allowing the hoofs to become overgrown, as often occurs in sheep on rich, low-lying pastures, owing to the horn not undergoing sufficient wear, favours the onset of the affection, as the superfluous horn becomes deformed, turned up at the toes, and splits, allowing dirt and infection to gain entrance to the sensitive tissues. The virulence of the causal organism becomes increased by its sojourn in the foot, thus accounting for the rapidity with which the malady spreads after a single case is established, and explaining why it has been described as a contagious disease, although it does not spread directly from sheep to sheep or even from one foot to another in the same animal, as has been proved by putting affected sheep with those not affected in a clean, dry place.

SYMPTOMS.—Lameness first attracts attention, and it varies in degree according to the stage of the disease. It is always well marked, and in typical cases the affected foot is not allowed to touch the ground. The animal commonly rests on the knees when grazing, and always does so when both fore-feet are attacked. If the hind- and fore-feet are involved, the animal is almost always lying, only changing its position when it has consumed all the grass within reach. The disease may commence in any part of the foot, wherever the bacteria have gained entrance, but it usually begins towards its inner aspect near the heel, where the first indication of its presence is separation of the horn, exposing the sensitive tissue, which appears inflamed and covered with a whitish exudate. After a while it becomes ulcerated and angry, and excessive granulations form as the result of the irritation caused by the edges of the separated horn. The horn becomes overgrown and curved for want of wear. If the infective process is not checked, necrosis of the ligaments and tendons and arthritis may supervene.

TREATMENT.—The first indication is to take measures to prevent further spread of the disease by isolating the affected animals and moving the in-contact subjects from the infected area to a clean, dry place after disinfecting their feet by walking them through a bath containing a reliable disinfectant, such as a 2 per cent. solution of copper sulphate or Jeyes' fluid. The sheepfold must be lime-dressed before it is used again. If the feet are overgrown, they should be pared. For the sheep slightly affected, the use of the bath mentioned once or twice daily is sufficient to effect a cure. Those in which the disease is well established require individual treatment. The separated and overgrown horn must be removed, and the inflamed tissues treated with an antiseptic or slightly caustic preparation. If there be a protruding mass of granulations it should be excised. Sulphate of copper ointment is an effective application, but when cauterisation is not necessary, iodine ointment, 1 to 20 of lard or vaseline, is preferable. It is essential to keep the patients in a dry place after being dressed. To maintain the dressing in contact with the lesion and to protect the latter from dirt and moisture, it is advisable in severe cases to put on a leather or rubber boot. G. B. Lancaster (*Vet. Rec.*, May 31st, 1947) says that in his opinion the best treatment for foot-rot in sheep is a vaccine of fusiformis necrophorus, curing 90 per cent. of the cases, 50 per cent. of which require only one injection. If there are wounds he advises, locally, a solution of aloes, spirit, and linseed oil.

Dermatitis of the Interdigital Region—" Scald "

This may affect the majority of the sheep or lambs in a flock. Its cause is not always very clear. It may be due to frosty dews, when irritation from mud cannot be blamed. The inflammation is usually fairly acute, and makes the patients very lame. The pain which it causes prevents the animals thriving, and brings about loss of condition, particularly in young lambs.

TREATMENT.—Cure is rapidly effected by the use of lead lotion or other astringent solution. Dressing with boric acid has a soothing and beneficial effect, and may be sufficient to cure the condition. The cause, if evident, must be removed.

AFFECTIONS OF THE FEET IN THE PIG

The pig may suffer from sore feet as the result of being driven some distance by road, especially when the animal is fat and heavy. The degree of inflammation varies in different cases. It is manifested by the usual symptoms. The pig is lame and inclined to lie down on the road. If infection gain entrance through a breach in the horn, suppuration may supervene and may eventually cause shedding of the hoof. Then intense inflammation of the digital region and constitutional disturbance ensue.

TREATMENT.—Keep the animals at rest on soft litter, and if the inflammation is severe, apply cold water and astringent lotions to the feet. Pare away separated horn, and apply an antiseptic protective dressing to the exposed tissues. Administer laxative medicine to counteract febrile disturbance.

Affections of the Interdigital Space

The interdigital space may be affected with " scald," or a wound, or a suppurating or necrotic lesion, as in the sheep, and must be dealt with accordingly.

" Foot and Mouth Disease " is a specific disease affecting chiefly cattle, sheep and pigs, which need not be dealt with here.

AFFECTIONS OF THE FEET IN THE DOG AND CAT

Open Wounds of the Paws

The paw is frequently wounded by treading on sharp bodies—sharp stones, glass, tacks, thorns, etc.—the commonest seat of injury being one of the pads, but the interdigital region may also be wounded A foreign body may be lodged in the tissues. The lesion will vary according to the depth and extent of the injury. It causes marked lameness.

TREATMENT is on the general principles of open wounds. When the wound is punctured and small, it may be necessary to examine each pad separately to find it. A foreign body should be searched for and, if found, removed. Antiseptic lotion and powder and a pad and bandage are indicated. Occasionally the wound is callous when submitted for treatment, especially when affecting the pads. Excessive horn may have then developed at the level of the wound in the form of processes with intervening sore spaces. The abnormal horn should be excised, and the ulcerated part cauterised with silver nitrate, after which a dry antiseptic and protective dressing should be applied.

A circular wound of the paw or metacarpal or metatarsal region is occasionally met with as the result of a rubber ring or a piece of cord or a wire snare being fixed round the limb, the ring or ligature becoming embedded and hidden in the tissues and causing suppuration. The indication, therefore, in a wound of this kind is to search for a ligature and remove it when found. Healing will then rapidly ensue. It may have been in the limb for months before the case is brought for treatment.

Contused Wounds

Contused wounds caused by crushing of the paw by the wheel of a vehicle passing over it are fairly common, and are usually complicated by fracture of one or more of the digits and destruction of a considerable amount of soft tissues.

The TREATMENT is to remove shreds of dead tissue and loose pieces of bone, clip the hair in the vicinity, and immerse the foot in a warm antiseptic bath repeatedly until the wound granulates, when a dry, protective dressing will be sufficient. The latter should be renewed daily. If a digit or digits are irreparably damaged, amputation thereof must be performed.

Sinuses

A sinus may form between the digits, due to the presence of a foreign body or a piece of necrotic tendon or bone in its depth, or occasionally to the cavity left after the bursting of an interdigital abscess or cyst refusing to heal. The procedure in every case is to open up the sinus to its bottom and remove the cause of the condition. A separated sesamoid bone has been found as the cause of the trouble, and its removal was followed by immediate recovery and disappearance of the lameness, which had been in existence for months.

Burns and Scalds

The dog's or cat's paws may be burned or scalded at fireplaces, and must be dealt with as described in the section on " Burns and Scalds."

Inflammation of the Pads

Inflammation of the pads in the dog often results from the animal running a long distance by road or over rough ground, such as stubble or ploughed fields, especially in dry weather.

SYMPTOMS.—When the dog is running the inflammation may not be very noticeable, but after he has rested for a while it becomes obvious, the animal being very tender on his feet, showing general lameness, and evidently suffering pain. He lies stretched out and hesitates about putting weight on the feet. The pads are found to be hot, swollen, and painful.

TREATMENT consists in rest and the use of antiphlogistic applications, cold water and astringent topics being indicated when the case is recent. If the horn be worn down to the flesh, antiseptic foot-baths are advisable to prevent septic complications. When the pain is severe, warm solutions of belladonna or opium or a warm decoction of poppy-heads may be used as an anodyne.

Separation of the Nail

The nail may be torn off or partially separated by violence in an accident, causing intense pain and lameness. When the separation is slight, the nail may become adherent again ; if not, it should be removed. If the phalanx be injured, it must be disarticulated and the resulting wound dressed with an antiseptic pad and bandage until it is healed.

Inflammation of the Nail Matrix

This may be acute or chronic. It is caused by injury—viz., a contusion or open wound—or by eczema extending from the interdigital region.

SYMPTOMS.—A painful swelling is formed at the coronet, which may also become ulcerated or the seat of small abscesses. There is marked lameness.

TREATMENT consists in applying warm antiseptic lotions, such as 1 or 2 per cent. solution of lysol or cresyl, or 1 in 1,000 potassium permanganate, and painting the ulcers with tincture of iodine, and opening abscesses and disinfecting their cavities. When the condition is due to chronic eczema, the internal administration of Fowler's solution of arsenic is indicated. In rebellious cases, amputation of the terminal phalanx is the best treatment.

Ingrowing Nails

The nail of the dew-claw, not being subjected to wear, often becomes curved and grows into the pad, causing acute pain and lameness.

The TREATMENT is to cut the offending nail with a bone forceps or rowelling scissors, applying the instrument to the sides of the nail, as its application above and below might cause splitting of the horn. This must be done periodically. An alternative procedure is to amputate the dew-claw. The dew-claws may be easily excised with the scissors during puppyhood, and the operation is often performed on whippets and greyhounds, in which the dew-claw may interfere with racing, owing to its catching the opposite limb when the dog is running. In dogs getting insufficient exercise, the ordinary claws become too long and require to be shortened, the pressure of the jaws of the forceps being applied laterally.

Horny Callosities

These sometimes form on the dog's pads, and may become fissured to form a tuft of horny processes. They cause a varying degree of lameness.

TREATMENT is not satisfactory. It consists in paring away the horn as much as possible, using warm antiseptic baths, and applying iodine and glycerine, or carbolised glycerine, or ichthyol ointment.

Interdigital Cysts or Abscesses

These are common in dogs, especially the long-coated varieties—spaniels, retrievers, and setters. The cause of the condition is evidently bacterial, but no specific organism has been discovered in connection with it, and why some individuals are more subject to it than others cannot be explained.

SYMPTOMS.—An inflammatory swelling gradually forms in one or more of the interdigital spaces of one or more feet, causing lameness, which may be very slight or well marked. The dog frequently bites or licks the affected part. The swelling, if not opened, bursts eventually, discharging a watery liquid. The resulting cavity may soon heal, or persist for want of drainage or on account of its lining failing to granulate. It may close for a while, after which the cyst or abscess reforms. Successive cysts may form in different spaces.

PROGNOSIS.—Recovery occurs rapidly in some cases on bursting or opening and draining of the cyst or cysts. Other cases are very obstinate to treat, the cysts forming repeatedly, despite the adoption of the usual surgical measures.

TREATMENT.—Rubbing in tincture of iodine over the swelling when it is forming sometimes prevents its development. When the cyst is present, treatment consists in opening it up completely and curetting its lining or destroying it by the application of silver nitrate stick. The application of tincture of iodine to the lining of the cavity may be sufficient to promote granulation and cicatrisation, and should be tried before using caustic preparations. The use of an autogenous vaccine has proved disappointing, but may have a good effect in some cases.

APPENDIX

I

EXAMINATION OF HORSES AS TO SOUNDNESS

The examination of horses as to soundness is a comparatively simple matter for the veterinary surgeon who is so well versed in the practical application of a competent knowledge of the anatomy and physiology of the horse that he has little difficulty in recognising aberrations from the normal concerning them in the course of his examination.

The newly fledged veterinary surgeon and even the matured veterinarian are not always in this happy position although they may have had a distinguished collegiate career, because they may not have taken the trouble or had the opportunities or time to apply their knowledge to the living animal by repeatedly inspecting and palpating regions subject to abnormalities or by observing at every opportunity the performance of functions liable to undergo alteration as the result of disease, for example in :

1. The locomotory system—watching the horse at rest, walking, turning, backing, trotting, and galloping.
2. The respiratory system—to listen to the respiratory sounds at rest (auscultation, using the phonendoscope), when startled (" grunting "), and during fast exercise or heavy haulage.
3. The circulatory system, including the pulse and cardiac sounds and rhythm (auscultation) at rest and after exercise.
4. The other systems as far as their functions can be observed.

Examination of the eye is not sufficiently practised by students or young veterinary surgeons to enable them to become familiar with its various structures as they appear in the living animal. Frequent practice of the use of instruments (retinoscope, ophthalmoscope, bi-convex lens) is essential to avoid mistakes in diagnosis of deep ocular affections.

The next requirement for the veterinary surgeon who wishes to become proficient in the examination of horses is to have a thorough knowledge of the pathological conditions that can be detected in the procedure and to examine all the horses that he comes in contact with to ascertain if any of these conditions are present and thus help to make himself expert in the matter.

The veterinary student is handicapped in that in the majority of colleges he has little time or opportunity for the practical application of his knowledge of the normal and abnormal animal and must rely upon himself to obtain the facilities outside the college, by spending some time with a veterinary surgeon engaged largely in equine practice and by frequenting horse shows, fairs, sale-yards, and race meetings. Notwithstanding that the veterinarian has fulfilled all the foregoing requirements, he will be by no means infallible in the art of finding whether a horse is sound or unsound, because an abnormality may be so slight (and yet serious) that it may be overlooked or be impossible to detect. This raises the point of negligence in the examination of horses for which the veterinary surgeon is liable and may be mulcted in heavy damages. It therefore behoves him to leave no loophole for this charge by exercising extreme care and omitting no detail to arrive at a correct decision. He may make mistakes and give a wrong opinion, but so long as negligence cannot be proved against him in his procedure he is not liable. There is always the danger, however, of the judge giving he verdict against him ; hence the advisability of joining a veterinary defence association as a protection in this and similar contingencies.

Definition of Unsoundness

The following extract from the judgment of Baron Park (1842) is generally taken as constituting the definition of unsoundness. " The rule as to soundness is that if at the time of sale the horse has any disease which actually does diminish the natural usefulness of the animal so as to make him less capable of work of any description, or which in its ordinary progress will diminish the natural usefulness of the animal, or if the horse has either from disease or accident undergone any alteration of structure that either actually does at the time or in its ordinary effects will diminish the natural usefulness of the horse, such a horse is unsound."

Remembering this definition, the veterinary surgeon can use his judgment as to what specific conditions constitute unsoundness. From the point of view of heredity, which is important in the examination of animals for the stud, there may be differences of opinion, but there is general agreement that the following conditions are hereditary : cataract, whistling or roaring, ring-bone, side-bone, spavin, navicular disease, shivering, stringhalt, and defective genital organs.

Procedure or method of Examination

The examination of a horse as to soundness must be methodical, done in stages of the same sequence on every occasion. The following are the stages usually adopted :

(1) *At rest in the stable*, where—

(a) His general condition and behaviour are observed, whether he happens to show any stable vices or favours a limb by resting it or shows evidence of stringhalt or shivering on being made to come over.

(b) A note is taken of its description—colour, breed or class, sex, age, height, and markings, using the terms prescribed by the Royal College of Veterinary Surgeons, a list of which is obtainable from that body on application (see also pp. 1013–17). A horse that has come a distance by road to be examined should be rested and not disturbed in any way for half an hour, " until the veterinary surgeon is ready to carry out the examination," a reason for this being that the horse standing for some time after a journey may show a lameness which appears only when the animal has walked or trotted after resting (spavin, navicular disease, rheumatism), and which passes off with exercise.

(c) The heart and lungs are auscultated, the character of the breathing is observed (broken wind), and the temperature is taken if considered necessary.

(d) The eyes are examined for defective vision and opacities without and with an instrument (opthalmoscope, retinoscope, bi-convex lens) remembering that an animal may be blind although the eyes appear to be normal.

(e) The hearing may be tested should the horse appear to be deaf.

(f) If the subject is a stallion or brood mare the genital organs are carefully examined, including the mammary gland in the mare.

(g) The mouth, including the incisor and molar teeth (superficially at least), is examined.

(h) Grunting the horse, if in a safe, roomy loose box, is practised.

(2) *Having the horse taken outside in a good halter or snaffle bridle*, and—

(a) Walked up and down for about 40 yards, turned short in a circle, right and left, and backed for stringhalt and shivering.

(b) Trotted slowly up and down, without excitement, on hard, level ground in a quiet place for the same distance, watching him carefully when turning.

(c) Standing square on a level surface with plenty of room for the veterinary surgeon to walk round the horse at a few paces methodically inspecting every region from the head to the tail on both sides and then palpating various parts, beginning on the near side at the head—

    (1) from the poll down the face, everting the inner wing of the nostril and the lips, exposing the teeth and interdental space ;

    (2) the jowl and chin ;

    (3) the top of the neck from the poll to the withers ;

64

(4) the side and under aspects of the neck and sternum, raising the jugular vein ;

(5) the back, loins, and croup ;

(6) the lateral and inferior aspects of the chest and abdominal walls ;

(7) the fore limb from the withers to the foot, anteriorly, laterally, and posteriorly, examining especially for splint, ring-bone, bobba bone, side-bone, sprained tendons, and synovial distensions, grease in hairy-legged horses, and affections of the feet ; then, having flexed the knee and supporting the fetlock with the right hand, the left hand is passed between the fore limbs from in front and the thumb pushes the back tendons aside from the knee to the fetlock feeling for splint again ; the same is done on the outside, reversing the hands ; finally the lateral cartilages and foot are carefully examined ;

(8) the fore foot having been given to the groom, the right hand is passed beneath the abdomen gradually up to the inguinal region and then along the hind limb from the angle of the haunch in front and the tuber ischii behind to the foot in a manner similar to that adopted in the fore limb, examining specially for spavin, bog-spavin, thoroughpin, curb, ring-bone, sprained tendons, and grease in hairy-legged horses in which it may be overlooked in its early stages ; the tail and dock are examined and the former raised to expose the anus, vulva, and perinæum ; the fore foot is then released to enable the examiner to lift and inspect the hind foot ; lifting the hind limb also serves now as a test for shivering. The same procedure is gone through on the other side.

(3) *Examination of the wind*, including—

(*a*) Grunting or " bulling " the horse, which is held alongside a safe wall on good footing (not concrete or pavement), or in a place prepared for the purpose, with a large mat suspended on the wall, and the halter, shank, or reins somewhat slackened to give the animal room to spring forward when he is threatened with a stick or handkerchief to frighten him to make an expiratory effort and cause a prolonged grunt if the larynx is more or less paralysed, preventing closure of the glottis.

(*b*) " Coughing " the horse by pressure on the larynx.

(*c*) Cantering or galloping the horse either in the lunge or saddle, in a calm atmosphere if possible. The horse may be ridden by the examiner—generally considered the better way—or by another person, who rides the horse first in a large circle and then in a small circle round the examiner both ways, and finally in a long, straight gallop, preferably up an incline, to stop close to him. When lunged the horse is sent round in a ring to the right and to the left. In every case the horse is kept going until he blows distinctly. Care must be taken that the cavesson or bridle and lunging rope or rein are strong and properly adjusted. If there is wind the veterinary surgeon stands with his back to it when the horse is approaching him.

An alternative method of testing a carthorse's wind is to cause him to pull a load or a heavy vehicle with the wheel locked up a long, stiff incline until he blows. Yet another way of testing a light horse's wind is to exercise him on soft ground on three legs, a fore foot being securely strapped up, Rarey fashion. This method has been practised by dealers, being a severe test which quickly brings out a noise if present. It seems rather risky, from the danger of coming down or catching the tied-up fore foot with the hind one when plunging forward. The author has seen it adopted successfully with Army remounts before and after the " roaring " operation.

(4) The heart should be re-examined after this exercise, when its beats will be more distinct and abnormalities more easily detected. The grunting test may also be repeated.

(5) In an exhaustive examination of a horse or if there has been some doubt as to whether the animal was lame when trotted, he may be allowed to rest in the stable for a while after being tried for the wind and then jogged again, when lameness, if present, will probably be accentuated. The grunting test may also be repeated.

Vices

Vices are to be considered but cannot always be detected ; the rule is that the vendor must give a guarantee that the animal is free from same.

Blemishes

A horse may have blemishes which do not constitute unsoundness and which must be mentioned and stated as being of no consequence or not likely to interfere with the animal's usefulness.

Useful Unsound Horses

Horses may be affected with conditions for which they must be cast as unsound and yet work perfectly sound, e.g., curb, spavin, peri-articular ring-bone, side-bones ; this probably accounts for so many veterinary certificates being read out at certain sales to the effect that horses are affected with some of these conditions but are " otherwise sound," never mentioning the word unsound. Another way of describing such horses in a certificate is to say they are sound except for some of the affections mentioned. Horses unsound in the wind are sometimes referred to as whistlers or slight whistlers and otherwise sound.

Certificates

Certificate is the name given to a signed statement by a veterinary surgeon that he has examined a particular horse, of which he gives a complete description, including defects, whereby the animal can be identified at home and abroad, and that he has found the said horse to be sound or unsound, without any qualification. There should be no room for doubt in the certificate as to the soundness or unsoundness of the animal. The client, or purchaser at a sale should not be left to draw his own conclusions by such phrases as " a slight whistler, otherwise sound," which a layman might take as meaning the horse is sound ; " sound except for a small splint," which might be taken as meaning that the animal is unsound because of the small splint.

Fraser (Lambourn, Berks) in an excellent article on the "Examination of Horses as to Soundness " condemns the use of this ambiguous phraseology and insists that the horse should be stated to be either " Sound " or " Unsound."

Form of Certificate.—

It is convenient to have printed forms such as the following :

CERTIFICATE.

No. ....   [*Name and address of the Veterinary Surgeon*]

[*Date.*]

I have this day examined at the request of [Name and address of person —description of the animal, including colour, breed or class, sex, age, and height]. *The said* [repeat the kind of animal—horse, mare, gelding. colt or filly] [has or is] [mention the form or forms of unsoundness if any] *and is in my opinion* [sound or unsound].

Identification Marks.

Signed......................M.R.C.V.S.

(If the certificate is not on a printed form it should be legibly and neatly written on good notepaper.)

II

COLOURS AND MARKINGS OF HORSES FOR IDENTIFICATION PURPOSES (as recommended by the Royal College of Veterinary Surgeons)

Colours

Black.—Where melanistic pigment is general throughout the body coat, limbs, mane and tail, with no pattern factor present other than white markings.

Black-brown.—Where the predominating colour is black, with muzzle, and sometimes flanks, brown or tan.

Brown.—Where there is a mixture of melanistic and chocolate pigment, without yellow, in the body coat, with black limbs, mane and tail.

Bay-brown.—Where the predominating colour is brown, with bay muzzle, black limbs, mane and tail.

Bay.—Bay varies considerably in shade from a dull red approaching the brown to a yellowish colour approaching the chestnut, but it can be distinguished from the chestnut by the fact that the bay has a black mane and tail and almost invariably has black on the limbs. The following three shades will suffice for description : *Bay* (includes bright bay) ; *Dark Bay ; Light Bay* (includes mealy bay).

Chestnut.—This is a whole colour of which three shades may be named : *Chestnut* (includes bright chestnut, golden chestnut, and red chestnut) ; *Dark Chestnut* (includes liver chestnut and mahogany chestnut) ; *Light Chestnut* (includes sorrel).

Blue Dun.—Where the colour of the body coat is a dilute black, evenly distributed over the body (giving a blue colour) with or without dorsal band (list) or withers stripes. Always black mane and tail. The skin is black.

Yellow Dun.—Where there is a diffuse yellow pigment in the hair with or without dorsal band (list), wither stripes, or bars on the legs. The striping is correlated with dark pigment on the head and limbs. When striping is absent the limbs will approximate to the colour of the body coat. The skin is black.

Cream.—Where the body coat is of a cream colour, with unpigmented skin. The iris is deficient in pigment ; it may even be devoid of it, giving the eye a pinkish appearance.

Grey.—Where the body coat is a varying mosaic of black and white hairs, with the skin black. With increasing age the coat grows lighter in colour. As there are many variations of grey according to age and season all of them should be described by the general term grey. In horses of this colour any distinctive hoof markings may be useful for the purposes of distinction.

Roans.—Roans are distinguished by the ground or body colours, all of which are permanent.

Blue Roan.—Where the body colour is black or black-brown, with an admixture of white hair which gives a blue tinge to the coat. The limbs from the knee and hock downwards are black.

Strawberry or Chestnut Roan.—Where the body colour is chestnut with an admixture of white hairs. The limbs are not black.

Bay or Red Roan.—Where the body colour is bay or bay-brown with white hairs which give a reddish tinge to the coat. The limbs from the knee and hock downwards are black.

Piebald.—Where the body coat consists of large irregular patches of black and white. The line of demarcation between the two colours is generally well defined.

Skewbald.—Where the body consists of large irregular patches of white and of any definite colour except black. The line of demarcation between the colours is generally well defined.

Odd Colour.—Where the coat consists of a mixture of more than two colours tending to merge into each other at the edges of the patches with irregular body markings not classifiable under the head of Piebald or Skewbald.

Note.—(1) Where there is any doubt as to colour, the muzzle and eyelids should be carefully examined.

(2) The term "whole coloured" is used (e.g. in Suffolk breeds) where there are no hairs of any other colour on the body, head, or limbs.

Markings

The variations in markings of horses are infinite and cannot therefore be comprehended by a limited number of terms without certain arbitrary groupings. In some cases a combination of the terms given below must be resorted to.

Limbs

White Coronet.—Where the hair immediately above the hoof is white. Describe the situation of the white marking as far as possible.

White Heel.—For the purpose of description of marking the heel is to be taken as the back of the pastern extending to the ergot. Where the white is confined to one or both the bulbs of the heel it must be specified.

White Pastern.—For the purpose of description of marking the term " Pastern " is to be taken as extending from immediately below the fetlock joint downwards. Any variation of the extent of the white should be specified, e.g. half pastern, three-quarter pastern.

White Fetlock.—For the purpose of description of marking the term " fetlock " is to be taken as comprising the region of the fetlock joint and downwards. Any variation of the extent of the white should be specified.

Higher White Markings.—Though the term " Sock " has been in common use for a marking extending to about half-way up the cannon, and the term " Stocking " for a marking up to the region of the knee or hock, these terms have been so loosely used that the Sub-Committee recommends for the sake of greater uniformity and certainty that for white markings extending higher than those already defined the particular height to which the white extends should be precisely stated and any variations in the upper margin noted, e.g. " White to middle of Cannon or shank " " White to Knee or Hock."

HEAD

Star.—Any white mark on the forehead. Size, shape, intensity, and position of coloured markings on the white to be specified.

Stripe.—Many terms have been used to describe the narrow white marking down the face, not wider than the flat anterior surface of the nasal bones, e.g. rase, race, rache, reach, streak, stripe, strip, etc.

The Sub-Committee recommends for the sake of uniformity that one term only be used, and they select, as being most useful for the purpose, the term " Stripe." The stripe may be a continuation of the star, or it may be separate and distinct from it. Where there is a star and a stripe and the stripe is not continuous with it the stripe should be described as " interrupted stripe "; and where star and stripe are continuous as " star and stripe conjoined "; where no star is present the origins of the stripe should be defined.

The termination of the stripe and any variation in breadth, length, direction and coloured markings on the white should be described, e.g. " broad stripe " " narrow stripe."

Blaze.—A white marking covering almost the whole of the forehead between the eyes and extending down the front of the face, involving the whole width of the nasal bones. Any variation in direction, termination, and coloured markings on the white should be described.

White Face.—Where the white covers the forehead and front of the face extending laterally towards the mouth. The extension may be unilateral or bilateral in which case it should be described accordingly.

Snip.—An isolated white marking, independent of those already named and situated between or in the region of the nostrils. Its position should be specified.

Lip Markings.—Should be accurately described—whether embracing the whole or a portion of either lip.

White Muzzle.—Where the white embraces both lips and extends to the region of the nostrils.

EYES

Wall Eye.—The term should be used exclusively where there is such a lack of pigment in the iris as usually to give a greyish white or bluish appearance to the eye. Any other important variations from the normal colour of the iris should be noted.

Showing the White of the Eye.—Horses which " show the white of the eye " should be so described.

BODY

Grey Ticked.—Where isolated white hairs are sparsely distributed irregularly in any part of the body.

Flecked.—Where small collections of white hairs occur distributed irregularly in any part of the body. The degree of flecking may be described by the terms " heavily flecked " " lightly flecked."

Black Marks.—The term should be used to describe areas of black hairs on white or any other colour (see " Ermine Marks ").

Spots.—Where small, more or less circular, collections of hairs differing from the general body colour occur, distributed in various parts of the body. The colour of the spots must be stated.

Patch.—This term should be used to describe any larger well defined irregular area (not covered by previous definitions) of hairs differing from the general body colour. The colour, shape, position, and extent should be described.

Zebra Marks.—Where there is striping on the limbs, neck, withers or quarters.

Mane and Tail.—The presence of odd coloured hairs in mane and tail should be specified.

Ermine Marks.—The term is used to describe black points on white, usually occurring on the coronet, but as this marking can easily be described as " Black Marks " it is recommended that the use of the word " Ermine " be discontinued.

Dappled.—The Sub-Committee recommends that this term be discontinued, as it is a seasonal and not a permanent marking.

GENERAL

Mixed.—The term " mixed " should be used to describe a marking consisting of the general colour mixed with many white or lighter coloured hairs.

Bordered.—To be used where any marking is circumscribed by a mixed border, e.g. bordered star, bordered stripe.

Flesh Marks.—Patches where the pigment of the skin is absent should be described as " Flesh Marks."

NOTES

1. *Adventitious Marks.*—There are many adventitious marks (i.e. not congenital marks) which are permanent, e.g. saddle marks, bridle marks, collar marks, girth marks, and other harness marks, firing and branding marks, scars, tattoo marks. Wherever these occur they should be described. Horses that have been docked should be so described.

2. *Near and Off.*—As the terms " Near " and " Off " are not recognized abroad, it is recommended that in certificates referring to horses for export an explanatory note defining " near " as " left " and " off " as " right " should be inscribed at the foot of the certificate.

3. *Routine.*—It is recommended that the following order of examination should be adopted:

Colour.

Breed.

Sex (where the horse has a registered name it should be inserted here, followed by name of sire and dam).

Age.

Marks on head (including eyes) in the order shown.

Marks on limbs, fore first, then hind, commencing from below.

Marks on body.

Remarks on mane and tail.

Adventitious or acquired marks.

INDEX

Angler's inhaler, 789
Anker's guarded knife, 341
Anophthalmia, 496
Anorchid, 398, 740
Ano-rectal fistula, 696
Anterior tibial neurectomy, 449
Anthrax, 55
Anti-back-breaking apparatus, 163
Antisepsis and asepsis, 193
Antiseptic agents, 218
Anus. *See* Rectum, 690
    congenital anomalies of, 690
    preternaturalis, 665
    spasm of, 710
Aorta (posterior), thrombosis of, 898
Aponeurosis of the hip, ossification of, 883
    of the thigh, ossification of, 883
Appendages of the eye, 519
Arecoline for choking, 629
Arterial thrombosis, 90
Arterial hæmorrhage, 87
Arteries, affections of, 85
    ligation of, 243
    open wounds and contusions of, 85
    rupture of, 88
    thrombosis of, 90
    torsion of, 244
Arterioles, crushing of, 244
Arteritis, 90
Artery forceps, 244
Arthritis, closed, 143
    deforming, 143
    dry, 143
    gouty, in birds, 143
    ossificans, 143
    post-partum, 142
    purulent, 139
    rheumatoid, 141
    traumatic, 139
Articular rheumatism, 141
    windgalls, 865
Artificial eye, 290
    hyperæmia (Biers), 260
Astigmatism, 496
Astragalus, fracture of, 927
Atheroma of false nostril, 545
Atrophy of muscles, 72
Auto-cauteries, 254
    for dividing tissues, 232
Autoplastia, 245
Avertin, 196

Bacillus of Nicolaïer, 46
    Septicus, 45
Back, affections of, 637
    abscess on, 638
    broken, 649
    galls on, 637
    hæmatoma on, 637
    ricked on jinked, 646
    sitfast on, 637
    wounds on, 638
Balanitis in the dog, 750
    in the horse, 750

Balanitis in the ox, 751
    in the pig, 752
Balano-posthitis, 750
Bandages, 226
Barrier and Siedamgrotzky on mechanism
    of sprained tendons, 841
Bees, stings by, 31
Bernadot's and Butel's apparatus for pre-
    venting broken back, 160
Biceps, rupture of, 803
    (coraco-radialis), 803
    sprain of, 803
    femoris, rupture of, 880
        displacement of, 881
        operation for, 882
Bicipital bursa, inflammation of (bursitis
        intertubercularis), 803
        purulent bursitis of, 805
Bier's hyperæmic treatment, 260
Biflex canal, inflammation of, 1000
B.I.P.P., 27, 220
Black pitch, 113
Bladder, affections of, 717
    amputation of, 726
    calculi in, 724
    endoscopia of, 721
    foreign bodies in, 722
    functional disturbance of, 717
    inversion of, 725
    paralysis of, 728
    passing catheter into, 718
    prolapse of, 724
    puncture of, 432
        in the horse and ox, 432
        in the dog and the cat, 432
    rupture of, 722
    stone in, 724
    tumours of, 727
    wounds of, 721
Bleeding. *See* Hæmorrhage
    local, 321
    operation for, 317
        See Phlebotomy
Blemished knee, 834
    operation for, 456
Blepharitis, 522
Blepharoptosis, 520
Blinds, 150
Blood stones, 94
    transfusion of, 29 and 322
Bobba bone, 874
Boccar's operation for stringhalt, 486
Bog spavin, 929
Bone, affections of, 105
    caries of, 129
    contusions of, 105
    fractures of, 107
    instruments for operations upon, 232
    necrosis of, 130
    open wounds of, 106
    pinning, 116
    saws, 204
Bowed tendon, 843

65 +

Necrosis of bone, 130
Needles, suture, 233
Nembutal anæsthesia, 199
  dosage, 202
Nephrectomy, 485
Nephrotomy, 484
Nerves, affections of, 99
  blocking, 801
  compression of, 99
  contusion of, 100
  section of, 99
  tumours of, 101
  wounds of, 100
  wounds of, 100
Nesfield's treatment for leucoma, 507
Nettle stings, 40
Neuralgia, cervico-occipital, 102
  dorso-costal, 102
  facial, 102
  lumbo-abdominal, 102
  traumatic, 42
Neuritis, 101
Nicking, 438
Nose, bleeding from, 546
  cyst in, 545
Nostrils, affections of, 541
  necrosis of cartilages of, 542
  tumours of, 544
  wounds of, 541
Nystagmus, 519

Obturator lameness, 894
  paralysis, 894
Occlusion of anus, 690
  of os uteri, 769
  of urethra, 730
Ochromus anthropophagus, 64
Œdema after castration, 372
  malignant, 45
  of head, 542
Œsophagocele, 634
Œsophagotomy, 315
Œsophagus, affections of, 623
  dilatation of, 633
  diverticulum of, 633
  ectasia of, 633
  exploration of, 623
  obstruction of, 628
  paralysis of, 636
  parasites in, 635
  passing probang into, 623
    stomach tube into, 625
  stricture or stenosis of, 633
  tumours of, 635
  wounds of, 627
Omentum, descent of, after castration, 371
  after laparotomy, 348
  function of, 348
Omphalocele, 672
Onchocerca reticulata, 65
Onyx (keratitis), 505
Oophorectomy, 402
Opacities of the cornea, 506

65*

Operating table for horse, 162
  for dog, 169
  theatre (horse), 148
    (dog), 149
Operation by blunt dissection, 241
  crushing, 241
  elastic ligature, 214
  tearing, 241
  thermo-cautery, 241
Operative surgery, 147
  technique, 228
Ophthalmia, specific or recurrent, 510
  sympathetic, 517
Optic nerve, atrophy of, 516
  inflammation of, 516
  papilla, 516
    atrophy of, 516
Orbicularis palpebrarum, paralysis of 519
Orbit, affections of, 525
  contusions of, 525
  fracture of, 525
  tumours of, 525
Orchitis, 744
Os calcis, fracture of, 926
  pedis, fracture of, 959
    osteo-periostitis of, 964
  uteri, occlusion of, 769
Oscheocele (scrotal hernia), 673
Ostitis, 118, 128
Otacariasis, 531
Othæmatoma, 526
Otitis, 529
Otorrhœa, 529
  ceruminous, 529
  eczematous, 529
  glandular, 529
  of distemper, 529
  parasitic, 531
Ovariotomy (bitch and cat), 414, 415
  (cow), 409
  (goat), 413
  (mare), 402
  (pig), 413
Ovaro-hysterectomy (bitch), 417
Overreach, 765
Ox, control of, 157
Oxygen and ether as anæsthetic, 189

Pads, callosities on, 1006
  inflammation of, 1004
Palate, fissure of, 581
Palmar (deep) neurectomy, 453
Pannus, 504
Panophthalmia, 517
Paracentesis thoracis, 322
Paralysis, 103
  local, 103
Paraphimosis, 753
Parasites in the eye, 519
  in kidney, 717
  in larynx, 618
  in œsophagus, 635

PRINTED IN GREAT BRITAIN BY WILLIAM CLOWES AND SONS, LIMITED, LONDON AND BECCLES
FOR BAILLIÈRE, TINDALL AND COX.